About the Author

Jessica Owers is the author of the heralded *Peter Pan: The Forgotten Story of Phar Lap's Successor*, winner of the 2012 Bill Whittaker Award for Best Racing Book in Australia. Her writing has appeared in *Inside Breeding, The Thoroughbred, Breeding & Racing* and *Outback* magazines, along with numerous other racing books and publications. She holds a combined honours degree from the University of Stirling, and has worked as a sub-editor in publishing and a riding instructor. She lives in Sydney's eastern suburbs with her husband, restaurateur Maurizio Lombardo.

JESSICA OWERS

SHANNON

BEFORE BLACK CAVIAR,
SO YOU THINK OR TAKEOVER TARGET,
THERE WAS SHANNON

EBURY
PRESS

An Ebury Press book
Published by Random House Australia Pty Ltd
Level 3, 100 Pacific Highway, North Sydney NSW 2060
www.randomhouse.com.au

First published by Ebury Press in 2013

Addresses for companies within the Random House Group can be found at
www.randomhouse.com.au/offices

National Library of Australia
Cataloguing-in-Publication Entry

Owers, Jessica, author.
Shannon: the extraordinary life of Australia's first
international racehorse/Jessica Owers.

ISBN 978 1 74275 024 8 (paperback)

Shannon (Race horse) – Biography.
Race horses – Australia – Biography.
Race horses – Australia – History.
Horse racing – Australia – History.

798.400994

Cover image © Hollywood Park, supplied courtesy of *The Blood-Horse*
Cover design by Blue Cork
Typesetting and internal design by Xou, www.xou.com.au
Printed in Australia by Griffin Press, an accredited ISO AS/NZS 14001:2004 Environmental
Management System printer

Random House Australia uses papers that are natural, renewable and recyclable products
and made from wood grown in sustainable forests. The logging and manufacturing processes
are expected to conform to the environmental regulations of the country of origin.

For Sonya

Contents

Success is not final, failure is not fatal: it is the courage to continue that counts.

– Winston Churchill

PART I

1

1938

It began on 15 February 1938, a little after sunrise and a little way off the Australian coast. Two English stallions, one bay, the other chestnut, stood in the deep straw of their makeshift stables, clumsy canvas concoctions on the deck of the steamship *Port Auckland*. Six weeks at sea, tilting on the skin of the oceans, leaning away from a Europe plunging towards war, the horses were restless. But that day, the *Port Auckland* slowed to a tired chug, inched into Sydney Harbour. It steamed under the Bridge to Glebe Island, shuddered into Wharf 3, then dropped her moorings and was still.

Crew hurried across the decks, hollering in coarse Cockney accents dry with sea salt. Down on the wharf, a battalion of trucks and hoists waited. The two stallions, wide-eyed, hot and sweating, were swung over the side onto Australian shores. It was a tick past 8 am.

No one, early on that Tuesday morning in 1938, knew the significance of the horses' arrival. They were just imports, two of hundreds that year scurried away from a burgeoning war. Only later, so many years later, would it be understood.

The horses were Midstream, sire of Shannon, and Emborough, sire of Bernborough.

2

Sire

Midstream's life had begun in England in 1933, the year Adolf Hitler became dictator of Germany. Born into a warm, balmy English summer, he was a spindly bay foal like any other, all splaying legs and confusion. His dam, Midsummer, was a winner of five races in the mid-1920s, but Midstream's class was in his sire line. He was by Blandford, an impossibly brilliant stallion who, by the foaling of Midstream, had produced successive winners of the coveted Epsom Derby.

He was an awkwardly conformed sire. Blandford was short in the pasterns and stood over in his knees, and conformation flaws rankled both sides of his pedigree. But he was staggering in the covering shed. By 1938, as Midstream carved his way across the oceans aboard the *Port Auckland*, Blandford had sired four English Derby winners and an Arc de Triomphe winner. His progeny had notched up classic races in England, Ireland, France and America, and he was a three-time champion sire. He was one of the rarest sources of classic stamina that Europe had ever seen. Even in later years, as speed strains arrived to his breeding shed, Blandford's talent for producing classic winners could not be extinguished. His progeny excelled over the 10-furlong average.

Such was Blandford's strike rate, when Midstream was foaled anticipation hung on him as it does the child of brilliant parents. Bred by Anthony de Rothschild at the palatial Southcourt Stud in England, Midstream looked a decent derivative of his sire. He was of the same mahogany colouring, with a similar thin blaze down his face and two hind socks. He had an Arab-like throw to his nose, and he was classically conformed – good neck, powerful shoulder, and thankfully straight through the forelegs. Sent to trainer Thomas 'Ted' Leader at Sefton Lodge on the Newmarket gallops, Midstream learned to ply his trade, and quickly.

On 2 October 1935, he won his first outing, the Boscawen Stakes at Newmarket. It was a five-furlong spurt up the famous straight, and the win was impressive. Midstream was stepped up in company. Tackling the Middle Park Stakes two weeks later, he faded to 11th of 13 horses, though he lost no fans. Nine days later he was the 13/8 favourite, dead-heating for first in the Criterion Stakes, and he finished his two-year-old season with two wins (including the dead-heat) from three starts, all over five and six furlongs.

In the European spring of 1936, Midstream was sent on a three-year-old's classic campaign. He tackled the 2000 Guineas, finishing 12th of 19, then the Derby, fading to 19th. In the St James's Palace Stakes he was last of five, but by late July of that year he was springing into form. He ran third in the Sussex Stakes, then won the Wykeham Handicap Plate at York over a mile. He ran two further seconds before spelling, and his trainer concluded that in Midstream, Blandford had sired a robust miler. Ted Leader decided he would not ask the colt to go further than the mile again.

On 13 May 1937, Midstream debuted his four-year-old season in the one-mile Newmarket Handicap. Ridden by his regular pilot Richard Perryman, he surged to victory for a £1000 victor's purse. Midstream raced a further five times that season, claiming two firsts and two fourths, his wins coming over a mile and then six furlongs. By September, he had proved himself a consistent race-horse, though not brilliant. He had run 17 times for six wins and three places, and £2580 in prizemoney.

Midstream's breeders had held on to him with the prospects of his being a sire but the horse's race career had been average. The de Rothschild standards were high. They kept only the best for breeding, so Midstream was consigned to the December bloodstock sales at nearby Newmarket. It would alter the course of horseracing in Australia.

—

About this time, many thousands of miles away in the Hunter district of New South Wales, Australia, Percy Miller went scoping for a stallion. When it came to thoroughbreds, Miller was an expert prospector, sifting through lines, tossing the average and unperformed, obsessed with English pedigrees. Master of Kia Ora Stud, the pre-eminent bloodstock breeding operation of Australia, Miller was intelligent, vivacious and impatient. On his farm, sat in a fertile hamlet between Scone and Aberdeen, he stood only imported stallions and, in 1938, that included Medieval Knight, Constant Son, Christopher Robin, Double Remove, Piccadilly and the wildly successful Pantheon, famous sire of two-time Melbourne Cup winner Peter Pan.

Miller was only too aware that bloodline trends shifted, and he paid close attention to the game in England. He recorded the hot sires of the day, and noticed where others were falling away. He also knew that his own stallions were getting along; Medieval Knight was lacklustre, Constant Son had got only a handful of stakes winners, and Pantheon was 16 years old. Miller needed an injection of new blood, and there was but one horse barnstorming the European industry. Blandford.

Miller contacted his London-based bloodstock agent, the ageing but insightful Clarence Hailey. The two men had a long history of buying English stallions for export. They had conspired on a dozen or so sires for Kia Ora, most recently Double Remove. And in late 1937, Hailey had been expecting Miller's telegram requesting a son of Blandford for Australia. There were, after all, breeders from Argentina to South Africa knocking on Blandford's door. But the Australian had money, influence, a long record of importing English horses and absolute faith in 71-year-old Hailey. Miller gave a single instruction to his friend: 'Get me the best-looking Blandford that you can'.

Hailey pored through the catalogue for the December bloodstock sale. He visited yards, filed through young stallions and picked over their pedigrees. He looked dozens of horses up and down, checking for straightness, soundness, turning them over like diamonds. A few days before the Newmarket sales, he tele-grammed Miller with two differing propositions – Midstream, whom he felt was the best-looking Blandford on offer, and another horse, a Gainsborough colt called Emborough that had great bone and a versatile racing record.

Miller was enchanted with Midstream immediately. The four-year-old had all the charisma he was looking for – a beautiful pedi-gree by the sire of the moment, a record with wins, and Clarence Hailey was adamant that he was put together perfectly. Sons of Blandford were also thin on the ground in Australia. Miller tele-grammed his approval to London. Price would be no objective.

The matter of Emborough, on the other hand, hung over him. On paper, he seemed a nice horse. He was by Gainsborough, a very smart stallion, had won the Harewood Handicap at Doncaster, then the Autumn and Manchester cups. He was bred on close lines to the Epsom Derby winner Mid-Day Sun, along with the 1000 Guineas and Oaks winner Exhibitionist. But Miller knew that finding space for Emborough at Kia Ora would be a problem. He was concerned he had too many stallions already. He decided to decline the purchase of the horse, but he mentioned Emborough to a friend of his, Queensland stud master Andy Maguire.

Maguire ran Kialla Stud in a south-east corner of Queensland, and he had said to Miller many months before that he wanted to import an English stallion to rejuvenate his flagging stock. If Miller was cherry-picking the bloodstock sales in December, could he bring a horse in for Maguire? Miller thought Emborough might be just the ticket. With Maguire's interest confirmed, he telegrammed Clarence Hailey to proceed with two separate pur-chases; Midstream and Emborough would be bought separately at Newmarket, but they would be shipped to Australia together.

On the cool, biting Tuesday morning of 7 December 1937, Clarence Hailey joined some of Europe's big-gun breeders at the famous Newmarket sales. They included Captain Federico Tesio, an exceptional Italian stud master, and the Hon. George Lambton, private trainer for the Earl of Derby. Scattered everywhere,

English, Irish and French breeders pitched for young horses. Bloodstock agents poised for their buyers, cards close to their chests. The atmosphere was like any big sale Hailey had gone to in the last 50 years – animated and competitive, even if talk of war was thick in the air. By the close of trading that afternoon, he had secured Midstream for the good price of 3500 guineas, or £3675. He had also arranged for the sale of Emborough. Immediately, Hailey booked passage for the two horses aboard the Port Line steamship *Port Auckland*, departing from Hull in two weeks' time, sailing through the Suez and Indian Ocean, with a brief stop in Melbourne before easing into the Pacific and on to Sydney. It was aboard this ocean-going steamer, on its open deck under a clumsy canvas awning, that Midstream, bound for Kia Ora and with Emborough in tow, found his way to New South Wales on 15 February 1938.

When Percy Miller clapped eyes on the Blandford four-year-old, it was £5300 later, the accumulated cost of importing the horse to Australia. Miller liked what he saw. Midstream was a very muscular stallion, about 16 hands, plenty of substance about him, and six weeks at sea had hardly turned a hair. He looked fit and full. With the horse installed on a train to Kia Ora, three hours north-west of Sydney, and Emborough on his way to Queensland, Miller took the time to assess his investment.

Midstream's purchase was a significant string in Kia Ora's bow. At that time, there were only 10 sons of Blandford in Australasia, and only one other at stud in New South Wales, so Miller had plenty of sales material at hand. Blandford, and hence Midstream, represented a resurgence in the old Sterling bloodline, which fell straight back to Eclipse, the grand, undefeated sire of the 1700s. But even without the Sterling influence, Blandford was a headline all of his own. Miller knew that even if Midstream went the way of Medieval Knight or Christopher Robin – that of medi-ocrity – the hype surrounding his debut progeny would recoup his purchase price within the first two years.

And so it was that Midstream, and not Emborough, came to

stand at Kia Ora Stud, a solid son of Blandford installed in New South Wales. Oblivious to expectation, pound notes or a world creeping towards war, he began his stallion duties in September 1938.

He was brilliant right off the blocks.

3

Kia Ora

In the soft, waspy spring of 1940, the plump bellies and swayed backs of 102 broodmares dotted Kia Ora's hills. They were daughters of such stallions as Magpie and The Welkin, producing mares with long, solid pedigrees. They were the likes of Society, an ageing, seen-it-all New Zealander and the dam of AJC Derby winner Talking. They were Manumit, the mother of VRC Oaks and Wakeful Stakes winner Session, and even Bareena, who was from a half-sister to the all-conquering Melbourne Cup winner Artilleryman. Picking their way across the sloping flanks of Kia Ora, these matrons looked like swollen carthorses in long grasses. They were, in fact, the life and soul of Percy Miller's stud.

Among them was Idle Words, an unimpressive blood mare of average proportions and dirty brown colouring. She was by Magpie out of the unraced mare Peptamint, and there was nothing outstanding in her dam line. Peptamint had not produced a single stakes winner, and the only claim on the family tree was that Peptamint's dam, Mint, was a half-sister to the producer of the 1000 Guineas winner Brown Betty. As such, there was nothing lucrative about Idle Words when she was foaled at Kia Ora in 1932.

She was leggy like every other foal, not big or impressive. She was consigned for sale with the Kia Ora draft at the 1934 Sydney Easter Yearling Sales, and on Tuesday 3 April that year she had entered the auction ring at Randwick, toey and nervous and friendless. She was knocked down to local trainer Jack King for an honest 110 guineas.

Miller had 23 youngsters selling that day, and he had been far from pleased with their 131-guineas average. The entire draft, by impressive sires Magpie, Pantheon, Constant Son and Baralong, had been affected by strangles just prior to their shipment from Kia Ora. Months of careful priming and years of selective breeding went out the window as Miller estimated the outbreak cost him £10,000. It had been an expensive affair for the stud master, but it was as good a year as any for disaster. The Depression, plump on the loins of Australia, had dried up trading. Only the very best yearlings were in demand at the 1934 sales, and the overall average of 153 guineas made Idle Words' price tag somewhat palatable.

The bland little youngster was trucked to Jack King's Randwick yard and in her first season in training she started in the 1934 Gimcrack Stakes for two-year-old fillies, one of the premier races for baby females. She finished well back. Over the next four years Idle Words raced 27 times, winning little more than two welter handicaps at Moorefield and a mid-week in town. By 1938, when she was six years old, she was in the hands of Sydney trainer Chris O'Rourke for owner Claude McIntosh, but she was heading for the paddock. She had come to nothing on the track and, by a curious turn of fortune, the familiar long grasses of Kia Ora came calling.

Percy Miller had been reacquiring Magpie mares for a number of years. The formula had worked before. Mares by The Welkin had produced beautiful yearlings for Kia Ora in its early days, and Miller's initial broodmare band had been crafted around that great stallion. Now it was Magpie's turn and, though dead a few years, he was becoming a promising broodmare sire. With the help of a few racing associates, Miller was buying back many of the Magpie stock he had previously sent to the auction block.

Idle Words didn't have much of a racing record behind her, and outside of pedigree, Miller wanted the best winning mares, so the daughter of Peptamint wasn't high on his list. But Idle Words was a homebred, and encouraged by his good friend Clive Inglis, a bloodstock professional and an expert eye in the horse business, Miller went to the table at the 1938 Easter sales. He bought back the mare for the small fee of 75 guineas. She was returned to Kia Ora in time for the 1938 breeding season.

The following year she produced her first foal, a bay colt by Pantheon, and by the rolling around of the 1940 season, Idle Words was dry (she had missed in 1939). Miller pencilled into his books that she would go to the untried sire, the new boy Midstream.

—

When Percy Miller stood in the hub of his horse stud, he could look all around at gentle hills climbing away from him, at long, blotchy green pastures and the Pages River away in the distance. His fences dipped through gullies and disappeared where his eye could no longer follow. Kia Ora was vast and magnificent, nearly 2000 acres in all. It was perfect bloodhorse country, enviable almost.

Miller was a curious mix of genius and spoilt child. He knew horses, knew them so well he could recite pedigrees like they were poetry. But he was eccentric. He had moved into this corner of the Hunter in 1914, purchasing Kia Ora with his mother for £15,040. At the time, Miller was 35 years old and a wildly successful butcher. His meat business, turning out animal carcasses around the docks of Glebe Island, had made him a fortune. He owned several homes in Sydney, including the impressive mansion 'Fairfield' along the Windsor Road, and many city and suburban cold stores for his butchering business. Though limited in education, Percy Miller was an unlimited entrepreneur.

When he purchased his Hunter Valley land a few miles from Aberdeen, in February 1914, he had the curious habit of gazing greedily into the neighbouring property. Segenhoe Stud was next door (in fact, Kia Ora was a subdivision of Segenhoe), and Miller could see its exquisite bloodhorses roaming the pasturelands. Competitive, he wanted them too, so he steered away from the trotting scene in which he had invested for years, and he moved towards thoroughbreds.

From the outset, Miller determined that Kia Ora would be the best – his stud would have the best, breed the best and sell the best. His first sale of yearlings was a draft of only three, in the autumn of 1916, and 1917 wasn't much better. But under the persuasion of his good friend Richard Wootton, a very successful Australian trainer in England, he imported his first English stallion. Flippant, until the arrival of Magpie in 1919 (who proved the most important sire of his day and the foundation stone for the stud's later wild success), was the initial Kia Ora flag bearer.

The property, when Miller first bought it, was a sheep and cattle run, with brittle, worn fences and uneven pasture. There was hardly an outhouse standing. Of 1880 acres, 400 was flat or gently rolling land, cleared of scrub and dotted with ghost gums and ironbark. The rest climbed away into hills, making the whole place feel like its own valley. The name, also, had come with the purchase. For a few years, Miller referred to his stud as 'Kiora' (as it had been spelt by its previous owner). By 1920 or so, the stud had become 'Kia Ora'.

By 1928, the property was sending 103 yearlings through Sydney's Easter bloodstock sales, aggregating £28,000, a small fortune. By the mid-1930s, Miller had stood dozens of imported stallions on his farm, some of them dazzling, but most of them spectacular failures. So shrewd was Miller, however, that he didn't lose a penny on a single one: the carefully crafted hype around untried imported sires had buyers paying ridiculous prices for yearlings. It meant that in a single season, Miller almost always made back the purchase price of a horse he had imported.

He was respected around Australia as a master tactician. He appeared at major race meetings, eager to track the progress of his sires' progeny. He knew better than any man that a champion on the track spelt a spike in trade for Kia Ora, and he had experienced such with Magpie's Windbag (1925 Melbourne Cup winner and one of the best horses of his time) and Pantheon's Peter Pan. Miller also existed to make his stud the largest breeding operation in Australia, and he was relentless in his pursuit of it. Rivalry with his neighbours, notably the Widden Stud operation of the Thompson brothers, consumed him and exposed his eccentricities. Percy Miller, even at the age of 61 in 1940, was one of breeding's oddest characters.

He was tolerable only for a short space of time, rattling on about his horses, oblivious to his audience's maddening boredom. He refused to go to funerals, would shy from all social events, and he would not speak to his brother. Even when the two dealt in bloodstock, they would employ a middle man to diffuse the details. They would spend hours discussing an arrangement, sitting in the same room, breathing the same air, but always speaking through the middle man. Miller's obsession with outgunning his rivals often proved expensive for him. He thought nothing of falling out with long-time friends over foolish matters. On more than one occasion he impulsively bought a horse just so his competition wouldn't get it. When the Thompson brothers purchased the grey stallion Chrysolaus in the early 1920s, Miller was hysterical. Immediately, he commissioned for the purchase of a grey horse from England. The result – Sarchedon – was an enormous flop at stud. But despite his strangeness, Miller was exceptionally open-minded. He sought advice on almost every aspect of his bloodstock operation, and his right-hand man was Bert Riddle, manager of Kia Ora Stud. Riddle was efficient and disciplined, shared the same vision as Miller. By the time of Midstream's arrival in the summer of 1938, Kia Ora was the largest bloodstock producer in the country.

Percy Miller's temperament demanded a levelled, unflappable stud manager, which was exactly what Bert Riddle was. Installed at Kia Ora in 1916, as soon as the first thoroughbreds were walked onto the property, Bert was critical in the wheel of success. Despite his boss's eccentricities, for Miller was stubborn, complex and often impossible to deal with, the two men were a seamless team. Hailing from a long background in harness racing, Bert Riddle was as much a horseman as Miller was a wheeler and dealer. From 1920 onwards, there was no stopping their union.

During the height of the 1930s, Kia Ora had a crew of 24 tending to about 193 mares and eight stallions. As war approached, Miller curtailed operations to about 100 mares and five stallions.

The property had eight mare and foal paddocks that drifted over miles of limestone bedrock. At any one time, the broodmare band moved like wild horses, unkempt and out of sight, up to 60 in a herd. There was also a foaling paddock and 18 foaling pens, along with an 80-acre paddock for yearling colts and two 30-acre paddocks for yearling fillies. By 1940, after 25 years in this neck of the Hunter, Miller had done just what he had said he would – he had created the largest thoroughbred farm in Australia.

On a sticky afternoon that year in late November, Idle Words was led away from the paddocks. She walked along the stony paths towards the covering shed, where she was dressed and readied for Midstream. The covering shed was octagonal in shape, with a domed roof and white timber walls. It wasn't very big, just room enough for two horses and two to three handlers, but it had witnessed the spawning of several superstars, namely Strephon, Statesman, Windbag and Amounis. This day's covering promised nothing extraordinary. Midstream was still carving his name as a sire, and Idle Words was just a brawny addition to the string running loose in the hills.

As Midstream made his way towards the covering shed, he stepped with the contour of excitement. In summer, the Kia Ora stallions were stabled to avoid the heat and flies, so the Blandford stallion was toey, finding not only freedom from the dusty confines of his box, but the sexy whiff of a waiting mare. Pulling against his groom Jack Keown, Midstream bounced and whooped his way towards Idle Words.

The union was brief and unromantic. The stallion was barely off the mare when he was spirited back to the barn and Idle Words to a small holding paddock. Not Jack Keown, nor Percy Miller or the Kia Ora manager Bert Riddle, knew if the match would be successful. At the very least, over the next few months as Idle Words' belly fell downwards, they knew they would have a foal come spring.

The mare grew bushy and plump through the winter, and as September 1941 approached she was led away from the main broodmare band into a foaling paddock. In the last week of September she was restless and heavy, and Bert Riddle brought her into a foaling pen, close to the homestead. Late into the night of 29 September 1941, Idle Words, in the tall grass of Kia Ora, dropped a colt foal with a smudgy white stripe down his face.

—

Bert Riddle and Jack Keown hovered on the foaling-pen fence as the colt was squeezed out into the world. Idle Words glanced around at the foal, her second, then watched as Riddle and Keown strode over to cleanse and disinfect the youngster. Their job done, the two men left the pair in the darkness, and by morning the youngster was trotting around on his feet.

In the sunlight, Riddle recorded that he was a bay fellow, with a white sock on his near hind, a white band around his off-fore hoof, and a splash down his face that was wide and purposeful between his eyes, faded to a thin strip down his nose. Privately, Riddle thought the colt had a low-set appearance. Nothing robust or bullish about this one. For a week or so, Idle Words and her colt remained in the foaling pen, bonding under the shade of the ghost gums. They were then moved to a small barley paddock, where the young foal stretched his straight legs for the first time, gradually growing in confidence and bone. After 10 days they went to the broodmare band, and tens of acres of stout pasture and rolling freedom. The colt gambolled around Kia Ora for six months like that, until he was hustled into the 80-acre yearling paddock with all the other young males. He would remain there until the day he was trucked out of Miller's farm, about 12 months later.

He was bound for the 1943 yearling sales.

4
War and horse-trading

In the gritty, industrial suburb of Alexandria in Sydney's east, at a stroke after midnight in March 1943, a livestock train came to a thud against its railway siding. With steam whistling from the underbelly, boxcar doors swung open and ramps dropped, and the sound of horse hooves sliced the quiet city night. The Kia Ora yearlings, 48 of them, had arrived from Scone for the Sydney sales.

There were 19 youngsters by Midstream, and among them the little Idle Words colt. He was smaller than his half-siblings, narrower and closer to the ground, still low-set. But as the string set off from Alexandria, for they had to walk three miles to reach the Newmarket saleyards of William Inglis & Son, he came into his own. He was balanced and sensible, curious even about his new, dingy surroundings.

The horses pitched the sound of iron clear into the night, 192 neatly shod hooves splitting the sleeping suburb. As they clattered south-east along Alexandria's streets they brought folks out of bed. Curtains twitched in the windows of workmen's cottages, and front doors swung open to wish them luck. Kia Ora's handlers, about 25 of them, men with thick forearms and a horse on each side, sometimes two, nodded their heads in greeting. Then it was onwards to south Randwick.

The Idle Words colt followed the string as it headed towards Victoria Park Racecourse. He crossed Joynton Avenue and followed Epsom Road until the suburb of Kensington. Winding through the back streets, he made it to Anzac Parade and over the tramlines that went all the way to La Perouse. He walked briefly along Doncaster Avenue, lined with racing homes, then turned east along High Street until he met Botany Street. Swinging right, the entire team coolly, calmly walked south until they came to the junction of Botany and Barker. Turning left into Barker Street, they had only a little way to go before they arrived at the Newmarket saleyards, the home of Australian horse-trading. They were just in time for the shards of morning light that were breaking in the east.

—

The Kia Ora yearlings were late arriving to Randwick. Usually Bert Riddle shipped them a week after the New Year, and usually there were about 100 of them. But the war had brought normality to a skidding halt, and this year there was barely half the stock for sale. Fodder shortages and tightened belts had carved into every breeder in New South Wales. Even the yearling catalogue, which had always displayed each lot on a full page, was leaner. There were now two horses advertised on each sheet, not to mention that the 331 yearlings to go under the hammer were about half the normal output.

The federal government had made it very difficult for the racing and breeding industries. In 1942, a ban had been implemented on the carriage of racehorses by rail. It was quickly followed by a ban on the carriage of racehorses by float for distances greater than 25 miles. These restrictions meant that trainers were unable to get horses to race meetings, breeders were unable to get yearlings to markets, and the bloodstock industry was getting squeezed. Stud farms had to host paddock sales to shift stock, Kia Ora the first in New South Wales to do so.

Until February in 1943, Percy Miller had had no idea how to get his yearlings, the Idle Words colt among them, to Sydney. But at this time, the House of Representatives met and grilled the Prime Minister, John Curtin, over the asphyxiation of horseracing. Along with the curtailment of transport, Curtin had to explain why the first Saturday in every month had to be free of racing, and also his intentions to curb SP (starting price) betting. Racing, more than any other sport in Australia during this war, was taking a hard hit from politicians. Prime Minister Curtin stated that the race-less Saturday was necessary in order that the war effort be brought home to the average Australian. Regarding SP betting, he stated that the pouring of money into bookies' bags was also detrimental to the war effort. Curtin had placed an embargo on workers buying homes priced above £350. Did he plan, asked his opposition, to impose the same restrictions on yearling buyers?

Over the following weeks, the federal parliament debated the issue. Curtin was resolute that the sport had little place in a society at war. A quarter of all Australian men aged between 18 and 40 years were overseas fighting the cause. What impropriety it was to be cheering and gambling at such a time. On the other hand, the bloodstock industry was worth hundreds of thousands of pounds a year in horseflesh and manpower, and the war would not last forever. Curtin knew that if he didn't loosen the stranglehold, the industry would be on its knees long after peace was declared. Something had to be done.

On 6 March 1943, the Minister for Transport, George Lawson, declared a relaxation on the rail ban. He revealed that the carriage of racehorses was still prohibited but, as yearlings were not technically racehorses, they were exempt. As breeders hurriedly set about with booking passages in order to make the Easter sales in six weeks' time, Lawson added that the relaxation would only occur where it did not affect the war effort. In essence, only boxcars that would otherwise be empty would carry the young thoroughbreds to Sydney.

William Inglis & Son rolled its presses right away. The catalogue for the 1943 sale was dispersed around Australia by 12 March. It listed 331 yearlings by 62 sires. Midstream had the largest representation with 19. Kia Ora's draft had a total of 48 horses, challenged only by the 50 consigned by the Thompson brothers.

—

The daily swing began once the Kia Ora draft was settled into the Inglis complex at Newmarket. The Easter sales were due to commence at 10 am on Tuesday 20 April, resuming for the second session the following day, so the young horses had a month to adjust to their surroundings. For most of them, it was their first experience in a stable. The Idle Words youngster found the confinement a struggle. For the first few days he was listless and difficult, pawing the straw away from his floor and biting the woodwork. The new diet of hay and hard feed didn't help. He kicked and paced about his box, giving one of his hind fetlocks a decent knock. Bert Riddle knew the wound was superficial, but it became a touch swollen and ugly. Riddle treated it and hoped it would disappear in time for the buying inspections, but it didn't. When Newmarket began to fill with potential buyers – trainers and bloodstock agents, restaurant owners and pastoralists – it was obvious this particular Midstream was carrying an injury.

Percy Miller had prioritised his draft so that the best youngsters would sell first. The Midstreams were lots 70 to 79 on the first day, followed by the lesser fancied ones on the second day. Idle Words' foal was Lot 79, the last of the group on the first day of trade. Though a fancied colt, he was at the bottom of the pecking order. With a steady flow of people through the Kia Ora barn, only a few sidled past Lot 79. When they did, they saw an undersized bay colt with an untidy hind leg and an average pedigree, and they moved on. They entirely missed the sharp, intelligent attributes that Bert Riddle had seen since the day the horse was born. He had been keeping a close eye on the colt, had watched how he had settled into his environment. The horse was sensitive, needed time to adjust to his surroundings, but learned quickly. Bert Riddle was convinced there was something different about him. It was just a hunch he got from time to time with youngsters, and he shared his thoughts about Lot 79 with only one man.

His brother, Peter Riddle.

5

Peter Riddle

Peter Riddle was tall and drawn in the autumn of 1943, thinner than he should have been. His shoulders were angular and bony, the lines in his face deep and his eye sockets pale and purple. He dressed well, paid careful attention to buttoning his waistcoat and pinning his watch to his lapel, but the effort was lost. These days there wasn't enough of Peter Riddle to fill his clothes, so he looked thin in his drapes and old.

He was, in fact, 58 years of age. He lived in a neat brick cottage at 4 Norton Street, Randwick, just behind the Kensington pony track. Riddle was a horse trainer, and rented stables at 16 Bowral Street, Kensington. It was the racing hub of Sydney's eastern suburbs, just off Doncaster Avenue and just west of Randwick Racecourse. Though he had often had up to 20 horses in his yard during his time on Bowral Street, these days Riddle had half that. It was the limit of what he could manage.

He was a quiet, private character. Peter Riddle woke each morning at the crack of dawn, slipped into his clothes and drove his 1938-model Chrysler Royal the short trip to Bowral Street. As much as his health would allow it, he pulled the saddles from the tack-room racks and slung them over his small team. He brushed the straw from his horses' manes, or knelt on the floor to wrap their legs. He would follow his charges to Randwick for their morning workouts, sometimes striding along behind them, other times on a pony. When he was unwell, it took him time to reach the track. He would perch by the inside running rail, or hover on the roof of the tote building with the other trainers, always frail and a bit cold, but ever the gentleman. With never a bad word to say about anyone, Peter Riddle was one of the nicest, most liked identities in Sydney racing.

He was born at Kaarimba, Victoria, on 26 July 1884. Kaarimba was a rural outpost with little more than a post office, about 140 miles north of Melbourne. His father, Walter, had found himself there on the gold trail years before and, marrying local girl Catherine Smeaton, he produced six children in the Kaarimba district, Peter the second of five boys (Bert was three years his junior). Their existence was that of simple country folk. Walter worked in the wheat fields and grazed cattle and sheep as Peter grew up. When Peter was six, the family moved to Cowra, in New South Wales, where they took up the lifestyle they had left behind in Kaarimba. It was here that young Peter was introduced to racing horses. In 1897, his father paid 100 guineas for a nine-year-old trotting stallion called Picaninny, and with an eye to standing the horse locally he competed Picaninny around the trotting tracks of Cowra and Canowindra. Peter, all wide eyes and curiosity, was barely 13 years old.

He was his father's shadow as Walter evolved the family's interests in harness racing. Peter learned to hitch the sulky to his father's horses, learned how to drive them and guide them around turns, how to negotiate races. Soon enough, Walter relied on his boys to take care of the small team he had mustered. Peter, Bert and David (the eldest son) ran a good ship through the last parts of the 1800s, turning out Picaninny progeny and sweeping the local trotting scene.

From the outside, the Riddles were doing well. They were a large family, now seven children, but on the inside, the unit was falling apart. Catherine, Peter's mother, was violent and unhinged, having an affair. The boys often walked in on her beating Helen, the eldest of the children (affectionately called 'Nellie'). They had seen their mother dragging Nellie from a stool by her hair, or jamming her face against the wall. When Walter stepped in to protect his children, he was pelted with hot tea or jabbed with corkscrews, whatever his wife could get her hands on. On 3 February 1897, Catherine was on a bender. As Walter lay sleeping in the couple's bedroom, she burst into the room with a cup in her hand. Nellie, who had been in the room with her father, yelled out. When Walter sat up in bed, his wife threw a cup of carbolic acid in his face. The household erupted. David and Peter, barely teenagers, spirited their father to the Cowra hospital, where they learned Walter had lost sight in one eye and was impaired in the other. It was the last straw. Their mother left the family home that night, and by 1900 she was dead.

The incident left an ugly stain on Peter Riddle's adolescence. His mother's domestic violence and, through 1898, his parents' divorce battle became a lurid public affair. It filled the newspapers from Cowra to Sydney to Perth in Western Australia. Peter and his siblings were hauled into court to testify against their mother, and their evidence was documented across the country. There were headlines: 'Woman or Fiend? Accusations by a Husband', and 'Cruelty to a Husband'. The Riddle family laundry was on show for the entire country, and it appalled and embarrassed young Peter.

Walter removed his children from Cowra a few years later, relocating to Granville, on the outskirts of Sydney, around 1905. Most of the boys were young men by then, including Peter, but they followed their father and his stallion Picaninny to Sydney. Setting up an elaborate trotting property, with breeding paddocks and Picaninny sire sons, the Riddle empire grew quickly. David, Peter and Bert all displayed the horsemanship in handling and driving that their father had encouraged from them, and Peter in particular was hooked. He traipsed around the country tracks of New South Wales with his father's horses, competing in local shows at Orange, Forbes and Bathurst. In June 1907, he drove for the first time on a Sydney track. Competing at Ascot, a proprietary pony course at Mascot in the south-east of the city, Peter Riddle scored a treble with his father's horses, and he never looked back. His name was so well known among owners that he rode and drove many non-Riddle pacers.

Among the owners who sent their horses to him was Percy Miller. The irascible, interesting Miller had his trotting interests based at his mansion Fairfield along the Windsor Road. In 1912, Miller's number one driver (and Fairfield manager) was disqualified, and Miller went in search of Peter Riddle. Then 28 years old, and assisted by his brothers Bert and David, Riddle moved in to Fairfield to run the Miller operation.

The relationship was smooth and successful. There was something about the Millers and the Riddles that just worked. Peter Riddle, like Bert, was calm and inoffensive to Miller's high-strung, overwhelming persona. Riddle drove 101 winners before the end of 1914, shipping horses to tracks in Melbourne, west New South Wales and even New Zealand. But by 1915, Percy Miller's attention had wavered towards thoroughbreds. After purchasing Kia Ora, he extracted Bert from the Fairfield operation to run his new bloodstock interests. Slowly, he dismantled his pacing empire, selling off his trotters or leasing them out to Riddle. By 1922, it was all but gone.

Peter Riddle rented stables in various locales around Sydney for a few years, first at Canterbury then Mascot. With Bert in the Hunter, and David in Hobart running a string that his father had established there, he was on his own. It mattered little. Between 1911 and 1921, Riddle claimed the Sydney driver championship seven times. He had a plethora of brilliant trotters, including Homeleigh Dick and the outstanding Sheikh, with whom he reached his greatest heights in the sport. Off the tracks, Riddle remained private and withdrawn. He was not a flamboyant man, didn't bet or splurge on the drink. His horses were everything to him, and when he wasn't with them he was at home, poring through standardbred pedigrees or mapping out the driving season. But he did meet a woman, a local girl living in Windsor. She was Newcastle-born Linda May Casey, and she was the daughter of an engineer. They were married in February 1922, after which Riddle decided he needed a change.

The prizemoney for trotting had remained relatively poor in Australia and, attracted by better propositions in New Zealand, he shipped his new wife and a team of standardbreds to Auckland, then Christchurch. In 1924, he drove Sheikh to a gallant win in the New Zealand Cup, setting a new track record for two miles. But this, and other wins, failed to attract New Zealand owners. By 1927, after five long years in the Dominion, Riddle and Linda, with Sheikh and a select few of the string in tow, returned to Sydney.

This handful of years had wearied the trainer. He had a young daughter, June, who was five years old when they arrived back in Sydney. Sheikh was pushing along in years, and the state of trotting in New South Wales was not promising. Prizemoney was appalling, and the proprietary tracks were getting squeezed by the Australian Jockey Club. Trotting was running out of venues. Riddle had been up and down to Kia Ora since his brother had begun managing it, and Bert had kept saying the future was thoroughbreds. Percy Miller had no trotters in work by then, and Riddle had a long, labouring think about defecting to registered racing.

The transition wouldn't be as difficult as he first imagined. A few of the country's leading flat trainers had done it, including Lou Robertson. But Riddle was not a compulsive man, and didn't make his decision hastily. The light-harness sport was in his blood. For years it had been all he knew. Trotting was the thing his family had excelled at; from the Kaarimba districts to Cowra and Sydney, the Riddles had been stars of this code. They were breeders, trainers, drivers and conditioners, and if it weren't for the poor health of the sport, and a lingering back weakness, Riddle wouldn't have been leaving it.

Nevertheless, around the middle of 1927, Peter Riddle began making the transition to training thoroughbreds. He won his last trotting race at the proprietary course Victoria Park, in Sydney's inner west, on 6 February 1928, and by then he had dispersed much of his stock. He already held a permit from the AJC to train a single thoroughbred, but he applied for a No.1 trainer's licence, which would allow him to train at Randwick Racecourse. In August 1928 it was granted, and Riddle became an official licensed trainer at Sydney's largest racecourse.

He took up rental of his stables on Bowral Street that month. The block belonged to the widow of the late trainer Frank Marsden. The yard was tucked in from the street by a short laneway that then opened up into a narrow, L-shaped complex. The boxes ran down the left of the yard, then swung around to the west. They were simple brick, discoloured by age and sunlight, but airy and liveable for the horses. As Riddle moved into the swing of flat racing, his yard quickly became like that of any other Randwick trainer: head collars and lead ropes limp off stable doors, straw bales stacked in the feed room, a chalkboard of horse information hanging in the tack room.

The change of routine was significant. Riddle found himself rising very early in the mornings now, following his team to a much more crowded training session than he had experienced with his trotters. On any morning, the AJC dictated which track was open to morning gallops, be it the course proper where racing occurred, or the A and B training tracks, or indeed the inside tan or cinders. There were about 500 horses in training at Randwick Racecourse, so a constant stream of animals meandered around the tracks each morning, drumming short spurts or long, grinding canters. Riddle's team, which numbered about 10 in his early days, worked their way around with horses that included, by 1929, Phar Lap, Nightmarch and Amounis.

Riddle had transferred his trotting colours to his thoroughbred operation. His own horses would race in pale blue and black halves, black cap (his trotting cap had been yellow). While he intended to own many of his own racehorses, he had an enviable bank of owners starting out. Percy Miller had promised him patronage, along with Miller's brother Robert, who was a successful owner. Riddle also had the support of Hugh Cameron, who had once owned Sheikh, and Bob Byers, both of whom were trotting men he had carried over to thoroughbreds. For the first few months of his new career, Riddle did little more than tick over. He had some success with pedestrian runners, horses that could give him a good mid-week win, or a Saturday purse if he was lucky. One of such horses was Celebrate, whom he campaigned to some decent wins for many years. But Riddle was barely on his feet in 1931 when he was disqualified.

The incident involved his owner and friend, Bob Byers, and the horse he trained for Byers, Prince Elmo. Entered into the Second Division of the Juvenile Handicap at Canterbury Racecourse, a track on the west fringes of the city, on 18 March 1931, Prince Elmo, under jockey Alf Stanton, sat an easy third in running and finished the race in second spot. But the winning horse's owner and jockey suspected foul play by the Prince Elmo team and told the stewards as much. Riddle and his owner were hauled over the coals for improper practices, in this case failing to let their horse finish on, and their appeals came to nothing. Though the jockey left proceedings without so much as a slap on the wrist, AJC officials disqualified Riddle and Byers for 12 months. Neither man could train or own a racehorse for a year.

Riddle's nature was such that he didn't bleat his innocence all around Randwick. It just wasn't in him to argue or protest wildly. The stewards refused to accept his good character and clean record as evidence in his appeal, and so he was forced, as part of the disqualification, to disperse his racing stock. He sent almost 15 horses out to grass or to other trainers; some he simply sold off.

It was a blot on the trainer's spruce record. Riddle hated the publicity it invoked. He found himself in the same sort of scandalous headlines he remembered from 1898 – 'Turf Sensation: Three Men Sent Out', and 'Three Disqualified: Prince Elmo Case'. The incident was covered in the *Sydney Morning Herald*, the *Age* in Melbourne, and local rags as far as Townsville in north Queensland. Riddle feared that he was so early into his flat-racing career that he might be undone for good. But 12 months down the line, he slowly rebuilt his operation. The Millers, Byers and most of Riddle's loyal owners were unfazed by the disqualification. They sent him new horses, and some of the old ones, and the Bowral Street team began to hum again. Celebrate notched up some tidy wins at Randwick and Moorefield, and there were others. It wasn't unusual to see Riddle horses one-two in mid-week meetings. But as the seas smoothed, further public humiliation was just around the corner. In 1940, his wife Linda May was caught having an affair. After 18 years of marriage, she had grown bored and frustrated. As if history were repeating itself, Peter Riddle found her (like his mother had been) aggressive and impatient at home. He hated the fact that she was drinking wildly and swearing in their daughter's presence. When she began to disappear at night, Riddle suspected infidelity.

He hired a private detective to follow his wife, and her affair was quickly uncovered. On St Patrick's Day in 1940, he confronted Linda May in the little flat she had been visiting at Forest Lodge, finding her in bed asleep with a young man. He immediately petitioned for a divorce, landing himself not only in his father's nightmare from years back, but in the gossip pages of the tabloid newspapers: 'Trainer's Wife Preferred the Butcher Boy', sang the *Mirror*. The article threw up every embarrassing detail of that St Patrick's Day night, and for a conservative, private character like Peter Riddle, the incident was, for the second time in his life, mortifying.

With Linda May gone, he and June settled down in their brick bungalow on Norton Street. Life was comfortable, even with the onset of war. Riddle wasn't short of money, and he had property inheritance in the wake of his father's death in 1933. When June married in 1942, to a Frenchman living in Sydney named Andre Ozoux, Riddle took a live-in housekeeper by the name of Kathleen Cranney. He worried what people thought of this situation, a 57-year-old man with a young woman (Kathleen was 31) living in his home. He felt like much of his life had already been public spectacle, and he was naturally concerned this would be just another incident.

And so he ticked away into the early part of the 1940s, with a low public profile and more and more time invested into his stable. But the ageing trainer was yet to nab a champion, or a horse that remotely resembled one. He had sat in the stands through the 1930s as Phar Lap, Peter Pan and Ajax broke the hearts of his own humble team. With the cloudy, suppressive days of World War II, Riddle still was in search of that elusive horse, the one that every trainer begs for. Amid the distractions of brown-outs, rationing and a curtailment to his sport, he was beginning to think that horse wouldn't come at all.

—

When Bert Riddle told his older brother about the Idle Words colt, Peter Riddle had about 10 horses in Bowral Street. It was early 1943, and the trainer was increasingly unwell. He was finding his breaths were becoming short and tight, his chest constricted. In the beginning, his pain had occurred as he followed his string to the track each morning, or as he got stuck in with the lads back at the yard. These days, it was coming on at rest.

He was suffering from arteriosclerosis, or coronary sclerosis as his doctor called it. Somewhere in Riddle's chest, a blood vessel was narrowing due to fat deposition, and it was blocking the passage of oxygen to his heart. His tolerance for any physical exertion was getting worse as the months went on, and it worried him deeply. He was a horse trainer; physical labour was part of his job. He pulled out the yearling catalogue in March 1943. Flicking to Lot 79, he took a long read of the pedigree of this Idle Words youngster, the one his brother had been harping on about . . . bay colt, from the 8 family on Bruce Lowe's figures . . . the second foal from the mare, closely related to Manitoba and from the same family as the Derby winner Mid-day Sun. Bert was adamant about this one.

Riddle had visited Kia Ora on a regular basis, less so these days with his illness. He usually had a bird's eye view of the yearlings coming through, and this year he had the inside track on not only Lot 79, but also Lot 73, a bay colt out of the Spearhead mare Glade. Riddle believed that he could secure the Glade colt for a competitive price, though he suspected it wouldn't be a small price, and then pick up the Idle Words youngster for a few hundred guineas.

The trainer saw through early April with his usual busy schedule, tending his small team and preparing his tactics for the sales. It wasn't unusual for Riddle to appear among the top buyers at the Newmarket complex each Easter, and this year would prove no different.

6

The small fellow with
the big brain

Late on the morning of Tuesday 20 April, Peter Riddle pulled on a pressed white shirt and a pair of dark cotton trousers, matching jacket. He gathered up his yearling catalogue and a cluster of registration papers, and he left 4 Norton Street, heading east.

It was a calm, balmy morning over the eastern suburbs. Riddle crossed Botany Street and turned right. There were motor cars all over the roads, most headed the same way he was. He crossed Barker into Young Street, strode a little way down that crowded, bustling avenue, then walked through the gates of the William Inglis & Son saleyards.

Newmarket was alive with activity. It was just after 10 am, so the business of the annual Easter yearling sales had just kicked off. Riddle could hear the gravelly tones of auctioneer Reg Inglis as he boomed through the amplifiers up in the sale ring. Inglis was calling the early lots. Riddle wound his way through the throngs of buyers and vendors towards the amphitheatre. The Widden youngsters were just beginning to sell when Riddle took a seat in the crowd.

The sale ring was a large, open space that sat in the shadows of an immense fig tree. There was covered seating around half of it, while the other half, under the tree, was open to the elements. When people ran out of room, they planted themselves cross-legged on the grass where the horses paraded. Riddle had seen many a popular auction when the rows of onlookers were six and seven deep. On this day, it wasn't that crowded. Glancing around, he recognised many faces from the track: Bailey Payten and ex-jockey Maurice McCarten, and Frank McGrath was loitering. There were jockeys too, some unrecognisable outside of their silks, and stud masters and bloodstock agents. Some people were simply there for the spectacle, a few ladies in neat frocks enjoying the sunshine, and Riddle noticed the number of soldiers that had come along this year. Some were Yanks, others Australians. They were all in uniform, a blunt reminder that the nation was at war.

The conflict had muted the tone of horse selling only a little. Though the number of lots was down on non-war years, Riddle could sense buoyancy in the crowd around him. It was like a race day. He had spoken with other trainers in the lead-up to selling and almost all had large owners willing to outlay hefty sums on the right lots. War wouldn't keep them from buying yearlings this day, even if it was Adolf Hitler's birthday. Though rationing, a severe constriction on race days and wartime coverage were all sober reminders of tough international affairs, racing was one of those outlets in Australia that was able to forget about it all.

Within half an hour of Riddle sitting down, the first Kia Ora youngster went into the ring. Reg Inglis had no need of introducing Percy Miller's bloodstock; the Kia Ora reputation was as solid and established as the fig tree hanging over them. The first colt, Lot 71 (Miller had withdrawn Lot 70), was by Midstream out of a sister to Melbourne Cup hero Hall Mark. She was knocked down for a respectable 450 guineas, and with only one horse to go before the Glade colt, Riddle was getting nervous.

He positioned himself in such a place that the Inglis bid-spotters could see him. They already knew of his interest in Lot 73 – it was their job to know such things. As Lot 72 left the ring for 300 guineas, the Glade colt trotted nervously into the crowded auditorium. Sharp, short shouts began to ring across the crowd as Reg Inglis called the horse to the high hundreds. Miller nodded his head for 1000 guineas and the spotters were silent. Without another call, the colt was Peter Riddle's.

There wasn't a better feeling for a horseman than knowing he had secured a valuable animal. As the colt left the ring, Riddle had barely time to bask in it when it was time to concentrate all over again. Though Lot 73 had been his prize for the day, Lot 79 wasn't far off.

The little colt entered the ring without much of a fuss. Immediately, Riddle could see the straight-shooting, unfussed attitude that his brother had been taken with. When other youngsters had pulled and reared at their lead ropes, this fellow stopped short every time he was startled, sizing up the intrusion. Then he would calmly walk on when the threat had passed. Though there wasn't much of him, and one of his hind legs was bandaged over that superficial wound, there was a lot to like about this one.

Inglis began his energetic sales pitch, reciting Lot 79's pedigree. 'He's out of a winning mare. Do I have 300?' A spotter's call sailed into the air, Riddle's bid. 'I've got 300, do I have four?' he sang. 'Do I have four for this son of a promising sire? Only the third crop. Do I have 400?' Another bid was pitched into the ring.

'Four hundred, I've got 400 for the colt.' Inglis could get little more from the crowd. The spotters twitched at the edge of the ring, glancing between the interested parties. No one spoke. 'Give me 25,' Inglis sang into his microphone. 'I'll take 25 on him.'

Riddle nodded his head and the bid spotter hollered, raising his hand to the auctioneer. 'It's 425 then,' Inglis yelled, anxious to extract more for the colt. 'A fine colt by a promising sire, he's from Kia Ora folks.' But there was nothing left to bleed from the audience. Reg Inglis brought the gavel down on Lot 79. 'He's gone to Peter Riddle, thank you sir.'

The colt was headed for Bowral Street.

7

The little Irish horse

Lot 79 found himself, the morning after his sale, in box number seven at Peter Riddle's yard. That day, and most of the days that followed it, began exactly the same.

Before the birds stirred, before the clatter of delivery vans or flatbed milk trucks, the stable shook off sleep. From the feed room began the clang of buckets and scoops, the dumping of rolled oats and grain. Boot heels clunked across the gravel under the rusty calls of lads and exercise riders. There was the kettle whistling, and the throaty nickering of impatient horses. Everywhere, like a permanent air-borne stain, the smell of molasses and stretched leather. Routine.

In those early days at Bowral Street, the small colt found himself in the leathery, pale hands of Riddle's foreman, Barney O'Brien. O'Brien was an honest seed, an ageing fellow (51) with miles on the clock. He had big ears and a magic touch with young horses. He knew how to soak the best from them, knew how to prune them into good racehorses. He had been a leading rider in the western districts of New South Wales moons ago. O'Brien was the reason that Riddle kept most of his yearlings in the yard during the breaking process, rather than sending them away to have them started under bridle and saddle.

O'Brien spent hours with the new horse. This boy, he knew, was something interesting, something special to the boss. He slowly worked the youngster into a saddle on the Randwick grounds, in the round yards on the southern end of the track. As the colt grew muscle and mass, O'Brien began to lean on him, first a little weight, then a lot. Within a month, Lot 79 was carrying the old foreman around the training tracks at a slow, wayward, often distracted, trot.

Because of the horse's light frame, O'Brien didn't rush him. Instead, he encouraged the smart out of him. He allowed the horse to think about his surroundings, to pick at grass under the running rail and nose his lead pony. He brought the horse to the track during the two-year-old jump-outs in the late mornings, and he rode him when it was wet, dry or windy, quiet on the course or frantic in the early mornings. If the colt played up, O'Brien would pat the hot neck and mutter, 'Calm yourself, Jerry. I've no time for your games now.'

The old foreman had nicknamed the youngster 'Jerry'. In part, it was because Idle Words' foal was somewhat plain, neither flashy nor impressive enough for anything grander. For the most part, though, the name stemmed from O'Brien's admiration of Randwick trainer Jerry Carey, whom O'Brien thought the most astute judge of horseflesh. 'He's a good judge of horses, and this one is the best I know, so I named him after Jerry,' O'Brien recalled years later.

As the strapper got the colt used to his 'Jerry' tag, Peter Riddle made his way to the office of the Australian Jockey Club (AJC) at 6 Bligh Street, Sydney. He went there to register his new yearlings with the Registrar of Racehorses, the custodian of all thoroughbred identities in New South Wales. He had had to decide on names for each of his youngsters, unique tags that might represent their pedigree, or their looks. Sometimes, though, he just liked the feel of a name. The promising Glade yearling became Beltana, and another purchase, a filly by Le Grand Duc, became Gipsy Lady. Riddle had purchased the top lot on the second day of the Inglis sales, a colt by Golden Sovereign out of the Windbag mare Jenny's Bag, and that animal became Randolph. But Lot 79 got the most appropriate name of all. With his sire Midstream firmly on Peter Riddle's mind, the Idle Words colt was christened 'Shannon', after the long, willowy river that wound through western Ireland.

—

In any year, the arrival of upcoming two-year-olds to the track has every racing man sitting up and paying attention. In 1943 it was no different. When Peter Riddle and his fellow trainers trotted out their new recruits that year, turf reporters scribbled furiously in their pads, calling out to exercise riders for the name of the youngsters, stretching their memories for the pedigrees and sale records. Owners took mental pictures of potential good 'uns, and punters, clock-stoppers and average Joes lined the running rails in the mornings, seeking out the stars of tomorrow. It wasn't long before they found a few.

Shannon began to turn heads early in his two-year-old preparation. In part it was because he was undersized; there just wasn't that much to him. But as he began to gallop, as he learned how to run like a thoroughbred should, it became clear he would be very, very good. He had neat action, the kind of motion that was efficient and straight. Each of his legs moved in such a way that he covered a lot of ground with minimal effort. He wasn't a high stepper, or an extravagant mover. Shannon was an economic galloper, a horse that got the job done with simple rhythms. Each morning, as he plied his trade around Randwick under Barney O'Brien, he got better and better at it.

By July, Peter Riddle was training the colt at the barrier. Each young thoroughbred at Randwick had to learn how to jump away with a race field, so the AJC hosted two-year-old jump-outs to teach the young horses about the starting strands and the New South Wales standing start. With O'Brien's cool hands on the reins, Shannon was taught to stand in a line with other horses, directly in front of the five-stranded tapes that stretched across the track. He learned about the fine line between standing still while remaining toey enough to leap away as the tapes flew up in front of him. He was a smart colt, and he learned the process quickly.

Towards August, Barney O'Brien began to relinquish the morning workout to a qualified jockey. Riddle elected ex-Queenslander, now Sydney hoop, Fred Shean for the job. Shean began to partner Shannon a few mornings a week around

Randwick and, under the experienced, disciplined guidance of a professional jockey, the colt began to shape into a proper race-horse. On 26 August, Shannon and Shean sprinted two furlongs on the course proper in 26¾ seconds. The pair went with Riddle's other two-year-old colt, Bravo, a very promising youngster that had been born at Kia Ora to Bert Riddle's mare Derring Do. Bert had retained the colt rather than consigning him for sale with the others, and Bravo had arrived at Bowral Street just after the yearling sales. He and Shannon did most of their work together, and Riddle quickly discovered that these two were his standout two-year-olds.

By the first few weeks of September, Shannon was stretching over half-miles in the morning. Riddle began to ask quicker sectionals of him. On 9 September, Shean got three furlongs and nine yards, running with Bravo, in 38 seconds. It wasn't a dazzling time, just good enough to be solid.

The formula for sectionals in horseracing came from the belief that it takes an average horse 12 seconds to cover a furlong. During trackwork, the rule was a useful one as it helped clockers, trainers and jockeys to measure how standard a gallop was. In a race, the rule was less applicable because the pace was slackened off after the initial jostle for positions, then picked up in earnest inside the last three furlongs. But, over six furlongs, a horse carrying a standard weight and running to the 12-second rule would complete the distance in 72 seconds, or 1:12. During morning laps, if a horse ran a half-mile (four furlongs) under 48 seconds, it was considered a good clip.

On 14 September, with about four months of schooling behind him, Shannon lined up for a public jump-out at Randwick. It was late morning, long after trackwork had wound up, and trainers, owners and turf reporters queued along the rail by the winning post to witness the spectacle. Shannon, under Fred Shean, was due to trial with Bravo and Silver Flare, a colt by Melbourne Cup winner Marabou. The three horses lined up beside each other at the half-mile post, which sat just before the bend into the home turn. Vintage AJC starter Jack Gaxieu would send them away.

When they set off, Bravo and Silver Flare sprung away from the ground. Shannon took a second to go after them, but entering the straight he was poised widest, albeit last, in stride and moving easily. They covered the first quarter in 25 seconds, and down the straight Shannon began to haul himself over his rivals. By the furlong post he was in front, hard held. He whizzed over the line in 49½ seconds for the half-mile.

The time was respectable, though not the fastest of the trials that day. That honour belonged to a son of Golden Sovereign, Majesty, who had been tagged already as the boom two-year-old of the season. Majesty had clocked a shade over 48 seconds for his heat, and he stole most of the headlines that morning. Even the famous turf scribe 'Cardigan' (Bert Wolfe, who had escorted Phar Lap to Agua Caliente in 1932) described him as the 'raciest two-year-old' he had seen for many years. Nevertheless, of Shannon, the *Sportsman* noted, 'In our modest opinion, Shannon, trained by Peter Riddle, will prove one of the smartest youngsters of the season.'

The Midstream colt began to thicken and grow, though he was almost always smaller than his rivals. Frank McGrath, the old, respected hero of the Australian turf and the former trainer of Peter Pan and Amounis, fondly called Shannon 'the little Irish horse'. But the colt's size became an afterthought through September 1943. Shannon won another trial for colts and geldings that month, lining up against Bravo, a very promising Victory Lad, and 12 others. It was the biggest field he had yet met on a racecourse. Once again hard held by Fred Shean, the colt hauled himself through the four furlongs in 48½ seconds, winning by three-quarters of a length to Victory Lad, Bravo finishing a half-length back in third. Two days later, Riddle trucked him to the proprietary track Ascot, a former pony racecourse, where Shannon ran the same time for the distance, the best of the morning.

The old trainer kept the springs tight on his young charge. Shannon breezed over half-miles a few mornings a week, sometimes three furlongs, then loped in easy canters on the other days. He wouldn't, in fact, go the full distance of his first race start (five furlongs) until the race itself.

Riddle planned to debut both Shannon and Bravo in the AJC Breeders' Plate on 9 October. It would be the first day of the spring carnival at Randwick, the second race off the bat. The Breeders' Plate was an event for two-year-old colts and geldings over five furlongs under set weights, so every horse would carry 8 st 5 lbs. Along with Shannon and Bravo, the race had attracted both of the star colts Majesty and Victory Lad, along with eight other rivals. In the final few days before the meeting, the Sydney newspapers rallied to those two. *Sportsman* wrote, 'Though Majesty appears to overshadow the rest of the two-year-olds this spring, we want you to keep Victory Lad in mind.' The newspaper forecast the Breeders' Plate finish as Majesty first, Cragsman second, Victory Lad third, and neither Shannon nor Bravo appeared of interest.

It wasn't that Shannon and Bravo looked unimpressive. In fact, both colts had been openly impressive in their trials since September, in particular Shannon. Rather, it was that the opposition in the Breeders' Plate was very, very good. Majesty, Victory Lad and Cragsman were top-class youngsters. They had all been prominent in their public trials, were all by fashionable imported sires, and many of them had faced off in the jump-outs. Majesty, also, had top Sydney jockey Darby Munro aboard. He was nicely bred, had been educated to a tee, and was yet to lose a trial.

As race day slid up, Peter Riddle didn't read the newspapers. It mattered little to him that his stars had been overlooked. A trainer preferred things that way; it took the pressure off, allowed him to get on with the job of training. So Shannon continued to breeze his good work in the early mornings, sliding under the radar right up to the day his career began.

8

The Sydney Turf Club

Wartime had Sydney by the throat with the rolling around of the 1943 spring carnival. Almost everyone in horseracing was affected, from the owners and trainers down to the feed man on Doncaster Avenue. It wasn't just the curbing of race days (the compulsory race-less Saturday in every month). It was the little things, the things that affected everyday living. In the papers daily there were recipes that required neither butter nor eggs. The RSPCA ran a series of advertisements on how to feed pets in the wake of meat rationing. Mutton and lamb supplies to Sydney had been cut for October (due mainly to the shortage of workers at abattoirs), while the Milk Board had issued warnings to its vendors about selling milk tokens on to customers. Everywhere, there were cuts to spending, cuts to supplies. Items like silk stockings, paper even, had become luxuries the working class just didn't have anymore.

Prime Minister Curtin counselled his public in early September that any relaxation in the control of goods would involve a weakening of the war effort. 'This does not mean the people will be asked to continue to sacrifice their living standards indefinitely,' Curtin said. 'The government is laying the foundations of a great social security scheme.' It didn't feel like it to many of the tired citizens of Australia. They needed an outlet from the obnoxious, unceasing talk of conflict, and they found it at Randwick Racecourse.

Record betting poured into Sydney's famous spring couple – the Epsom Metropolitan race double. The bag-swingers reported tickets of £2000 on the event, and many smaller bets had come from servicemen in battle stations. The AJC was expecting a huge turnout for the carnival, which would commence on Saturday 9 October, with the AJC Derby and Epsom Handicap the following Saturday, and the Metropolitan occurring on the final day of the meeting. 'All we want is fine weather,' commented AJC secretary George Rowe in the lead-up to opening day, 'and figures will reach amazing proportions.'

The figures he was hollering about were attendance, totalisator receipts and bookie betting. Rowe, who had helmed the AJC as secretary since 1932, rolling his club through the Depression and now the war years, was sensing a big event for Sydney headquarters. In part, it was because people were tired. 'Racing is an outlet for the nervous strain and stress on a war-working community,' commented the *Sydney Sportsman*. 'For some time past, despite the battering and ramming to which it has been subjected, it has become a real craze with the populace.' Racetracks had been enjoying a fat spike through the turnstiles since war broke out. Sydney's citizens were tired and overworked, underpaid and underappreciated. They worked longer hours for less pay, less food and less of the finer things in life. And they recouped these losses at the races, where they could cheer and make merry, forget the national despondency. As much as Prime Minister Curtin was ashamed that a gambling sport was counselling his citizenry, it was, and he couldn't change it.

From the AJC's point of view, this was good news. The war was bringing crowds into the racecourse, but in 1943 the club had another reason to hope for the best possible carnival. As of August, it had been competing with the newly formed Sydney Turf Club.

In years prior (since the formation of horseracing in Sydney in fact), the AJC had had a monopoly on registered racing with its headquarters at Randwick Racecourse and, from 1922 onwards, an additional venue at Warwick Farm (racing had not begun at the Farm until 1925). The AJC also controlled the Hawkesbury Race Club. These tracks were far from the only racing locations in the city, though. There were dozens of proprietary (privately owned) racing clubs dotted around, including Rosehill Racecourse on the western fringes of Sydney, Canterbury and Moorefield. There were also the pony courses Kensington (across the road from Randwick),

Victoria Park (in Zetland), Ascot, and the popular training track Rosebery (on the southern end of the eastern suburbs). By 1943, these courses were racing under the rules of racing governed by the AJC, and they were known as registered proprietary courses.

All these individually run clubs and their individual agendas were a bugbear for the sport. For years, reformation had been simmering. On 5 May 1943, it finally came when the Sydney Turf Club Bill was moved in the New South Wales Legislative Assembly. Its objective was to establish a genuine non-proprietary racing association that could acquire any or all of the Rosehill, Canterbury, Moorefield, Ascot, Victoria Park and Rosebery race-courses (the latter two were military-occupied, as was Kensington). It was entirely up to the new club which course, or courses, it wanted.

As the 1943 spring carnival swung around, the newly formed Sydney Turf Club (STC) was yet to acquire a racecourse. Estimates were that the club would require £50,000 a year to operate, and sporting newspapers were questioning where the dosh would come from in the event that race days could not generate it. The New South Wales colonial secretary, J. M. Baddeley, had interjected that a government guarantee could be imposed. This promoted a score of criticism from taxpayers. 'There are thousands of people in the community who are not interested in horseracing and there's no reason why they should be forced to help carry the STC baby,' sang the *Sportsman* newspaper. From the AJC's perspective, the success of the STC was vital. For decades, the parent club had been trying to clean up the proprietary racing scene in the state. In particular, it had wanted rid of the pony tracks. The STC would smarten the organisation of racing in the city, and it would have little impact on racing at Randwick and Warwick Farm. But the wheels were taking their time in turning. It would be January 1944 before the new club hosted its first race day.

The STC, nevertheless, had appointed a very impressive board of directors. These men, responsible for wading through a sea of red and tangled tape, had been personally selected by the premier,

W. J. McKell, and represented a powerhouse of Australian racing and breeding. Among them was the chairman of Tattersall's Club, William Walter Hill (who became chairman), George Ryder, Henry Tancred, Herbert Thompson (of the famous Thompson brothers), and Bert Riddle. Riddle's inclusion was a marvellous endorsement of his work at Kia Ora Stud. If he had needed a stamp of approval from the highest body in the land, this was it. He had been cherry-picked from hundreds of racing and breeding men across the state, and of him Premier McKell said, 'His appointment recognised the natural link between breeding and racing.' Bert Riddle's clever, managing mind and his natural way with horses would go a long way in the first steps of the STC.

9

'It was bad luck'

Early on the morning of Saturday 9 October, the first of 65 race-day trams rattled away from Circular Quay. Trundling through the choked streets of Sydney, nudging weekend shoppers and city traffic, the tram gathered racegoers like Mother Goose. By the time it bustled onto Anzac Parade, the main arterial road that would take it straight to Randwick Racecourse, it was full, carnival patrons spilling out its sides and swinging off the back.

War was on, so racegoers were somewhat demure in simple frocks and second-hand stockings. There was age and wear on men's coats, in their trousers and shoes. But this didn't mute the spirits of any who had paid up to go to the races. Crowds were animated and cheery as they filed through the racecourse turnstiles in the tens of thousands. Sprinkled around this tram-riding working class were Australian and American soldiers, smart and tailored in military uniforms, pressed to a detail.

Randwick was impressive during these big carnivals, an old hand at the game. The racecourse itself had been granted to the AJC by the state government (for the yearly rent of a single peppercorn), and racing had begun there in May 1860. Since then, the big, majestic track had hosted every champion thoroughbred that Australia could muster – The Barb, Carbine, Poitrel, Gloaming, Beauford, Phar Lap, Peter Pan. It had a top itinerary of races throughout the year, some of the biggest in the country, including the Sydney Cup, AJC Derby, Epsom and Metropolitan handicaps, and the Doncaster. Alongside Flemington in Melbourne, Randwick Racecourse was the epicentre of Australian horseracing.

The course sat on a flat field of ground on the western fringe of Randwick township. It had three grandstands – the Official (or Members') Stand, the Grandstand, and the St Leger – and they faced east, into the morning sun. The track itself was a mile and three furlongs around on the course proper, was about 100 feet (30 metres) wide at its narrowest point and had three chutes – at the mile start, and then at the seven-, six- and five-furlong starts. Behind the stands were dotted the race-day amenities of all race-courses: tote buildings, betting rings, tearooms and kiosks.

On this first day of spring carnival, the course began to buzz by midday. George Rowe had predicted 60,000 people, and the caterers were in full rhythm for lunchtime trade. Beer was limited, but it didn't matter to the crowds. They hovered about the bookie umbrellas and the tote windows, enjoying the patchy sunshine with whatever beverage fell into their hands.

The Breeders' Plate, which would feature Shannon (Bravo was not paid up, Riddle concluding the colt needed more time to mature), was the second of the day at 2.20 pm. It was the first prolific two-year-old event in the season, a five-furlong sprint under 8 st 5 lbs, and 12 had accepted. Outside of Shannon, there was boom colt Majesty, along with Victory Lad and Cragsman. None had run a race before.

Peter Riddle arrived at the course with his horses. Aside from the two-year-old, he had his stable star Modulation running in The Shorts at 3.35 pm. Modulation was a neat, nuggety four-year-old by Manitoba that had been a standout colt, winning the St Leger in the autumn, and he was favourite for the following week's Epsom. Riddle was very protective of the horse, as he often was with his top horses, and he was a little suspicious of the Randwick going on this day. The track, he suspected, would be heavy. Every trainer, in the lead-up to the big meetings, paid especial attention to the ramblings of the state meteorologist. In 1943, Peter Riddle was listening to David Mares. For weeks now, Mares had been recording torrential downpours over Sydney. The last week of September had been sickeningly wet, rain bucketing into the rain gauges at Observatory Hill. Over the proceeding 10 days, with persistent showers, the track hadn't the time to recoup; Riddle expected it was gloop at certain points.

By the running of the first race, Barney O'Brien was readying the young Shannon. The race-day stalls sat on the northern end of the course, inside the wall that bordered busy Alison Road. Behind him, the bay colt heard the rumbling of heavy traffic, of buses, motor cars and crowds milling near the turnstiles. In front of him, the curious, idling public and the busy energy of strappers, trainers and owners. O'Brien led Shannon to the saddling paddock about 20 minutes before race time. The youngster was twitchy and curious, normal behaviour for a maiden thoroughbred. The racecourse wasn't new to him, but the crowds were. There were thousands of people hanging over the paddock railings, watching him walk past, most of them looking around for Majesty. There were voices pitching odds into the masses, hands and pencils in the air. '6/4 odds-on Majesty, who'll have it? You sir, right then.' Shannon was trading at 7/2 against.

Because Shannon belonged to Peter Riddle, the old trainer, for this race at least, had no owners to entertain or reassure, but he was nevertheless agitated. Only 15 minutes before, he had made the hasty decision to scratch Modulation from The Shorts. Ted Bartle, Modulation's regular pilot, had gone around in the first race and on weighing in had declared the track very heavy. He had relayed this report to Riddle and Modulation's owner, AJC timekeeper William Kerr. Riddle waved the press away after the scratching became public, but Kerr was a friend of the newspapermen. 'Peter Riddle told me he can keep the horse fit with track gallops,' Kerr told the posse of reporters that hovered around the paddock, 'whereas one slip on today's going might have undone all the good work for the Epsom.' Riddle had ordered Modulation back to Bowral Street, and now he diverted his attention to the Breeders' Plate.

The first two-year-old race of the season was worth £1137 to the winner. It wasn't an old classic, not like the Derby or the St Leger. It didn't even fit into the traditional realm of 'classic'. First run in 1906 and won by the undefeated New Zealander Boniform, the Breeders' Plate had since had the likes of Wolaroi and Heroic amongst its winners. The 12 horses entered in 1943 were very good two-year-olds. In addition to Majesty, there was every reason to suspect that Riddle's colt and Victory Lad would train on into smart three-year-olds.

Fred Shean, in Riddle's blue and black racing silks, guided the young Shannon to the five-furlong chute with a subdued canter. The going was gluey but, like Bartle, Shean had been through it already in the first. No jockey would be out to break records with these babies.

Jack Gaxieu was on his starter's podium when he called the jockeys to order. Shannon had drawn the widest alley in the field, and so he stood without a horse on his nearside. Down the track before him lay a short trip onto the course proper, then a straight run of almost two and a half furlongs before the turn for home. The Randwick straight was just over two furlongs long, with a gentle climb to the winning post inside the furlong pole. When the tapes flew up, Shannon jolted out of his standing start into an untidy rhythm. Partly because of the going, partly because of first-race distraction, it took a few strides for the colt to find his balance. When he did, Fred Shean eased him out of the chute in about fourth place.

Settling onto the inside of the track, Shannon bowled along as the field lumbered towards the turn. He had plenty in the tank, was concentrating on the task, and had given his jockey no cause for concern. Shean had been coaxing and educating the young horse for weeks now, and it was paying off. Not even the going, deep and squelchy to the fetlocks, was bothering Shannon.

The 12 horses began to slip their moorings as they swung into the home turn, stretching out a little further and covering the turf a little quicker. Towards the back, runners were already off the bridle. Shannon, sixth as they galloped past the Leger stand, motored away with the leaders, but a little too quickly. His acceleration was so swift and easy that he found himself on the heels of Silver Flare, and Shean was forced to check him, knocking him right out of rhythm. The colt shifted to better running room, but the race was already on in earnest. Victory Lad was powering down the straight. Majesty, who had snuck along the rails, was poised second, not even a length off the leader Cragsman.

Shannon zipped past the furlong post in a new gear. Victory Lad had shaken off the field and was two lengths clear, then three. He had moved incredibly quickly. But Shannon was travelling faster, and he drew alongside the leader as the winning post came close. The pair heaved and thrashed through a final effort, Shean tucked low over Shannon, George Moore driving and pushing on Victory Lad. They gushed over the line together four lengths clear of Majesty.

Shannon lost his first race by a head.

—

A stride or two over the line, the Midstream colt powered right past Victory Lad. The winning post had come a fraction too soon for Shannon, and there was no doubt in the minds of those watching that he had been the fastest horse. The time was a respectable 1:02½ for the muddy going, more than four seconds outside the five-furlong Randwick record (58¼ set by All Love in 1940). The official margins were a head and four lengths.

Peter Riddle was pleased. The trainer had set the colt a big task for his first race. He could have eased Shannon into competition with a kinder run against lesser opposition, like a maiden handicap in November or December. But the horse had not been beaten in trials, and Riddle knew a good one when he had one. The son of Midstream had only confirmed his trainer's faith in this sloppy, untidy renewal of the Breeders' Plate.

Shannon earned £260 for his effort, but he returned to Bowral Street a tired horse. That was nothing unusual for a maiden, but the ground had been very heavy over the final half-mile, and Shean had gone through the worst of it, on the rail. The scrimmages had also been a feature of running. Barney O'Brien spent the afternoon soaking the mud out of the colt's legs and belly, and ironing out the jars and jolts he might have got. The following morning Shannon trotted up sound and cheerful.

The big story out of the Breeders' Plate in the days that came was the defeat of Majesty, the odds-on favourite who had fallen over the line four lengths behind Victory Lad and Shannon. For weeks the boom colt, that had also been the highest-priced yearling at the 1941 sales (he was sold 16 lots after Shannon), had been given every superlative under the sun, but after the race many of these superlatives were taken back. The horse's trainer, Fred Cush, told the press that his horse's loss was one of the biggest shocks he had experienced in horseracing. The cheap yearlings had trotted all over the pricey colt. Victory Lad had cost a mere 180 guineas at Shannon's sale (lot 173 on the second day of trading), and his trainer, Dan Lewis, told the press, 'I knew Majesty would have to be all that was being said about him to win.' Nevertheless, many felt that Victory Lad himself was lucky Shannon had run into a wall passing the Leger stand. *Truth* newspaper said, 'As fast as Victory Lad finished, Shannon finished faster. Another stride would have seen Peter Riddle's colt taking the bows.'

The trainer didn't say much after the race, as was Riddle's way. 'It was bad luck,' he told the *Telegraph*. 'Fred Shean told me that he was cut right out when going for an opening near the Leger. He had to check Shannon and bring him on the outside.' In the week that followed, most everyone agreed with him.

The ageing trainer had a bag of offers arrive on his doorstep for Shannon. They came from competing trainers, prominent owners and wealthy businessmen who saw a potential star and wanted to pounce before the iron got too hot. After Shannon won a race, his price would escalate, but even now, in the infancy of the horse's career, the offers that came for him were double, triple, quadruple what Riddle had paid for him. The old trainer wasn't interested. He had waited years, decades even, for a colt of this calibre. If Shannon proved himself the racehorse Riddle suspected he was, the offers would be small change before the season was out. And anyway, it wasn't about the money: Riddle had grown very attached to Shannon, and the colt's prospects excited him, gave him a reason to see through his failing health. There was just no temptation to sell.

10

The glamour horse of south-east Queensland

In the meanwhile of Shannon's track debut, there was a thoroughbred in the backblocks of Queensland, a bush horse that was harvesting some real attention. He was three years old, thickly set, an extravagantly conformed chocolate colt. He had Hollywood hair, long and tousled, unusually beautiful for scrub country. He was a first-crop foal by Emborough. He was Bernborough.

He was foaled at a bush property in the Darling Downs, to a mare called Bern Maid. At eight months old, he and his dam were dispersed to the Bach brothers, Jack and Frank, who settled the pair at their property in Oakey, west of Brisbane, before on-selling the foal to Albert Hadwen. Hadwen, in whose colours Bernborough would race, sent the colt to the Toowoomba yard of trainer J. J. Mitchell in mid-1941, and by the middle of 1943 the chocolate-bay had won almost all his starts – seven victories in nine outings.

It was an impressive tally, even for a bush horse. Bernborough, who was as striking and strong as he was talented, began to inch his way down the Australian coast, his fame and feats reaching Sydney and Melbourne. He became a local superstar in Queensland, the glamour horse of sunshine racing, and his fame came as much from his looks and action as his record. Bernborough was a massive colt, with a long, floaty galloping stride. His mane hung neatly over his near side, never a hair out of place, and his forelock was silken and impressive. He also had a unique signature in his racing: breaking lazily and then charging in the late stages to win by arrogant margins.

Bernborough's two-year-old career was glittering, and logical progression would have seen him graduate from Toowoomba's country circuit to the big leagues of Brisbane racing, eventually on to Sydney and Melbourne. But early in his career his fame was replaced with notoriety as Bernborough and his owner became embroiled in a long, lofty battle with the Queensland Turf Club (QTC).

The Bach brothers had been found guilty of a ring-in, attracting the attention of QTC officials and detectives who pored over every inch of the Bachs' racing affairs, including the sale of Bernborough to Hadwen in June 1940. So exposed were the Bach brothers that any business they had conducted around the time of the ring-in was picked at and examined, and the QTC was less than impressed by the particulars surrounding Bernborough's sale. In a bizarre rule that allowed them to bar any horse from racing without stating a cause, officials did just that: the Bern Maid youngster was suddenly box-bound, ineligible from competing on any racetrack in Queensland.

Hadwen took up the case with the Toowoomba racing officials, producing a receipt that clearly showed he had purchased Bernborough six months before the Bach's ring-in incident. The horse was cleared to race in Toowoomba, but the ban was upheld by the QTC and Brisbane Amateur Turf Club (BATC), and the AJC followed suit in Sydney, meaning Bernborough could race only on the Toowoomba circuit. It was a claustrophobic fiasco for such a talented animal.

Hadwen leased Bernborough out to a third party in 1943, to a storekeeper by the name of Francis Joseph Roberts. Roberts had nominated the then three-year-old for the Toowoomba Cup on 24 April, and Bernborough was odds on, as tight a favourite as the race had ever seen. Attendance for the event was unprecedented. Thousands of racegoers fell through the turnstiles to see their idol, hanging off the rails and loading up with the bag swingers. There was an air of buoyancy, despite the grip of war. It was something only a racehorse could do, drawing people out of their doldrums at the hardest of times with the promise of victory and cheer.

At 1.55 pm, not long before the jump, mayhem broke over

Toowoomba when Bernborough was scratched from the race. Roberts, who was hauled before the stewards, was forced to explain himself in quick order. 'I scratched Bernborough because I didn't want to take the risk of breaking him down up that hill (the home straight),' he pleaded. Roberts produced a £25 betting slip he had placed on his horse, hoping this would convince the stewards he had had every intention to run Bernborough. It didn't. Hadwen's horse was refused nomination for any races at Toowoomba, effectively barring Bernborough from racing anywhere in Australia for nigh on six months.

The horse became Queensland's biggest racing headline. Newspapers up and down the state decried the situation. 'Although he (Bernborough) is credited with being Queensland's best horse, apparently he is not to have the chance of proving it,' said *Worker* newspaper in early September. Bernborough's nomination for the winter meetings in June was rejected by both the QTC and BATC, and Albert Hadwen was slowly losing his wick. The horse had come back into his ownership, but by the time Shannon was debuting in Sydney in the two-year-old events of October 1943, Hadwen was coming around to the cool, blunt reality that Bernborough might be more trouble than he was worth.

11

'One up with plenty to play'

Albert Hadwen's problems were a world away to Peter Riddle. Back in Bowral Street, the ageing trainer had his mind squarely on the two-year-olds Bravo and Shannon.

In the lead-up to Saturday 23 October – Shannon's second scheduled start – Riddle patrolled his stables each morning with a bridle slung over his shoulder, oily saddle rag in his hand. He looked distracted; in fact, he was concentrating doggedly. Oiling the smooth, beaten leather over his shoulder, he tossed in his mind the tactics for Saturday's racing. Both Shannon and Modulation were due to race on this, the last day of the AJC meeting.

The weather had been fine for over a week, and Shannon had responded to the firm morning going with impressive workouts. Each day, he was clocking among the top times, though rarely asked to sprint further than two or three furlongs. During spurts, Fred Shean noticed the colt had wised up in his action. Shannon seemed to better understand where to put his feet, and how to lean into corners, when to move for the winning post. Shean eased him down each morning in 26¼ for two furlongs, 36½ for three. Track watchers, who had followed the small colt since his first appearances at Randwick, were certain he was a sure thing for Saturday.

Shannon was entered in the first race on the card, the five-furlong Canonbury Stakes. It wasn't a rich stake like the Breeders' Plate. First prize amounted to only £880, £200 for second, but it was a popular two-year-old class for colts and geldings, and the field had 18 entries. They included Majesty, who would be out for vindication after his poor showing in the Breeders' Plate.

Across Sydney, Shannon was first pick for the Canonbury. He had not given Peter Riddle a single headache. The trainer knew the colt was a potential star, for he'd been in the business of horses long enough to know the good ones from the brilliant ones. But the Canonbury Stakes wasn't going to be a jaunt for the Midstream youngster (it would be, after all, only the colt's second race). Riddle knew that Majesty had hated the soft going in the Breeders' Plate, and with firmer footing he may well be the expensive starlet he had been suggesting all along. Silver Flare and Buckle were also lining up again. Riddle had watched Buckle clock the fastest three furlongs at Randwick on Thursday morning, three days before the race. The chestnut youngster had hauled his rider past the winning post in 37 flat, hard held.

The signs became a little more ominous on race morning when a heavy wager was placed on Billy Cook, Majesty's jockey, to win the first two races on the card. Such was the market confidence in Majesty that he would start just outside favouritism for the Canonbury: Shannon was 7/4 against, Majesty 2/1, with Buckle 7/1 and the next closest was Silver Flare at 20s. It was a two-horse event.

No one knew that better than Fred Shean as he lined Shannon up for the Canonbury jump on Saturday afternoon, 23 October. He was positioned in barrier 14, with Majesty a few horses inside him. Majesty's owners had ousted jockey Darby Munro and replaced him with Billy Cook, who was known across the east coast as the strongest of front-running riders. The signals were loud and clear to Shean that Majesty, in this firm footing, would jump to the front and stay there.

The tapes flew up at a tick over 1.15 pm, and Majesty did just what Billy Cook asked of him. He dug his feet into the turf and leaped into the lead, roaring into the one and only turn like a scalded cat. Shannon, settling fourth in running, had a lot to do to catch him.

The Canonbury field approached the three furlongs in a tight bunch behind Majesty, who had opened up two and some lengths in front. Shean crouched low over Shannon and asked him to move around the group, and the Midstream colt responded with tactile agility. He clawed into Majesty's lead with such fleetness that at the furlong pole he had reached the leader's girth buckles. But Majesty had slipped away with too much lead too early. When the winning post came the expensive colt had a half-length advantage over Peter Riddle's colt. The two youngsters, a smart five lengths clear of every other runner, slipped over the line in a ridiculously quick 59 seconds, the fastest five furlongs ever clocked by a colt in Australia.

Among the crowd of 55,500, Peter Riddle stood a little disappointed and a whole lot frustrated. Shannon was in bridesmaid shoes yet again, and by the same maddening margin. If Majesty hadn't slipped away going into the turn, Shannon could have closed the space by the post – but that was racing. Riddle thought he might instruct his jockey to ride closer to the speed from now, and it wasn't all bad. Two races over differing surfaces and Shannon had been right there when it counted. It was just a matter of time and experience for this one.

Majesty's owner, Monte Walker, was mouthy in his analysis of the Canonbury Stakes. 'I think I got the cream of the sales in buying Majesty for 1600 guineas,' he told the reporters who hustled him for post-race comment. Riddle was inclined to disagree, but he was too polite to say so publicly. He'd seen these boom colts time and again. They came along with all the fanfare attached to their sale price, they won a race or two, then fizzled off and ended up in India. Over all his years with trotters and gallopers, Riddle never attached talent to a price tag.

—

October rolled into early November with warming spring temperatures and renewed vigour in racing. In the south, it seemed like Melbourne had altogether forgotten there was a war on. Unofficial estimates on Melbourne Cup Day saw 120,000 people slip into famous Flemington for its biggest day of the year, cheering on Dark Felt to victory after emptying the bars of liquor and the bookies of tickets. The tote windows saw the most money ever exchanged, and when the city workers arrived at the track in the early afternoon, just in time for the big race, the crush between the tote building and the grandstand was so severe that women fainted on their feet.

The frivolities at Flemington were a sign that Australia needed an out from war talk. Everywhere, the vestiges of conflict could be seen. In Sydney, 'brownouts' were a depressing part of daily night-fall. Shop fronts, street lamps and even tram lights glowed a dull, dirty brown. For a few months it was okay, but after a few years it was dragging on the morale of the city. Bars closed at six o'clock to shuffle people off the streets, and only select establishments could entertain citizens into the night. Mostly, these were filled with soldiers and sailors and the wealthy echelons of Sydney society. The rest of the city just had to get on with it.

And they did, but there were problems. Amid the working classes in the factories and abattoirs and down on the wharves, there was an additional and new uneasiness. Refugees were pouring into the city every month from dismantled towns in Hungary, Austria, Poland, Ukraine and Russia. Finding themselves in warm, safe Sydney, these displaced souls came up against an awkward, almost polite, wave of racism. Tagged as 'reffos', though few meant it as a slight, they were accepted and tolerated. Nevertheless, when their backs were turned, Australians muttered, 'They'll take the jobs away from us, just you watch.'

If Peter Riddle was worried about these changing social tides, he never let on. He had his own rainbows to chase. His health was faltering, even in these warming spring months. His stoop was a little heavier in the mornings, and he was letting go of many of the stable chores he had always enjoyed. More and more, Kathleen, his live-in housekeeper, was at his side, merging her duties from cleaner to carer. Riddle worried constantly how this looked to outside folk, how inappropriate it probably seemed to upstanding Catholic locals, and he thought he would marry Kathleen soon enough, just so he could stop worrying about it.

In the yard, Shannon was kept ticking over. The two-year-old was on song for another three starts this campaign, after which he would have done enough. Riddle planned to spell him after that, probably with Modulation and Bravo before they came back in for the autumn. Shannon would line up in the Two-Year-Old Stakes at Randwick on 20 November, and then the Kirkham Stakes a week later. He would finish with the December Stakes as late as Boxing Day.

Barney O'Brien kept the young horse healthy and happy. Their daily routine began much the same as for every other thoroughbred at Randwick.

Before first light, O'Brien crept about the yard with a mug of boiling tea to his lips and a kind word for each of the horses. When dawn arrived, the team was often on its way to the track. On the mornings when Shannon was just loping, when he didn't require the smooth, guiding hands of Fred Shean for burning sprints, O'Brien tucked his overworked, tired old legs into the irons and cantered Shannon wide around the course proper, or trotted him smartly across the tan or cinders. The colt rarely gave trouble, possessing, O'Brien marvelled, a sensible brain between his ears.

It was just as well, because in the week leading up to the Two-Year-Old Stakes, Sydney weather took a turn. The day before the race, temperatures were far below normal and rain fell onto Randwick in miserable heavy inches. While Majesty's connections, who were lining their colt up again, went into a spin about the going, Riddle sat back and watched the odds swing towards him. Shannon slid into 11/8 favouritism because he had already shown wet-track form.

There was additional information behind this favouritism. Majesty was carrying a penalty into the Two-Year-Old Stakes, meaning he would lumber 8 st 12 lbs to Shannon's 8 st 5 lbs. The excellent filly Tea Rose was also nominated, a lithe little chestnut that had won her last start at Rosehill in record time. She also would carry a penalty (8 st 7 lbs), and so Shannon's lot was looking pretty good.

On the morning of the race, Riddle stepped out on the turf

in his gumboots and sank to his ankles in some parts. The track was soft, soft enough that a horse with a weight advantage had even more of an advantage, and this was promising for Shannon. The rain had stopped over the eastern suburbs, but it was a cool and cloudy spring day. Riddle hurried back home to Norton Street to rug up for what would be a chilly afternoon beneath the grandstand.

With a stiff wind over the course proper, the track was drying out by the running of the Two-Year-Old Stakes at 1.50 pm. Shannon and Fred Shean cantered to the five-furlong chute (the horses were, in fact, racing five furlongs and 14 yards) and mingled with the other 11 runners. Starter Jack Gaxieu gathered them up, ordering the young horses into their spots. The two-year-old fields were often the hardest to straighten for a standing start, but this time they gave little trouble.

Shannon had drawn wide again in postposition 12. On his inside was the talented Tea Rose, and Majesty was in five. Shean looked out from under the peak of his helmet silk. The chute was the same straight run into the home turn, largely flat until the short climb to the winning post. He thought that the outside draw might not be such a terrible thing in this going. His colt had a soft weight and was good in this firming turf. More than these, though, Shean was determined that Majesty and front-running Billy Cook wouldn't get the bounce on him this day.

The course-clerk ponies backed away from the field and Gaxieu sent the two-year-olds away with a resounding 'Go!' From his wide draw, Shannon leapt into a gallop, bustled by Shean across the track to settle with Majesty in the opening sectionals. In fact, so sharp was the response from the Midstream colt that Shannon dragged Majesty out of the first furlong, covering so much extra ground.

In the stands, even Riddle was surprised as he watched Shannon tow the field into the turn and down the straight. There was simply no stopping the horse. Shean had only to ride hands and heels and Shannon shot away from his rivals with appalling ease . . . a length, two lengths, three lengths. Ticket holders cheered the heavy favourite all the way to the line, and Shannon galloped over it in a painless 1.01 for the five. It was the easiest £557 Riddle had ever collected.

Leading bookie Jim Hackett, climbing off his box in the betting enclosure, shook his head and prepared for a flurry of thirsty ticket holders. 'I don't know how they're going to beat him next Saturday,' he said aloud, referring to Shannon's starting in the Kirkham Stakes. Hackett had suspected all along that Shannon would towel Majesty in this race. He had opened the horse at 5/4 in the betting, closing him at 11/8. Majesty had been kept at a safe 2/1, but the expensive youngster hadn't even run second. Tea Rose had filled that spot three lengths off Shannon, and Majesty had dawdled home another three lengths third. Shannon had run his rival over by six lengths. In their three meetings now, he had finished ahead of Majesty twice.

Riddle's colt trotted back to the paddock with unassuming grace. He was the kind of horse that didn't know how to be arrogant. If he knew he had won, he didn't show it. All sorts of cheers floated over the railings at Fred Shean, as was the norm when a favourite is ridden home, and Peter Riddle shook his jockey's hand. Barney O'Brien stepped up and led Shannon away.

Reporters jostled in on the trainer. 'I thought my colt was certain to turn the tables on Majesty today,' he said, 'but I didn't expect him to win as easily as he did, to be honest.' A faint crack of a smile emerged on Riddle's lips, but no one noticed it. Among the press boys, Riddle wasn't known for exciting outbursts. The trainer confirmed Shannon's entry in next Saturday's Kirkham, then he waved the reporters away.

Monte Walker could find no excuse for Majesty's hiding. Even Billy Cook was stumped. He told the papers that his mount was well beaten before the turn. Across the racecourse that afternoon, the general consensus was that the battle of the star two-year-olds had been firmly won by Peter Riddle's much cheaper, much more consistent youngster.

—

In three starts, Shannon had notched a win and two closing seconds. His prizemoney total was £1017, well over twice his purchase price. He had won every trial he had contested, and consistently blasted among the sharpest workouts each morning. And his Randwick win was even more impressive on analysis. On the slow track, adjusting his time of 1.01 for the five furlongs and 14 yards (removing the 14 yards), Shannon ran a minute dead for the exact five. He was an outstanding prospect in 1943, and Riddle wasn't the only one to know it.

The last patron had hardly slunk out of Randwick on Two-Year-Old Stakes day when the trainer was approached with a concrete offer for Shannon. Details were kept out of public notice, but the proposer was a known racing identity with a large string of horses in another stable. He had his eye on Shannon as a 1944 Derby prospect, and dangled £2000 in front of Peter Riddle.

'After today's performance I am convinced that he will win the two-year-old classics of the current season. It was the best two-year-old performance I have seen this year,' the mystery buyer told the *Sunday Telegraph*, though not a single detail of his identity was printed. Peter Riddle was only amused, certainly not tempted. He revealed that he had been receiving offers for Shannon since 15 October, the day before the Breeders' Plate. 'That offer was made on behalf of a Victorian owner who said put your own price on him, no limit,' Riddle told the *Telegraph*. 'No offer will be considered though. I think he is too good to sell.'

Any man could do the sums. The £2000 offer was decent for a young, inexperienced racehorse, decent by any standards. That money could tide a man over and then some, pay his rent in a semi-detached brick cottage in the suburbs for years. But Peter Riddle didn't need the money. The ailing trainer couldn't see any logic in selling a horse that was on the improve. Shannon, he suspected, was the horse a trainer waits for, the youngster that every battling horseman waits a lifetime for. And he was already very attached to the colt. Perhaps it was because the horse was so talented, perhaps because he was so tractable and kind to handle. It was definitely that he belonged to the trainer, for every guinea of that 425 guineas sale-price had come out of Riddle's pocket. And, in the cloudy mess of his failing health, Shannon was a reason to get out of bed before the birds, a motive for seeing another day through.

In the week leading up to the Kirkham then, Riddle plied his star through the usual routine. Working with Bravo, Shannon drilled three furlongs without shoes on Thursday morning (it was a habit of Riddle's to work his horses without plates). Breezing on the A grass, the pair dashed right along the rail in 37 seconds, Shannon on the outside. A little after them came Tea Rose, hard held for the distance in 40 seconds. Watching the action, the *Sportsman* clocker scribbled in his notepad, 'Shannon is by far the best colt racing on Saturday. Looks a very safe investment.'

Bert Riddle had ventured down from Kia Ora for the week, for Bravo was making his race debut on the same card, in the first race off on Saturday, the Hoxton Park Juvenile Stakes. There wasn't much of Bravo. The colt was pint-sized but famously brave. Clockers felt there was little between him and Shannon from what they'd seen in morning workouts, and so bookies had him as pre-post favourite for the Hoxton at 6/4. It was probably warranted. The day before the meeting, Shannon and Bravo, breezing in their familiar one-two tandem, cruised over a soft track at Randwick in 37 seconds. It was three-quarters of a second faster than any three-furlong sprint that morning, and beat by a full second the best time of the older horses.

'Shannon will be odds on', sang the *Sportsman* the morning of the Kirkham Stakes. Only seven horses had been paid up for the race, and they included the top colts along with Tea Rose. Shannon was 2/1 on, Majesty 5/1, and the filly was second option at 4/1. Few punters were taking a bite out of the Majesty apple.

At five furlongs and 14 yards, the Kirkham was a standard two-year-old event. It wasn't a rich race, only £787 to the winner, but it was a benchmark feature late in the spring. It was often the last or second-last race for the top juveniles before they were spelled. It was also a favourite's race, making it an old-fashioned brain freeze for the bag-swingers. In its previous 10 editions, only one winner (Haddon Hall in 1942) had not been a first or second favourite. The reason for this run of fancies was that, this late in the spring, the outstanding two-year-olds had had plenty of racing to prove themselves. Shannon, Majesty and Tea Rose had each run multiple times, and while Shannon and Tea Rose had consistency rippling through their records, Majesty had been hot and cold. The Kirkham Stakes was, therefore, a relatively easy race to call.

When the Hoxton Park Juvenile got underway, Randwick Racecourse was buzzing with patrons. It was a light and breezy day, which was fortunate as rain had clattered down the previous evening, drenching the track. Solid money was bouncing through the bookies' bags and tote windows, and as Bravo led from start to finish in the Hoxton, the favourites' roll was underway. Bert and Peter Riddle watched their little colt gallop home by nearly two lengths in his first racecourse start.

The Kirkham Stakes was due off at 2.45 pm, and as Barney O'Brien circled Shannon in the parade ring, in the cool, windy shadow of the old grandstand, Peter Riddle stood with Fred Shean in conversation. The jockey was watching the horses, arms folded and head cocked, listening to the trainer. Riddle, in his race-day crisp white shirt, dark suit and tie, peered out from his fedora, muttering things Shean already knew. Don't get trapped on the rail. Give him room to see. Let him win as he likes.

The jockey crossed the paddock towards Shannon, and O'Brien slung him aboard. The three-minute bell clattered across the betting enclosures, and racegoers began to stream towards the rails and stands, vying for a look at the hyped two-year-old. Calmly, lazily almost, Shannon trotted out of the paddock and onto the turf for his preliminary gallop. Shean guided the colt up the straight, then swung him back down past the grandstand and Leger and around the turn to the chute. Nothing fazed the horse. He milled with the Kirkham field as the tapes dropped across the track.

Three minutes after post time, Jack Gaxieu sent the youngsters away. Shannon, in postposition two, leapt off his hocks into an early lead on the rails. Only front-running Majesty was inside of him.

The two colts blitzed through the first furlong together, and as they screamed past the half-mile pole the rest of the field were strung out like butcher's sausages behind them. Coming out of the turn, Shean, travelling quietly, could see that Majesty was in trouble. Billy Cook had raised his whip and was calling on the speedster for more fuel. As they straightened for home, only two furlongs travelled, Majesty was already spent.

The tiring colt fell outwards as he ran out of steam, carrying Shannon away from the rail. But Riddle's horse was travelling so easily that Shean had only to shake his hands and Shannon picked up, kicked away. Tea Rose, who had managed to come around Majesty and slip along the rails, got within a length of Shannon, but that was as close as she, or any horse, came. The son of Midstream saw the winning post ahead, and straight as a child at Christmas he stretched his neck out and powered down the Randwick straight. He stopped the clock in the Kirkham Stakes at 1:01½, two lengths to the good of Tea Rose.

An almighty cheer rose up from the stands and the Flat as favourite backers kissed their winning tickets. Shannon had come home at 2/1 on, in some places 5/4 against, while Majesty had plugged home in fourth, beaten by third-placer Hawk Craig. The time was a very good one too, considering the soft track and Shannon's weight of 8 st 5 lbs. Tea Rose had carried a full five pounds less.

Bert and Peter Riddle shook hands with half the racecourse as they waited for their horse to trot in. Shannon swung back in to scale with a light step and loose rein, none the worse for the run. Peter Riddle collared Shean for a blow-by-blow description of the race, as was his way. Shean was used to it. 'Majesty went with me all right,' he told the trainer, 'in fact, at one stage he was up a half-length on me. But I knew that my fellow had it on him. There wasn't the slightest cause for concern.'

As the riders filed back into the jockeys' room and the

paddock began to fill for the next race, only Fred Shean was left to face reporters. One testy journalist ventured that Tea Rose had been hampered by Shannon's shifting off the rail, and that were it not for that, the filly would have won the Kirkham Stakes. Shean politely scoffed at the suggestion. 'If I had wanted to, Shannon could have won more easily,' he said. 'My mount raced right away from the others in the last 100 yards.'

Shean made his way back to the jockeys' room, thought about this exciting Midstream colt. Shannon, in his eyes, was as good a two-year-old as he had ever ridden, possibly the best. The colt possessed remarkable early speed from the tapes, and acceleration when the whips were up. The papers were all saying he was the star juvenile of the season, and Shean had piloted him in each of his four runs now. It was a promising partnership promising big wins. Eight long years ago, Shean had ridden his first feature winner at Randwick. That day in 1935, he had travelled from his Queensland base to ride the gelding Lough Neagh to victory in the Tramway Handicap. Shean had fond memories of old Lough Neagh, the chestnut gelding that had raced on until the age of nine. The jock remembered him well, remembered the £100 that Lough Neagh's trainer had slipped him for the win. Shean had been 31 years of age, probably old to be starting out on the Sydney metro scene, but that 100 quid had felt like a lottery win. 'That horse was a game ol' bastard,' Shean often recalled, 'he never knew when he was beat.'

The Queensland hoop didn't ride another winner on Kirkham Stakes day, but he slid home that evening with the confidence that he was Shannon's first-call rider, and that was rolled gold in his trade. A jockey can wait his whole career to partner a champion, and when he finally gets one it can be snatched from him by suspension, injury, a million possibilities. A man could go mad worrying about it, but Shean, level and confident, wasn't such a man.

12

'I think Bravo is the better of the pair'

December rolled into Sydney, soft and muggy. The city was glorious at this time of year. Days were long and oily, pickled by hot skies that climbed forever. At night, the black, glassy folds of high tide lapped the gullies and sandy bays of the enormous harbour. In this corner of the Pacific, where summer came at the end of the year, where Christmas was a platter of roast beef and pudding at 100 degrees in the shade, the damp, dirty headlines that fell out of miserable, war-carved Europe were almost unreal.

On 16 Bowral Street, Shannon lilted in the still humidity of box seven. In these early December afternoons, the yard was quiet and deserted in the heat, waking again for three o'clock strolls when the southerly had often snuck in. The colt had been in now for over nine months, the stretching pastures of Kia Ora a mere memory. Usually, this late in the year, the good horses had left Randwick for a deserved spell. In 1943, there were two reasons Shannon had been kept in.

The first was the transport ban imposed on the racing industry. No trainer could truck his horses further than 25 miles, be it for a race meeting or a spell. The ban had put a terrific strain on spelling properties outside of the radius, on float drivers and owners and trainers alike. Racehorses were staying in longer to avoid all the complications associated with sending them out. The second reason Shannon and his stablemates were still racing into December was prizemoney. Purses were nowhere near what they had been before the war. Shannon, who had raced four times this season for the smart record of two wins and two seconds, had won a mere £1804. Only a select few races these days were worth four figures to the winner. So, to recoup the expenses of racing a horse, owners were racing their animals longer and oftener.

For Peter Riddle, keeping Shannon in was down to a number of things. It was prizemoney and it was transport, but it was also because the trainer enjoyed the two-year-old sprints late in the year. He believed they were a strong opportunity to fit young two-year-olds for racing without the high pressure of spring events. Usually, these late races were a little easier to win, but this year, with the war reversing much that was normal, they were more competitive. Shannon and Bravo, both entered for the December Stakes on Boxing Day, which was worth a lucrative £1160 to the winner, would face their old foes in Tea Rose and Majesty.

Riddle had a plan to get Shannon to the post in shipshape order. After the Kirkham Stakes win, he mapped out a start in the Voluntary Aids' Handicap at Randwick on 11 December for the colt. This meeting was a Red Cross benefit, hosted by the AJC to raise funds for the Red Cross charity, and over the five furlongs and 14 yards it was a standard two-year-old event. Riddle didn't attach much lustre to it, as he saw it simply as a tune-up for Shannon on the road to the December Stakes.

However, the trainer began to stress over his two star colts clashing. Riddle was in a unique position among Randwick ranks; he had the two outstanding youngsters of the season, owned one of them while his brother owned the other. At some point there was going to be a conflict of interest, and Riddle knew it was inevitable. As that conflict approached in the mould of the December Stakes, the old trainer grew more and more uncomfortable.

Riddle didn't want the horses to meet in competition because he believed that Shannon was the better of the pair and the protective big brother in him didn't want to spoil Bert's party. Though many of the newspapers were saying there was next to nothing between the colts, Riddle knew better. In trials, the trainer had put much more weight on Shannon's back and he usually ran him on the outside of Bravo. The results of the trials were deceptive; Shannon had had a lot more work to do than his stablemate.

Riddle was also conscious of the penalty Shannon would

carry into the December Stakes. The colt's win in the Kirkham had given him a five-pound disadvantage, meaning he would meet Majesty on level weights (8 st 10 lbs). Bravo, on the other hand, would carry 8 st 5 lbs, and Tea Rose would be even more favourably weighted with 8 st. Though Riddle believed that Shannon would have the measure of Majesty on level terms, he worried about the other two.

Into the first week of December, fate intervened. Late on the morning of Saturday 4 December, as Riddle prepared for a race meeting at Rosehill, Shannon was startled in his box and kicked out at the partition wall. The rattle of the kick had Barney O'Brien scurrying to the colt's door, and a quick inspection found a minor abrasion on the near hock. The trainer was called, and Shannon trotted up relatively sound before Riddle left for a Rosehill race meeting in his Chrysler Royal.

He wasn't too concerned, but in the early evening he returned to check on the colt. O'Brien led the horse out of box seven and Shannon hobbled like an old carthorse, doing his best to avoid laying any weight on the left hock. Trainer and foreman were alarmed. In the hours of the day, the injury had had a chance to bruise and swell, and immediately all plans for the rest of the month came to a grinding halt.

On Monday morning, Riddle scratched Shannon from the Voluntary Aids' Handicap, but he held out hope that the colt would be right for the Boxing Day meeting. It was, after all, three weeks away. Over the weekend, the colt had responded to treatment for the hock injury. It had been iced, then rubbed with liniments and wrapped. O'Brien had been changing the dressing at will, and Shannon hadn't been lame for long. Into the week, he was moving soundly, trotting up clean. Riddle worried, nonetheless, that the colt would miss fast work for a week. It was a significant setback on the road to the December Stakes.

He thought he would sit the next week out to see what condition the colt was in. In the meantime, Riddle sent Bravo out for the December Nursery on December 18. His brother's little horse bolted home by two and half lengths under 9 st 5 lbs. A huge rush in the betting just before the jump had sent Bravo out favourite at 11/8 against, and it was a strong galloping performance. 'If both Riddle's colts are trotted out in next week's December Stakes, it is our opinion Bravo would be favourite,' commented *Truth* newspaper.

If Peter Riddle disagreed with that, he kept quiet. Shannon wasn't pleasing him at home, missing out on valuable gallops and looking a little rough around the seams, while the bruising was taking longer than expected to heal. He had blistered the wound, so it looked unsightly, probably more than it actually was. After Bravo's win at Randwick, the trainer made the decision to scratch Shannon from the rich December Stakes. It was a shame, but Riddle felt Shannon was too valuable an animal to push at such an early age.

With the horse out, the newspapers went to work on making much of Bravo, helped along by AJC handicapper G. F. 'Fred' Wilson, who came out with some interesting observations after Bravo's Nursery win. 'Before today I didn't think there was much between Bravo and Shannon,' he said. 'However, Bravo's win was so pronounced that he clearly established himself as a colt of real class and, despite Shannon's proved ability, I think Bravo is the better of the pair.'

Riddle found all this talk rather amusing. It was typical of the papers to make much of the stable rivalry, to create headlines around which colt was better. When the *Telegraph* came calling for comment, the trainer said, 'Bravo seems to be making steady improvements, and it is hard to guess whether he or Shannon will be the better in the autumn.' The *Telegraph* maintained that Riddle, once certain of Shannon's superiority, was now unsure of it. Nothing was further from the truth.

Riddle didn't waver in his faith that Shannon was a better horse, despite Bravo's roll of form. The trainer planned to keep the colts apart on the track as long as possible, but where many would interpret that as avoidance, in fact it was because of Riddle's loyalty to his brother. Both colts had the opportunity to clean up the autumn races, so why would he place them in the same race? It made no sense.

He didn't plan for the colts to meet until the Sires' Produce Stakes on 8 April in the following year, the race that was the decisive target for all top two-year-olds in Sydney. Before then, the youngsters would be rested and brought back in for a number of autumn races. On current form, Riddle knew Bravo would be a formidable opponent for Shannon, but no matter what the papers said, no matter how much they elevated Bravo above the Midstream colt, the trainer knew Shannon's future was stronger. He just knew it.

On Boxing Day, Bravo was humiliated in the December Stakes, trailing home three lengths third behind Majesty and the super filly Tea Rose. It was an unpopular loss across Randwick, as Bravo started 2/1 on for the win. 'Backers think either Bravo is not as good as they thought him,' commented the newspapers, 'or he is beginning to train off.' Riddle thought it was a good time to put his two-year-olds away.

Very late in December, on a balmy morning after breakfast, an old horse float thrummed to a halt outside 16 Bowral Street. The ramp fell onto the pavement with a dull thud, and Barney O'Brien led Shannon up and into the belly of the old truck. The engine kicked over and wound its way out of Sydney.

Shannon's nostrils filled with the dank smells of industrial Parramatta and western Sydney before the truck swung north-west towards the district of Richmond. Gradually, the colt caught the whiffs of summer grass and the distant, pine-heavy Blue Mountains. The air was fresh and crisp, the space vast and rolling. Shannon had arrived at the spelling farm of Messrs Cornwell and Ridges.

For the next month, Midstream's little bay colt felt the sun burn his dappled hide, and the occasional summer rain drench him through. He spent hours of the lazy afternoons with his neck outstretched in the long pastures, picking the grass under his nose and batting away the march flies. He was a horse again.

13

A short neck or four lengths

Good fortune can shield a man only a little, and as 1944 fell open, no man knew that better than Peter Riddle. He had money in the bank, a small stable of brilliant racehorses, but his body was failing him. His breaths were often strained and shallow now, his shoulders hurt from the effort of everyday chores. Shifting a straw bale, stooping to wrap a horse's legs, these were things that left him feeling like he was 105. He wasn't even 60.

Riddle had heart disease, its slow and steady onset crippling him. Medically, his arteries were closing. Blood supply to his heart was obstructed, meaning that, at any point of the day, it was singing out for more oxygen. He had intermittent chest pain, often set off by emotion or exertion. Sometimes it lasted a few seconds. Sometimes it went on for half an hour.

The trainer's daily routine took longer and longer to get going. No one noticed it more than his daughter June. Living with her father in Norton Street (her husband was fighting in New Guinea), June watched Peter Riddle struggle to get out of bed before the birds, struggle to keep up with the string as they headed to the track each morning. She insisted he reduce the team, imploring her father to stay away from the sales and cull the horses that weren't earning their keep. She stressed that training horses was an enormous draw on her father's energy, but she couldn't make him stay away from the yard.

In a way, Peter Riddle's decline went hand in hand with an exhausted Australia, a country that, with the turn into 1944, was expecting the hardest year in living memory. Shortages, sacrifice and inconvenience, these were part of Sydney's every day now. Even the Great Depression and the stripping recession of the 1890s couldn't keep up with this war. It was five long years now and counting.

Pope Pius XII expected peace in 1944, and many shared his optimism that January. But with the hopes of peace came the fear of conclusion and how the world might get there. 'The cornered German people will struggle bitterly to the last,' predicted the *Telegraph*. 'Hitler may persuade them to use gas. He will certainly bring out his secret rocket gun, now known to be more than a bit of propaganda.' Australia, even from its remote Pacific parking (though it wasn't remote enough from Japanese threats), was panicking.

Across the nation, citizens wondered if, for the first time, they would feel some of the privations that their European allies had grown accustomed to. Post-war diseases, which wiped out almost as many people after the Great War as it did during the war, were on their minds. Coal was scarce, rubber tyres almost extinct. Eggs, fish and poultry were unusual luxuries. Meat rationing was the latest punishment, following along from butter rationing. Regardless of peace rumours and calming prophecies from the Vatican balcony, relief for the working class was nowhere in sight.

'From long habit we are wishing each other a "happy new year",' said the *Australian Women's Weekly* on New Year's Day, 'but in our hearts, we know 1944 can hardly be that.' The popular magazine predicted that the year might bring 'the fierce exultation of victory, release from strain and satisfaction in duty done. Even the high joy of reunion'. But editorials across the nation on 1 January all carried the same message: peace, perhaps, but resilience to see things out to the bitter end.

Randwick's racing theatre had been hit hard. There were cuts to prizemoney and curtailment of race days, but there were the hidden tensions too, the ones not immediately obvious on the outside. On Bowral Street, Riddle was absorbing the increased cost of grain, straw and hay. Horseshoes were in thin supply in his tack room, owing to the federal control of primary industries. Treats for the horses were non-existent; carrots, though not in short supply, were reserved for humans, and apples had hit a ceiling price. As many people worried into the long nights about how they would feed their pets, horse trainers had the lead-weight concern of feeding an entire stable of valuable bloodstock.

The worry was pressing on Riddle, and he was one of the lucky ones. He wasn't doing it especially hard, due to astute investment and a spate of good wins lately. Nevertheless, his health had proffered new insecurity. He became protective of June and Kathleen, of providing for them. And possessions, assets, grew in importance. Shannon included.

—

The colt stepped back into Riddle's yard in late February, probably later than was normal for a horse on an autumn campaign. Most of the big guns aiming for the high titles came back in early January, but Shannon had gone out later. He had spent just about a month on the farm at Richmond. When he rattled off the horse float and into the yard, he looked round and tidy from his holiday. He wasn't a horse that carried much condition, but he had grown quickly, as two-year-olds do.

He was a lovely horse to look at. Not too tall, about 15.2 hands high, with good length through the barrel and a straight neck. There wasn't a single angle on him. Gently curved and even, he was built like neither a stayer nor a sprinter. In temperament, Shannon was cooperative and tractable. He was a mature two-year-old; nothing fazed him. He ate well, slept well and didn't spook or shy on the way to the track in the mornings. Even when the string walked along the congested, lively route to Victoria Park Racecourse, a notoriously fast track for morning work a mile or so from Randwick, he was calm and well behaved.

By early March, Riddle had him sparring again with Bravo. The pair was breezing half-miles in 50¼ seconds, Bravo usually pulling Shannon home by a head. The smaller colt had a head start on his stablemate. Bravo had gone out for only a brief spell, and hadn't lost much of his race fitness. He would be ready for competition a little earlier.

The trainer expected to debut Shannon in the Services' Handicap at Randwick on 18 March. The meeting was in aid of the Australian Comforts Fund, a wartime civilian organisation that provided free comforts to the fighting-fit Australians in battle zones. The AJC was planning an enormous turnout for the worthy cause. Tote expectations sat at £150,000, a phenomenal amount of money. AJC secretary George Rowe had ordered every tote window be manned for the six-race meeting. He had also cut out a race (there were usually seven races on a Randwick card), believing that the spacious intervals between races would encourage more money through the tote as people had more time to bet. About five per cent of the investment would go to the Comforts Fund: £7500 if expectations were met.

The transit authorities had scheduled extra trams and buses to ferry crowds on race day, so that by the jump of the first race there were scores of people pouring into Randwick. George Rowe watched as 45,000 racegoers paid their way through the turnstiles, while another 8000 servicemen and women tagged along. It was a 50 per cent increase on the Red Cross meeting held on 11 December, and Rowe calculated £22,000 to the Comforts Fund. It was a remarkable contribution from the racing community.

Shannon was due to line up at 2.50 pm, the second race on the card. It was a six-furlong event from the Randwick chute, just under a furlong further than the colt had ever travelled. The going was good. Sydney was basking in a mild and balmy start to autumn, so the track wasn't a problem, but the field was enormous. Twenty-three horses were going to post for the £552 purse. Shannon and Victory Lad, who had pipped Riddle's colt in his very first race, were top weights with 9 st 5 lbs. The lightest weighted was Wellington with a full two stone less.

Fred Shean eased Shannon into position down the six-furlong chute. There were horses everywhere, and Jack Gaxieu had his hands full with them, barking orders here and there, ordering jockeys into their correct spots. It was going to be a tough break, and when the webbing flew up it was messy. Shannon, in postposition 19, was swallowed up by a surge of horses charging towards the rail.

Shean settled the colt in ninth place as they moved out of the chute. There was just nowhere to go. Shannon had horses on his inside, horses on his outside, and the jockey could only hope that out of the home turn the field would fan out, or he would be able to go wide. Neither happened. As the 23 horses spread into the straight there was no hole to crawl through, and Shean had to check Shannon to prevent him running onto the leaders. The horse wasn't fit enough to come again, so when the first horse dashed past the winning post, four lengths to the good of the field, Shannon was fifth, blowing hard.

It was a fighting effort. With 9 st 5 lbs first-up since a rest, the bay had run only a half-length behind the second-placed horse. Victory Lad had lumbered home in 11th. But as the horse trotted back to scale, tired and gusting air, the stewards swept in on him, questioning Fred Shean.

They wanted to know why the jock had checked the horse in the straight. From their observations, Shannon had been travelling untroubled down the straight and would have been in the mix of the finish if Shean hadn't checked him. 'I was about to go around two horses when they shifted out,' he told the stewards, shrugging. 'I checked him, hoping to get a run on the rails.' The officials were satisfied.

Barney O'Brien led Shannon back to Bowral Street a short time later. Peter Riddle followed after them. The old trainer was satisfied with the run. He hadn't expected a win, and neither had the books. Shannon had gone off at 12/1. In light of a bad draw, a huge field with a big weight and pasture fat still clinging to him, Shannon had done well. He had needed the run, and he would strip fitter for it next time out.

Riddle had just about two weeks to clean out his charge's pipes. The colt's next two starts were the Fairfield Handicap on 1 April and the rich Sires' Produce Stakes a week later. All roads led to the latter race, which would boast the best juveniles in New

South Wales and a tempting purse of £3068 to the winner. The race would be over seven furlongs, and was open to two-year-old colts and fillies alike.

To win it, a horse had to be sharp. The Sires' Produce was the richest two-year-old event in Australia. The VRC version was run in early March, and was worth almost £1000 less. First contested in 1867, the race was as old as Randwick Racecourse. But those were days when two-year-old racing was infantile. Most horses began serious racing for the three-year-old classics and went onwards to the great staying tests of the year, the Melbourne Cup, Caulfield Cup, Sydney Cup. Nowadays, speed was king. With the cost of racing horses spiking every year, owners were looking for a quick return on their animals. Two-year-old races had exploded in popularity, and with them the prize value.

The Sires' Produce Stakes had been won by a tally of top juveniles in recent years: Mollison, Ammon Ra, Hall Mark, Ajax, Reading and Yaralla. Each had gone on to brilliant track careers, proving the Sires' was a champions' race. Though a classic race, in the traditional sense of the word, was restricted to three-year-old events, the AJC Sires' Produce Stakes was a classic of the two-year-old season, and Peter Riddle worked towards it with dogged determination.

Shannon had to be ready to win by the running of the Fairfield Handicap on 1 April, and on race day he looked fitter and primed for a tussle. Riddle had set him at Victoria Park and Rosebery tracks since the Services' Handicap, and the horse had tightened up. He looked much lighter than he had 10 days before.

The Fairfield had been so well patronised in 1944 that it had two divisions, and Bravo was running in the first while Shannon would contest the second. It was over the unusual distance of six furlongs 20⅔ yards. Brittanic, who had won the Services' Handicap, was lining up as the 7/4 second-choice. Shannon, who had caught the eyes of track watchers in the run-up to the race, was paying 5/4 odds on.

He jumped well, settling third as the 13-horse field moved

towards the half-mile. Shean bustled him into the lead as they snaked around the turn, running girth to girth with the filly Birthright. When they entered the straight Shannon had wrestled the lead away, and inside the furlong he had gone for home. But wide on the course, lumbering 7 st 1 lb to Shannon's 8 st 13 lbs, Liberality came. His finishing spurt was so intense that Shean hardly saw him coming. When they hit the winning post Shannon had gone under by half a neck. Liberality had come home at 20/1.

Across Randwick, odds-on backers scowled and hooted the result. The bag-swingers threw their hands in the air, feigning sympathy. 'Oh well boys, out for the count then', they said, as scores of punters flung their tickets away in disgust. Then they snapped their bags shut.

As Shannon trotted back to scale, Fred Shean absorbed much of the ring's discontent. It wasn't the first time the colt had fallen at odds on, and whether it was by a short neck or four lengths, it made no difference to the gambling man. But the turf student saw things differently. Shannon had had to give Liberality 26 lbs in the Fairfield, and 11 lbs to Brittanic, who had finished one and a half lengths away third. The horses had run 1:13¾ on the good track, which was three-quarters of a second faster than the race's first division earlier in the day (Bravo had run third). If horses tire accumulatively, it is certainly accelerated by weight. It was generally felt among racing men of the time that a horse had a neutral zone carrying weight, in which it was unaffected by the pounds in the saddle. That zone was felt to be about 8 stone before weight began to tell. It varied between horses, some being able to carry poundage better than others, but most turf men were conclusive that a horse weighted well over 8 stone, pitted against a much lighter weighted runner, would have to work much harder in the dying stages of a contest, given that the weight is so much heavier at the winning post than at the starting tapes.

Shannon, also, had drawn postposition 12 in the 13-horse field. On the six-furlong Randwick track, the inside horses, who can sprint the first two furlongs in a spritely 23 seconds, have a

significant advantage over the outside horses when they settled
down. From his outer alley, Shannon had conceded the inner
horses a one-and-half-length advantage over a half-mile. There was
no doubting that in a field with more than a dozen runners, as had
been the Fairfield and Services' handicaps, the outside marble was
a bad draw. So, as Shannon had bolted across the track to contest
the lead very early in the Fairfield, he had run some impressive
sectionals in the early part, and with the accumulated burden of
his big weight, his half-neck loss was very commendable.

The *Sunday Telegraph* agreed. 'Connections are yet to decide
whether Liberality and Brittanic will contest the AJC Sires'
Produce next Saturday, but neither would appear to have a chance
of beating Shannon in the race.' The newspaper realised, as did the
smart punter, that Shannon would meet the pair on level weights.

14

The 1944 Sires' Produce Stakes

At midday on 8 April 1944, the Randwick Racecourse tramlines were clogged with comings and goings, trundling old 'toast racks' and express cars packed tight since Circular Quay. It was a hot, stale day, much too warm for the time of year, but the track was glittering because of it, and full.

It was Easter Saturday. St Leger day. The card boasted the Sires' Produce, the Doncaster and the St Leger, an epic day's racing in Sydney. The bookies were in full swing on their pedestals, hollering odds and calling the specials for the big ones. The air over the ring was polluted with shouts and whistles, pointing fingers and pound notes flying here and there. Official attendance would later record 82,400 people, which was double the figure from 1943.

They came from country regions and local suburbs, handing over 1/3 to get in. A man who came by horse was charged an extra 3d, or 6d to park his car. To access the saddling paddock he paid 15/-, a woman half that, while the St Leger reserve demanded 3d from men, women and children alike. Many bought their tickets on the trams, and others paid their way into the Flat. If the punt were good that day, they would pay to move into the Leger, and if the punt were very good, they would find themselves in the paddock by the end of the day.

Shannon's race would jump at 1.55 pm. Twelve horses were lining up, and the field was excellent. Liberality and Brittanic had paid up, but they were small change for Riddle's colt. Bravo was contesting, as were Victory Lad and the excellent Tea Rose, and these three made the Sires' Produce the most competitive race Shannon had yet contested.

All colts in the race would carry 8 st 10 lbs, and fillies 8 st 8 lbs. Shannon was paying 2/1 against. On this event, there wasn't an odds-on choice in sight. Tea Rose was paying 7/1 alongside Brittanic and Victory Lad, while Bravo was showing 8/1. Cliff Graves, vintage turf reporter with the *Telegraph*, had selected Shannon, Bravo and Victory Lad in that order.

At 1.30 pm Shannon followed Barney O'Brien into the parade ring. In the dense sunlight he looked rich and full, dapples on his hindquarters and speckling his flanks. He carried number two saddlecloth, so he circled the paddock behind Bravo, who carried number one. Liberality was behind him, and Tea Rose carried 10, many horses behind. Shannon, as usual, was calm and orderly despite the overcrowded scenes around him.

The rail around the paddock was choked with people, all stretching to get a look at the two-year-olds. Many more patrons were pouring out of the luncheon room and the oyster room. Miss Bishop Caterers, who had been contracted to fill the bellies of Randwick racegoers for over a decade now, were running low on bread and scones for afternoon tea. But as the Sires' Produce was the first feature race of the day, followed by the Autumn Stakes, the Doncaster and then the St Leger, the eating pavilions were emptying out as Shannon went to post.

He left the parade ring at a relaxed trot, loping down to the seven-furlong chute on a long, loose rein. The chute was on the far east end of the track, directly opposite the grandstands and inside the steeplechase course that flanked Wansey Road. It was a straight run of about two furlongs before the first turn, then about two furlongs into the turn for home. Shannon had drawn barrier 11 of 12 horses, wide again, but the extra distance would give Fred Shean more time to slot in before the turns.

Jack Gaxieu was shuffling the field by 1.55 pm, but two-year-olds were diving in and out of position all around him. It was a chaotic start at 2 pm on the tick. On Shannon's outside, Scaur Fel was left two lengths at the jump.

Shean bustled Shannon along to an early position as the field sorted itself down the chute. Cragsman had taken an early lead with Gay King on his flank, but Shannon had broken from his outside draw so smartly that he was following the two leaders as they spilled onto the course proper. Running a strong gallop, they turned over the first two furlongs in 22 seconds.

Shannon covered the ground in easy, stretchy strides. The going was good, so the colt had no troubles with his feet, and Shean hovered quietly over his neck, waiting for the turn into the straight. As it neared, in a narrow space between Shannon's ears, Shean urged the colt to pick up. The horse's neck dipped a little more, the rolling motion of his body a little more pronounced. He came up on the pacemakers quickly.

But as the field swung into the straight, things got messy. On the rail, Shannon sat a length and a bit off Cragsman on the inside, with Gay King on that colt's outside. Cragsman, tiring, veered suddenly across the track, jolting Gay King so severely that jockey Ted Bartle, on Gay King, swung right out of his saddle. Just as he was about to right himself, Darby Munro's mount Victory Lad cannoned into him from behind. Bartle had no chance. He came over the side of Gay King and lay in a heap on the Randwick turf. Munro pulled up Victory Lad, and the rest of the field, riderless Gay King included, surged on without them.

The scuffle had left an enormous hole on the rail for Shannon to charge through, and he did. Shean rode hands and heels down the straight, and opened a two-length advantage within strides. But Tea Rose had avoided all the trouble too, and she went with Shannon all the way.

The two horses boxed out the last furlong like two old warriors, Shannon on the inside, Tea Rose on the outside. Neither horse would give in. The grandstand crowds were thunderous, cheering on the colt as favourite, cheering the filly for her determination. But Shannon was winning the contest of wills, stretching his perfect neck out as they bolted under the judge's string.* He prevailed over Tea Rose by an official half-neck, and the pair had

---

* The judge's string was a white cord that stretched over the track from the judge's box to the winning post. Often referred to as the 'overhead finishing line', it helped the judge decipher a winner in a close finish.

gone three lengths clear of Bravo, who had finished strongly from midfield to snatch third.

The time of 1:25 for the seven furlongs was three seconds outside the Randwick record, but the trouble in the straight had slowed the closing stages considerably. In recent years, only Ajax and Hall Mark had run faster incarnations of the Sires' Produce, in 1937 and 1933 respectively, so the time was respectable for young horses. As Shannon trotted back to scale, cheered by tens of thousands of happy punters lining the rails and the infield, and as an ambulance crew hovered over Ted Bartle further down the straight, the stewards readied to question jockeys about the rough finish.

Fred Shean had been clear of the incident, so after he stripped Shannon and weighed in correctly, the red flag was raised over the semaphore board (indicating correct weight). It was followed by the red-on-white flag (totalisator pays out), and an almighty cheer from the Randwick crowd. At 2/1, Shannon had returned very nice odds, and lines of punters filed their way across the track from the Flat, paying their way up into the Leger and onwards to the saddling paddock if their luck held out.

Peter Riddle showed little emotion as he greeted Shannon in the ring, but privately he was elated. It wasn't just the prizemoney attached to the win: £3068. It was the prestige of owning and preparing a two-year-old classic winner. As an entire, Shannon was now far more valuable a sire prospect, not to mention a racehorse. However, the pardonable pride of saying the colt was his was where Riddle took most satisfaction.

The win hauled Shannon's earnings to £5022. From seven starts he had the fabulous record of three wins, three seconds and a single unplaced effort. Of his runner-up finishes, the margin had been no more than a half-length. It wasn't a flawless record, but it was consistent at the highest level. As the bay was led away from the course by Barney O'Brien, Riddle swayed after them, wondering now if he should run the colt in the Champagne Stakes the following Saturday.

The Champagne was usually the next port for Sires' Produce winners, but Riddle had been telling himself that Shannon wouldn't run in it if he won the Sires' Produce. He didn't think his colt would be represented in the weights, as Shannon would carry a 10-pound penalty into it, while Bravo would go in with 8 st 10 lbs. Though Bravo had finished no closer than third today, Riddle believed his brother's colt was smart enough to edge out Shannon with his weight advantage. The trainer also suspected that Shannon was not as sharp as he had been in the autumn, despite today's very good win. No, he wouldn't change his mind. Shannon wouldn't run in the Champagne.

Barney O'Brien walked the colt back to Bowral Street a little later in the afternoon, Peter Riddle following along when the racing was over and the sun had fallen far west of Randwick Racecourse. He was exhausted by the time he made it home to Norton Street that night. It was getting harder to stay afloat during race days; his shoulders ached and he felt steamrolled. The excitement of Shannon's win had wiped him out.

In the next few days, he shipped the colt to Richmond for a few weeks of grass and grain. Bravo, who could manage only third in the Champagne behind Scaur Fel and the gritty Tea Rose, joined him soon after. The two colts sprouted thick woolly coats and grew into their bones as winter settled in. Back at the yard, Peter Riddle felt the onset of the cool months as only a frail, sick man can.

15

The Abbeville Affair

Winter had a firm grip on New South Wales when Fred Shean took the train to Newcastle one morning late in July. He was heading to one of the last meetings of the season, to the Newcastle Jockey Club's Cameron Handicap on 29 July. The race was a seven-furlong event around Newcastle's Broadmeadow racetrack, and Shean was riding the second-choice Hall Stand. The heated favourite, a nondescript, plain bay gelding called Abbeville, was the mount of fellow Sydney hoop Noel McGrowdie.

The race went off as the market predicted. Hall Stand and Abbeville punched out a magnificent duel down the home straight, with the fancied Abbeville prevailing by a long nose. It was a sensational tussle for the £1050 purse, popping the track record by a full second. Veteran jock Andy Knox, who had been riding Precise at 7/1, closed home back in fourth. There were no enquiries from the stewards, everything stood squeaky clean. Shean and Knox rolled home to Sydney.

McGrowdie jumped into a motor car with Mr Porter, a friend of Abbeville's trainer, Randwick-based Tom McGrath. On the long drive to Sydney down the Pacific Highway that night, McGrowdie confessed to Porter that he had been approached in the jockeys' room to throw the Cameron Handicap, to 'ride dead' so that Abbeville might lose. It came with a £600 bribe and a neat promise of silence. McGrowdie, in a spin as to what to do, had told no one.

The morning after the race, Porter met Tom McGrath for a round of the links and a chinwag. He told Abbeville's trainer about McGrowdie's sensational confession, and McGrath was disgusted with what he heard. On Monday morning during trackwork, he cornered McGrowdie about Porter's story, and the jock came clean.

He repeated the story to the trainer, word for word. Immediately, McGrath approached Newcastle secretary Jack Hibberd, who then notified the club's stipendiary stewards, and a can of worms spilled open on the world of New South Wales horseracing.

Abbeville had been backed for the Cameron Handicap to the tune of tens of thousands of pounds, so many thousands that McGrath had stationed an armed guard on the gelding as soon as he had left Sydney for Newcastle four days before the race. Aub Fulford, a champion bare-knuckle fighter, had watched over the horse through the long nights until the morning of the Cameron. Poised beside him was a double-barrelled shotgun, just in case. Plenty had ridden on Abbeville's win, plenty enough to try to make him lose.

Newcastle stewards showed up to the AJC offices at Randwick on Tuesday 8 August 1944. It was only eight days into the new racing season. They were there to hear McGrowdie's evidence. Abbeville's rider had been called in for a preliminary hearing, but so had Fred Shean and Andy Knox. Shean told the waiting press that he was mystified as to why he had been called in, that he suspected he was being asked for evidence. Knox also said he had no clue as to what was going on. But McGrowdie's testimony that day proved damning for both of them. McGrowdie accused Fred Shean of approaching him in the jockeys' room with the £600 offer, admitting he had no idea who had put Shean up to it.

McGrowdie testified that Shean had sidled up to him before the running of the Cameron, stating he was delivering a message. 'I've been offered £600 to stop Hall Stand,' Shean allegedly confessed to McGrowdie, revealing the amount would increase to £1000 if Precise, the mount of Andy Knox, were to win. 'This offer applies to you too,' Shean allegedly told McGrowdie. The winning jockey testified that Shean had told him the monies would be handed over before they left the track that afternoon, but he had also admitted that he didn't want any part of it. McGrowdie said he had retorted that he had been laid a fortune to win the race, and that he, also, wanted no part in the incident.

Shean was grilled for a long time by the Newcastle stipes, enduring two hours in the offices of the AJC. Who had approached him to pass on the bribe, and why had he agreed to do it? Shean confessed that it was Andy Knox who had approached him, that Knox had asked Shean to pass on the bribe to McGrowdie. Shean testified that after McGrowdie had refused the offer, he reported back to Knox. 'No business Andy,' he had said.

When he left, the stewards were far from impressed. While McGrowdie was under heat for not reporting the issue on race day, Shean and Knox lay accused of trying to fix the outcome of the Cameron Handicap. 'There may or may not be something in the allegations, but I want to ensure that no discredit to Newcastle Jockey Club will remain,' declared Jack Hibberd that day.

As the three jockeys left the AJC compound, Andy Knox muscled up to McGrowdie, hissing 'informer' at him. Shean caught Knox by the arm and drew him away, fearing a confrontation that would only fuel the fire. Forty-year-old Knox, though often brilliant in the saddle (he had won the jockeys' premiership title in 1936), was no stranger to the stewards' room. He was bullish and confrontational, often arrogant, and known for the odd sulk. He had been riding at the top level for more than 26 years and was, in fact, planning his retirement from riding. On that day, he was bristling, wondering if the Newcastle Jockey Club was about to bow him out of race riding for good.

They did. By five o'clock on Tuesday 8 August, with the evidence of all three jockeys considered, the Newcastle stipes disqualified both Shean and Knox for two years. Their licences to ride were revoked under Rule 210 of the Rules of Racing, which stated: 'The stewards may disqualify any person who may corruptly give, or offer, any money, share in a bet, or other benefit to any jockey.' The disqualifications were binding across all Australian racetracks. Shean was floored. 'I couldn't believe my ears when they told me,' he said to the *Telegraph*. 'I got the shock of my life to find out I was actually involved. It was a bombshell. I will certainly appeal.'

Knox was cagey about his innocence. 'I may appeal in an

attempt to clear my name, but whether I do or not I have advised Shean to appeal,' he told the press. 'I've told him that I will give evidence in his support, and I feel this will absolve him at the hearing.' In the end, both Shean and Knox lodged appeals. They would appear before an AJC tribunal on 17 August.

McGrowdie, meanwhile, was under scrutiny about how the incident might reflect on him. He declined to admit that it was affecting him professionally, saying he had lucrative offers for the upcoming spring. But people wanted to know why he hadn't revealed the bribe before the running of the Cameron Handicap. 'What an invidious position I was in,' he responded. 'Say I had talked and then been beaten on Abbeville. What then?'

In the days that followed, he tired of the media quizzes. 'What can I say that hasn't been already said? My only request is that the matter shall now be dropped and forgotten.'

It wasn't. The Newcastle stewards impounded the betting books of five prominent bookmakers, requesting all evidences of straight-out and doubles bets on the Cameron Handicap. They ordered all five bookies to front an inquiry at 2 pm on 15 August, digging furiously to find the source of the £600 bribe. They suspected that huge liabilities, laid on the result of the Cameron–Newcastle Cup double, was the fuel behind the bribe, but they had to prove it.

Precise's owner, prominent Newcastle bookie Phil Jenkins, was summoned to appear at the inquiry. If the bribe did pend on Precise winning the Cameron Handicap, it made sense that the owner of Precise might be involved. All of Jenkins' ante-post and course betting books were brought into evidence, but were found to be undecipherable. The carbon copies were so bad that the stewards had to adjourn the investigation, demanding the originals so that the owner might be cleared of suspicion. Jenkins iterated that he had never been found foul in all his years as a leading fielder at Newcastle, and that his risks on the result of the Cameron Handicap were no more than £3000. This, he testified, did not represent anything excessive that might suggest guilt.

On the afternoon of 17 August, a dry, cool day over Randwick, Fred Shean and Andy Knox fronted an AJC committee in appeal of their two-year sentences. They had paid £10 each in appeal fees. The committee consisted of all the big guns of the Australian Jockey Club, including chairman George Main, chief stipendiary steward J. B. Donohue and secretary George Rowe. It also featured Newcastle stewards P. J. Ryan and Reg Mitchell, who had presided over the investigation to date. The relationship between Shean and Knox had deteriorated markedly. They didn't speak as they waited to enter the committee room, Knox first to give evidence.

The matter was very serious, more serious than any situation Shean had found himself in professionally. The jockey was 39 years old. He wasn't considering retirement, unlike Knox. Shean told the committee that any bribes had not affected his riding of the Cameron Handicap on 29 July; he had ridden Hall Stand into a gallant second place, just pipped at the line by the winner. He said the penalty was not justified, given that nothing had affected the outcome of the race. It was a weak case given the severity of the charge, but it was all he had . . . almost.

Shean had brought along Hall Stand's trainer as a character witness. Charlie McLoughlin testified that just before he boosted Shean into the saddle for the Cameron, he told the jock that the owners had opted to bet lightly on their horse due to his outside draw. 'I consider Shean tried to win on Hall Stand as hard as I have ever seen a jockey do,' he said. He was trying to reiterate to the committee that Fred Shean's riding of Hall Stand had been honest and dogged, that he had tried to win the race.

Twelve pages of evidence sat before the committeemen as they deliberated Shean's and Knox's appeals. The two jockeys were inter-rogated for 85 minutes, feeling the weight of racing's officialdom tick-tocking over their fates. When the committee finally revealed its decisions, the light was fading from the late-winter afternoon. Fred Shean's disqualification stood. Andy Knox was ejected for 10 staggering years.

The sentence fell on Knox like a cartoon anvil. He kept

shaking his head, slamming a rolled-up newspaper against his thigh in frustration. As he left the AJC offices, he kept muttering to himself, 'I can't understand this, I don't deserve it. They've done something dreadful to me.' When the press boys pushed him for comment, he said, 'Ten years disqualification means I will be too old to resume riding. I'm terribly upset going out this way after 26 years good riding. I can't believe it.' In temper and frustration, he bleated that he had been railroaded. Knox had never professed that he was innocent of the charges, but he said he had not been properly acquainted with Shean's and McGrowdie's evidences, and that this put him in a false position. 'I couldn't cross-question them fully,' he told reporters that night. 'I was railroaded by the jockeys I thought pals, and crucified by the AJC.'

Fred Shean was relieved, grateful even, that his own sentence hadn't been increased, but his disqualification banned him not just from riding; he would not be allowed to set foot on a racecourse anywhere for two years. The sentence also stamped him as a partner to Knox's involvement, but Shean professed again and again that he was innocent. He told waiting reporters that night that all he was guilty of was passing on a message, and advising Noel McGrowdie to take no part in any skulduggery. 'Apparently these admissions got me into trouble,' he said, 'and now I have gone out, although I'm innocent.'

Shean was refunded his £10 appeal deposit and sent on his way. He was anxious to get home. His wife had been ill with worry about the entire affair, and as he drove away from Randwick Racecourse for the last time in a long time, he wondered what he would do. He wasn't short of money, having invested his turf winnings handsomely. But the shame of the incident was enormous. It made him feel sick, having always considered himself an upstanding, honourable fellow. Would people forever question his integrity now?

The 10-year disqualification of Andy Knox burned a hole in Sydney racing, as it was the heaviest sentence AJC chairman George Main had ever imposed on a hoop in his eight-year chairmanship.

'Knox's offence was very serious,' he said. 'I cannot disclose further information.' As the lightest top-jockey on the metropolitan ranks, Knox would be a terrific loss, and everyone knew it.

On Bowral Street, Peter Riddle was much more concerned about Fred Shean. As of 17 August 1944, Riddle had no jockey for three-year-old Shannon.

The trainer had been following the case closely, like most racing men. But *unlike* most racing men, Riddle had vested interest in its outcome. Shean's disqualification was a terrible blow to Shannon's progress. The youngster was a sensitive type. He had grown tuned to Shean's guiding hands, his light seat and gentle ways in the thick of a race. He wasn't a horse that would enjoy bullying or brash riding, and three-year-old colts often needed that cool hand more than they had as two-year-olds.

In the interim of the appeal, Shean had continued riding Shannon in early-morning trackwork (the colt had come back from a spell in early July), but now that he was barred from every racecourse in the land, Riddle had to source a new pilot. For a time, he wondered about ex-Queensland hoop George Moore, whom he knew well and who rode out for him a few mornings a week. He thought about Billy Cook, also, who had partnered Bravo. Whoever it was, it had to be someone that Riddle trusted absolutely, someone he knew would preserve his colt.

The decision fell out of his hands. As spring crept up on the harbour city with its pink, warming mornings, Peter Riddle fell so ill he could hardly stand. From a bed at Prince Henry Hospital in coastal Little Bay, he charged Shannon's care, and the jockey problem, to his brother Bert. It was the first puncture in an unsettling, unstable wheel that rolled Shannon towards his three-year-old spring.

16

The Demon Darb

Darby Munro had the feel of the cat that got the cream. There seemed always to be a slight crack of a grin on the corners of his mouth, a smirk that softened his thick, dark eyebrows but that made him seem cheeky, smug almost. He wasn't a big man, 5 ft 2¾ in, weighed 8 st 12 lbs when he wasn't making weights. He had thick, wavy hair pasted back from his face and a dark, swarthy colour to his complexion. He was exotic-looking for a Randwick jock, a man who might easily have been Spanish or South American.

He was 31 years old in the spring of 1944. Darby Munro lived in a tidy, expensively furnished apartment on Wansey Road, overlooking Randwick Racecourse. He was wealthy, a four-figure earner. He had things that most people didn't have: flyscreens, patio furniture, a wireless. In fact, his lifestyle was more like that of a movie star than a popular metropolitan jockey. He drank, smoked, ran red lights. He was a big personality in a very big black Cadillac.

Though married, Munro was a handful. He probably wasn't faithful. He would stumble home at sinful hours of the morning, the smell of grog and the smudge of rouge too obvious to hide. Some mornings he didn't even make it out of his car. He would be found incoherent across the back seat of the Cadillac, ruffled and half comatose. Darryl Cook, a Munro sidekick, remembered dragging the jockey out of his motor car on so many race mornings. 'Take whatever's in my pockets, son,' Munro would drawl. Sometimes it was mere shillings. Other times it was more money than a working man would see in a month.

Darby Munro had so much racing in his pedigree that he might have been part thoroughbred. In the early days of the

1900s, his father had been the head trainer at St Albans Stud near Geelong. Darby, along with his older brother Jim, ran ragged around the yard, pulling on horses' tails, scooting between their legs. From the minute he had been old enough to talk, Munro's preoccupation had been racehorses. By the age of five, he was mouthy and confident, bawling out the stable crews for dressing a horse incorrectly. His mother grew weary of sheets going missing from the linen press. 'I always knew where they'd be,' she said. 'Darby would be using them to bandage the legs of his pony.' Constantly, she worried that he would run a horse up the wrong way, that his little body would be trampled by some cranky beast on a hapless morning. 'But they never did,' she said. 'Horses loved him; they knew he loved them.'

Munro's father nicknamed his son 'Darby' when the boy was little more than knee-high. The name didn't come from an association with racing derbies (as legend tells), or even from his uncle, who was also a David. The nickname came from little Munro's handshake. Darby's handshake was so firm and powerful that his father used to say he could break out of manacles (manacles were handcuffs, dubbed 'darbys' by the convicts that wore them). The jockey would forever be known as 'Darby' thereafter.

By the time he was 10, Darby Munro was riding out his father's horses in the early mornings. He had been well schooled. His father would hitch a racing saddle to a fence rail, no more than two inches thick, and force his son to climb aboard. Darby would find the irons and hover above the saddle, balancing on that rail while swapping his whip hand, riding with the winning post square in his imagination. Because of it, his coordination and balance on a racehorse became second to none. And it was during these dawn workouts on the St Albans gallops that Eric Connolly noticed him. Arguably the biggest punter in Australian horseracing, a one-time trainer and full-time king-hitter in the ring, Connolly was swish, sophisticated and terribly smart.

The young Darb fell into Connolly's circle. An impressionable teen, Darby learned to walk like Connolly, dress like him.

He learned the value of money from him too. It was a unique introduction to adult life, and Darby was hardly a teenager when Connolly relocated him to Melbourne to ride track trials. Still too young to race ride, Munro hopped aboard Manfred, Rampion, Pantheon and Bicolor. These were outstanding heroes of the roaring twenties, and a sweet introduction to life at the top of horseracing.

By 1944, Munro had become Australia's money rider, its most prolific big-race jockey on the circuit. Based in Sydney, Darby was a horseman of no compare. They called him 'Mr Wonderful'. There was no jock that could judge a race like him. He could push a horse through the eye of a needle, anticipate when a hole was coming in the field and burst through it. He was known for finding room in a race finish where there was none. He would holler his way through it, properly frightening the younger riders out of his way. And he seemed to know exactly how much horse he had underneath him at all times.

Horses ran for him like no other rider, for he was strong and bullish in the saddle. That famous balance was never better on display than in a tight finish, when it seemed like he was flailing and bouncing when in fact he was centrally poised, never shifting his weight from the centre of the horse. He wasn't stylish or graceful as some jocks were. He wasn't demure with his hands, or forgiving with his whip. He wanted to win, and by lord he would win if he could. In the saddle, he was just like he was on the ground – big and loud and compulsive.

Some days, he was positively hated. No jockey in Sydney was more vilified than Darby Munro. He would trot back to scale amid heckles and jeering if he lost on a favourite. People instantly concluded he had pulled the race. Sometimes they were right. On certain occasions, the abuse was inflammable. Small-time punters would telephone his home, roaring abuse into the receiver. Munro refused to get a silent number. The following week he would ride a big winner and the cheers would come. Crowds of racegoers would surge on the weighing enclosure; often Darb blanked them, other days he raised his hat to them. His skin was thick. He knew the mob was fickle.

Over the years, he had grand associations with champions. His most famous win had been aboard the redoubtable Peter Pan in the 1934 Melbourne Cup, when the pair had top weight and the outside draw on the worst track Darb had ever seen. He rated the win as the most courageous of any horse he had ridden, and believed Peter Pan to be the greatest handicapper he knew, his great rival Rogilla (Darb's most famous 1930s association) the greatest weight-for-ager. When Munro had an opinion on a horse, he voiced it. Writing for the *Argus* newspaper in 1949, he declared weight-for-age champ Ajax a 'fake': 'I know this will start something,' he declared, 'but I rode against Ajax several times and I think he was greatly overrated.' Munro had ridden many great champions, but forever he would testify greatness as a horse that could win one or both of the AJC and VRC derbies, then run a good Melbourne Cup.

No one had ever seen, or heard, anything like Darby Munro. His personality came through a doorway before he did. There was crookedness about him, like he wasn't quite as straight as the stewards would like. He was devilish in a horserace, determined and fiendish in a finish. But that wasn't why he earned the nickname 'Demon Darb'. It was the rogue in him that earned him that title, the part of him that raised the ire of stewards. But they rarely got him for anything. A short suspension here, a warning there was all he had got over the years. Still, his brother Jim (a trainer by 1944 but before that one of the country's most accomplished, most decorated jockeys) pleaded with him not to ride in Melbourne. 'Jim always thought they were after Darb,' remembered Daryll Cook. 'He'd always tell him not to ride down there.'

Munro was a celebrity. He would arrive at the boxing on Friday nights in Sydney, cheered as he took his seat. He spoke to anyone. Whenever he was around, people came. His aura was magnetic; folks trailed him like pilot fish. Even his routine was famous. He rarely ate breakfast, instead swallowing a mug of hot tea before straying to the track, often until midday. For lunch, it was a grill of lean sausages and bread. For dinner, a roast joint or fish, usually reeled in by a friend earlier that day. Munro never wasted to meet his mounts (he suffered from stomach ulcers). Instead, he fixed himself to his thin diet and sweated off at the Turkish baths on race mornings, or at Wylie's Baths in Coogee. At best, he could skinny down to 8 st 6 lbs, but that was his limit. He complained constantly that the minimum riding weight for hoops should be 7 st 7 lbs (not 6 st 7 lbs as stipulated by the then riding rules). Outside these hours, he smoked too much and drank too much. He fell out the doorways of Coogee's Oceanic Hotel, or swanky clubs in Kings Cross. Some race mornings he was so inebriated that he was still drunk when he began riding. Munro was black and white, brilliance and mess all rolled into one brawny, iron-like body.

—

From his bed at Prince Henry Hospital, Peter Riddle wondered if the Demon Darb might be the rider to replace Fred Shean. He wondered this late in the evenings, when the corridors fell silent to visitors, when June had left his room and driven home to Randwick, when the doctors had come and gone and left him with little but worry. Kathleen was his wife now. The pair had married on 3 June when Shannon and Bravo had gone out to Richmond. It was a marriage of convenience, little else. He was fond of Kath, but relations between her and his daughter were strained. Riddle was stressed and tired from the whole thing.

He watched from the wings as brother Bert brought Shannon into his three-year-old season. The bay colt was due to debut in either the Cape Solander Handicap or the Flying Handicap at Randwick on 26 August. The brothers hadn't decided yet which race they would head towards. By early August, Shannon was breezing around Rosebery. Nothing special: half-miles in 52 seconds, 50 and 49 seconds coming up to race day. The colt looked bigger now, less foalish, and he was developing a hell of a shoulder. He had retained his neat, even proportions and his heel had cleared up during his spell. He gave Bert no troubles leading into race day, but he was still carrying pasture fat. As the Cape Solander was a far more competitive race, fielding Bravo, Tea Rose, Victory Lad and Cragsman, Bert Riddle opted Shannon for the cheaper Flying Handicap. There was no way the colt would win the Solander in his dawdling condition.

Peter Riddle waited for race-day reports on 26 August. Bert had commissioned ex-Queensland hoop William Martell to ride both Shannon and Bravo in their races. Martell was 26 years old, and a relatively seasoned hoop. He had acquired his jockey's licence in Brisbane in 1938. He was sensible, professional, though not gifted like Shean or Demon Darb. He had ridden Peter Riddle's horses before, but not these high-profile three-year-olds.

The matching was not a success. Bravo, although race fit, was beaten out of a place in the Cape Solander, and when the tapes flew up for the Flying Handicap, nine minutes after the advertised start time, Shannon was left two lengths behind. When the field settled onto the course proper from the chute, the colt was third last. Three times in running he ran into interference, checked and straightened and then bumped again. With a flat horse and a bad spot, Martell didn't know what to do. So he did little, and Shannon faded until he was 12th passing the winning post. It might have been lack of fitness, and it might have been lack of confidence from Martell, but the race was a poor start for last year's champion two-year-old. Riddle was less than satisfied.

A day or two after the Flying, the frail trainer took leave from his hospital bed and drove to Wansey Road to see Darby Munro. He and Darb were old, old friends. They had history that went back to the late 1920s. During that time, young Darby had been having a stale time of things. He had barely started professional riding when he broke his ankle, then came down with an infection followed by measles. When he was on his feet again, Sydney racing had virtually forgotten him. It was a competitive time to be a jockey; his brother Jim reigned supreme, along with Jim Pike, Billy Duncan and Maurice McCarten. But Peter Riddle hadn't forgotten him. It was 1929, and he approached Munro to be his stable jockey. He secured the youngster a licence to ride on the pony circuit, and Munro saluted with a string of wins on Riddle's horses, in particular on the talented sprinter Sweet Oration. Munro would never forget it was Peter Riddle who had set him on his way again.

The jock knew Riddle was in a bind because of the Abbeville affair, and when the trainer asked him if he would partner Shannon in his next race, the Hobartville Stakes on 8 September, the jockey agreed. The pair arranged that Darby would pilot Shannon in the Hobartville, and if the colt's form were satisfactory he would consider staying aboard for the AJC Derby on 9 October. In between those races was the Rosehill Guineas on 23 September, but Riddle didn't push that. One race at a time, he thought, as he made his way slowly back to Little Bay.

And so, early on the morning of 31 August 1944, under a temperate and clear Thursday sunrise, Darby Munro climbed aboard Shannon for the very first time. The colt felt different to him, a little narrow but neat. Every new horse felt different, like driving a new car. The seat was different, or the steering lighter. On that morning at Randwick, in eyeshot of Barney O'Brien and Bert Riddle, Darby Munro took hold of Shannon's mouth and coaxed him onto the B grass. The colt was a little thick in the girth, a little too podgy to be impressive, but the Demon found him smooth and even, with a suggestion of coiled speed somewhere below that skin. As horse and rider cantered away into Randwick's broad turns, a famous partnership had been born.

17

Pipedreams of fortune and glory

In the life of a good Sydney three-year-old, all roads led to the AJC Derby. The race was the pinnacle of the spring calendar, the most expensive and esteemed classic of the year. Like its English counterpart, it was a stiff mile and a half in the early months of the racing season. Some said it was a stallion-making race, others a measure of thoroughbred greatness. Either way, at the essence of the Derby was its bringing to light the best three-year-old of the year.

The AJC version had begun in 1861. The race was as old as the Melbourne Cup, but its concept was far older. It mimicked England's Epsom Derby, the most hallowed of turf contests and, since 1780, the greatest turf prize in the world. A man dreamed about winning the English Derby, even if he wasn't English. It was the richest race in the Old Country, but the reward of winning wasn't just money: it was glory and fame in thoroughbred halls.

Traditionally a spring race, the Derby put 8 st 10 lbs on colts, 8 st 5 lbs on fillies. For years, the AJC renewal had allowed geldings to nominate, but not since 1931 had a gelding been allowed to race in its classic. (That decision, controversial down to its bootstraps, wouldn't be overturned until 1957.) At its core was the idea that the Derby should extract the best stallion prospect for the breeding industry, and England had stuck true to that root. But Australia had had a few very high-profile Derby-winning geldings, including Phar Lap and Gloaming. By ostracising geldings from the race, the AJC (and the VRC had ruled similarly) was sticking true to race origins.

In 1944, the AJC Derby was worth £3882 to the winner. For Peter Riddle, there was one pressing concern: would Shannon stay the Derby's mile and a half?

Midstream had been questionable beyond a mile, but Blandford, Shannon's grandsire, was unquestionably a classic-distance producer. Everything in Shannon's paternal line suggested he would go a mile and a half. There were even fewer questions on the dam side. Idle Words, by Magpie, was stoutly bred to go the distance. Magpie had produced winners of the Epsom Handicap, Caulfield Cup, the Doncaster, AJC and VRC derbies, Craven Plate, Melbourne Cup and AJC Plate (over two and a quarter miles). He had been the pre-eminent sire of the roaring twenties. But Midstream's weakness over the classic courses in his three-year-old year in England left a couple of niggling doubts in Riddle's mind. As yet, Shannon hadn't been asked to go further than six furlongs. He would step up into seven at his next outing, but the Derby was an altogether different ask.

Because each horse was required to carry a standard weight, regardless of ability or conditions, there was often a wide gap in the weight-carrying ability of the Derby field. As a result, the best-backed horses often won. Significantly, the horse that could stay the distance was the major influence in the Derby betting market. In the case of the VRC Derby, run the Saturday before the Melbourne Cup in early November, several races had occurred in a horse's preparation to demonstrate to punters that he could go the mile and a half. Because the AJC renewal was run early in the spring, a horse had few race tests to prove itself. It was a difficult hurdle for any trainer with a horse under stamina questions.

From his sick bed, Riddle planned to send Shannon to the Derby through two significant races: the Hobartville Stakes over seven furlongs 26 yards at Randwick on 2 September, then the popular Rosehill Guineas (nine furlongs) three weeks later. He was also considering the Canterbury Guineas and Clibborn Stakes in between. The races offered a gradual climb in distance, and in the Hobartville, Shannon would carry the Derby weight of 8 st 10 lbs. It would also be the first time Munro would pilot the colt in competition. With an £833 first prize, it wasn't a rich purse, but the Hobartville was an esteemed run-up to the bigger prizes.

The line-up for the 1944 Hobartville would include Riddle's pair of Shannon and Bravo, and Victory Lad, Majesty and the two fillies Scaur Fel and Tea Rose. The usual suspects. Tea Rose, who had been alarmingly brilliant since resuming from her two-year-old successes, was fancied favourite at 3/1. She was simply on fire. The day that Shannon had slumped home in the Flying Handicap, the filly had carried 8 st 12 lbs to third place in the Cape Solander, with the winner and place-getter carrying a stone less than her. 'It was a mammoth performance,' said the *Sportsman*, 'and we expect her to win the Hobartville. She is more forward than Shannon, and when they met in the autumn she was almost his equal.'

The Midstream youngster had a week between his Flying Handicap run and the Hobartville. It wasn't a lot of time to open his pipes, to work off some of the condition that still hung about him this early in the spring. But after Darby Munro had accepted the ride on the colt, Sydney's top jock had whistled the cobwebs away within a few days. Munro's hand was so firm and confident on a horse, so cool and disciplined even in trackwork, that by Saturday 2 September, race day, Shannon was visibly fitter.

The colt drew position nine in the 11-horse field (Scaur Fel had been scratched after falling ill). Tea Rose was widest from the rail. With little to no rainfall for days, the going was good (though the AJC had watered), and as the horses circled behind the starter's podium, the sharks were circling too. In the ring, Shannon had drifted from 5/2 to as much as 4/1 in spots. Riddle's staff couldn't believe their eyes. Even the boss, recovering in bed at Norton Street, had been confident the colt was the goods.

In fact, when Shannon had entered the saddling paddock, punters had taken a long look at him and walked away. He had breezed so well in the lead-up to the race that he was right back to his natural frame, which was very light. The punting public was still not impressed, and had stopped backing him. Rumours got to the bookies that Shannon was in no fit state to win a race, and coupled with a desertion of betting on him, the price drifted. The *Sunday Telegraph* would describe it as 'one of the biggest betting drifts ever associated with a classic event'. Peter Riddle knew Shannon had fooled the ring.

At the tapes, the three-year-olds were skittish for Jack Gaxieu. Cold Shower, second off the rail, misbehaved and brought a few minutes delay upon the field. When they jumped, it was 1.59 pm, four minutes over start time.

Shannon skipped away from the start with a quick spurt under Darby Munro. The tempo was strong from the outset, and as the field bunched out of the chute onto the course proper, he settled third. Majesty was coasting along up front, opening his lead into the first of the two turns. Shannon rolled along with Vermeil, Victory Lad and Bravo around him. No one was going after the leader too early.

When Majesty belted past the half-mile, the chasing pack began to close. Shannon, on the rails, was out of room, and Munro chose to ease the colt back to sixth and go out. When they moved into the turn for home, Shannon had slipped into running room on the outside of the field, and with the straight laid out before him, the Demon Darb tucked into his mount and rode for home. Shannon accelerated away.

He shot past Cold Shower, Bravo and Victory Lad, and as the crowds in the St Leger cheered the flying bay, Shannon took Vermeil, then Majesty, to account. Business-like in his pursuit of the lead, the colt motored away by a length, then two. Only Cold Shower could go with him. At the winning post, Shannon had a one-and-three-quarter-length advantage, and he snatched the Hobartville in the slick time of 1:25¾. Minus the 26 yards of the distance, the seven furlongs had been run in 1:24½.

It was an excellent win, but not a popular one, though punters knew they had only themselves to blame. Tea Rose, the 3/1 favourite, had come home second-last. As Shannon trotted back in, Munro ignored the jests that came his way. As usual, the punters were speaking through their pockets. He shook hands with Bert Riddle, weighed in with the stewards, and left to consider his options for the AJC Derby. At that moment, Shannon looked a good prospect for the blue riband, but Munro wouldn't be held to a ride just yet. He would wait a little longer before confirming things.

The Hobartville brought Shannon's tally to £5855 in nine races. It was his fourth win, and suggested a promising spate of racing ahead. But more often than not, things went awry in horseracing.

—

In the spring of 1944, the Sydney Turf Club, having acquired Rosehill Racecourse, had a few problems. The first was a swarm of bees. Hundreds of the insects had set up camp on the paddock scratching-tower, amid the pansies and wallflowers and red poppies. George Evans, the course caretaker, had been trying to shift them for two years, but that spring they had arrived with enforcers. 'They've come with fighter escorts this time,' Evans said. Appealing for help in dislodging the swarm, Evans prepared his racecourse in the meanwhile. The Guineas meeting was coming up on 23 September, and Rosehill was blooming. The track looked like a bowling green.

In late August, the STC's spring plans were scuppered when the railway authorities announced a ban on race-day trains. Horses and greyhounds were prohibited from carriage aboard passenger and goods trains due to coal shortages, leaving trainers with few means to transport their animals to Rosehill's Guineas meeting. The STC immediately applied to the AJC for the use of Randwick, and a meeting of the AJC board took place on 1 September. The problem with the request was that Randwick already had 10 meetings in its books for the following two months, due to wartime occupations at Warwick Farm, Ascot and other tracks. Hawkesbury, too, had applied to headquarters to host its 30 September meeting at Canterbury track.

The AJC granted the STC request, mostly because the Guineas meeting was the club's major spring event. Rosehill secretary Reg

Rowe was relieved about the ruling, but told the *Telegraph* that the meeting would resume at Rosehill if coal restrictions were lifted. As the days ticked towards 23 September, and no such relief was in sight, Sydney trainers resigned to racing at Randwick.

The decision made little difference to Peter Riddle. In fact, it made his life easier. Though he was no longer in hospital, he was in poor health, weak from even standing. He hobbled to the yard the morning after the Hobartville to inspect Shannon, conferring with Barney O'Brien and brother Bert. On Monday 4 September he withdrew his colt from the Canterbury Guineas, to be run on 9 September, declaring his worries about backing his horse up so quickly. 'He's a little on the light side, and I'd be afraid that an immediate run over nine furlongs would set him back,' he said.

On 8 September, the Prime Minister rescinded his ban on transport for racing fixtures, meaning that the Rosehill venue could go ahead. With wind in its sails again, the STC decided to instigate a new concept to its Guineas meeting: the field for the three-year-old Rosehill Guineas would parade in the saddling paddock for conformation and soundness rosettes. The committee believed that the awards would benefit the breeding of thoroughbred and utility stock, and would add a gala-like atmosphere to the meeting. Immediately, trainers had their reservations about fussing with fizzy three-year-olds right before an important race, but no complaining was about to change the STC's minds.

With three weeks between runs, Shannon had plenty of time to sharpen up, and sharpen up he did. His morning work was so impressive in the lead-up to the Guineas that he became that elusive figment in horseracing – a moral. On 21 September he went six furlongs at Rosebery with stablemate Modulation, defeating the older horse by a length in 1:16, wide out on the course proper. Trackmen watching the gallop looked at their watches and declared that if Modulation had been able to extend Shannon, the colt would have demolished the Rosebery course records set by Gold Rod and Hall Stand. It was a cracking trial, as Modulation was not only an experienced campaigner, he was also a fancy for the Epsom. After the gallop, several of the big bookies took straight-out bets on Shannon for the AJC Derby. Curiously, though, his price shifted only a little, many bag-swingers opting for him. One declared: 'I thought Shannon looked very light in the Hobartville, and I doubt whether he is robust enough to stand a hard preparation for a race over a mile and a half. I think he's too small to carry 8 st 10 lbs.'

Peter Riddle read all the comments and remained defiant. He had trained Aeolus in 1938 to run second in the Derby, and that horse had been smaller than Shannon. The winner that year had been Nuffield, an excellent three-year-old, and Riddle didn't believe there was a Nuffield in the 1944 running.

The *Telegraph* was so certain of Shannon winning the Guineas that on race morning it predicted he would run close to the Rosehill track record, set by Rogilla in 1934. Within half an hour of the race, the colt was even-money, in some spots odds on. By 2.40 pm, with Rosehill packed tight with punters, racegoers and service folk, Shannon was the talk of the town. He entered the parade ring with Barney O'Brien, Munro and Bert Riddle nearby, and everyone wanted a look at him. As it turned out, they had a little too long to look.

The STC's little 'horse show' took place bang on schedule. The running of the Guineas had even been delayed by 15 minutes to accommodate the judging of conformation and soundness, and in the cool spring sunshine, the 16 Guineas horses went around and around the paddock, stopping here and there for inspection, turning in to stand still, then going out again. After 10 minutes, many of the youngsters were getting fractious, and trainers were getting concerned, then irritated. When the judges decided on their winners (Shannon was not among them), rosettes were pinned to bridles and a rail-side band struck up within feet of them. It was the last straw for many of the horses. Vermeil, a twitchy three-year-old at the calmest times, was walking around on his hind legs as his jockey climbed aboard. His antics began to upset other runners, so that by the time Darby Munro cantered Shannon down to the nine-furlong start, he had left a maelstrom of disorder behind him. Trainers and owners were hollering their discontent at Rosehill officials, and punters were lamenting a string of hot, tetchy horses going down to the start. Things got worse at the barrier.

Shannon had drawn postposition five, and the ill-tempered Vermeil was on his inside. For just under 10 minutes the field bounced on and off the tapes, horses ducking in and out, giving Jack Gaxieu all sorts of headaches. Vermeil, under George Moore, had had enough. He'd been on his hind legs for nearly 20 minutes. As Shannon walked up to take his place for the umpteenth time, Vermeil kicked him square in the belly, and a ruckus broke out. Every horse around Vermeil veered away from the line, except Shannon. The little bay was so buckled and winded from the kick that Munro was sure he was going down on the turf. He looked over from the saddle, expecting to see a broken leg.

Gaxieu ordered the field away from the tapes, then charged at Vermeil and Gay King (the latter also causing trouble). He sent the two colts to the outside of the field, then ushered a vet inspection of Riddle's colt. Darby Munro jumped off Shannon and pointed to the area where the colt had been kicked. Roy Stewart, track veterinarian, could find no visible injury. Shannon trotted up sound, though he was anything but spritely. Stewart passed the horse fit to run, and Munro climbed back aboard.

Gaxieu, exhausted and short of patience, called the field back in. But on the outside, Vermeil and Gay King were still going. They had begun fighting, rearing and lunging at each other, and dumped jockeys George Moore and Jack Thompson in the dirt. Then both colts charged back down the track riderless. The clerks of the course went after them like the cavalry. Even the late Banjo Paterson couldn't have written the script for the 1944 Guineas.

It was a full 14 minutes after the advertised start time when the field stood still at the tapes. Gay King and Vermeil had been caught and reunited with their pilots. They stood bedraggled on the extreme outside. Tea Rose had missed the trouble from her wide position in 15, and Shannon was toey and unhappy near the rails. When the webbing flew up, he skipped away with surprising speed, falling into second spot, but quickly the fire went out. Munro knew the horse was running well below par.

He allowed the colt to fall back through the field at his will, fearing something was amiss after Vermeil's kick. Shannon had drifted to 10th passing the six furlongs, and Munro hadn't even looked up to see who was in charge up front. He nursed Shannon into the turn for home, only to run into traffic. Good Idea, on his inside, leaned out and clipped Shannon's heels. The colt fell back again as they straightened, and Munro, admitting he had to try to win the race on the favourite, asked for effort. He was surprised by the response. Shannon gathered himself and broke into open running, closing on the leaders with quick efficiency. He wasn't going to catch Tea Rose, who had skipped away by two lengths, but Shannon bunched with the chasers as they crossed the line. He finished an eventful, even farcical, Rosehill Guineas in fifth place.

O'Brien whisked 'Jerry' away from Munro as soon as the saddle was off. Bert Riddle, too, hurried to the race stalls to inspect his brother's horse. Shannon wasn't lame, but to the old strapper he looked sore and tied up. Vermeil had lashed out with one hind foot, which was usually a faster, more damaging kick than when both heels were used. O'Brien also noticed that one of Shannon's racing plates was twisted from where Good Idea had run onto him.

The stewards called an inquiry into that interference, but found it to be innocent. They then had to deal with a stream of criticism from punters, trainers, jockeys and owners about the conformational judging before running. Tim Brosnan, trainer of Vermeil, said his colt had gone mad because of it. 'Neither the racing public nor breeders of thoroughbreds want it again,' he said. The papers suspected that £50,000 of public betting money had gone down the drain because of it. Even Bert Riddle, on the STC board, had to question the wisdom of the stunt. 'I could see by the way Shannon was travelling that he had been hurt,' he said. 'Munro told me that he was still affected when the field was finally sent off. It was a worrying situation for all of us.'

After the running of race six, stewards requested another inspection of Shannon in the race stalls. It was about two hours after the Guineas, and Roy Stewart once again found little evidence of lingering injury. There were no marks on Shannon's coat, and he was trotting up sound. He suggested that the colt had recovered well from the incident. Telephoning Peter Riddle, Bert relayed the incident. It was a worrying call for the ill brother, but he muscled up the ambition to meet the horse float at Bowral Street later that night.

It was well after 5 pm when Barney O'Brien drew Shannon into the belly of the horse box. Evening had settled over Rosehill, and the emptiness that swept a racecourse after a big day hung everywhere. Lemonade cups, race books and dead betting slips were homeless all over the ground, the grandstands littered with pipedreams of fortune and glory, or at least a taxi home instead of the train. As Shannon rattled the hour-long drive home, swaying in the back with faithful O'Brien squatting in the straw, Peter Riddle worried away the early night waiting for him.

18

The AJC Derby

In the days that followed the Guineas, the trainer could hardly stand. As much as Riddle wanted to follow his three-year-old to the track each morning, he couldn't manage it. Barney O'Brien was handling almost every aspect of the colt now, and the bond between the pair was solid. O'Brien fed the horse, rugged him, tacked him and warmed him up before trackwork. He worked him down, strolled him in the late afternoons and bedded him at night. With Riddle laid up, and Bert juggling duties between Kia Ora, the STC and Bowral Street, Barney O'Brien was virtually training Shannon in the run to the AJC Derby.

The colt bounced back from the Guineas quickly. He was a little tied up in the barrel on Sunday, but by Monday he was fit again and working Randwick. But, as is often in racing, luck wasn't on his side. Early on Tuesday morning, O'Brien picked up slight lameness in the colt coming out of his box, and Shannon caused a bit of a stir by opting for light exercise only. The press boys jumped on to the telephone straightaway to ask Peter Riddle what the problem was. Was it the Guineas kick? Something worse? Riddle reassured them that his colt was a little lame, nothing serious he hoped, and until Shannon had shaken it off he would go lightly for a day or so.

Riddle was playing down the setback. At this stage in a spring preparation, it was expensive to lose any day of good work, although Shannon didn't necessarily need fast work. That morning around Randwick, trainers discussed this, remembering the days when horses were blown out around fast half-miles every morning. It was rarely done these days, trainers surmising that modern horses couldn't stand up to the load, either because of weaker breeding resulting in lighter frames, or the shift away from the longer staying races* meant hard, long drills were no longer necessary. In Shannon's case, he was a lithe thoroughbred, but if he wasn't galloping consistently in the days before the Derby, he would be in trouble.

Riddle had contemplated running him in the Clibborn Stakes on 6 October, which would have set him for his first go at the Derby distance, but the lameness was a little more persistent than anyone had guessed and by Friday, Shannon was out of the Clibborn. O'Brien applied foments and poultices to Shannon's near-fore heel, which he discovered was scratched from an over-reach. It was a common problem in racehorses, caused by the hind feet clipping the sensitive heels of the fore feet, and usually it cleared up quickly. It was also a spot prone to infection if the ground was deep and muddy or dust climbed into the wound.

With persistent cleaning, Shannon's injury looked to be clearing up. Late in the week Darby Munro climbed aboard for an easy mile around Randwick in 1:54. 'He feels thoroughly sound,' Munro told the press after he jumped off. And the money came. The colt was rolled into Derby favouritism after a £1000 cash bet, a few points clear of Tea Rose, second choice, and Accession, Murray Stream and Removal, all vying for the prize. On Friday morning, Bert Riddle, who had caught the train down from Kia Ora the night before, took the horse to Rosebery for a half-mile in an easy 49½. He was satisfied, but not for long. As Shannon eased down, he became cramped up front, bobbing like a hobbled carthorse. When the heel was examined, it was red and tender.

The camp was exasperated. Peter Riddle had been admitted back into Prince Henry Hospital, and now the colt was lame again. Bert ordered more foments and poultices, and rested on his laurels for a few hours, refusing to commit to any program. 'He'll need a good hit-out tomorrow if he is to be fit for the Derby next Saturday,' he told the *Telegraph*. 'I am hopeful that he will come

---

* By the 1940s, Australian racing was moving away from the long staying races that had dominated its calendars for decades. An unofficial statistic states that by 1944, there were only four flat races in the country further than two miles.

through it well, and that he'll be fit to stand some solid galloping next week.'

The treatment worked well enough into the following days, and early on Tuesday morning Shannon, Bravo and Modulation were floated to Rosebery track. Darby Munro climbed aboard Shannon and worked the colt, tentatively, over a mile and a half. At the six-furlong mark, Munro asked for speed, and Shannon accelerated. Bravo joined in the gallop at the half-mile, but Shannon hardly noticed. He clattered away from his stablemate in an easy 1:20 for the six, 37 seconds for the final three, which was slick going at the end of a long run.

It was a promising workout, and Bert telephoned Riddle with the details. The sick trainer was pleased, but the brothers conferred on Shannon's realistic campaign.

The colt was also nominated for the Victoria Derby, which would take place the week before the Melbourne Cup. Traditionally, the Cup occurred on a Tuesday, but in 1944 (due to wartime restrictions) it would race on a Saturday, a week after the VRC Derby. Peter Riddle thought it unrealistic that he would get Shannon south. He couldn't accompany the horse to Melbourne, and owing to transport restrictions the horse would have to go by boat, which would antagonise a horse with lingering foot troubles and associated fitness issues. On Wednesday morning, therefore, Bert headed to the AJC offices to scratch Shannon from the VRC event.

On Thursday, just two days before the Derby, Bert Riddle repeated the trial and Munro took the colt around the Rosebery mile and a half again. Bravo joined in at the three-furlongs this time, and the two surged into the straight together. With less than a furlong to go, Shannon shot away, clipping the three in 36½ seconds. It was a smart gallop, and everyone watching from the rails, from clockers to strappers and trainers, agreed the colt looked the Derby winner. Jumping off, Munro declared: 'Doesn't matter how good Tea Rose is, Shannon will beat her.'

O'Brien took the reins and led the colt towards the stalls. The further he got from the track, the more the old strapper noticed it: Shannon was sore. By the time the colt was led up the ramp of the truck to get home, he was lame.

At the yard, Randwick veterinary surgeon V. E. H. 'Viv' Davis was called in. The problem was still the near fore heel, which was raw and tender. The trials had probably made it worse, stretching the wound. By later in the night, Shannon was comfortable again, but only because of veterinary treatment. If the Derby had been the following day, he would not have been able to run.

From Prince Henry, Riddle was inclined to scratch the colt. The lead-in to this race had been awful, from the Guineas incident to this foot trouble. Without being at the stable each day, he also couldn't figure out just how lame his colt was. And, if Shannon wasn't favourite, he would have been withdrawn by now. But the public had invested in Shannon's running. It was a taxing position for an owner.

The Riddle brothers agreed that the track trials were strong. Shannon could gallop freely when the heel wasn't bothering him, so they left the horse in the race and applied to the AJC for a race-day anaesthetic. The treatment would be applied to the horse's foot just before he left the saddling paddock, minutes before the Derby start time. The application went to the stewards, who would refer it to the track veterinarian, who would then assess if it were in the best interests of the horse, and also of the race, to allow it. In 1933, Hall Mark had won the Melbourne Cup with the help of an anaesthetic, and the good horse Limerick had run most of his life with the treatment. News of Shannon's application, though, sent the Derby market scrambling. His backers rushed to lay him against Tea Rose, who was the obvious second choice for the race. In the 24 hours prior to running, not a penny was placed on Shannon to win.

—

Derby Day was going to be sticky. Over Randwick at dawn, the sky was pink and still, and as the sun crept over the course it was over 86 degrees (30° C) in the shade. Trainers and strappers peeled off their jackets and ducked for cover as the mercury rose. By midday, the course was baking under a relentless, oily heat.

Shannon stepped into the sun early in the morning for a warm-up canter. His foot was packed in an antiphlogistine plaster, a mix of camphor, menthol, oil of wintergreen and eucalyptus oil that worked as an anti-inflammatory. At first, Shannon looked awkward and stiff, favouring the near fore. Everyone at the track watched him go around, from the stalls to the moment he trotted off on the B grass with Darby Munro. After a gentle circuit, he pulled up fine. He showed no signs of favouring the injury but, as he cooled off, it seemed he was again tender and feeling the effects of the abrasion. The Riddle camp called in Viv Davis.

The veterinarian inspected the colt at Bowral Street. He walked Shannon up and down the stable row, lifted his foot and looked into the wound. The heel had split. It was raw and tender. But Davis noticed that new heel was already growing on the old wound, and he treated the foot and repacked it. He told Bert Riddle to bring the horse to the track for the Derby, and that he would examine the wound again just before running.

Bert telephoned the news to Peter Riddle, who was too sick to make judgement. He handed the responsibility of the colt over to his brother, and Bert decided to race. Barney O'Brien didn't think it was the correct decision, but he didn't air that opinion. He put 'Jerry' through his race-day routine, and by midday the colt was at the track, sweating through the afternoon oil.

The Derby was due off at 2.25 pm, the hottest part of the day. The only reprieve was the grandstand shadow that had fallen over the parade ring by that hour. Shannon and 10 other three-year-olds made their way slowly around the enclosure, taking it easy in the stinging heat. A few were sweating white foam from underneath the saddlecloth. One or two looked exhausted. Tea Rose, pre-post favourite now at 9/4, looked fresh and unabashed by the temperatures.

The stewards had denied Bert Riddle's application for a race-day anaesthetic, pending a final examination of Shannon in the enclosure. Moments before the jockeys were called up, veterinarians Roy Stewart and Viv Davis inspected the colt and, as Shannon wasn't overly tender on the foot, they passed him race fit. The condition, Stewart reported, wouldn't affect his ability to race. The bell sounded for jockeys up, and Darby Munro strode over. O'Brien legged him up and wished him well. He snapped the shank off Shannon's bridle and sent the young horse on his way, worried down to the boots on his feet.

Down the road at Prince Henry, Peter Riddle sat up in his hospital bed, waiting for the Derby. A little radio was perched on his bedside table, a special privilege so that he might hear Shannon's race, and also that of Modulation. Modulation was running in the Epsom Handicap at 3.05 pm, right after the Derby. Riddle nervously tuned the crackling, muffled commentary so that he might hear the goings-on. He could make out the racecaller hailing them to post, but he couldn't feel the track: its shufflings, excitement, its heat. He missed it. The commentator relayed that the horses were at the tapes, a few giving trouble. Shannon was drawn barrier three, Tea Rose on his outside. It was 2.25 pm.

The Derby field jumped in the shadow of the grandstands, directly in the path of the St Leger stand. The cheer that sent them on their way was magnificent, a wave of animation that followed the young horses past the winning post for the first time and out of the straight. Shannon, settled midfield, hadn't leaped away as fast as he usually did. He was one off the rails in the middle of the bunch as they settled into the backstretch.

On Tea Rose, jockey Harry Darke was pleased with the pace. They were clipping moderate sectionals towards the six furlongs, which suited his filly. He was a length or two off the leader Lancaster Pilot as they swung into the half-mile, and Munro knew they were the pair to watch. But Shannon was nowhere near as sweet as he usually was. He wasn't lame in his action, Munro knew, but the fluidity, the ease in his action, just wasn't there.

Bending into the home turn, as Tea Rose came off the bridle and went for the lead, Munro couldn't shake a response from Shannon. Past the Leger, into the dying stages, the Derby was lost. Tea Rose was gone by two lengths, and the Demon Darb didn't push the colt. He sat up and eased the horse over the line, cantering home in sixth place.

In those days, radio callers ignored the colour and character of a race, reiterating only the result into the wireless. Peter Riddle, therefore, could only picture the Derby reception in his mind, his colt probably hobbling home, punters jeering at the Demon Darb for not trying on the heavily supported second choice. In fact, Darb was spared that, as Tea Rose had gone off the 9/4 favourite. Shannon had been 3/1. Neither had the colt hobbled home but, as he cooled off, he was getting there. Viv Davis took another look at the split heel, which was inflamed and tender. He reported to the stewards that he stood by his earlier assessment that Shannon wasn't hindered because of the injury. Logic knew better. Barney O'Brien knew better too.

The old strapper packed Shannon's foot and walked him back to Bowral Street. The pair left behind the heat and excitement of Derby day, and Tea Rose's epic victory. She was the first filly since 1898 to win the blue riband, and her winnings had now hauled her into contention for greatness. But the question remained nevertheless: would she defeat a fit, sound Shannon on any other day?

—

Peter Riddle rode the highs and lows of 1944 as best he could. Shannon had failed in the AJC Derby, but Modulation had stepped out half an hour later to clinch the Epsom for him under Darby Munro. Within days of the races, the frail trainer thought he might go home to Randwick, but his sickness was as dogged as Shannon's split heel. Doctors perched on the end of his bed, advising him to relinquish his horses and take it easy from now on.

Riddle knew, soberly, and better than his medics, that the vigour of training was almost beyond him now.

The Derby had been a disappointment. He didn't even know what had really happened. Since the Guineas, Shannon's preparation had been stop-start. There was the kick, and then the split heel. There was also the question as to whether Shannon had stayed the Derby distance. Munro hadn't pushed him to climb into the leading bunch when he knew the colt was spent, so Riddle didn't know if Shannon had been beaten by fitness, injury or lack of stamina. All of these queries bounced around his tired mind through the long, whitewashed hours in his hospital bed. He couldn't wait to get out.

The VRC spring meeting came and went. Darby Munro, sliding down to the southern city, slid home first in the Melbourne Cup aboard 3/1 chance Sirius. It was a significant win for the Demon Darb, and not just because he was a Sydney boy taking the Melbourne spoils. Sirius won by a gruelling neck, denying the plucky Peter a huge win. Peter was a son of Peter Pan, whom Munro had steered to victory in the 1934 Melbourne Cup. Darb had denied his old favourite the rare esteem of a Cup winner siring a Cup winner.

Riddle moved slowly to disperse some of his stable. It was a tough decision, an invidious one for a man devoted to racing horses. He would keep Bravo, and Modulation if he could, and certainly Shannon. Riddle had no intentions of ever selling Shannon, and probably the Midstream colt would be his last horse in the yard. In early November, he sent the three-year-old onto a truck and out to grass at Richmond, with plans to bring him back in for the autumn riches. But Riddle's plans were ambitious for a sick man.

Sydney wouldn't see Shannon again as a three-year-old.

19

Fellow citizens, the war is over

Fifteenth August 1945, a bright, chilly morning over Sydney. On the streets it was wintry in the shadowy draughts of Pitt, Elizabeth and Macquarie streets. But a little after 9 am, no one noticed. Citizens everywhere huddled around wireless sets inside shopfronts and department stores, in public bars flung open, in cafes and corner stores. Then they fell onto the streets delirious. War was over.

'Fellow citizens, the war is over', announced Prime Minister Ben Chifley, diplomatic and calm over the airways. 'The Japanese government has accepted the terms of surrender and hostilities will now cease. Let us remember those whose lives were given that we may enjoy this glorious moment and look forward to a peace which they have won for us.'

From every doorway across the metropolis, people fell out in excited stupor. Within minutes of the broadcast, as word spread like scrub fire, tens of thousands of Sydneysiders clung to the city's arteries. They screamed and hollered, hugged people they hardly knew, and people they didn't know at all. Street bands appeared out of nowhere, perching on the pavements and whipping up Nat King Cole and Bing Crosby. People danced and danced amid a blizzard of strewn paper from balconies, offices and factory bench-tops. It was delirium and hysteria, and it went on and on.

The city's trams and buses ground to a halt, and gradually all traffic was cocooned in crowds until there was nothing but people anywhere. They came from the suburbs, from the beaches. They deserted their jobs to join the revelry. Businesses across town shut their doors, and then the street vendors peeled into the throng. They sold flags, all models of Allied ensigns, and whistles, paper hats and rattles. An hour after the declaration of peace, Sydney's streets were swollen with 300,000 people.

Still more folks came. They poured into every available space, singing and chanting and backslapping. A hokey-pokey ring broke out in Queen's Square, while down along George Street towards the Rocks and Circular Quay, a conga line, hundreds of people long, weaved and plunged into William Street. On this day, a man wasn't a baker or wharf worker, a banker, jockey or trainer. He was just a man, for peace had levelled everyone.

At nightfall, a million people clung to downtown Sydney. Over 150,000 of them grooved and boogied in the Domain with station 2GB. The rest clutched any available spots in the streets and along the foreshore, as for the first time in six years, colourful fireworks burst into the skies over the Harbour Bridge. In notorious Kings Cross, only the Roosevelt, a nightclub, remained open for business. Over 1000 people crammed inside to dance away years of restraint. The rest partied on the street outside. Everywhere, citizens reunited with customs of old. The Anzac Memorial in Hyde Park, overladen with flowers and flags, was illuminated for the first time since 1939.

The following morning, the city awoke with a hangover and an enormous litter problem, but no one cared. A second day of jubilation had been meticulously planned, beginning with a march that navigated from Macquarie Street to Martin Place, George and Market streets, ending in the Domain. The police had closed the city to all traffic, and the postal service was suspended in the metropolis, while cafes and restaurants were also closed. From 9.30 am the city bowed to war's end in some way, either with processions, church services or gatherings at war memorials. A salute of 101 guns reminded everyone of the austere soundtrack of conflict, and then it was party time again. Sydney had never seen, not even with the Bridge opening in 1932, this many people corralled in her arms for a single occasion.

Across Australia, and across the Allied world, a giant shift had taken place, like a motor car suddenly thrown into reverse. The world was celebrating, but undercurrents of worry were obvious. Millions of people employed at munitions factories stood in limbo, uncertain of their paid fates as the need for bullets and armoury fell away. And it wasn't just machinery workers hit. More millions had toiled in warehouses making buttons for uniforms, or the comfort kits so precious to soldiers in the field. Overnight, the machines had stopped, and with it people's means to live. Australia had been the most mobilised of the Allied nations. One-seventh of the population was in uniform, and in the days that followed the surrender of Japan (fighting had ceased in Europe in May), so began the migration of service folk home from the Asian regions. Of the one million Australians who had served in the conflict, 40,000 would not make it back.

Demobilisation of the forces had begun before street sweepers moved in to Sydney early on 17 August. The federal and state governments had suddenly the challenge of converting a wartime economy back to one of peacetime, of switching industry to civilian requirements and dodging the windfalls of inflation that might come from complicated cessations in operating. Public notices had to be rewritten, law and order reassessed. Down to the little details, like brownout lighting and the re-juggling of the tram timetable, Sydney had to take stock.

For the most part, Australians were patient. But it had been a long, exhausting six years of rationing, going without and bare necessities. It would be a while before fountain pens became available, for example, or leather suitcases, watches and clocks. Chifley encouraged his citizens to show restraint, that the restrictions imposed on them might not be immediately relaxed. The *Sydney Morning Herald* advised, 'The need for unity and unselfishness is not less because the guns are silent.' Nevertheless, there was a grand suggestion of normality, which was all anyone needed.

Australia (as an inaugural Ally) had been at war for 2172 days, 612 days more than for World War I. It had been a sobering, scarring experience, so when life began to resume its prewar character, everyone was relieved. Few believed that things would be perfect right away. After all, most Sydneysiders had just gotten over the Depression when war had erupted in Europe in 1939. But the International Olympic Committee began planning the next Games, and Sydney–London flights resumed through Singapore (63 hours one-way). These were the things that gave hope and the suggestion of normalcy. In the horseracing sector, everyone looked towards the relaxation of red tape that had bound the sport for years.

Sydney racing clubs faced continued challenges despite peace. The Queensland government had lifted its rail ban on transporting racehorses, but the New South Wales government wasn't budging. There were fodder shortages across the state and racehorses, still, were vilified. 'It is unthinkable,' said a representative of the milk industry, whose carthorses were working on half-rations, 'that women and children should go short of milk in order that race-horses may be fed.'

The AJC and STC could cope with the transport ban. It seemed fair that the railways be used for vital services like the transport of fodder for working stock. The clubs reasoned that they could manage the field sizes at remote courses like Rosehill and Warwick Farm. But the fodder shortage itself was more concern-ing. Trainers across all tracks had slimmed down their teams, and they feared that the government, under pressure from competing industries, would plant further legislation on how they obtained feed, and how much of it. A remote Queensland paper, the *Central Queensland Herald*, put it perfectly: 'Trainers and owners will work out their own salvation, so long as they are left to their own devices and not subjected to official hindrance.'

But they weren't left to their own devices. The AJC, thought to be under the lean of state powers, placed some wilful bans across the sport in an attempt to appease the fodder problem. For example, no horse that had run unplaced in its previous six metropolitan races was eligible for nominations. Maiden, novice, encourage and trial races were slashed. And, most ludicrous of all according to trainers, after 1 August 1945 no two-year-old fillies were allowed in any race, anywhere. The response to that ruling was deafening. Turf journalists, radio commentators, owners, trainers, and average Sams on the street, decried it. 'Had there been the extreme shortage of fodder that was alleged, then some of the restrictions might have been justified,' said *Sportsman*. 'But there was positively no reason whatsoever to put a ban on fillies for the remainder of the year. It was a definite blow at the breeding industry.'

Fodder politics aside, when peace fell upon the world in August 1945, horseracing in Sydney was in sparkling health. Few industries had skated through the conflict like racing had, owing to a ludicrous demand for the sport that had brought people through the turnstiles and money through the tote windows. Officially, Sydney bookmakers had had their best years in the history of the nation's turf, and it had been so good that many of them, with a war conscience, were embarrassed. But that demand for racing – that human need to cheer and holler that had filled Randwick grandstands since war broke out – sent the sport into the post-conflict era healthier than it ever could have hoped for.

And so began the new racing season in August 1945. Peter Riddle was just on his feet. Stricken with persistent illness, unable to stand some days, or breathe others, he had left Shannon out throughout the autumn, seven months respiting in long Richmond pastures. When the colt came back in, in early June, Riddle went calling on the Demon Darb. It was time to make good on a promise.

20

Eyes on the Epsom

Way back in April 1944, when Shannon had run astray in the AJC Derby, Munro had climbed into his big motor car and driven south from Wansey Road. Straight all the way down Anzac Parade, he had arrived at Prince Henry Hospital's B-Block, where Peter Riddle was interred. The two men had engaged in a long confab.

Munro had asked the trainer about his plans for Shannon. Though the colt had lost the Guineas and the Derby, the jockey had lost no faith. To Munro, Shannon had only just begun to open up. He sensed a speedster in the colt, an acceleration genius. If Riddle planned to return Shannon as a four-year-old, the wily jockey wanted a piece of the cake.

Riddle explained his situation slowly. Under medical orders, he had to take leave of the training business for six months. That meant releasing some horses, and sending Shannon out for half a year. He expected the colt would return for spring racing in 1945, when Riddle would have his eyes on the Epsom Handicap, the big spring mile. At this news, Munro nodded slowly, his thick dark eyebrows clenched pensively. 'If he runs in the Epsom, I'm your jockey,' he told Riddle. The trainer agreed.

Munro left Little Bay that April day with queer excitement in his belly. It was unusual for a jockey to commit to a partnership so far down the line, but Darb was taken with Peter Riddle's little horse. Shannon was so easy to pilot, so tractable and pleasant, that he almost wasn't work. More than this, there was fire in the engine. And Munro would know. He remembered his powerball partnership with Rogilla a decade before, a horse that could leap to full throttle from a standstill. Munro knew what talent was, and knew when it hadn't matured, and Shannon was on ice.

He might be something almighty next year.

Now it was time for Riddle to collect on the debt, and in mid-August 1945, recouped in health and sailing on second wind, the old trainer telephoned Darby Munro. The jockey hadn't forgotten his promise – he rarely did – and the two men talked shop about Shannon's path to the Epsom. Though Darb was committed to the big ride, he wasn't committed to the races in between. Those rides would include the Campbelltown Handicap, the Chelmsford possibly, the Tramway and the Hill Stakes. The men agreed to take it one race at a time

—

Four-year-old Shannon was no beauty queen. He was like a teenager awkward in his bones. There were angles and recesses in his conformation now, big joints that distorted his frame, as if he was made of lollipop sticks. The trained eye knew he was blooming late. One morning, a clocker took a good look at the horse at Victoria Park. 'He has the neck of a chicken, an arm as skinny as an old fowl's, the ribs of a greyhound, and the rump of a goose,' he said. Fellow clockers chuckled. But the man added, 'He has the heart of a lion though, and oh boy can he gallop.'

Beauty was of little concern to Peter Riddle, and even less to Barney O'Brien. Shannon's 53-year-old guardian knew nothing of ugliness in his favourite horse, because Shannon was so pleasant and gentle that his temperament was all O'Brien saw. 'He's the sweetest horse I have ever handled, and I've been in the game for 35 years,' the old strapper said. 'He behaves like a big kid. Every morning and afternoon he has a frolic, playfully bites my ears and pulls my handkerchief out of my pocket.'

The bond between man and horse had become famous up and down Randwick. After galloping in the mornings, O'Brien spent the later hours before midday 'playing' with Shannon. The horse's favourite trick was whipping off the strapper's hat as he walked past the box, or leading him around the yard by his tie. Often, if O'Brien leaned against the stable door reading a newspaper, Shannon would nibble the sheets, eventually coaxing the entire paper out of O'Brien's hands until he stood blankly, newspaper hanging out of his mouth. Barney O'Brien could pull Shannon's tongue, walk under his belly, sit in the straw as he slept. It was a bond bound tight with affection.

O'Brien had carved out a specific regime for the Midstream colt. Shannon was fed five times a day (most horses ate three times a day, especially in light of fodder shortages). O'Brien sieved chaff, oats, corn and carrots, with lucerne tossed about the box regularly. 'I believe in letting him eat whenever he wants to,' O'Brien said. 'A contented horse is always a good eater, and the more water he drinks, the better. It helps keep him fit.'

Shannon was fit, but it was a wonder to outsiders. The horse slept a lot, and when he was under, nothing disturbed him. Usually, he was the last horse to poke his nose over the box door in the mornings (though he was the first to leave the yard for trackwork). His penchant for laziness was a yard joke. Shannon often ate and drank sitting down because he couldn't be bothered getting up. On the track, O'Brien believed the horse wanted to do just enough to get his face in front. On the way there he was often hard to hold, but job done he eased right up. Shannon didn't want to motor right away from the field. O'Brien believed he liked the company.

Riddle afforded his colt every whim. The walls of Shannon's box were painted light blue because the trainer believed it was 'easier on his eyes'. In the afternoons, Shannon was taken for a stroll in an entourage. Peter Riddle rode the stable pony on one side, and O'Brien rode Bravo on the other. On Shannon's heels trotted Rico, O'Brien's Alsatian dog and Shannon's best friend and bodyguard. The dog slept in the box with the horse every night, followed him to trackwork each morning and waited by the running rail for his return. For Riddle, it was added security. For Shannon, it was constant companionship.

The plain bay horse was a calm, tractable thoroughbred. But

where many lazy racehorses were pig-headed, often difficult on the racetrack, Shannon was sharp like a farrier's hatchet. In the yard, when the bandages came out, the colt's ears went up and he knew it was race day. On course, he was often more interested in the incidental clatter of proceedings than in the race itself. Thankfully, there was no firmer hand than Darby Munro's. Shannon never gave trouble at the barrier, never pulled his jockeys out of the saddle or tore at their sockets to get away. He was easy and contented, a product of both his temperament and the two men who handled him.

His 1945 preparation began slowly in late June, for it takes a few weeks to drop a horse out of a paddock and back into a race campaign. Shannon did slow, drilling work around Randwick, mostly with Barney O'Brien in the irons. When the fast work began in late July, the pros then jumped aboard. Into early August, Riddle shuffled between Darby Munro, Jack O'Sullivan, George Moore and Billy Cook. He also floated the colt between Victoria Park, where fast work was done, Rosebery, when it was wet, and Randwick, every other day.

Shannon gradually opened the pipes from three furlongs in 28½ seconds to five furlongs in 1:05½. By mid-August, the horse was so tuned he play-bucked Jack Thompson right out of the saddle, then set off around Victoria Park on his own. It was out of character for him, but the result of harmless high jinks. When Thompson remounted, Riddle ordered the horse over six furlongs, which Shannon ran, unfazed and unextended, in 1:23.

The map for the season looked something like this: Riddle planned to debut Shannon in the Campbelltown Handicap at Randwick on 25 August. His horse had a big weight – 9 st 1 lb – but it was over the sprint distance of six furlongs. After that, it would probably be the Tramway Handicap on 8 September. Again, Shannon would carry 9 st 1 lb, but if the Tramway were his last run before the Epsom on 29 September, a good burden over seven furlongs would fit him for the big one. Shannon was also nominated for the Hill Stakes in between these two, and the Peter Pan Stakes and George Main after the Epsom. None of these was a certainty. In fact, Shannon was also nominated for the Metropolitan, a stayer's test of a mile and five furlongs shortly after the Epsom. If Riddle thought his colt better suited for the longer race, he would scrap the Epsom altogether.

It was strange planning on the trainer's behalf, but something persisted in Peter Riddle that Shannon could stay. He felt the colt's AJC Derby run had to be written off because of the circumstances under which he had run it, and he maintained therefore that Shannon hadn't yet proved or disproved he could run a long race. Nevertheless, few shared Riddle's faith in his horse's ability to stick. Many thought the colt too weedy to carry weight over a sustained run.

Riddle publicly maintained that Shannon was aimed towards the Epsom, so when betting began on the famous Epsom–Metropolitan double, the colt was placed on the second line of favouritism behind Melhero and a fascinating New Zealand import, Sleepy Fox. Sleepy Fox was a new arrival for top Randwick trainer Bayly Payten, and it was widely held that he was uglier than Shannon. But he could move, this fellow. Sleepy Fox had won over all sorts of tracks up to a mile under heavy weights (in 1947 he would set the Dominion record for a mile).

On Monday 20 August, AJC handicapper Fred Wilson released the weights for the Epsom. Sleepy Fox toppled right out of the race with 9 st 11 lbs, a sure sign the handicapper fancied him. Shannon was allotted 8 st 10 lbs, four pounds less than weight-for-age, which reflected that the horse hadn't raced in nearly 12 months. But the weights were the least of Peter Riddle's problems. Despite Darby Munro assuring he would come good on his promise to ride Shannon in the famous mile, he was Bayly Payten's stable rider, and that meant he would be called up for Sleepy Fox.

It was a common problem in busy racing months, and one that Riddle was well used to. He knew that Munro's allegiance to Shannon was strong, but the jock would have to get a contract release to pilot him, and Munro himself might not be too enthused to do so. If Sleepy Fox was as good as everyone expected him to be, weight or no weight, he would be a fighting chance to win the Epsom. Why would Munro want to get off him?

The Campbelltown Handicap came up quickly at the end of August, and Shannon had been training for 10 weeks. Riddle privately held that the horse would debut well, such was his fitness, and he put a few pounds on an each-way result. In the market, Shannon was paying huge odds. On race day he started at 8/1 on course, but by post time he had blown out to 20s. Criticisms of the horse's size (with 9 st 1 lb on his back) had been reflected in the market, coupled with a rush for Warlock (who was carrying 2 st less). The books had listened, and Shannon had been set adrift.

The true rail was out at Randwick, so the Campbelltown was over a distance of 6 furlongs and 20 yards. Shannon had drawn the widest alley of 15; with two horses scratched earlier in the morning, the field was down to 14. Darby Munro settled the colt on the edge of the line-up, but horses on the rail were playing up. When they jumped, it was four minutes after the scheduled race time of 2.50 pm.

The featherweight Warlock leaped to the lead when the webbing went up. Munro didn't lift a finger. Shannon coasted away from his outside draw and crossed over to settle third, behind the leader and Gay King. They weren't too quick out of the chute, as the going was slow after a few days of rain. Nevertheless, Warlock was slick as he hauled the field towards the only turn, and Munro was wary that the lightweight might steal a run in the straight.

He clicked to Shannon to hurry up, and the bay picked up his game so quickly that Munro was almost left behind. Shannon moved up on Gay King as they came out of the home turn, and Warlock's jockey began to scrub away at his ride. Passing the Leger stand, Shannon was poised in careless rhythm, and Munro had hardly moved. As the cheers in the stand reached Darb's ears, he let his mount go, and Shannon moved off the line as if programmed. He slipped past Warlock and broke into a length lead, then two. As the winning post came, Darby Munro sat up and cruised home.

He had already won the Warwick Stakes that day, but Shannon had practically steered himself to victory in this Campbelltown.

The win occurred in 1:12½, and netted Shannon £865. Even Peter Riddle, less than confident with his each-way bet, was surprised at how easily his horse had won. Eleven months from the track had rubbed out none of Shannon's brilliance, and the colt had earnings of £6720 from 12 starts for five wins and three seconds. When the horse cooled off in the race stalls, fresh as summer rain, he suggested there was plenty more in the barrel.

Immediately, money came for Shannon's Epsom chances. It was that time of year when every race tipped the big betting market this way or that, so much so that the Epsom market could flip in a single weekend. But on Monday after the Campbelltown, the *Daily Telegraph* caused a stir when it ran the headline, 'Metrop likely mission for Shannon.' The paper quoted Peter Riddle as saying, 'I still think Shannon will stay and a programme of weight-for-age races would provide a good Metropolitan preparation.' Bookies expected a lull in takings on Shannon's Epsom, and punters expected bookies to promote Shannon to Metrop fancy. Neither occurred.

By Wednesday, Shannon was a clear favourite for the Epsom, money having poured into the books. The gambling man was confident that Riddle saw things this way: Shannon would no more run the Metropolitan than Phar Lap would. Things got more interesting the following Saturday when Sleepy Fox debuted in the Canterbury Stakes at the STC's Canterbury racecourse, slipping home in near course-record time unextended. Connections declared the horse would likely run in the Epsom, despite his big weight. Even Riddle had to admit that the Kiwi horse was hot.

With the Tramway approaching on 6 September, Fred Wilson issued Shannon with 9 st 1 lb again, and it was a subtle tip. The weight was 5 lbs over Shannon's Epsom weight, while every other Tramway entrant also entered for the Epsom had been given less. Sleepy Fox had gone down 2 lbs. The AJC handicapper considered Shannon's Campbelltown win a 7 lbs better performance than

Sleepy Fox's Canterbury Stakes win. In response, Shannon shot to first line of favouritism for the Epsom, backed into Metropolitan doubles for £60,000.

All this was very interesting to Darby Munro. The jockey had a big decision to make: Sleepy Fox or Shannon. The New Zealand raider would have a grandstand under his saddle to win the Epsom, and the race was still two weeks away. Shannon, on the other hand, would skirt in with 8 st 10 lbs, which had to improve his chances. And Munro was due for a windfall if Shannon came in, in gifts and winning percentages. The Demon Darb felt people leaning all over him for an answer. Billy Cook had proffered his services, while Fred Shean, whose Abbeville ban was about to expire, had also stepped out of the wilderness with an offer to pilot Shannon in the big event. Shean's history as Shannon's former pilot suggested the rekindling of a partnership that could cost Munro a tidy fortune. So on the night of Tuesday 4 September, with 25 days until the Epsom, Munro went with Shannon.

He telephoned Peter Riddle right away, and the trainer was pleased, relieved. Munro had come good on his promise. Riddle settled in that night, confident that he had the best rider for his in-form horse, confident that all was going well. Finally, he was able to look towards the next race without question marks.

The Tramway, in three days' time.

21

'The best Epsom trials the turf has ever seen'

Randwick, the morning before the Tramway, the course was buzzing with dawn trackwork. A soft fog rested over the B grass as several hundred thoroughbreds loped along, blowing through the early light into daytime. Their trainers leaned over the rails, squinting into the eastern sun. They looked like they were dawdling, or daydreaming. They looked like men who did this every day.

On that morning, Shannon worked an easy half-mile in 52 seconds. As he wound down, another horse was just setting off. She was small, only 15.2¼ hands high (with shoes on), a plain-Jane bay with a white coronet on her near hind and a smudge between her eyes. But she had heart space, a barrel that measured 73½ inches around, bigger than most colts. She was the five-year-old mare Flight, the first lady of the Australian turf.

She set off with Jack O'Sullivan, her regular pilot, and everyone watched her go. Flight was simple and economical during trackwork. She did nothing flashy, ambling so commonly that she looked like a poor sort of racehorse. Averagely conformed, she had a long neck and short hindquarters. In full training she was lean and light, hardly ever muscly. But her record was exemplary. Since debuting in a nursery handicap in December 1942, Flight had started 33 times for 13 wins, but she was unplaced only six times. Her winnings amounted to £15,375 after victories in the Champagne Stakes, Craven Plate, Colin Stephen Stakes and close seconds in the AJC Derby, and Doncaster and Metropolitan handicaps.

Flight was owned by Brian Crowley, an AJC committeeman who had breeding interests in the remote New South Wales flats of Merrywinebone. He was a wealthy fellow, finely educated at the lavish Scots College in Sydney. When Flight came along, he designed her racing colours as close to the Scots banner as the AJC would allow (dark blue and orange). At that time, Crowley's son, who was stationed in England with an RAAF squadron, had just completed his first solo flight. The racehorse was named in his honour.

She was foaled at Manildra in September 1940 to the New Zealand mare Lambent, by the Heroic sire Royal Step. Weedy as a youngster, she was sent to the 1941 Easter yearling sales. What occurred there became racing folklore. Flight was sold to Brian Crowley for 60 guineas, pocket change. She won eight times her sale price with her first start eight months later.

Flight was moody. As soon as trackwork was complete, she insisted on returning to the yard, and no one could coax her otherwise. Likewise, no one could get near her in her box beyond her strapper Arthur Watts. On race day, crowds around her stall would shy away when she flattened her ears or scowled at them. Her trainer, Frank Nowland, believed she was very private. Less kind, well-known turf journalist Cliff Graves later described her as 'an untamed shrew'. But her idiosyncrasies were tolerable in the face of her brilliance. She was a free-moving speedster that could sit off the pace or go with it. She could win on all tracks over most distances, and she was perilous in a close contest. She had clocked countless finishes where the margin was less than a half-length.

One of her downfalls was condition. After spelling, Flight took a long time to get shipshape again. It was because of this that she wasn't among the favourites for the 1945 Tramway Handicap. Those honours belonged to Shannon, Tahmoor and Victory Lad. Flight had had only one run since her winter spell (the Canterbury Stakes on 1 September), and she had finished third. Nevertheless, she shared top billing with Shannon for the Tramway. They would both lump 9 st 1 lb.

The race was an open-class handicap, and in addition to the favourites there were Modulation, Cold Shower, Tribal and

Britannic. Weight allowances meant a huge spread in the field. Silent, a useful sort who had run third in Shannon's Campbelltown, had slipped in with 7 st 1 lb, a full 2 st less than the top-weights.

On form, the Shannon camp hadn't to worry about Flight, but Peter Riddle worried anyway. Flight was a year older than the Midstream horse, and had almost three times as many starts under her girth. And, it was the era of good mares. Flight, Tranquil Star and Tea Rose, they had each been a force on the racetrack in recent years. Darby Munro, also, wouldn't be undervaluing her. He had ridden Flight into third place with 9 st in the two-mile Sydney Cup in the autumn. Munro considered her a moral beaten that day, as the saddle had crawled onto her withers in the first furlong and Darb had hardly been able to move on her.

Most believed that Flight wouldn't trouble Shannon this early in the season, though the *Sun* conceded that the colt didn't have opposition of Flight's calibre in his Campbelltown run. Probably, the newspaper was underestimating the mare, but its allegiance lay with Shannon. The *Daily Telegraph* took a similar tack. Its turf reporter had sat on the rails around Victoria Park early on Thursday morning, clocking Shannon in a five-furlong trial in 1:02 flat. 'On his work, he's a good thing for Saturday,' the *Telegraph* reported.

This was just what the bookies feared. They would be heavily stuck in Epsom doubles if Shannon won the Tramway. The colt had been backed all week with every popular Metropolitan candidate, and at the odds they had laid, many of Randwick's bag-swingers wouldn't be able to finance their liabilities.

On Friday afternoon, the soup thickened. A rumour that Shannon wouldn't run in the Tramway went viral. It circulated among bookies, eventually reaching radio station 2UW, which ran a 'Sports Parade' program on the evening before racing days. Peter Riddle happened to be listening when the announcer declared Shannon a non-runner for the Tramway. He went straight for the telephone but couldn't get past the 2UW switchboard. 'Where the report originated I don't know', he told newspapers later, 'but it was entirely without foundation. Someone has been throwing doubts about Shannon since the time he accepted on Wednesday.'

With all the hearsay, Shannon's price for the Tramway slipped to 3/1 on Friday night. By post time, it was even wider.

—

The paddock betting ring was almost empty when Shannon arrived at the chute for the Tramway. It was a few minutes off 1.50 pm, and the books fidgeted idly, Eric Welch among them. A lone, patient punter stood a few feet from him, hands in his pockets. 'I'll do 5/1 for Shannon,' Welch called to the man. 'Whatever you've got.'

The punter took a wad of notes out of his pants pocket and stuffed them into Welch's hand. There was £500 there. The men exchanged betting slips and the punter hurried away with a £2500 liability on Shannon. With two other bookies he had slips for £1000 and £1500. 'That's the most patient punter I've ever met,' Welch muttered aloud.

The rumours on Shannon's not running had blown his price right out, had netted patient backers the chance of a small fortune. Eric Welch had proffered 5/1 because his bag was full from other horses. Big punters had come for everything else, particularly Cold Shower, who was in with 8 st 10 lbs and was pre-post favourite at 5/2. (An enormous plunge of £50,000 had come for the horse.) He had won the All-Aged Stakes in the autumn, but he looked far from a winner this day. Cold Shower was so fractious at the barrier that he was upsetting Castle Frontenac, who was drawn in barrier 15. Shannon, in 16 (second from the outside), kept moving away, remembering the kick he had received in the Rosehill Guineas. Darby Munro swung the colt away from the line and asked Jack Gaxieu if he could start from the extreme outside spot. Gaxieu agreed, and called the field to order.

From the stands, it looked as if Shannon had been ordered to the outside of the field, which occurred when horses were unruly. It looked that way to Peter Riddle, too. As the Tramway field went on its way, the old trainer watched as Shannon pinged away and crossed the track to settle fourth, two deep.

In fact, Shannon had bounced away from the tapes faster than any horse. It was a messy start; Cold Shower had turned sideways when Gaxieu had pressed his lever, and had settled his chances when he collided with Silverelda. Flight, in barrier 12, had gone clear of the scrimmage and on settling down she was third behind pace-setters Ribbon and Petulance. Munro put Shannon to sleep one off the rail behind Flight, and they skipped out of the chute in that order.

From the outset, Munro knew that Flight would be his greatest trouble. The mare was travelling easily in front of him, as easily as Shannon. As they swung into the first turn, he eased Shannon alongside her, and the two horses ran in tandem approaching the half-mile pole. The blood was up, and the pace quickened. A clocker, perched high in the stands with his field glasses cocked, clicked his stopwatch into motion when Shannon ran past the half pole.

Tick tick. Munro moved the colt into the home turn, and sensing that Flight was about to move out to go around the leaders, he asked Shannon to go forward. The colt accelerated away, blocking Flight's path and she slammed into Shannon's shoulder. As Shannon was in higher gear he simply bounced away from the bump, but Flight was shaken right out of rhythm. As Munro pushed Shannon into the straight, the mare lost two or three lengths.

The Demon Darb took the opportunity and rode for home. Waving the whip at Shannon's face, he came up the rise of the Randwick straight buried in the colt's mane. Past the Leger stand, they were in front. And Shannon kept on finding. Within a furlong of the post, Flight had come again on the rails, but Peter Riddle's horse held her challenge. Flight was on his flanks but she couldn't get her head in front. Shannon sprinted over the line in 1:24½ for the seven furlongs 26 yards. Time adjusted, it was not far off the course record.

Up in the stands, the astute clocker clicked his stopwatch when Shannon won the Tramway. The horse had run 47¾ for the final half-mile. It was a staggering sectional with 9 st 1 lb on his back. 'He needs only to stay fit to win the Epsom,' the man said, shaking his head.

Shannon trotted in covered in sweat, but that was the only sign he had gone around. He wasn't blowing or fidgety, though the same couldn't be said for Flight. The little mare had a two-inch skin gash on her near-hind leg, a result of her collision with Shannon. Veterinarian Roy Stewart went with the horse to the stalls to dress the injury, but later reported that Flight wasn't lame. The wound was skin deep only.

The stewards called Munro in to explain the incident. 'I was making a forward move on the outside of Flight, who had a rails position just behind the leader, Ribbon,' the jock explained. 'I moved forward, but almost simultaneously Jack O'Sullivan came out from the rails to make a forward run. We collided, Shannon faltered, but Flight was the worse affected and she dropped back.' The stewards ruled that the incident was Munro's fault, but that it was accidental. The result stood.

The incident had been textbook Darby Munro. There was no rider on the circuit who could judge a race like him. He could look at a rival horse, pre-empt what the jock was going to do, ride all over him before he did it, and make the whole thing look circum-stantial. He was crafty and brainy and a terrific actor, and it won him countless races.

Shannon's Tramway margin – a long neck – was deceptive. Flight had had to bounce back from lost ground to get so close, but the result didn't record how easily Shannon was travelling inside the final furlong. Munro knew that Flight was close, but he had asked only enough of his horse to win the race, and Shannon had been holding the mare comfortably. 'Flight had every opportunity of beating him,' reported the *Sun* that afternoon. 'She made her run when Shannon began to improve, and although she battled on, she was being held.'

Shannon left the course fit and clean that afternoon. The Tramway was his seventh win in 13 starts, and netted him £714. It had been an efficient effort, nothing glamorous or flashy about it. But that evening, in post-race discussions, criticisms of the horse carried forward. Many believed him too small and wiry to withstand another outing before the Epsom on 29 September. Riddle didn't understand it. He knew Shannon was a small colt, there really wasn't much to him. But he had run a corker in the Tramway with a big weight on his back, and the time was excellent. He was also two for two this spring. 'I can't understand why some people think Shannon isn't strong,' Riddle told the *Telegraph*. 'He's not very big, but he's tough I tell you.'

———

Riddle didn't plan on running Shannon again until the Epsom, but he held nominations for two races in between: the Hill Stakes at Rosehill on 15 September, and the Arthur Dight Quality Handicap at the Hawkesbury meeting, to be hosted at Rosehill on 22 September. He thought Shannon was wound enough to see through to the Epsom without another run, but in the days after the Tramway he had a long think about that. Shannon was sparkling during trackwork, but three weeks between runs might be too long.

Riddle sat down on the Tuesday after the Tramway and studied the form for both the Hill Stakes and the Arthur Dight.

The Hill Stakes would have a field of no more than eight, and the stiffest competition would come from the Metropolitan favourite, Removal. It was also a weight-for-age event, so Shannon would line up on equal measure with most of the field. If he opted for the Hawkesbury race, the contest would be much tougher. The field would be bigger and he would be penalised by the handicapper. Given that Shannon's target was the Epsom on 29 September, Riddle thought it would be foolish to give the colt a hard run. So he opted for the Hill Stakes, declaring the horse on Wednesday morning at 11 am, just before Flight was scratched from the Epsom.

The mare's connections didn't admit they were avoiding Shannon. Flight had been allotted 9 st 3 lbs in the Epsom; she would have been giving the colt 7 lbs in the big mile. The Tramway was a good indication that Shannon would have had the measure of the mare, because they had been equally weighted in that race and Shannon had finished ahead of her. Flight's owner instead declared for the Metropolitan, which made Shannon an even sharper favourite for the Epsom.

Riddle was treating the Hill Stakes as a workout for Shannon rather than a competitive contest. Speaking to the *Sun* newspaper the day before the race, he said, 'Shannon's backers in the Epsom should not be upset if he wins or loses tomorrow. He's in because he may as well have a gallop in a race as on the training track.' Because of this, Riddle was not upset when it transpired that Darby Munro could not pilot his colt. The jockey was committed to Removal, the Metropolitan favourite, from Bayly Payten's yard. Instead, Riddle engaged Jack O'Sullivan in the absence of Flight.

On race morning, Removal went wrong. On veterinary advice, Payten scratched the horse from the Hill Stakes. Darby Munro picked up his telephone and called Peter Riddle, and asked if he might pick up the ride on Shannon now that he was free. Riddle agreed, so long as Jack O'Sullivan would relinquish the mount. He did, and with Removal out and Munro back aboard, Shannon slipped into odds on for the Hill Stakes. He was 10/9 on when racing began at Rosehill that afternoon.

Of the 30,000 people who flowed through the turnstiles, none predicted the dramas that would transpire throughout the day. They began with Guineas favourite Blue Legend, whose float broke down on the way to the course and left him stranded. At 3.40 pm, the barrier tapes failed for the start of the Theo Marks Camellia Stakes. A handful of runners dragged the tapes down the track, two horses dumping their riders. Jack Gaxieu called out to jockeys to come back, but most of the field finished the course, oblivious to the chaos behind them. When Immediate ran past the post the winner, a chorus of protest sprung up from trainers. STC stewards ordered the race be rerun at the end of the card, but the hot favourite Melhero was scratched for the rerun after inspection. Because stewards also ruled that all bets stood for the rerun, costing backers of Melhero a small fortune, Rosehill turned into a bear pit. Riddle had never heard such a pitch of jeers and hoots.

The old trainer had had Modulation in the Camellia (the horse was unplaced), so he watched proceedings very carefully. Every jockey was hauled before the stewards, while two were treated for injuries. But when plucky Immediate won the rerun, proving that the best horse *had* won first time around, Modulation crept up to take second spot. The entire fiasco made Shannon's earlier run in the Hill Stakes an absolute afterthought.

He had broken from barrier seven with characteristic dash, settling third in the field of seven behind Mayfowl and Cold Shower. The Hill Stakes was 8½ furlongs, and Munro settled the colt easily. Shannon ran along with a loose rein, perfectly settled, until the home turn. Entering the straight, Munro lifted his hands and asked the horse to go on. Shannon ranged up to the leader, then simply ran past him. At the post, he was two lengths to the good of the field, coming home in 1:45, three-quarters of a second wide of the distance record. It was the softest win of his career, and he was jaunty as he trotted back to scale.

At 10/9 on, Shannon was cheered as only favourites are cheered. He hadn't caused an ounce of stress for his Epsom backers, and for Peter Riddle, the win was on song with the horse's progression towards the big mile. Shannon had run 48½ for the last four furlongs of the Hill Stakes, with the first four run in 49¾. 'Shannon was easing up on the post,' noted the *Sunday Telegraph*. 'It was apparent to spectators that he won with more in hand than the two lengths margin.'

The win hauled his earnings to £8224, and he remained unbeaten as a four-year-old. Across Sydney, black-market bookies went grey. Shannon was looking so strong for the Epsom that he was the shortest-priced favourite since 1933. Racing officials guessed that as much as £200,000 had been laid on doubles resting on Shannon. 'They have not the means to pay, these unlicensed bookmakers,' an official said. 'If the fancied horses win, they will vanish.'

As Shannon left the course for the hosing dock, about an hour before the brouhaha of the Camellia Stakes, turf scribe Cliff Graves hung back with retired trainer Fred Williams. Williams was an old pillar of Randwick Racecourse, had associations with some of the finest horses in Sydney's long racing past. He cast his mind back to the five Epsom trophies he had won, beginning with Greenstead back in 1920. He turned to Cliff Graves and said, 'Shannon's wins this spring . . . I think they're the best Epsom trials the turf has ever seen.'

22

The hardest of races

The day of the Epsom, 29 October 1945. Peter Riddle stood beneath Randwick's Members' stand, demure in a dark wool suit, neatly pressed white shirt and tie. His hair was brushed and parted beneath his hat, his leather shoes buffed and spick beneath the folds of his trousers. He had field glasses, his trainer's badge pinned to his jacket, and an AJC race card in his hand.

The card had replaced the usual race booklet. There was a paper strike going on, so only the minimum details could be found on the Epsom runners that year: weight, draw, trainer. There were no weight-for-age scales or records charts, details of catering or stewards' information. The cards had been in vogue 40 years before, when they had been 6d to a book's 1s. They were still 6d, and they slipped around the crowd of 78,000 like hymn cards.

Peter Riddle was cool as he watched Shannon parade. Inside, down deep where hard men stash their soft side, he was jittery. Months of work had arrived at this moment, and triumph and failure pressed on him in equal measure as he stood beneath that grandstand. He had a proven racehorse, and the hottest public favourite in over a decade. But with that came pressure and strain, the fear of defeat. He thought he'd be used to it after so long in the game, but he wasn't.

It was 2.40 pm, 15 minutes to post time. There were people everywhere, packed tens deep against the parade rail. A sea of bodies was crammed from the turnout of the straight all the way down to the Leger stand. There were thousands more bobbing around in the Flat. The bookies' trade was rip-roaring, and people were impatient and bored in long lines behind the tote windows. The best about Shannon was 2/1, and long before the jump operators knew they had unprecedented trading. By the close of racing that day, punters had thrown a record sum into the tote coffers.

Shannon looked as ordinary as always in the parade. It was extraordinary that out of his small, plain frame could burst phenomenal easy speed. He wore saddlecloth number five, and strolled along behind second-choice Immediate. Every so often, he pricked his ears into the crowd, or stopped to stare down over the thousands that lined the home straight. Nothing bothered him, as nothing had ever bothered him. Only when Darby Munro was slung onto his back did he come up into his bridle, waking up to the contest at hand.

There were a few pounds of lead under his small, rawhide saddle. (The Demon Darb had to get down to 8 st 5 lbs for rides later in the meeting, so he was lighter than Shannon's 8 st 10 lbs.) He didn't wear boots or bandages, and his mane and tail hung loose about him. As he set off for his preliminary gallop, he looked small and foalish over the turf. Thousands watched him go, including Peter Riddle, who had climbed into the stand for a better view.

The trainer was confident in Shannon's steel. The horse had ability to stick and an arrogant turn of foot, and he was fit on winning. Still, the Epsom wasn't the Hill Stakes or the Tramway. There were 17 horses in this field, and the lightweights would make Shannon carry every bit of his load. He had also drawn alley 16, second widest. Silent, whom Riddle feared was Shannon's greatest danger (Silent was trained by Jim Munro, Darby's brother), was drawn in five with more than 2 st less on his back (7 st 8 lbs). Riddle predicted that Shannon would jostle for shelter for the first two furlongs down the back, and he hoped that on settling Munro would have switched him off to save fuel. But there were no guarantees from barrier 16. The pair might run three or four deep all the way into the home turn, and in an Epsom that might be fatal.

As the horses circled behind the tapes at 2.50 pm, a hushed buzz settled over the Randwick crowd. Though the Derby had been run half an hour before, the Epsom was the big betting event, the race that spawned doubles dreams or dashed them. People all over the course looked anxiously at their tickets, giving up on talk. Trainers and owners stood still, counting the beans of chance. Some had withdrawn their horses because of Shannon, others hadn't even nominated because of him. But in these last moments before contest, when anything could happen in the following two minutes, it was never a one-horse race.

Shannon stepped into line at 2.55 pm, five minutes over time. On his outside was Silverelda; on his inside Abbeville, the horse at the centre of Fred Shean's disqualification and who was top weight with 8 st 13 lbs. Bragger, trained by an upcoming Randwick starlet called T. J. Smith, had drawn the rails, and midfield was Melhero (from the Camellia Stakes drama), Victory Lad and Cold Shower. As the horses halted before the tapes, a line of famous faces stared down the Randwick mile: Billy Cook, Jack Thompson, George Moore, Darby Munro.

Jack Gaxieu sent them away at 2.56 pm to the tick. Darby Munro leaned onto Shannon as the colt threw his front feet in the air, and the pair pinged away from the tapes with the rest of the field, raising a fair gallop. But from alley 16, with only one horse outside him, Shannon was isolated early. Bragger and War Eagle had leaped into a quick lead with Immediate trailing them, and the trio took off like march hares.

Munro shook up Shannon as they came out of the chute. The leaders were blazing down the back of the course; they would pick off the first half-mile in 48½ seconds. Coming out of the two fur-longs, Shannon was eight or 10 lengths off the pace. Munro was scrubbing the ears off the colt, pushing him to move along, but the horse had nothing. Trapped four wide, Shannon moved into the first turn 11th of 16.

Munro was getting desperate. He had been riding hard from the first furlong, but Shannon had no power, nothing close to the gears he had used in his previous three outings. He had made no improvement as they swung away from the five pole, and though Munro didn't stop trying, he gave up hope of victory. Shannon was covering so much extra ground on the fringe of the field, and at this speed over a mile the cause was lost. Up in the stands, Peter Riddle thought so too.

Horse and rider scuttled towards the half-mile as Immediate and Bragger went like scalded cats up front. Darby Munro drew on his iron nerve, and he slipped his whip into his inside hand and gave Shannon a crack into the final turn. Suddenly, Riddle's horse morphed into something extraordinary. Shannon woke up, took hold of the bridle from Munro's hands. He dropped into a lower gear, gathered himself, then accelerated away from his stupor.

The response was so unreal that Shannon ran right around the horses in front of him, and momentarily Munro thought they might win it. But the field was into the home turn, and the inside horses fanned out so wide that Shannon was run right off the course. He was seven or eight horses deep straightening up, and his jockey swore blindly. Nothing had gone their way. Mid-stride, Munro made a lightning decision. He could spare Shannon the last three furlongs, or he could ride his lights out. Shannon was galloping so brilliantly into the straight that Munro chose the latter. The Demon Darb tucked into Shannon's neck and riding onto the outside rein, he hauled the horse around the traffic and clear into the middle of the straight. Shannon had lost at least four lengths going so wide, but there was no other way around.

Riddle's young horse saw open pasture in front of him and went for home. His gallop was so stirring that inside the final furlong he was up on the leaders. But Immediate had tired, and running legless had fallen out. Munro had to check Shannon sharply, then start riding all over again. He was flailing, urging and pushing and hollering. He had no idea what horse was on the rails. Shannon's neck rose and fell with his front legs, his heart bursting to reach the winning post. As he swept past it, deaf from tens of thousands of voices roaring him home, he just prevailed. Shannon won the 1945 Epsom Handicap by a neck.

They had run home in 1:36¼, and past the judge Munro sat up on the colt, his muscles tired and his lungs short of breath. He was exhausted. He glanced across the track to see that it was Billy

Fellows on Melhero nearest to him, though nearly half the width of the track separated them, with his brother's horse Silent a little further back. Neither Darb nor Fellows had any idea which horse had made it home first, but the Randwick cheers gave them a clue. Dudley Smith, the AJC judge, had posted Shannon's number on the semaphore board, and punters all over the track wielded their delight like feverish schoolkids.

Peter Riddle, too, was short of breath. He knew his heart couldn't handle the adrenaline, so he waited in the stands for a few minutes, his shoulders heaving, his head stooped. By the time he looked up, Shannon was trotting back down the straight towards the paddock, and to the old trainer, the horse looked spry and sound after his marathon. Riddle took a deep breath and left the stand, picking his way down the stairs towards the ring. When he arrived, a sea of people greeted him: brother Bert, an elated Percy Miller, club committeemen and fellow trainers, and on the side-lines, away from the hysteria, Barney O'Brien.

O'Brien tried hard to suppress his ecstasy, for men didn't jump up and down in those days. They smiled broadly and briefly, shook hands or exchanged a slap on the back, then it was business as usual. But as Shannon trotted in with Darby Munro, O'Brien couldn't suppress his delight. He gave Shannon a rough rub on his sweaty neck, and slapped Munro on the knee. Darb tipped his hat to the crowds that cheered still, and he slipped off Shannon to weigh in.

The jockey was in awe of the Midstream horse. Never, in years of riding, had he known a horse to sustain so much top speed for so long. As he loosened the girth, sliding the saddle and cloths off Shannon, he still couldn't believe it . . . four wide, then seven or eight wide, then checked, then victory. Outside the jockeys' room, he spoke about the win. 'Shannon jumped well, but he couldn't have beaten an egg early. I was riding so hard at the five furlongs that I didn't think I had a bolter's chance of winning. At the three, Shannon took hold of the bridle for the first time and I felt then that he was starting to gallop like I knew he could. But I still didn't feel confident. Only in the final furlong did I feel he would win.'

Billy Fellows wondered if the judge had made the right call, so close was Melhero to Shannon at the finish. Fellows thought he had won the Epsom passing the post. 'Shannon was so wide out that I could not judge whether he was in front or behind me,' he told the *Telegraph*. Shannon's win was incredible even to him. Melhero had had a terrific run, never left the rails and didn't meet with a single mishap. Dudley Smith, the judge, declared after the race, 'Shannon caught Melhero a few strides from the post. He came home like a train. There was no doubt about the result.'

Amid the post-race mess, Munro confessed to Riddle that Shannon was the best horse he had ridden in a long time. 'I would have won by a whole lot more but for Immediate swinging off the course,' he told the trainer. 'He just kept going and going with that amazing burst at the end.' Words between the two men were brief. Riddle had seen everything from the stands. He knew.

He was giddy with relief as he accepted the Epsom sash. It was well after 3 pm, and the sun was sliding behind the grandstands. They stood in the shadows therefore, he and Darby Munro, Bert Riddle and Percy Miller close by. Barney O'Brien walked Shannon in small circles near the crowd. The moment was surreal for the trainer, reward for sickness, perseverance and faith in a young horse. It was the best moment of his training life.

He followed O'Brien and his horse back to the stalls, watching as Shannon took a long drink at the trough and cooled down in the hosing bay. All was right. The colt was none the worse for his tough race, and his weedy exterior surely cloaked an iron constitution. Shannon was undefeated this preparation, four from four now. His Epsom purse had brought him £2900, tipping his overall earnings to £11,124. That was the price of a small home in the suburbs, and more money than any horse had ever earned Peter Riddle.

As Barney O'Brien got ready to walk Shannon home to Bowral Street, Flight was narrowly defeated in the Colin Stephen Stakes. Her vanquisher was a promising horse called Russia, a chestnut five-year-old by the imported sire Excitement. From the stalls, O'Brien could hear the hoots for Darby Munro, who had ridden odds-on Flight into defeat. The ride had been flawless, and the mare went down by less than a neck, but such was the fickleness of the punting public.

Shannon and O'Brien strolled home, entering the yard before the last race had been run at Randwick. O'Brien turned the straw in Shannon's box, filled the manger and scattered lucerne about. He pried Shannon's racing plates off, wrapped his shins in bandages and rugged him, then he led him into his blue stable. Finally, the old strapper sat down outside with Rico, the Alsatian.

O'Brien had been with Shannon every moment of the Epsom prep. For the three nights leading into the big race, he had slept outside the stable with a pitchfork at arm's length. He had seen nothing of his wife or children for weeks, going home only to eat dinner and then trundling back to the yard to watch his horse. With Shannon bedded down, sound and safe and victorious, O'Brien took a deep, tired breath.

23

The horse will tell me

Bert Warburton, turf editor at the *Sun*, had a hunch after the Epsom Handicap, and he threw it out there for his readers on 4 October. 'Shannon looks a better mile-and-a-quarter horse than a miler.' The suggestion was reasonable. Warburton believed that Shannon, this preparation, had mixed weight-for-age racing with handicaps, over distances from six to eight-and-some furlongs under varying weights, and he had won each test with plenty in hand. 'He stayed right on in the Epsom after beginning slowly, and he won the Hill Stakes very easily, a race beyond a mile in distance'. The *Sun* editor was convinced that Shannon could stick.

Riddle agreed. He had always maintained that Shannon could stay beyond a mile, but the horse was yet to have that button pushed. His only runs further than the distance were the Rosehill Guineas and the AJC Derby, and as both races occurred under interference and injury, they didn't answer any stamina questions. But one week after the Epsom, Shannon was due to run in the Craven Plate. Over one and a quarter miles, the race would be his first extended trip this preparation.

The Craven Plate was a pillar of Sydney racing, a contest so heavy with champions past that it was almost incomparable on the calendar. First run in 1867, it boasted among its early winners Yattendon, The Barb, Glencoe and Tim Whiffler, Chester, Trident, Abercorn and Carbine. Since the turn of the 1900s there had been Wakeful, Gloaming, Beauford, Windbag, Amounis, Phar Lap, Peter Pan and Chatham. Flight had won it as a three-year-old in 1943, while Tea Rose had clinched it in 1944. The Craven Plate was a champion's race because the best horses usually won it, and in 1945 Shannon looked its obvious winner.

Most of the press boys fell into Warburton's corner, that

10 furlongs wouldn't be an issue for Shannon. The *Sydney Sportsman* predicted: 'Shannon to cop Craven shekels.' But the AJC timekeeper, William Kerr, who was also Modulation's owner, didn't think Shannon would last the extra two furlongs. Modulation was nominated for the Craven Plate, and had claims to winning it. He, too, was an Epsom winner, but he was also a St Leger winner, at one and three-quarter miles.

The 1945 Craven field was excellent, a gathering of some of the best weight-for-agers on the Sydney circuit. In addition to Shannon and Modulation there were Flight and Russia, fresh from their tussle in the Colin Stephen Stakes. There were also boom horses Repshot, who would be right at home over the distance, and Immediate, who had been a respectable fourth in the Epsom. Shannon would go in with 9 st, giving a pound to Flight, while Russia and Modulation would carry 9 st 4 lbs. Shannon, deservedly, was favourite at a loose 6/4, with Flight next at 3/1 and Russia was wide at 8s.

Peter Riddle was satisfied that Shannon had held up after the Epsom. It had been a tough race, and the horse had come home a little distressed, but he had rested on Monday and bounced back into work on Tuesday. By the middle of the week he was firing on all guns. On Thursday, he went to Victoria Park with Bravo where the pair worked the course proper. Going over the kikuyu well out from the rails, Shannon clipped a half-mile in 50 seconds flat, held to stay with his stablemate. 'He's absolutely fine,' Riddle said after the gallop. 'It was to be expected he would be a little distressed after the Epsom because he was set the hardest task for an Epsom winner I have seen in a long time. But he's right as rain now.'

Shannon was on song for the Craven Plate, but so was Flight. The mare was heading to the Melbourne Cup in early November, with a run or two in southern races in between, possibly the Cox Plate and the Mackinnon Stakes. She had turned over some nice gallops during the week, including a five-furlong dash with speedy Victory Lad in 1:03¼. Though she had been heavily campaigned already (the Craven Plate would be her sixth start in the spring),

Flight sat second choice behind Shannon, somewhere between 3/1 and 7/2. 'She adds interest to what should be a very interesting race,' commented *Sportsman*. 'She should be the danger.'

Peter Riddle wanted to eliminate as many dangers as possible from Shannon's Craven bid, and at 12.45 pm on race day, two hours before the jump, he scratched Modulation. William Kerr had been keen to see his horse take on Shannon, believing that the Midstream colt was vulnerable over the 10 furlongs and that Modulation stood his greatest chance of downing his stablemate if ever he was going to. But Kerr had absolute faith in Riddle. 'I leave the matter entirely to Peter,' he said.

The Craven Plate was due off at 2.30 pm, and with Modulation out the field was down to six. The race was the key attraction of the day, though attendance was down. Some 48,000 filed into the racecourse against 55,000 in 1944. Nevertheless, the weather was clear, though cool, without a hint of rain. The course proper would be quick, played out by the first race that turned over five furlongs in a slick 1:01.

Shannon, as seemed his fate, had drawn a wide alley. He stood in postposition seven (in to six with Modulation's withdrawal) as Jack Gaxieu called the field in. Immediate was the only horse on his outside, while Flight jogged on his inside. Then came Russia, Repshot, and Accession was on the rails. Without any trouble, the six-horse field set off at the advertised time.

Flight leaped into an early lead as they left the chute, and Darby Munro guided Shannon across to the rails, settling second with Immediate on his outside. The pace was moderate, Flight taking 27 seconds for the first two furlongs, but going down the back of the course she picked things up. The first half-mile went down in 51 seconds, and the first six in 1:15. She had drawn a two-length lead on Shannon when she swung out of the back straight towards the half-mile.

Munro kept Shannon within reach of the mare, and as they turned for home he had no fears of Shannon fading. When they straightened, the horse moved up to challenge, but passing the

Leger Flight sprouted and raced right away from him. Her turn of foot was quick and brilliant, and Shannon had no answer for it. Perhaps he was tired from the Epsom effort, perhaps five races in six weeks was too much. Flight went out by one, then two lengths, and cruised over the line in a smart 2:03, only 1¼ seconds slower than the Australian record for 10 furlongs. Shannon stuck well for second as Russia ran on a length behind him for third.

Riddle's horse slowed quickly after the post, and Munro knew he had had enough. Trackwork was one thing: a horse could still impress in the early mornings, as Shannon had the previous week, but it was race day that always found them out if they were tired. As Shannon trotted back to scale behind Flight, Munro ignored the jeering crowd. Some punters bleated about Shannon's loss, but the majority were after Flight. 'What happened in the Metrop?' a few called, angry at the mare's last-start 12th in the Metropolitan. But the stewards dismissed any calls for an inquiry and the result stood.

Racing students were underwhelmed. Flight's win had been the seventh upset in eight weight-for-age races that spring. Even turf writers felt that the weight-for-age form was mediocre. There was merit to that, given that the Craven Plate was Flight's first win of the season in five starts. But she would prove her brilliance in a few weeks' time by winning the Cox Plate, an emerging weight-for-age championship in Australia. It had simply taken her a while to get her running shoes on.

Riddle was disappointed that Shannon had been beaten, but he respected Flight, knew her depth. 'It was no disgrace to be beaten by a champion mare like her,' he said in the post-race interviews. The trainer knew right away that Shannon was trying to tell him something. The horse was honest. He did everything he was asked until it was beyond him, and the Craven Plate was a signal that he had had enough. 'Shannon knows when he's beaten. He tells me when he wants a rest,' Riddle said. The trainer confirmed that he would send his horse for a spell, bypassing the rest of the spring. 'Shannon is lazy. He likes these long spells between races.'

Munro hung up the blue and black silks that afternoon and suited up for the later races. A little before 4 pm, he sent Flying Cloud off for the one-mile Kia Ora Stakes. The pair had gone only a furlong when they stumbled over two fallen horses in front of them, sending Munro crashing to the dirt. The jock curled up in the grass, eyes clenched shut as the back of the field leaped over him like springboks. Two other jockeys lay sprawled nearby as ambulances rattled towards them. The incident left the first two horses dead, and Munro was spirited to the racecourse casualty room, where a huge crowd milled awaiting news of his condition. He was pale and shaken as he stumbled out and towards an ambulance, stooped stiffly underneath a blanket. He had a dislocated shoulder and a broken wrist, and would be lucky if he was riding again before Christmas.

24

The Bernborough surge

With some fanfare, on the afternoon before Shannon's Craven Plate, the reddish bay Bernborough had entered the Inglis ring at Newmarket. His Queensland owner had shipped him down to Sydney to be sold, for he was still barred from racing anywhere outside of Toowoomba. A fat crowd had gathered to watch the auction, see what all the fuss was about. Bernborough was sold for 2600 guineas that afternoon, to the ritzy Sydney restaurateur Azzalin 'the Dazzlin' Romano.

The sale generated a lot of speak around Randwick. Bernborough had been in Sydney for several weeks already, cantering along the same beat as Shannon in the mornings. He was in the care of trainer Harry Plant, and had made strong impressions since his arrival. Post-sale, the horse slipped into the colours of Azzalin Romano, and on 8 December 1945, with Shannon six weeks into his summer spell, the Queensland horse debuted in Sydney in a Flying Handicap at Canterbury. He was unplaced, going down to Peter Riddle's Bravo after considerable interference. But the loss was quickly, painlessly forgotten. Jockey Athol Mulley was instated to ride the horse, and Bernborough set off down an extraordinary path of 15 straight victories that would bewilder the sport.

He won the Villiers by five lengths at Randwick on 22 December, and the Carrington Stakes a week later. Into January 1946 he won the Australia Day Handicap, then shipped to Melbourne where he won the Futurity and the Newmarket back to back. By the time the Sydney autumn races swung around, Bernborough had won five straight. Nothing seemed beyond him, not weight – he had carried 10 st 2 lbs in the Futurity – nor draw or track. He had broken the steel of the broader community, implanting himself as the darling of the racing game, injecting Phar Lap-like energy into racing headlines. The 'Toowoomba Tornado' they called him, or in many cases, just 'Bernie'.

He was breathtaking to look at. The son of Emborough was masculine and athletic, and a giant at 17.1 hands high. He was evenly proportioned from poll to withers and withers to dock, with a girth of 72 inches. During trackwork he was graceful and stretchy, often curled over onto his bit like a grand prix horse. His forelock, at any time, tumbled long and tousled over his face. Athol Mulley squinting and lost in the streaming Bernborough mane became a famous snapshot.

By the emergence of autumn 1946, Bernborough was the superstar of Australian racing. Azzalin Romano was beating away the postman, flooded with fan mail from every nook of the nation. On the track, the horse looked unbeatable, and Mulley was feeling the pressure that came with big champions. Only 22, he wasn't made of the same stuff that drove the Demon Darb. Mulley worried constantly, about threats, about losing on the public idol. Some weeks he would just disappear out bush. 'I was worn out and tired,' he would recall. 'The pressure would get too great, and I'd just run away from it.'

———

With the turn into 1946, Peter Riddle followed Bernborough closely. Here was a new obstacle for Shannon, a horse more imposing than Flight, fitter, stronger, much more lethal. Bernborough looked like he was made of iron, picking off the Futurity and Newmarket handicaps in the space of a week. Hats off to this fellow, Riddle thought. He must be a machine.

Expectations were that Shannon would come back to racing for the autumn of 1946, but Riddle had niggling doubts about doing so. Weakness was creeping up on the trainer again. He had been fighting fit in the spring, but he wasn't feeling strong into the hot, oily days of January and February. These were the months when Shannon needed to come back in to fit for the autumn events, which would kick off in March. But Riddle's chest was bothering him, and he was losing weight again. He tried to stay robust and positive, but he was battling his body and he knew it would be a hard road guiding Shannon through the cooler, wet months.

The trainer also had pressing financial concerns. Far from running out of money, Peter Riddle had the problem of having too much of it. His investments in stocks and property kept him in the green, so far in fact that the horses were almost a hobby. By mid-February, his yard was down to only two – Shannon and Modulation – when his brother sold Bravo to Indian interests. Shannon's spring wins alone had netted Riddle £5569, a small fortune. Because he was the horse's owner and trainer, the only cut from the winnings was the nominal fee for Darby Munro, plus a sling to Barney O'Brien. Therefore, Shannon's earnings, atop other incomes, slung Riddle right up to a higher tax bracket.

He never publicly said so, but the trainer hinted that he did not want his champion 'used up for the benefit of the government'. Riddle decided that the best course was to leave Shannon out for the autumn, then bring him back for the following spring (and a new financial year). He said he was content to limit Shannon to four or five races a season, citing 'personal reasons'. Few owners with an exciting turf freak like Shannon would be so sparing with him, so money – losing lots of it to income tax – was almost certainly Peter Riddle's incentive.

In part, it was the trainer's concerns for his estate. He was no fool. Riddle knew his illness would take his life eventually; he had spent the best part of two years inside Prince Henry Hospital. He wanted June to be secure after his passing, and Kathleen too. Handing over an enormous chunk to the taxman in his final years wasn't part of his plan. But people thought Riddle's handling of Shannon eccentric. They thought it protective, many even asserting he was afraid of Bernborough. But Riddle stuck to his guns. Personal reasons.

Shannon, therefore, lolled in long grasses as the autumn wound up. Bernborough won all and sundry in his absence. He started with the Rawson Stakes, then took the Chipping Norton and the All-Aged, all in Sydney. In early June he went to his old haunting grounds of Queensland, winning two races, including the Doomben Cup. By the time August rolled around and he had been given a brief rest for the new racing season, Bernborough had won 10 straight. He had made Azzalin Romano a household name.

The Italian had a few definite ambitions for his horse, the first to establish a winning sequence of 20 races. The record was 19, held jointly by Desert Gold and Gloaming. Romano had impressed upon his trainer, Harry Plant, his faith in the horse getting to 20, provided he trained on with the same brilliance that he had shown in '45. Among this sequence of 20, Romano wanted the King's Cup. An esteemed race on the national calendar, the King's Cup, that year, would be at Randwick (it was alternately held in each state of Australia). But to win it, Bernborough would have to bypass the Caulfield Cup, as the two races were too close together to compete in both. The King's Cup was a quality handicap with a maximum burden of 9 st 5 lbs, whereas Bernborough could get the grandstand in the Caulfield Cup. Because Romano's primary goal was to hit 20 successive wins with his horse, the King's Cup might be the easier route to that ambition.

For the meantime, Azzalin Romano trod water, taking things race by race, refusing to commit to much. It brought him right up to the warming days of August 1946, when Shannon was well and truly returned from rest, and pointed towards a brilliant spring.

25

'Little, if anything, inferior to Bernborough'

Early August was hot in Sydney, like the first month of a still summer when the flies move in. The mercury was reading record temperatures: nearly 83 degrees (28° C) on 12 August, the hottest August day and night on record. The city was approaching 33 consecutive days without rain, an all-time dry spell for Sydneytown. At Randwick, the grass tracks were stiff and brittle as the city, and the state, plunged into testing drought.

In the early mornings, horses appeared on track well before first light, dodging the sting of morning heat. Many of the top animals left Randwick altogether, floating to the spongier Victoria Park where they could work fast sectionals without jarring up or developing shin soreness. Still with thick winter coats, most of them pulled up sweating and puffed out, much like their trainers. But everyone was settled in; it was going to be a broiling spring.

Shannon had come in from Richmond in late May, had been working into fitness slowly for two months. He was a bigger horse now, just above 16 hands. His hind-end wasn't so impressive, a little short for the breed, but he had grown one of the most outstanding shoulders of any horse. From the base of the neck it plunged deep and long to his forelegs, with the ideal slope of 45–50 degrees. Perfect shoulder conformation meant that galloping concussion was dispensed in the front end and not absorbed, placing less stress on the front legs. At top speed, a mature racehorse could place 100 times the force of gravity on his feet with each stride, so correct conformation in front was vital for soundness.

A mature five-year-old now, Shannon looked robust for the first time in his life. In fact, he threw right back to Blandford, who was similarly put together. When the trackmen began to arrive at

Randwick to time the morning workouts in the run-up to spring, they were surprised at how much the horse had grown. The weediness that had characterised Shannon since his two-year-old days had deserted him.

Riddle began to ask for fast work just as the weather climbed, so with George Moore in the saddle Shannon headed to Victoria Park most mornings in August. The trainer had the routine down to an art: Shannon would set off for five furlongs on the course proper, often going as much as 48 feet off the rails, and at the three-pole Modulation would join in. The pair would turn over the following fractions quickly – 38 for the three, 12 for the final furlong – but Shannon was always hard held to stay with his stablemate. Riddle rarely let his horse rip right away from Modulation, and Shannon rarely wanted to anyway.

On some mornings, Shannon and Bernborough drummed the same five furlongs. They cut two very different pictures, the Queensland horse gross and stylish, Riddle's charge plain, relaxed and economical. Riddle himself often shared the rail with Harry Plant, sometimes Azzalin Romano shadowing them. The trainers were growing accustomed to the Bernborough circus; wherever the horse showed up, a bandwagon soon followed.

At that early stage of the spring, Riddle had no concrete plans for Shannon. The horse had been away from racing for a whole season, but track workouts were suggesting he might be as sharp as 1945. If so, Riddle wanted him to defend his Epsom title; given that the handicapper wouldn't have any autumn performances to measure him on, Shannon might go in to the big mile well weighted. But when the Epsom weights were released, Shannon tipped heaviest with 9 st 9 lbs.

Fred Wilson, AJC handicapper, had not been hard on the horse. He had measured Shannon right up to Epsom traditions. Chatham, who had won his first Epsom with 8 st 13 lbs in 1932, had been given 9 st 10 lbs for his second go (which he won), so Wilson rated Peter Riddle's horse thereabouts with Chatham. Nevertheless, in the 81-year history of the Epsom, only two horses had won with more than Shannon's assigned weight: Chatham, and Marvel in 1891.

Shannon had copped a 13 lbs rise on his Epsom weight of the previous year, which was one of the biggest increases awarded any horse on the road to a second Epsom. Riddle said, 'Mr Wilson is a fair handicapper, and I respect his judgement. But I've made no decision yet about actually running him.' Riddle had guessed that Shannon would get no more than 9 st 7 lbs. 'If Mr Wilson thinks him a 2 lbs better horse than I do, I'm glad to accept it.' Nevertheless, the Midstream five-year-old still fell into outright favouritism. A purported plunge of £400,000 was made on him into the Metropolitan result, which infuriated Riddle, given there were no assurances the horse would start. 'The whole thing is not only ridiculous,' he said, 'but amazing that people could fall for such a story. I don't know what the bookmakers are up to these days, but one thing I do know is that they are always on the look-out for dead money.'

Riddle had only a grey idea of what races Shannon would compete in through the spring. He was nominated first-up for the Warwick Stakes and the Campbelltown Handicap on 31 August, and the Hill Stakes and Theo Marks Quality at Rosehill three weeks later. The Epsom meeting would occur on 5 October, with the Monday races two days after that. Beyond that, Riddle was unsure if Shannon would spell or stay in for the Craven Plate, possibly even the King's Cup, on 12 October.

From the get-go, Riddle had a dilemma. He had maintained that Shannon would start his spring in the Warwick Stakes, a seven-furlong event at Randwick, over the Campbelltown. Bernborough's camp had the same plan. Romano's horse was fresh from his Queensland efforts and hadn't been out nearly as long as Shannon. He was still carrying autumn fitness and would be hard to beat. Riddle didn't like the idea that Bernborough might break Shannon's heart so early in the season, which was likely because Shannon was not race fit. But if he opted for the Campbelltown, which Shannon had won first-up the previous year, he would carry the grandstand. Fred Wilson had given him 9 st 11 lbs for the six furlongs of that contest. 'It might be too severe first-up,' Riddle told the *Telegraph*. 'I might decide upon the Bernborough race.'

He didn't. On the Wednesday before the meeting he scratched Shannon from the Warwick Stakes, opting for the Campbelltown Handicap. Though the weight bothered him, he felt that exposing Shannon to Bernborough so early in the season would do his horse no good. Riddle believed that a ripe Shannon, over a mile, would be a match for Romano's glamour horse. But he was unapologetic about controlling when such a match might occur. 'Plans are being made from race to race,' he told the press. 'We'll tackle Bernborough later on if I think it's fit.'

The newspapers didn't tow that line. Said the *Daily Telegraph*: 'Shannon will contest the easier Campbelltown Handicap. Bernborough's presence has influenced Shannon's Epsom preparation, and if Bernborough keeps him out of weight-for-age events, Shannon's connections will find it hard to place him.' The *Telegraph* was referring to the weight-for-age Hill Stakes, which Shannon had won the previous year on his road to the Epsom. He was in the field again this year, but so was Bernborough.

Riddle had a feeling that the entire spring would go like this, headlines about him avoiding the megastar and picking off the easier events with his racehorse. But there were so many rumours about Bernborough heading to the Caulfield Cup, to the Melbourne Cup, to America, that likely the opportunity to meet the Queenslander would peter out very quickly. Bernborough was not nominated for the Epsom, Shannon's target, and so the only race in which they could possibly meet, under conditions and fitness that favoured both of them, was the King's Cup on 12 October. And that was so far down the line that Riddle refused to think about it.

After scratching Shannon from the Warwick Stakes, he pressed on into the final few days before the Campbelltown. On the Thursday he floated Shannon to Canterbury Park racecourse, the STC's secondary track to Rosehill, where the horse galloped six furlongs in an easy 1:19½. The work itself was secondary; Riddle had brought Shannon to acclimatise him to the new fixed starting stalls. The STC had been the first club in Australia to employ the stalls, fixing them to the six-furlong chute at Canterbury. They consisted of timber-panelled boxes with the six-strand tapes dropped across the track in front. Rosebery had been using them in trial gallops since February, but Canterbury, on 16 March 1946, had been the first track in the country to use them on a race day.

They were a big change for the sport. Not since the strands had replaced the flag start moons ago had an apparatus altered horseracing so much (the totalisator excluded). Jack Gaxieu believed he would be able to send fields away much more smartly with them, while Sydney's jockeys were supportive of their introduction. Darby Munro found his mounts went in quietly and jumped away quickly, and had much more running room in the first 50 yards. But while the benefits of the apparatus were obvious, in their infancy the stalls provided a few headaches too. Some horses leaned against them on walking in, refusing all urgings to stand upright for the jump. At Rosehill, in one of the earliest race-day uses, Alderman, an affable brown gelding, lay down twice upon walking in, thinking he was heading into a loose box.

Shannon approached the stalls at Canterbury with Darby Munro in the saddle. Riddle wanted his horse to associate the contraption with competition, with a racing mentality rather than a schooling mentality. Riddle rode along on the stable pony, and Modulation was also on hand, and after tractable Shannon had had a good look and a sniff, he walked through the stalls with the tapes up a few times. Then he was asked to stand still inside them, until finally he jumped away for six furlongs. He wasn't a fussy horse, and probably would have gone away from them on race day without prior education. But Riddle wasn't that sort of trainer.

Friday, the day before the Campbelltown, Shannon took it easy. The newspapers didn't. They were in overdrive about his comeback. 'Shannon's class should carry him through despite his 9 st 11 lbs,' commented the *Sun*. 'He is a naturally smart horse when fresh.' Bert Warburton, writing for the paper that day, said, 'Shannon's chances in this race are favoured to the exclusion of all others because he is considered little, if anything, inferior to Bernborough.'

While the Queensland superstar had five horses to dispose of in the Warwick Stakes, Shannon had 19 in the Campbelltown. They included Victory Lad, who was nearest in the weights with 9 st 5 lbs, and the good horses Blue Legend, Murray Stream and Puffham, all well under 9 st. He was giving Victory Lad 6 lbs, and the lightest-weighted horse well over 3 st. For once, Shannon had drawn an inside position in barrier six, which could be a tough marble in a tight field. The race would go from the six-furlong chute, but they would travel on the outer course, covering 19 yards further. Though Shannon was better than all the horses in the field, this renewal of the Campbelltown wasn't an ideal race for him first-up in 10 months.

—

Randwick was buzzing at 1.30 pm the following day when Bernborough stepped into the paddock for the Warwick Stakes. It seemed like the city had crowded into the racecourse to catch a glimpse of the horse. Some 47,500 paid up to enter, an increase of 10,000 on the previous year. They crowded the rail as the equine headline warmed up, hollered to him as he cantered his preliminary, and fell into blue fury when Athol Mulley came within a neck of getting him beat.

Mulley took a tight hold of Bernborough in the final 50 yards of his race, standing in his irons and easing the horse right up when they had gone out in front. Magnificent, a boom four-year-old, dug so deeply into Bernborough's lead that only a neck separated them at the judge. Mulley got away with it, but he was put across the coals by the stewards.

Bernborough had been 4/1 on, and serious punters were peeling themselves off the concrete by the time Shannon stepped out for the Campbelltown. The parade ring was crowded for the fourth race of the day, 19 horses walking in succession. Shannon was number one, with about a stone of lead under his saddle. He looked very well, but his weight worried the ring. He had started at 4/1 in the morning, but at post time he had eased to 5/1.

Jack Gaxieu managed to get the big field away at 2.38 pm, eight minutes behind schedule. Shannon was slow to move from the barriers, and as insider Gay King shot into a quick lead out of the chute, Shannon eased into a rhythm in ninth or 10th place, halfway back through the field.

They rattled past the half-mile and Shannon went wide into seventh spot. He was still 10 lengths off the leading pack as they straightened for home, but Munro had had half the race to gauge how well Shannon was going. The horse was full of running, hardly noticing the load on his back. Coming up the rise of the straight, Darb tucked into Shannon and rode with hands and heels, coolly gathering in the field one by one. Puffham, who had taken over the running, was clear by a length, but Shannon was wound up and cruised past him, unextended, a stride before the line. He won the Campbelltown Handicap by a half-length in the spiffy time of 1:11½, or 1:10½ for the true six.

It had been an armchair ride for Munro, who had judged the early pace, sat back and simply pressed the button to go wide to win. 'I had a perfect run,' he said after the race. 'I only needed to keep him going and shake the whip to win. He was racing like the winner three furlongs from home.' The Campbelltown broke a losing duck for Munro also; he hadn't ridden a winner in Sydney since the autumn.

The pair was given a hearty cheer when they returned to scale, and Riddle stood in the ruck waiting for his horse. Reporters swarmed around him. 'That was a perfect Epsom trial,' he told them. 'He won as he liked, and all going well he will start in the big race.' The press clamoured for further comment, but Riddle waved them away. He wasn't feeling well, and he felt suddenly worse in the hoopla. After checking on Shannon and conferring with Darby Munro, the trainer sat down on a bench under the eaves of the Members' Stand, breathing heavily. A moment later he collapsed.

People rushed at him from all directions, finding him conscious but overcome. He was lifted to his feet as he babbled that he was all right, and shuffled into the casualty room to lie down. The fifth race came and went, then the sixth, and Riddle was no better. He was white when Barney O'Brien deserted Shannon in the stalls to come and check on him. O'Brien urged race-day officials to summon the on-course doctor, and the AJC broadcast an urgent call for Dr Stratford Sheldon. Sheldon was alarmed when he saw the trainer, convinced Riddle was having a heart attack. He ordered an ambulance right away, and Riddle was sped back to Prince Henry.

Shannon's trainer had postponed rest and treatment to get his horse fit for his Campbelltown comeback, and he was paying a high price for it. The hospital declared his condition serious on arrival, allowing only June and Kathleen a few minutes to see him. Later on in the night, he was moved to the cardio ward that he knew so well. He greeted an old friend there, Newcastle Jockey Club committeeman Bert Light. The two were similar cases, and among their medical team was Prince Henry's superintendent, Dr C. J. Walters. Walters was particularly interested in Riddle's and Light's cases, and not just from a medical standpoint. Walters was an old friend of Sydney racing, and on several occasions had consulted on equine illnesses that had baffled ordinary veterinarians.

Riddle was too laid up to read any of the press that resulted from Shannon's Campbelltown win, which was a shame as the headlines were stirring. Cliff Graves, writing in the *Sunday Telegraph*, said, 'With the exception of Bernborough, Shannon is the best miler we have seen in New South Wales for a long time.' Bert Riddle took leave again from Kia Ora to oversee Shannon, and as Peter Riddle improved slowly at Prince Henry, he guessed he would be back at the yard before the Epsom on 5 October. Barney O'Brien and Shannon were such a smooth operation by then that the old trainer worried little about his horse erring in his absence.

Into the following week, the racing columns were dominated by superstar speak: whether Bernborough, Shannon and Flight would meet in a race that spring. Bernborough was the outstanding champion, while Shannon had returned to his lethal best, and Flight, though yet to debut that spring, had won five races in the autumn. All three were nominated for the Chelmsford Stakes on 14 September, but Shannon was nominated for a number of races into the Epsom, the Chelmsford just one of them. The papers, and the racing public, were growing desperate to see the three clash. But the Bernborough camp changed their mind every five minutes, declaring on 3 September that their only certain program was the King's Cup on 12 October. A day later, that plan was binned. 'Public exasperated by Bernborough riddles,' ran the front page of the *Sun* that weekend.

Shannon's spring plans suddenly opened up. Riddle had had little intention in aiming for the Chelmsford, with or without Bernborough, and with that horse out of the King's Cup, any chance of the pair meeting had vanished. From his hospital bed, the trainer had to map out Shannon's route into the Epsom, for there were myriad races he could contest: the Hill Stakes or the Tramway, and also the Theo Marks Quality Handicap. While Shannon had gone through three races before his Epsom effort the previous year, this year Riddle thought he was in better shape and needed fewer hit-outs. He leaned towards starting the horse only once more before the Epsom.

But the game threw the trainer a curve ball on 14 September. Darby Munro, riding a horse called Double Mint in the first at Randwick, was pitched clear of his mount after they stumbled over a faller, Lord Dundee. Lord Dundee's jockey, Jimmy Duncan, a popular little lightweight of 35, lay sprawled on the turf as Munro came to. Both riders were clattered back to the casualty room in an ambulance, but Munro watched his friend slip away before they even arrived. Duncan was pronounced dead by Dr Stratford

Sheldon, likely from a fractured skull. It was a terrible thing for Munro to witness.

Randwick racecaller Lachie Melville found it difficult to keep on with the program that day. He was a close friend of both Duncan and Munro. Flags around the course were dropped to half-mast, and at the official announcement of Duncan's passing over the amplifiers, racegoers dropped their hats and stood mute with shock. Darby Munro had only abrasions to his back and required two stitches for a deep cut to his left leg, and he could have continued riding. But he was so disturbed by the tragedy that he dismissed the rest of his rides and went home.

Racing was still recovering from the incident on Monday afternoon. Darby Munro, probably sunk with depression, had become ill. His arm had swollen after a tetanus shot, and the cut to his leg, though requiring only two stitches, had been deep enough to expose the bone. The jock didn't eat well enough to promote any sort of healing, and towards the end of the week it was infected. Riddle had decided to start Shannon in the Theo Marks Quality at Rosehill on 21 September, opting out of the longer weight-for-age Hill Stakes. With Munro sidelined, he had to source a new pilot.

It was like deja vu. Riddle had been in hospital when Fred Shean was ousted by the Abbeville affair, and that time he had allowed his brother to engage a new rider. This time, he took full charge of the search, seeking out George Moore for the ride.

Moore was a Queensland expat, a very smart jockey who had transferred to Sydney early in the war from Eagle Farm. He was young, only 23 years old, but Riddle saw mammoth potential in him, thought he would be a Sydney force within a few years. (He was right. In 1949 George Moore would accept tenure with upcoming trainer T. J. Smith, and the pair would become a bewildering force in 1950s racing.) Riddle had invited Moore into his fold very soon after the young rider's arrival in the harbour city, and Moore had been riding Shannon and Modulation in track gallops since 1943. The jock accepted the ride on Shannon in the

Theo Marks, delighted to borrow the limelight from the Demon Darb. Riddle advised him to stand by for the Epsom also.

Shannon remained in both the Theo Marks and the Hill Stakes for the 21 September meeting at Rosehill. Riddle was reserving the right to change his mind about the best option for his horse. The Bernborough camp had contradicted their plans yet again, deciding that the Chelmsford (which Bernborough won the day Jimmy Duncan was killed) would not be his final Sydney race (as they had predicted). It would be the Hill Stakes instead, and so Riddle was faced with the same predicament as he had had three weeks before: run Shannon ragged making a race of it with Bernborough in the weight-for-age event, which might spoil his Epsom chances, or send him to the handicap event where the field was larger and his weight potentially heavier.

Closer inspection of the weights made Riddle's choice easier. In the Theo Marks, Shannon would carry the top weight of 9 st 5 lbs. It was 6 lbs less than his burden in the Campbelltown, and 4 lbs less than his Epsom weight. The reason for this lay with the Theo Marks being a quality handicap, which meant there was a maximum top weight, in this case 9 st 5 lbs, and the rest of the field was handicapped down from that. In the Hill Stakes, on the other hand, Shannon's allocation would come from the weight-for-age scale, but with penalties slapped on. Shannon would carry a few extra pounds for his win three weeks before, as Bernborough had (the Queensland horse would carry 9 st 11 lbs). In the end, the Theo Marks looked a far safer road for Shannon's Epsom chances.

So, on the afternoon of 21 September, Shannon cantered to the seven-furlong start of the handicap race. It was bright and balmy at Rosehill after a day of welcome rain. The track was giving underfoot, so that the first three races ran outside the Rosehill record by two or more seconds. George Moore, in Riddle's pale blue and black silks, was under instruction to win the race, not race the clock.

As the 14 horses milled at the start for the Theo Marks, Rosehill officials prepared for an important moment. Shannon's event was the first stakes race to be recorded by the track's new photo-finish camera, which had been installed only that week. The camera was housed 20 feet above the line, in a tower that sat opposite the winning post. The judges remained on the first floor of the tower, overlooking the finish. The STC, since the close of war, had leaped ahead of the AJC with its modernising of its tracks. Along with the camera that week and the starting stalls on all STC tracks, the club had also introduced an official sheet of acceptances, displaying a comprehensive tally of race acceptors, their weights and postpositions. Formerly, the press had had to compile its own data, so the club's innovation was welcomed with collective relief across the newsrooms.

Shannon took a good look at the fixed stalls in the chute, but he walked in and stood soundly before the jump at 2.33 pm. He had drawn marble 11, with stablemate Modulation almost widest. When the strands flew up, he jumped away in contention, and Moore settled him midfield.

The pair ambled along into the first turn, but Shannon was full of beans and Moore swung him out to get a clear passage. At the five furlongs, the horse was six deep on the track with no cover, and though Moore tried to steer back to the rails, no one let him in. The jockey sat quietly after that, allowing Shannon to find his own lane, and the Midstream horse loped along in the centre of the track. Coming into the straight, he had moved up into the leaders with such derision that Moore didn't move until the final furlong. He gave Shannon one short crack with the whip, and the horse motored into top gear so quickly the jockey was almost left behind. He spurted into the lead, wavering briefly towards the rail before Moore corrected him, and he sprung over the line a half-length ahead of the pacemaking Dowborough. The clocks stopped. Shannon had annihilated the Rosehill course record by 1¼ seconds, or 1:22½ for the seven.

When George Moore saw the time posted, he couldn't believe it. Was it possible that Shannon was travelling that quickly so effortlessly? Later, Moore would advise the connections of Young

Veilmond, his Epsom mount, not to bother lining up for the big mile. 'After riding Shannon today,' Moore said, 'I don't think anything has a chance against him at Randwick.' The win hauled the horse's earnings just shy of £13,000, and it was his sixth win in seven starts. But it was the ease with which Shannon won the Theo Marks, giving the second-placed horse 25 lbs, which stirred racegoers.

The *Sun* described the effort as 'shattering from an Epsom viewpoint. Shannon covered 50 yards more than any other runner, yet still won and broke the seven-furlongs record'. Moore said he had not ridden a greater miler than Shannon. The horse was named for another handicap event at Rosehill the following Saturday, but as the Theo Marks wrapped up, Bert Riddle didn't think they'd go there. 'Although I can't say for certain, I don't think Shannon will race again before the Epsom,' he told reporters. 'He did not have an easy race today, and another next Saturday might prove too severe.' Bert would confer with Peter Riddle about that, but both men agreed that Shannon was in top order and did not need another run to peak him for the Epsom. Therefore, the horse had two weeks to tide over before the big race.

Peter Riddle managed to get out of hospital. He cut a frail figure as he arrived back at Bowral Street to oversee Shannon. But in temperament, he was robust. He climbed aboard the stable pony each morning to follow his star to the track, and in the long fortnight intervening the two races, the son of Midstream sparkled.

26

Those crazy press blokes

At first light each morning, on the crisp, dewy surfaces of Randwick or Rosebery or Victoria Park, thoroughbreds puffed and snorted their way along the running rails. They ran in rhythms. One red apple, two red apple, three red apple. They ran in pairs, or in groups, sometimes solely. Their footfalls clapped over the turf drum-like, in beats of four, three if they were cantering. Then they disappeared around the next bend. Routine.

On top of the tote buildings, in the stands, glasses pitched, or draped over the running rail, the clockers watched. They were the four or five press boys who came all year, then the additional five or six who sprung each spring. They were the touts who kept the bookmakers supplied, and the independents trolling for a kill in the ring. Each of them was dedicated, a tireless recorder of vital but mundane detail.

Trackwatchers knew how to identify a thoroughbred, every thoroughbred. Without silks or saddlecloths, and through dull, sleety mornings or dawns drenched in mist, they knew a horse's snip or stocking, the breeder's mark on the near shoulder or the grey hairs at the tip of the tail. They had trawled the yearling sales, scribbling notes on pedigrees . . . dark bay, dapples on the quarter, sock on the off hind, and so on through hundreds of lots. They skulked around yards getting to know those that hadn't sold in a sale ring. The expert clocker never forgot a horse once he had seen it. Ever.

They timed fast gallops with incredible accuracy, a system smoothed by decades of practice. A clocker carried two watches, often four, and some, if there was a desk to lay them out, had six in front of them. Timing the work of 10 or 12 horses going together, clockers divvied responsibility. Each would call a different horse's time, 'seven in 1:33, first four in 52', and another would identify the horse, its jockey and winning margin. A clerk would jot the details, then coolly, modestly, they would move on to the next group.

The clockers came to the track in long, camel coats or short-sleeved pressed shirts, whatever it took. They showed up in the rain, the driving sleet and the torturous sun, with pencils, notebooks, binoculars and stopwatches. Ted Hush, trainer of Russia, glanced over at them one sodden morning. 'I thought we trainers were fools being out in this weather,' he said, 'but look at those crazy press blokes.' When horses were on the track, the clockers rarely spoke, bleating only numbers, names, or scribbling out fractions without drawing their eyes from the turf. Mostly, they remained nameless, for it was thankless work, reserved only for the passionate on a payroll. Nevertheless, it was they who moulded starting prices, who fed the newspaper inches in the run to big carnivals. It was their tireless, unfettered attention that recorded Shannon's every move into the Epsom.

The bay was obvious to them; he might have been albino, so recognisable was Shannon. Clockers knew his jaunty trot, the way he cantered on a long rein, the angle of his nose as he came onto the bit. The way he came off it when his rider pushed him out. On 24 September, two weeks to the Epsom, a fresh spring morning, no rain, they timed him over five furlongs at Victoria Park. 'Middle grass, 24 feet out. Shannon 1.03, first two in 24.' The afternoon headline: 'Shannon's dazzling speed over five.'

On 3 October, the clockers recorded Shannon's final trial before the Epsom. It was a warm morning at Victoria Park, double figures before the sun was even up. They watched Darby Munro, riding again since his Randwick fall, spurt over the middle grass, wide on the outside. Giving Modulation a short start, a lighter rider and the inside run, Shannon and Munro picked off the stablemate and surged clear. They turned the distance over in 1:02¼, the final three in 37 seconds.

The *Daily Telegraph*'s trackman headed back to his Castlereagh

Street office that morning, telling the turf editor that, in his opinion, Shannon was sharp enough to extend Bernborough over a mile. He would know: he had watched both horses every morning for months. He explained that the time Shannon clocked that morning was equivalent to 1:01 on the inner rail, which he found remarkable given Shannon had so much in reserve pulling up. The *Sun* sat in a similar camp about the horse's chances. 'No horse could have trained on more perfectly than Shannon, and only bad luck will prevent him winning his second Epsom tomorrow.'

The job of the faceless clockers was done, months of tracking, watching, calculating in aid of a big race. They would rest the following morning, enjoying the fruits of their labour on race day: a short price in the ring, a beer and a pie. They would start again the following week, towing reporters into the know about boom horses, or a champion out of tune. As long as the thoroughbreds came, so they would come too.

Randwick fell silent the eve of the big mile. Trackwork was over, the bar and lunchrooms were stocked and ready. Course officials had the turf in shipshape order. The strip of grass along the rail, affectionately known as the 'Randwick oasis', had been quarantined long enough, and the following day it would be opened to racing. Caretakers had watered it through, and thought they might go over it again in the early morning. The grass was left uncut, so it was a little long, but it would offer more cushion, even if it would tend against fast times.

Everything was in place for history.

27

The 1946 Epsom Handicap

Darby Munro woke very early the morning of the Epsom. He was jaded; it had been a tough few days. He pulled on his daks and shuffled to the living room, took a long look out the window over Randwick Racecourse. It wasn't light yet, the horses hadn't arrived for their race-day stretch over the tan. Munro headed to the kitchen, made a pot of steaming tea.

He wasn't riding until the Derby that day, the Epsom right after. He had turned down rides in the earlier races. It was unusual for him to do so, but it was his first day back racing since Jimmy Duncan's death, and that incident had hit him hard, harder than any other in his long career on horses. But as the Demon Darb flipped on the gas, grabbed a cup, poured his tea that morning, it wasn't Duncan's death that badgered him, or even the lingering infection in his leg. It was the phone calls that bothered him the most.

They had started a few nights ago, at midnight after he and his wife had just come in from the pictures. At first, he'd thought it was a wrong number, so he'd let the telephone ring out. But when it kept going, he picked it up. 'Is that you Darby?' came a gravelly voice on the other end.

'Yes.'

'What would you say to £15,000 to stop Shannon on Saturday?'

Munro wasn't new to the racing game. He'd had these sorts of calls before, the kind that change the direction of the day, or keep a man awake at night. They almost always circled around odds-on horses, animals that stood to lose someone a lot of cash. The turf annals were riddled with these sorts of rackets, but when they arrived on a jockey's doorstep, with their cold calls and seedy

171

undertones, it was never fun.

'This is no time for jokes,' Munro said into the telephone. 'Who's speaking?'

'Never mind who's speaking', the voice said. 'Would you be interested?'

Munro hung up the receiver. He knew it wasn't a prank call, but he couldn't help thinking that anyone serious about such a thing would not call at such an hour. They would call at a time when they knew a jockey would be coherent enough to respond, coherent enough to listen to the finer details of the offer and perhaps be tempted. But two days later, at about 8 pm, less than 48 hours to the Epsom, the caller tried again.

'I'm offering you £15,000 to stop Shannon,' he repeated. Munro went to interject, but the voice spoke over him. 'There's no catch in this. If you agree, you'll get 15 grand before the race. Name the place, and the money'll be there for ya. We'll take your word that you'll go through with it.'

'Listen,' Munro said. 'I don't know who you are, but whoever you are you've come to the wrong place.' He hung up.

Munro told Peter Riddle about the calls the following morning. The trainer would appreciate the gravity of them. Riddle already had a guard stationed on Shannon at Bowral Street, and Darby Munro's mystery caller affirmed the need for one. Though Riddle was concerned about his jockey's news, knowing well that £15,000 was a hell of a lot of money (though it was only a grain of sand in Epsom liabilities for the books), he was also inclined not to be too worried. He trusted Darby Munro absolutely. The jockey was not going to pull Shannon in the big race.

'They didn't know what they were asking you Darb,' Riddle said. 'There isn't a jockey in the world who could stop Shannon in the Epsom and get away with it.'

Munro had lived for days with this on his mind, the confidence that Shannon was a certainty if ever there had been one, and the unsettling knowledge that people wanted to stop him. As Munro stood in his kitchen idling with the tea bags, he knew it was all down to him now. Peter Riddle's job was over, Barney O'Brien's too. Darby Munro rarely felt pressure, but he felt it at that moment the morning of the 1946 Epsom.

—

He stood with Peter Riddle at 3.30 pm as the Epsom horses paraded in the mounting yard. The trainer didn't say much: 'Settle with the pack, don't let the leaders get the jump on you into the turn, watch out for Blue Legend.' They were things Munro already knew. Probably, the field would try to make Shannon carry every ounce of his 9 st 9 lbs. Munro thought an early pace would suit the lighter-weighted fancies Blue Legend and Magnificent, who were second choice in the betting. But Shannon was so versatile – front, back, middle of the pack – that even if they clattered through the early fractions, he believed his mount would stay with them, even with his big weight.

Shannon was 5/4 on in the betting, the shortest-priced favourite ever to go out for an Epsom Handicap. Millions of pounds had been plunged on him around the country in one-off bets and doubles bets into the Metrop result. For months, well back into August, he had been favourite for this race. Leading Randwick bookie Tom Powell despaired when he thought about it. 'Shannon represents one of the biggest risks I've ever had in a double. I think he's my worst risk actually, because I can't see any escape. In most big races there are usually several horses who seem to have a chance of beating the favourite, but there doesn't seem even one danger to Shannon here.'

Most of the racecourse thought the Epsom was sewn up before it had even been run, and on an average day, Darby Munro would have felt the same. But there was something in the air. He had lost the Derby by a half-head on the evens-favourite in the previous race, and trotted back to an angry tirade from mouthy punters. The winner had been a 33/1 shock. Headquarters just didn't feel like it usually did. It was fizzy, unfriendly. There were

66,400 patrons jostling for the tote windows and bookie stands, frustrated and impatient with the queues and delays. Women were elbowed aside in the panic to get on before the jump. The bars were packed tight, ran out of draught beer before the Derby had even been run. Bottled beer was overpriced, toilets congested. 'Back to jungle law,' one patron had said.

Munro strode over to Shannon with Riddle in tow. It was 3.30 pm, 10 minutes to the jump. Shannon was easy and relaxed, oblivious to the thousands of people who crammed the ring and their animated, pitchy chatter. Peter Riddle legged his jockey into the saddle and looked up at him. 'Well son, only an accident can beat you.' And then Darb was on his own.

Barney O'Brien snapped the shank off Shannon's bridle, and horse and jockey trotted out of the mounting yard onto the course proper. There was a nervous buzz over the racecourse crowd, a familiar feel before a big race. Shannon cantered his preliminary well in hand, then Munro turned him around and loped him down to the mile start. Away from the sea of faces and twitchy fingers clutching odds-on tickets, the jockey relaxed a little. Out here it was easier, just a carpet of grass before him and a whole lot of horse under him.

At the mile chute, 15 horses walked in small circles waiting for Jack Gaxieu to sort them out. Shannon had drawn barrier 15, with fancied rivals Magnificent and Doncaster winner Blue Legend the only runners on his outside. Jack O'Sullivan was aboard Magnificent, Eddie Fordyce on Blue Legend. Both jocks had strong instructions to track Shannon's every move, to race him into a tight finish with his heavy load. Magnificent had 9 st 4 lbs on his back, but Blue Legend had only 8 st 9 lbs, a full stone less than Shannon. Munro didn't give either horse a chance of worrying Shannon on average luck, but if any runner were going to, it would be either of these two.

Back in the stands, Peter Riddle took his place in the box, his binoculars hovering. He was nervous. These big-race moments were never easy, and now he knew getting too excited was a risk to his health. He looked straight across the crowded Flat to the chute, horses bobbing behind the barrier. Shannon was there, Darb in the now famous blue and black silks. Riddle calmed himself. It was like the 18 previous Shannon races, he told himself, but of course that wasn't true.

The racecaller hovered before his binoculars too. Lachie Melville had been calling Epsoms and Derbies and Sydney Cups at Randwick for more than a decade. He was conservative, unexcitable and very accurate in his calls. There was nothing he hadn't seen. He had been studying the Epsom charts since Thursday, verifying the runners and the pronunciation of their names, memorising their colours (though he knew most by heart now) and their jockeys. In those final minutes before the Epsom Handicap, he set his eyes on the odds-on favourite Shannon.

Bob Skelton was watching the favourite too, with a bird's-eye view from outside the pressroom in the trainers' stand. Skelton, at 64, was an ex-trainer and owner, and a big-bet punter without peer. His plunges were infamous the length of Australia: in 1924 a Sydney newspaper had branded him 'the greatest and gamest punter in the world'. Skelton was a big fellow, had a huge belly that rivalled only his vocal cords. But he was a sound judge of horse, and an expert assessor of track gallops. He could clock a horse better than anyone after decades of living off the talent, and as Jack Gaxieu began to shuffle the Epsom field, Skelton poised his stopwatch in one hand, pitched his binoculars with the other.

'Bring them up now!'

Gaxieu drew the horses towards the barrier. Darby Munro nudged Shannon forward. On his outside, Magnificent and Blue Legend came up, but Shannon was toey. Perhaps he was reading Munro's nerves, or the antsy Scotch Gift was irritating him. In postposition 12, Scotch Gift, a lightly weighted outsider, was giving all sorts of trouble. For a long few minutes, the troublesome mare lunged and plunged her way out of the line. Shannon grew so hot from her antics that he, too, reversed right away from the barrier. Munro swung him around and walked him away from the tapes, planning to walk him back into line calmly. But Shannon was uncharacteristically upset. As Scotch Gift played up a few yards away, a clerk of the course rode up and took hold of Shannon's bridle in an attempt to settle him. They were three or four lengths behind the field, and what followed next altered Epsom history.

Jack Gaxieu, red in the face from a fractious field, saw a line of 13 horses and sensibility left him. He sprung the tapes up in a moment of rushed, furious impulse, and then he saw them: Scotch Gift flat-footed and obstinate, and Shannon turned sideways against a clerk pony, the odds-on favourite, backed for millions around the country, left half a furlong.

Deafening despair rose up from the grandstands as Randwick realised Shannon had been left at the start. Peter Riddle almost sat down, and Lachie Melville could only call on in disbelief. Darby Munro's chest leaped when he heard the clatter of the barrier-rise. He felt as might a dying man, like the flashing recollection of his life would arrive in a second or two. Instead, before Shannon had even rustled an inclination to follow the field, Munro had knee-jerk responses: give up, or go after them. He went after them.

Darb yanked Shannon's head away from the clerk of the course, untangling him into clear space. They were so wide on the course that they were practically on top of the outer rail. When Shannon reached the barrier, Munro hunched low into the horse's mane and threw his hands out, hollered, 'Ha, ha! Go!' Shannon leaned onto his hindquarters then sprang off them, sensing right away his rider's panic. He shot off. Bob Skelton, his binoculars pinned to Shannon's little silhouette, clicked his stopwatch as the horse rattled away from the ashen Jack Gaxieu, still on the starter's podium.

Shannon burst into a maddening gallop down the back of the course, quickly crossing to the rail with Munro hunched low and quiet over his neck. The jockey was cursing wildly into the wind, but was almost blind with despair. There was Buckley's chance, Munro thought, that any horse could sustain this speed for a mile with 9 st 9 lbs on his back. Shannon was chasing the stragglers in top gear, flying out of the chute like a scalded cat. When they met the course proper, the pair was more than 10 lengths off the tail of the field.

Munro's thoughts were clouded with images . . . of fortunes lost because of Gaxieu's blunder, of the jeers that would greet him when he got back a loser. Jesus, what had happened? If Shannon hadn't been moving so quickly, Munro might have fainted with frustration. But the Midstream horse was going like the clappers, leaping headlong into the empty space between him and the tail end of the field. As they swung out of the first turn, past the five pole towards the turn into the straight, Shannon was careering onto the heels of the back marker. Munro couldn't believe it.

The half-mile swept past them and Shannon kept going, dashing past the trailing horses into the turn. He was in the pack now, and Munro realised suddenly that Shannon wasn't going to run out of steam. This mighty horse was going to keep on running and running, so the jockey decided to ride for dear life.

He crouched low into Shannon's mane and rode onto the right rein, steering the speeding animal towards the rail. Munro knew that there was no shot at victory from an outside lane. He could only win from the inside, so he prayed that a hole would open and they could push through. And as they straightened, Shannon shot through on the rails, landing firmly in the middle of the field at the top of the straight. Munro had no clue which runners were around him as he began to dig into Shannon with hands and heels. The horse was relentless, picked off one opponent after another. The folks in the Leger were hysterical, but the jock didn't hear them or see them. Munro saw only the furlong post looming, and he guessed they were three lengths off the leaders. Only then did he draw the whip and ride like the Demon Darb of old.

Shannon lifted beneath him, finding reserves that only champions possess. He had been travelling at his top for seven furlongs, but it didn't matter. He motored into the leading division with crazy speed, and Munro didn't even look up. He pushed the horse into the line of leaders; Young Veilmond was on the rails, Puffham was next, Shannon diving and surging next to him, with Blue Legend on the outside. And no jockey was riding harder than Darby Munro. With every stride, Shannon left Puffham behind, but Blue Legend went with him. Munro's left hand rose and fell with his whip, pleading with his horse to get up. Shannon inched ahead, his nose rising with Blue Legend's, falling with it. And then they were over the line. Click. Bob Skelton's stopwatch ground to a quick halt.

Randwick was in dumb shock, a kaleidoscope of hysteria and outrage muting every racegoer. Munro dropped his hands and let Shannon slow down; like the people in the stands, he had no idea who had won. He was exhausted, overwhelmed by the animal beneath him. He had been riding competitively since 1927, but no horse in Munro's 19 years had run like that for him, hell-bent from barrier to post with so much lead on his back. It was the greatest effort he would ever know. So when a howl rang up over the racecourse, he was devastated, for he knew then he had lost.

On the semaphore board, the judge had hoisted the numbers: Blue Legend by a half-head to Shannon, Young Veilmond another half-head third.

Lining the rails around the mounting yard, punters were dispossessed of their senses. They hooted and jeered and hollered abuse, and as Blue Legend trotted in, their resentment climbed. When Shannon and Munro came in, it got far worse. They demonstrated viciously, throwing their tickets at the jockey and jostling as if to climb over the railing. They hesitated only when a line of police stood in their way. Albert Davidson, a 29-year-old storeman from Darlinghurst, was among them. He hollered abuse at Munro, swearing at the jockey, drawing on every unpleasant tag under the sun. A policeman hauled him over the rail and dragged him away, arrested him for using indecent language. After Munro had hurried into the jockeys' room, another man broke the police cordon and went after him, hollering, 'I'll fix him this time!'

Darb was beside himself in the sanctum of the jockeys' room.

He could still hear the jeers on the other side of the door. Riders milled all around him, asking him what had happened. None, bar Eddie Cracknell on Scotch Gift, had seen the debacle of the start. On Blue Legend, Eddie Fordyce had known only one thing: – Shannon hadn't been beside him at the jump. Munro explained the incident in stunned vocabulary. 'I can't believe it. He let them go when I wasn't in line.' Jockeys couldn't believe it either, and they wouldn't until they saw the footage later on.

Munro stayed put inside, shaking his head as the race played in his mind over and over again. Six inches. That's how much Shannon had lost by, a paltry half-head. Munro couldn't imagine by how far Shannon would have hosed home if he had been allowed to jump with the rest of the field. Had someone got to Jack Gaxieu, he wondered, the same man who had tried to get to him the week before? It just didn't make sense. How could Gaxieu not have seen him, and Scotch Gift too, the horse that had started all the trouble? Scotch Gift had been left even further than Shannon, and had finished last. Munro wasn't surprised when the stewards called him to an inquiry.

Jack Gaxieu had crossed the mounting yard to a torrent of abuse too. He would never forget it. He had been starting races at Randwick since the spring of 1930, but he had never blundered a race as badly as this. Shannon's defeat was his fault, and he had to explain that to the stipendiary stewards. He was glad when he left the angry mob behind and entered the inquiry.

'I became confused when Scotch Gift upset the field,' he told the stipes. 'I honestly thought Shannon was up when I let the barrier go.' The stewards recorded that 'Gaxieu said it was a fact that Shannon, after being in line, was back about two lengths from the machine, but he (Gaxieu) did not realise this until the field was despatched, his attention having been concentrated on other horses that were restless'. Munro thought Shannon was further back than two lengths, but he waited his turn. 'Both riders were caught unawares when the barrier went up,' Gaxieu added.

It didn't explain how the starter, with all his experience,

had missed Scotch Gift. Even if Gaxieu had genuinely thought Shannon was in line, how had he lost sight of the horse that was causing the most mayhem? If Shannon was two to three lengths behind the field, as Gaxieu testified, then Scotch Gift was six or seven lengths back. How any man, let alone the official AJC starter, could have missed either of them was stupefying.

Munro was indignant when he stepped forward. 'The people are wrong in blaming me for this defeat,' he said. 'The starter left me completely. I was four or five lengths behind the barrier, not even expecting a start when Mr Gaxieu said "Go". That meant I was caught flat-footed. I had to move up to the barrier before I could get Shannon going, and then muster racing pace. To be honest, I almost thought of not chasing the field.' Munro told the stewards he was 12 to 16 lengths behind the last horse in the field (Scotch Gift excluded) when he got going. 'I was never hopeful, but to get so close was a marvellous performance by the horse,' he said. 'I think, with one more stride, I would have won the race.'

The stipes cleared both Munro and Cracknell of blame before the two jocks had even left the inquiry, but they kept Gaxieu behind. They ordered Lachie Melville to broadcast that the riders were exonerated, but Melville was given no details, and racegoers were furious that the true facts of the event were not released so that people might calm down. The remonstrations, therefore, continued. Blue Legend was afforded next to no applause at the awarding of the sash, and his owner, Mrs Herbert Field, had little to say. 'It might have been a fluke beating Shannon,' she said, 'but it was still a great performance for my horse to win with 8 st 9 lbs.'

Gaxieu's lot remained up in the stewards' room, but the chairman of the AJC, Alan Potter, would later declare that no official inquiry would occur into the mishap. Though the starter's admissions to the stewards were disconcerting, little could be done. The result couldn't be changed, the race couldn't be run again. It was just one of those things. But the turf editor of the *Sydney Morning Herald* took a different tack. 'The Epsom start was an occasion, above most others, when the preciseness and efficiency which brought Mr Gaxieu to the front as a starter should have functioned at its best. A starter should not have knowledge of the betting on the horses sent to his barrier, but this time it was impossible for Mr Gaxieu not to have known that Shannon was a hot favourite. Therefore, it was a time when it meant something to racing that Shannon should have the equal chance the starter usually gives every horse. And it was galling that this should be the occasion when Mr Gaxieu should spoil his record.'

The weight of the incident was heavy on Jack Gaxieu, and he expressed his regret to Munro as the crowd continued to call for blood 20 minutes after the race. Munro shrugged it off. 'Oh, it's just one of those things,' he said. Chief stipe J. B. Donohue said on record that he had never seen, in all his experience, a race ridden with such judgement. 'It was the greatest exhibition of riding I have seen. Munro rode as though there was no other horse in the race.' Alan Potter, too, was overwhelmed. Like most on course that day, he had not looked at any other horse once Shannon had set off after the field. 'Munro got to within a half-head of being a national hero,' he said. 'It was a pity he was beaten by that half-head.'

Nearly 40 minutes after the sensation, Munro had to emerge into the mounting yard to ride Silver Link in the Colin Stephen Stakes, and the ugliness began all over again. 'How are you going to throw this one, Darb?' people jeered. Still the abuse came at the jockey, along with betting stubs, wrappers, food, whatever was at hand. Extra police had been called in, so that 10 constables lined the fence between the public reserve and the official enclosure. Munro wore his most steely expression, refused to look at the crowds, but he thought he might never get over this. Peter Riddle didn't stick around. He left the course with his racehorse.

The tide of public abuse disgusted many racegoers who, like Riddle, thought the remonstrations unfair and over the top. Opinion slipped around the course that nuisance horses like Scotch Gift, a 100/1 no-hoper, had no right to be in the race. Others contended that Gaxieu had made a false start and should have called the field back in for a restart, as he had done with the

Camellia Stakes the previous year. Many more complained that the AJC could have avoided all of this if it had prioritised the installation of the starting stalls and the 'magic eye' photo-finish camera, as had the STC. 'The AJC must accept responsibility for an incident that mars the prestige of racing,' said a *Telegraph* editorial. 'Starting gates would have prevented any possibility of the disgraceful Epsom start that meant the defeat of the hottest favourite in the history of the race. Had photo-finish equipment been installed there would have been no ground for the doubts that exist about the judge's placings in the sensational finish.'

—

It felt like the longest day of his life. Darby Munro rode only three horses the day he lost the Epsom, but they were the hardest three he could remember. A weaker man would have thrown in the towel on this unforgiving game, but Munro was no such man. He had felt the sting of public indignation before, knew well the fine line between being a hero or a heel on big race days. But Shannon's defeat was different, raw. He carried it like a grand piano on his bony shoulders.

It mattered only a little that people had leaped to his defence. Jack O'Brien, turf scribe for the *Telegraph*, said, 'Personally I think Munro rode the best race of his career, and I don't say this because Shannon made up his ground and finished only half a head behind the winner. I say it because Munro had to overcome the psychological reaction of being left at the post. The accomplishment of both horse and rider deserved a better result.' It was true. Munro did deserve a better result after throwing his all into the run, and it was demoralising that the racegoing public had not appreciated his trying. He had only done so because of their money. If Shannon had not been so heavily backed, Munro would have trotted him back and spared the horse, and himself, the withering effort. That evening, in the quiet of his home, Munro wondered why he had bothered.

Nothing would change the result of the 1946 Epsom Handicap. He knew, as everyone did, that Blue Legend had got away with murder. That horse, though a Doncaster winner, had gone with the field all the way and had scrambled home by a nose, while Shannon, with a stone more and a 50-yard disadvantage, had run him to six ridiculous inches. In his wildest dreams, Darby Munro would never ride a race like it again.

Big Bob Skelton knew that, had the evidence to back it up. It was there in front of him, on the bald face of his stopwatch. The Australian mile record was 1:34¾, set at Flemington six years before. Shannon had destroyed it. Skelton had clocked him to run the 1946 Epsom in 1:32½.

Nearly 70 years on, it would remain the fastest mile ever recorded at Randwick.

28

Mr Wonderful

Shannon must have been made of steel and concrete. The morning after the Epsom, though he should have been stiff and wiry, he was fresh as summer rain. He stepped onto Randwick's tan for an easy jog under Barney O'Brien, light and stretchy and in good spirits. He wasn't jarred up or jaded, didn't need his feet pared or his joints rubbed. It was like he hadn't raced at all.

He was nominated for the George Main Stakes the following day, the traditional Monday meeting of the spring. There were only three to oppose him, but they were good ones: Flight, Magnificent and Modulation. Riddle had toyed with the idea of scratching his horse, given that Shannon's Epsom would have knocked a normal constitution sideways. But Riddle saw no need to do so. He was more concerned about Darby Munro. The jockey had been advised by his physician not to ride in the George Main because his leg wound was still infected and swollen. Just squeezing into breeches and boots had caused Munro a lot of pain, and even if Shannon went on into the George Main, Munro was no certainty to pilot him.

Riddle had placed George Moore on alert, but he really hoped that Darb would be fit to ride. It wasn't for Riddle's own selfish intents; he wanted to give Munro a shot at redemption, a victory that might claw back some of the public favour he had lost on Saturday. Riddle, like most in the racing business, knew that Shannon had been robbed in circumstances that were far beyond his jockey's control. But Riddle had known Darby Munro for a long time. Everything was cold comfort in the breeze of public hatred.

The trainer had deserted Randwick shortly after the Epsom. He just hadn't wanted to hear it. In all his years on the turf, Riddle had never heard such monstrous demonstration from the punting public. They had a right to bawl someone out; the way Shannon had been left was a clear breach of racing protocol. But Munro had ridden Shannon to win, and he had deserved a better reception for such masterful handling. Riddle had thought the ride remarkable, the signature of a genius in the saddle. His only regret, aside from his horse losing, was that Darby Munro had not been rewarded with a win.

The George Main Stakes proffered a chance to make amends, and Riddle wasn't the only one thinking so. The books had installed Shannon at odds on in ante-post markets. Flight was 7/2 against, with only change coming for Magnificent and Modulation. No one thought the quick turnaround would do Shannon any harm, and on Monday morning when Darby Munro elected to ride (he would ride only Shannon that day, opting out of all other offers), the pair became a certainty for the second time in as many days.

The Demon Darb kept his cap low as he left the jockeys' room for the George Main Stakes. It was 2.15 pm, a dull and indifferent day over the eastern suburbs. A weak shower of rain had watered the course overnight, so the going was good. As Munro strode over to Shannon, was legged into the saddle by Peter Riddle, he was caught unawares by Randwick. An ovation of cheers and claps rose from the public reserve, sweeping along the racecourse apron and up into the grandstands. From the official stand to the Leger, patrons stood from their seats, clapping the jockey who, only 48 hours before, had been their villain. It was unprecedented. Riddle smiled, patted the jockey on the knee. Something rose in Darby Munro as he headed, once again, for the famous mile chute.

Shannon stood soundly in alley 4 with Flight on his outside, Magnificent and Modulation hugging the rails. The George Main was a weight-for-age contest, so Shannon carried 9 st 3 lbs, giving Flight 5 lbs. With only four in the field, there wouldn't be much jostling for a run, so Munro wasn't stressed about the start. Though the Epsom bungle was clearly on his mind, he knew Gaxieu couldn't repeat his error if he tried. The only concern, therefore, was that Flight was toey to get started, and when the tapes went up she punched into an early lead.

Shannon was slowest away from the machine by half a length, but into running he was all over Magnificent and Modulation. Munro swung him out and around those two, and Shannon settled on Flight's flanks, allowing the mare to dictate the war. They opened a length on the trailing pair, Flight clipping the first half-mile in 47 seconds. She was galloping strongly, but Shannon stalked her, a menace on her wings.

They clattered into the home turn together, and Munro shook the whip at Shannon. The horse exploded. The response was instant, like water tossed on an oil fire. Shannon bounced away from Flight with reckless abandon, leaving her behind in a matter of strides. And he kept on going . . . a length, two lengths, then three. Inside the final furlong he was out by seven. His run was so withering that Munro took a peep over his shoulder then eased right up, sauntering past the winning post six lengths clear. Shannon had run the mile in 1:34½ . . . a new Australasian record.

Clockers, at various stations around the track, stared at their watches. Was it possible that the horse had run that quickly so easily? Shannon had clipped the last half in 47½, eased right up, which meant that if Munro had ridden him out he could have gone 1:34 flat. It was phenomenal. The sectionals were even better. Unofficially, Shannon had run the first seven furlongs in 1:21¾, which shaved a quarter of a second off the long-standing Australasian record of 1:22. He had also equalled Randwick's six-furlong record of 1:10. In addition, his time for the mile shaved three-quarters of a second off the Randwick record. Though he had slowed right down, Shannon's running of the last furlong in 12¾ seconds indicated just how fast he was travelling into the straight. 'Pushed right out, he could have run the mile in 1.33¾,' said the *Telegraph*. Overall, Shannon had equalled or broken four time records in his George Main.

The racecourse became the Randwick of old as Munro trotted his charge back to the enclosure. Patrons cheered the heroes en masse, waving their hats in the air and hanging over the rails to cry 'well done'. Perhaps it was their way of undoing Saturday's carnage, perhaps they just appreciated a good spectacle. Either way, Munro gave them a quick wave and a grin. 'Are you happy now, Darb?' called a reporter.

'Of course I'm happy,' he retorted. 'Who wouldn't be?'

Up in the Members' stand, one cheeky patron was laughing. 'Now he's happy. He'll dismiss that tank he came to the races in and go home by tram.' Everyone, the length of the racecourse, was glad to see the Demon Darb, Mr Wonderful, back on the right side of the mob.

His post-race comments were matter of fact. 'I was determined to ride Shannon today, even if I had only one good leg. I wanted to atone in some way for Saturday's incident, even though I think by now everyone knows it wasn't my fault. Shannon showed today he is a great horse. He would give Bernborough the hardest race he has ever had at a mile, I tell you.' Reporters scampered away from Munro, tomorrow's headlines in tow.

For Riddle, the George Main Stakes emphasised the tragedy of the Epsom result. Shannon was unbeatable in his current state, and only Gaxieu had got the better of him, just. Though the 1946 Epsom was a good story for the dinner table, it was a thorn in Riddle's side, though he didn't publicly say so. Another trainer would have jumped up and down about the race, demanded an inquiry and insisted his jockey lodge an appeal. But Riddle was no such trainer; that sort of excitement was beyond him these days. He followed his horse back to Bowral Street after the George Main, watching his every step, checking for soreness, over-exertion. There was nothing, nothing but steel and concrete under the flesh and blood.

The George Main Stakes had been the first time Shannon had run right away from a field, and though Riddle didn't put much merit in winning margins, holding that Shannon was always better than the bare result, the win was visually and statistically impressive. Shannon was loaded with speed, had an easy way of going that only exceptional horses had. But he usually did just enough to win, dawdling along to the line like a kid on his way to the school gates. In the public's perception, therefore, he was no Bernborough, who won like a steamroller (the Queensland horse had won his 14th consecutive race the day Shannon lost the Epsom). But suddenly, after the George Main, the public were inclined to wonder if Shannon might be right up to Bernborough's class.

On paper, Riddle's horse had broken track records in his last three outings: a Rosehill record for the Theo Marks, the unofficial blitzing of all times in the Epsom defeat, and the four records he had broken or equalled in the George Main. Bernborough was blazing a similar trail down in Melbourne. The logical conclusion was that Shannon would go to Melbourne for the VRC carnival, running into Bernborough while he was there. Riddle conceded that his horse was fit enough and race-ready for a clash with the 'Toowoomba tornado', saying he looked forward to them lining up over a mile at weight-for-age. But it wasn't going to happen that spring. The trainer could barely leave Randwick without medical assistance, let alone endure a 14-hour rattle on the Melbourne Express. But he had thought about going. 'I have until tomorrow week to nominate him for the principal Victorian races,' he commented after the George Main, 'but I don't think there is much chance of it happening.'

The likely targets in Melbourne would have been the Mackinnon Stakes on Derby Day over a mile and a quarter, where he would certainly meet Bernborough, and the Linlithgow Stakes over a mile on Cup Day, both weight-for-age. But as much as these events would have suited Shannon, Riddle would never have made the trip. His physician had been laid up with a broken leg, and the only way the trainer would have considered travelling was if his doctor could have travelled with him. Riddle was only weeks out of hospital from coronary failure, and it was unreasonable to expect that a clash between the two great horses would supersede his health. Anyway, the trainer believed there would be time enough in the autumn for the two horses.

While Riddle toyed with the idea of sending Shannon out in the aftermath of the George Main Stakes, the King's Cup loomed on 12 October. He had put the race on the back-boiler for weeks, refusing to commit to it without first seeing how Shannon pulled up from his Epsom program. But given that the horse was firing, by Tuesday Riddle thought they'd give it a shot. The only problem was that Shannon remained an unknown at a mile and a half.

—

The story behind the King's Cup begins in 1927, when the Duke and Duchess of York attended the races at Flemington on a thin April afternoon. The race card included a unique event, a race that carried a rich stake and a £100 gold cup gifted from the king of England. Called the King's Cup, the race was an instant success, so much so that the visiting royalty suggested it occur every year. The king committed to donating a yearly trophy, with the race going to states in rotation. The details were spun up later in the year when delegates from the leading metropolitan race clubs around Australia (bar the Northern Territory) met in Melbourne to hash out the details. They decided that the King's Cup would be a race of a mile and a half, a quality handicap with the maximum tonnage 9 st 5 lbs, and the minimum 7 st. In addition to the gold cup, the stake would be no more than £2000 and no less than £1000. States would host the race in order of population, beginning with Melbourne, so that Sydney got the event in 1928, Brisbane in 1929, and so on until Tasmania finally played host in 1931. Winners of the event included champions Limerick, Phar Lap and Rogilla.

The race had not been run since 1939, holding over until the war ended. That meant that the 1946 renewal at Randwick would be a celebrated occasion, and the AJC had thrown a winner's purse of £1635 at it. Shannon had been allotted the maximum weight of 9 st 5 lbs, and of the seven other horses that would go to post, only Good Idea, a Melbourne Cup fancy, came closest with 8 st 11 lbs.

Russia, with good handicap form, had slid in with 8 st 9 lbs while Flight had nearly a stone less than Shannon on 8 st 7 lbs.

When it became clear that Shannon would contest the King's Cup, the books took a risk and advertised him at odds against, about 9/4 in most places. No one was sure if the Midstream horse could go the mile and a half, including Peter Riddle. 'It will be purely experimental,' he said. Shannon's only run over the distance had been the Derby in 1944, when he had placed well back, so punters were reluctant to come for him. The connections of Cordale, the Metropolitan winner, were very confident. They expected their horse to win the race, virtually ignoring the fact that Shannon was in the race at all. 'Cordale should beat Good Idea in the King's Cup. We expect that's how it should go.'

Flight's trainer had a different view. He thought the mare was just at her top, that the George Main beating had made her fitter and the extra distance of the King's Cup would play in her favour. 'Flight meets Shannon on 7 lbs better terms than the George Main,' Frank Nowland said. 'When they met in the Craven Plate over a mile and a quarter last year, Flight beat Shannon by two lengths. Shannon has yet to prove that he is as good over the longer distance, and he will be flat out conceding her 12 lbs over a mile and a half.' The clockers agreed. They watched the mare register the fastest five furlongs of the morning two days before the race, and conceded that slick as Shannon was, he would be all out to beat Flight in the King's Cup.

The newspapers thought so too. The *Telegraph* picked Flight as its choice, from Good Idea then Shannon. The *Sydney Sportsman* opted for Good Idea from Shannon and Flight. Only Bert Warburton of the *Sun* maintained that Shannon would stay. 'Shannon, the horse of the moment, and at least equal to Bernborough, should win the King's Cup, adding to his already great record. He is the type to be anywhere his rider desires, and if the pace is not too slow he should not pull too hard. Actually, he'll run the race to suit himself and win accordingly.'

Tactically, Riddle thought Flight would lead. The Nowland

camp would be hoping to make Shannon carry his extra 12 lbs all the way, knowing their mare could steal a break from the half mile, open a lead, and leave Shannon with too much to do while he was tiring. But if that were to be Flight's plan, Riddle guessed the pace, at least, would be strong. If they went at a funereal gallop, Shannon would be in trouble. Therefore Riddle hoped that Flight would make the pace, because he knew that Shannon was fit enough to chase her down. It was just a question of stamina now.

The King's Cup would jump at 3.20 pm, and the day of the race it was stiff over Randwick, very hot and getting hotter. The eight-horse field was sticky as it made its way into the enclosure, and by the time Shannon made it to the start he was sweating between his hind legs and down his neck. Darby Munro adjusted his grip on the reins as his hands slid up and down the sweaty leathers. Even beneath the light sheath of breeches and silks, the jock was perspiring.

Shannon sprang from the start like a schoolboy leaping with the bell. From barrier two, he cruised into fourth spot out of the straight for the first time, and went to sleep into the back part of the course behind Quadrant and Flight. They went through the first half-mile in 52½, the mile in 1:41. As the field swung out of the five furlongs and towards the home turn, Munro woke his horse. He had spared Shannon by placing him well from the barrier, tucking him in behind the speed and saving precious fuel. He urged Shannon up beside Flight as they straightened, and the horse hardly came off the bridle as Flight surged into open running. Shannon motored past her into the lead and kept going, opening a length, then two lengths. A mile and a half, and it was all the same to him. He loped over the line two and a half lengths clear in the King's Cup.

It was the easiest of wins. Munro had hardly crouched in his irons, hardly raised his whip to Riddle's horse. Shannon was machine fit at the end of his spring campaign, and nothing in the state could stay with him. Peter Riddle took the ornate King's

Cup trophy from the state governor, General John Northcott, and handed it to Darby Munro beside him. A long ovation stirred Randwick racecourse, and Mr Wonderful was back in the familial grip of adoration.

The King's Cup was worth £1635 to Shannon, bringing his winnings to £16,344. It was his 12th win from 18 starts. But Shannon had raced 10 times in the last two seasons for eight wins and two seconds, a phenomenal record for a mature racehorse that would have been even better were it not for Jack Gaxieu. Riddle felt very satisfied as he took possession of his splendid trophy, and not just for the sake of another win. Any myths about Shannon's staying ability had been dispelled once and for all, and that gave the frail trainer more satisfaction than the rich cheque on its way into his bank account.

Later that afternoon, Bernborough won his 15th straight race by clinching the Caulfield Stakes in Melbourne in track record time. He was on song for the Caulfield Cup the following Saturday, Mulley declaring it 'already won'. But Sydney paid little heed – it was just too hot. The city sweated through its hottest October evening in years, a brassy and livid night come after a day of fierce summer. In his blue box on Bowral Street, the King's Cup winner drowsed through it, waiting for first light when the mosquitoes would go to ground.

29

Two horses, no race

Riddle thought his horse had done enough, but in the late afternoon a day or so after the King's Cup, he received a telephone call. Danny O'Mara, chairman of the Brisbane Amateur Turf Club (BATC), wanted him to bring Shannon to Queensland. O'Mara proposed a match race with Bernborough on 23 November, at Doomben over a mile under weight-for-age conditions. The purse was £5000, making it as rich a contest as that week's Caulfield Cup.

Azzalin Romano had barely stepped off a plane in Melbourne when the match race was thrust in his face. Fred Pilbrow, turf editor for the Brisbane-based *Courier-Mail*, was on assignment for O'Mara to press out the potential interest from the Bernborough camp. In the Menzies Hotel downtown, the two men picked over the idea. The race would be high profile, one that would have the nation talking, and Romano admitted he was interested. The stake was huge. But he would have to talk to Harry Plant, who was very quick to railroad the plan. 'Bernborough has already travelled 3000 miles this season, and by next month he will have been racing continuously for 10 months. Adding another trip to Brisbane would send his mileage to 4400, and that might overdo it, even for a great horse like him.' Plant added that the Queensland club would be better off with a rich autumn race, open to all comers. 'It would prove a great attraction,' he said, 'and it would appeal to me at that time of year.'

Plant was wise to refuse. Concerns were quietly surfacing among racing men for the heavily raced Bernborough, who was carrying grandstand weights every time he stepped out to race and who had been on the trot since sporting Romano's silks on 8 December 1945. He had raced five times already that spring, with the Caulfield Cup, Mackinnon Stakes and a nomination for the Melbourne Cup still on his book. He had a staggering 10st 10 lbs to lug in the Caulfield Cup, and 10 st 9 lbs allotted for his Melbourne Cup, the heaviest impost since Phar Lap in 1931. People wondered if there was a bottom to this horse at all, and if so, when it might be reached.

With the refusal of the Bernborough camp, Peter Riddle's decision was simple. He, too, declined the Doomben match for the same reason he wasn't carting Shannon to Melbourne: his health. He told O'Mara that he wouldn't hesitate to let Shannon gallop it out with Bernborough if his physician could have travelled with him to Queensland, but that wasn't possible, so neither was the match race, at least until the autumn. O'Mara's grand plans for a Shannon–Bernborough clash blew away with the southerly that rushed into Sydney that night.

Shannon went out as Bernborough went on into the Caulfield Cup that weekend with the heaviest weight the race had ever seen. From the jump, it was obvious to everyone that the field was out to beat the Queensland horse. Crowded, jostled and sandwiched in running, Bernborough was left an impossible task in the straight and managed only fifth. It was a sensational upset, an expensive one for loyal punters and devastating for Azzalin Romano. Trainer Harry Plant was livid, and in the coming days the wheels began to fall off the dream. Bernborough was scratched from the Melbourne Cup, Plant declaring that the horse would never race in a handicap again. He sacked Athol Mulley, replacing him with ex-Brisbane hoop Billy Briscoe.

The eyes of horseracing rested on the new partnership on 2 November 1946 when he sat astride Bernborough for the Mackinnon Stakes. The pair was 4/1 on ahead of Flight, poised for a facile canter around Flemington in a small five-horse field. Out of the home turn, Bernborough was in cruising speed as he began to gather in the front-running Flight. Then the big horse bowed in running, veering outward and bobbing and duck-ing in that awful way that horses do when they have shattered a foreleg. Bernborough had displaced the sesamoid bone in his near fore, rupturing the ligaments that bound it. Next to no one at Flemington saw Flight stroll past the post in the Mackinnon. Hundreds of people, instead, dashed frantically down the course to see the stricken Bernborough, or craned their necks to watch the horse ambulance amble away with him. In the days that followed, Romano dug deep to save his horse, and Bernborough responded well. By early December he was on the mend, but it was a tragedy for Australian racing that he would never gallop again.

Peter Riddle couldn't believe it when the news reached him. Racing men were hardened to losing horses, but the erring of one so good, one right at the top of the sport, was hard to digest. Shannon and Bernborough would never meet on the track. The trainer wondered if the big weights and long months had finally taken their toll on the iron horse. Had Bernborough been hawked around a little too much? As the seven-year-old stallion knitted his injury, boxed in Melbourne with a tally of physicians watching his every move, the question of his future hung over the country. Would Romano stand him as a stallion, or sell him to a stud master in the Hunter region, even Queensland? In the end, the owner did neither. Ever wooed by the big dollars of the United States, Azzalin Romano sold his champion to American film magnate Louis B. Mayer, of MGM fame, who had been knocking on the door of Australian bloodstock for a while. Bernborough would go to Mayer's Kentucky breeding string at Spendthrift Farm in the early months of 1947.

30

All the rest and residue

The autumn of 1947 blew into Sydney with its cooling nights after a long, dry summer. It was welcome in Bowral Street, where the straw was dry and brittle and the air smelled like months of grease and sweat. The flies disappeared, the trees in the street outside wilted and grew thin as March pushed into April. And Peter Riddle was down to one horse as health, and taxes, got the better of him.

Tom Kerr had put Modulation through the sale ring for 1500 guineas, so only Shannon, in stable seven, stood in Riddle's yard. The lads were gone, the boxes rented out to other trainers. Riddle was going against medical advice even keeping Shannon, though he had decided not to race the horse through the autumn again. 'I'd be lost without one to train after being among them all my life,' he said. 'I've given up looking after a team, and Shannon is now my hobby. If I were to dispose of him, I could scarcely hope to get another as good.' Shannon was keeping Riddle's spirit afloat, but the ailing trainer was fielding offers for his racehorse from all over the world.

American J. Burke Clements, a chairman from Helena, Montana, had made ventures in December to lease Shannon for racing in the United States. In a letter, Clements proposed to Riddle a six-month lease of the horse for $10,000 (about £3500) in which Shannon would run in six races between May and December 1947. The agreement suggested that half the sum would be paid on Shannon's arrival to US shores, with an option for Riddle to claim 10 per cent of prizemoney on the final three races over the remaining lease balance. 'I would consider purchasing outright,' the American wrote, 'but I presume you would not want to sell.' He was right. Not only was Riddle not interested, he was offended.

'The offer is ridiculous. It is an insult to my intelligence and an insult to the ability of my horse,' he said. 'If Shannon retains his form he could win that much money here in a few races next year without all the worry of sending him to America.' Riddle believed the arrangement was all in Clements' favour, and it annoyed him. 'I don't think I will even bother answering the letter,' he said. He didn't.

In the new year, Harry Plant gave it a go. He had travelled with Bernborough to America to settle the big horse at Spendthrift Farm, and returned with all sorts of plans. 'In America I saw good horses, but none to equal Shannon,' he said. 'I am certain that if he were taken there he would prove a sensation.' Plant approached Riddle on behalf of another set of American interests, who had told him to go to any price. They planned to ship Shannon to the US where he would be prepared by Bernborough's trainer for an American campaign. Plant went to £30,000, a phenomenal amount of money, but he ran into the same wall as had Clements and all the others before him – Shannon was not for sale, no matter the price.

Out of the autumn races, the horse whiled away the approach of winter on Bowral Street, fresh from a spell and in light work in the crisp mornings. The Queensland clubs were trying very hard to entice him north for their winter races. Shannon was nominated for the Doomben 10,000 on 5 July, and the Doomben Cup a week later. He had big penalties in both, over 10 st. He was also named for the King's Cup, which would occur on 13 August in Brisbane. But in early June, Riddle stood shivering on the rails of Victoria Park, watching Shannon turn over his first piece of fast work in months. The horse was sluggish, blowing his way through the final furlong. Riddle sent a telegram that afternoon to the BATC, advising his horse was out of the Doomben events. 'I could have left him in longer in the hope he would improve,' the trainer said, 'but there is only three weeks remaining before the 10,000. Out of that period, almost a week's work would have been lost through travel.'

There were few excuses for Shannon not being fit. He had

been in from his spell for weeks, and if Riddle had applied the acid early, the horse could have been good enough to freight to Brisbane. Something was wrong, and as June marched onwards Shannon idled in his box. Riddle arrived later and later at the yard each day, gave fewer instructions to Barney O'Brien. He was impossibly pale and thin by then, a shadow of his robust old self. But the spirit lingered, the enthusiasm and affection for his horse still obvious when he entered the yard in the mornings, his attention to duty still visible when he followed him to the track. But Riddle was slow and frail and ill, and he knew, as did his wife and daughter, as did Barney O'Brien, that it was Shannon who had kept him going for two years. But it was borrowed time that finally ran out.

Peter Riddle shuffled into his sitting room on 4 Norton Street the night of 29 June 1947. It had been a wintry Saturday, hardly warm enough to stay outside. His chest hurt from stooping in the cold for so many hours, but he ignored it, settled into his lounge to read. Kathleen was quiet beside him. Without warning, his heart cartwheeled. In seconds, he couldn't breathe for the pressure, then he couldn't see. His panic was silent and momentary as his life slid away, and then he lay still. An enormous coronary occlusion, it had been quick and quietly violent. Shannon's trainer was dead.

—

A long procession of racing folk followed Riddle's coffin from Kinsela Chapels in Taylor Square to the Eastern Suburbs Crematorium in Botany. It was 1 July, and the shock of the trainer's death had hardly settled, but it didn't stop the newspapers. The *Sydney Morning Herald* ran a story that day: 'Shannon might end in U.S.A.' The article stated that 'prospects of Shannon going to America to complete his racing career are considered to be strong'. Riddle had been dead less than 48 hours, but the fate he had wanted least for his horse was suddenly looking the most likely.

Speculation was endemic about what would happen to the

horse. It was on everyone's mind as they farewelled the trainer that Tuesday afternoon. June wondered about the fate of her father's most treasured possession. Darby Munro was there, grieving for the partnership that he and Riddle had forged over a decade before. Barney O'Brien was lost. He didn't know whether to press on with Shannon's training or wind it up. The yard was lonely without the affable, kind trainer, and it saddened the old strapper each morning when Shannon stretched his neck over the box door, waiting for Riddle to walk in, to pull out the saddle and send him off to the gallops. He, along with most of Randwick, waited for news of what would come next.

Peter Riddle had made his solicitor and his brother Bert the executors, or trustees, of his estate. He left his Chrysler motor car and his inheritance from his late father's estate to his daughter, June. Kathleen got the Norton Street home and everything inside it. She began to dispose of her late husband's possessions almost immediately, and it was a surprise to June one afternoon when she learned that Shannon's King's Cup was sitting in the window of Hardy Brothers downtown. She hurried to the York Street store to claim it, buying it back for the price Kathleen had hawked it for. June had little contact with her stepmother again.

Shannon's fate was more complicated. Riddle's will bequeathed 'all the rest and residue of my estate, including all my racehorses and racing equipment, unto my trustees to sell by public auction'. The old trainer had wanted Shannon to be sold. The monies accrued from the sale would pay debts outstanding on the estate, including funeral expenses and a £7 grocery bill with the local store in Kensington. The rest would be divided equally between Kathleen and June. Bert Riddle and his co-executor, Felix Finn, kept the details of the will private, refusing to disclose that the trainer had wanted his horse sold. A stream of enquiries, therefore, came their way: would Shannon race on in the interests of the estate, would he be sold privately, or sold to America? It wasn't until early August that they revealed the Midstream stallion would be sold, and they confessed that it had been a difficult decision to arrive upon, though it hadn't been their decision at all. Felix Finn, who had known Peter Riddle for a long time, was public about the emotional importance of the sale. 'There was never a chance of Shannon being sold if Peter had lived,' he said. 'The horse was the apple of his eye. He recognised in Shannon, from the outset, a champion, and whenever he spoke of him he disclosed the bond that existed between him and his horse.' Finn wished the new owner every success. 'I trust that Shannon will more than fulfil the cherished hopes and ambitions of his late owner,' he said, 'and carve, if he has not already done so, a memorial to Peter Riddle.'

The particulars of the sale were handed over to William Inglis & Son under the tutorage of managing director and senior auctioneer Reg Inglis. 'I am certain that no sale has ever approached in importance the projected sale of Shannon,' Inglis said. 'The comparable example would be that of Heroic at 16,500 guineas (in 1925). I would not attempt to guess that Shannon will not bring that or more.' The sale was scheduled for Newmarket on Wednesday 20 August, at 3 pm, hurried so that the horse might meet any spring engagements. It would be a unique event, the only occasion at Newmarket where a single thoroughbred would be sold.

'Odds are being freely offered against the Shannon sale establishing new figures,' commented the press in the run-up to 20 August. Heroic's 1925 price was an auction record, but the highest price ever paid for a thoroughbred in Australia was £19,000, coughed up for dual-Derby winner Talking in 1936. 'Those laying the odds point out that there are very few men in Australia who would be prepared to pay a gigantic price for a six-year-old so highly rated in the handicapping lists.' The observation was correct. Shannon's time on the track would be limited due to his age, and though he was an entire and stud potential existed, it was impossible to measure the value of that. For example, it would take a long time for the horse to earn a return via stud fees if he sold for astronomical sums. And that is presuming he would prove a decent sire. On the American end, there were complications too.

The new US racing season would not kick off until January 1948, and if that buyer were to stand the horse at stud, he would have to wait until the following year, 1949, to establish him. In other words, an American buyer would have a long wait for a return on their purchase, even assuming the crossing from Australia would not affect Shannon.

With Sydney all a-chatter about the impending sale, Shannon remained with Barney O'Brien at Bowral Street. The pair was transferred to the charge of trainer William Henderson, whose horses occupied the adjoining boxes in the yard, and Henderson's staff took up Shannon as one of their own, mucking and feeding and chipping in with his chores. People came and went all around him – potential buyers, veterinarians producing soundness reports – but he remained calm in his strapper's familiar, safe hands. O'Brien was to keep the horse just fit, nothing was to be asked of him. The estate didn't want strains or bruises or blemishes on him going into the auction ring, so Barney O'Brien and Shannon pottered about, stretching their legs in lazy gallops in the mornings, strolling in the cool afternoons. If the winds of change were not so darn strong around them, these might have been the best days of their lives.

31

'Any rich man . . .'

The halls of the Newmarket complex were stained with famous names: Amounis, Chatham, Flight, Bernborough. Each had left their mark somewhere, a scuff on the wall or a dent in the woodwork, a chip on the stone floor somewhere beneath the shavings. But none on their day had been more hotly spoken of than Shannon, for whom rivers of people poured into Barker Street on Wednesday afternoon, 20 August. It was a carnival, a circus of 4000 racing folk and curious public. They were press boys, Cinesound cameramen, Sydney gentry and average Sams skiving from the glassworks to watch the show. They came singly, in groups, occupied fence posts, the limbs of the famous fig tree, and they swamped the sale ring, 20 deep around. They waited.

William McDonald was among them, a bookmaker known up and down the aisles of Randwick Racecourse. He had co-owned the gallant Winooka in the mid-1930s, and leased Abbeville. He had deep pockets and a face built for the poker table. He told few that he was interested in Shannon, but he was probably outclassed. There were some heavy players around him, including Maurice McCarten, high-rolling jockey turned trainer. He was representing George and Harry Tancred, Sydney racing men (and brothers) with interests in shipping Shannon to the US. Ossie Porter had a similar plan. He was Victoria's leading owner, had flown to Sydney especially and was confident. 'I have always wanted to own a champion, and this is my opportunity,' he said. 'I don't care how high I have to bid. The sky's the limit with me.'

Porter was neatly dressed and connected. He had 20 horses in training in Melbourne, including the Caulfield Cup winner St Fairy, who had won him a mint. He was also savagely sure of himself. He would famously say after his retirement, 'The bookies will always win out – unless of course you're born lucky, like me.' Porter had told the press all about his plans after securing Shannon: four races in Sydney before a stint at the rich Santa Anita Handicap in California. He even named the races. He bleated about talking to Darby Munro. 'Munro told me Shannon was perhaps the greatest horse Australia had produced. He also told me that Shannon was the best horse he had ever ridden, so that was good enough recommendation for me.' But even Porter was in over his head. Sitting beside the auctioneer's platform, with his bidder Maurice Grogan and a bottomless pit of currency, was Sydney's peerless W. J. Smith.

Sixty-five-year-old 'Knockout' Smith was enormous, as much in stature as standing. He was thick everywhere (though not tall), from his neck to his shoulders and down to his forearms, with silver curly hair and sharp little eyes. As a youngster, he had been a bullish fighter, keeping his corner with his bare knuckles and brutish size. It was this talent that had earned him his nickname 'Knockout'. The story went that he had run into a group of mouthy, drunken Germans in a crowded bar at the break of World War I, and had laid the group flat with a handful of swings – five knocked cold, one hospitalised and a few walking wounded. No one ever stood over William John Smith.

He was not book-learned, departing school at the age of 13 to work at the 'bots', the Melbourne Glass Bottle Company, as a water boy. After a rocky start, running onto the wrong side of management due to his union involvement, he had climbed into senior roles in South Australia, then Melbourne and eventually Sydney. With a sharp wit for business and a work ethic learned on his feet, Smith organised one merger, then two and three, until he chaired Australian Consolidated Industries, employer of more than 7000 people with a £2.5 million annual payroll, and one of the most important wartime producers of glass, plastics and packaging. With fortunes earned, Smith didn't slow down. Even at 65, his mind moved like a march hare, one project to the next with ageless energy. His face was still jaunty and healthy, his torso rock solid. If a paunch popped out, he got busy with the dumbbells and early morning swims off Seven Shillings beach. He was a creature of habit, demanded a half-bottle of Great Western every evening and a walk down Wolseley Road. Smith's character entered a room before he did, big as all outdoors. He was tough, could be irritable, the sort of personality that came with rising from nothing. He had sent competitors to the wall, put the fear of God up anyone who had to deal with him. But he was vastly human. 'Well, 'e's never allowed a glass worker to have a pauper's funeral,' his men said of him. 'If you did your work, you'd get on with him.' Even union officials, men he had sacked, many of whom he had scuffled with, spoke of the 'big fellow' in good humour.

Smith had plunged into the racing game in 1917 with a horse called Tony Bin. In 1931 he had formed a partnership and raced under the name F. Smithden. He had owned the very smart Kuvera in the Peter Pan era, and he had used this horse as the flagship of his new thoroughbred nursery, a patch of about 4000 acres a mile from Scone in the Hunter Valley called St Aubin's. The stud moved at Smith pace: within a year or two it had new fencing, irrigation and pastures under oats and barley. It also had a one-mile training track for home-sprung yearlings, with barrier starts and a straight finish. In a short space of time, Smith had installed some very impressive stallions – Manitoba, Victoria Derby-winner Hua, and the impressive New Zealander Beau Pere. This horse, a superstar sire, was the catalyst for a stunning new business arm that had brought Smith ringside for Shannon's sale that afternoon.

Smith had been travelling the globe for years with Australian Consolidated Industries, in particular to the US where he had forged strong ties with famous Californians. These friendships coincided with a surge of American interest in Australian bloodstock, and Smith saw an opportunity that had gone untapped back home. He arranged for Beau Pere to be sold from St Aubin's in 1941 to the Hollywood film mogul Louis B. Mayer. Smith netted 10 times what he had paid for Beau Pere, and it began a series of high-profile exports. Even though Australians were disenchanted at the exodus of favourite horses to the 'Yanks', Smith possessed such a business acumen that he saw past sentimentality. A few days after Peter Riddle's death, he plunged again. Paying 13,000 guineas at auction for Ajax, star weight-for-ager of the late '30s, he opened the horse up to US interest. As he sat with Maurice Grogan waiting for Shannon on 20 August, Smith was winding up the sale of Ajax behind the scenes. He had sold the horse to millionaire magnate Charles Howard, of Seabiscuit fame, for about $100,000.

The presence of Knockout Smith in the sale ring, waiting for Shannon with his bidding man, was enough to make a potential buyer turn for the door. A few bookies were ringside, giving 6/4 about Smith taking the horse home. Not even the weight of money behind Ossie Porter, or the combined heft of lawyers and bankers, was enough to persuade anyone that W. J. Smith would be outdone. Maurice Grogan was locked and loaded. He had been given a blank cheque to buy Shannon, and he wasn't worried about the speed of the sale, the number of bids or how high Ossie Porter might push him. He sat, with Smith, alongside Reg Inglis's platform as the clock ticked towards 3 pm.

The crowd was lively, chatting furiously about the sale, watching the newsreel cameras placed at pivotal positions around the ring. Each person had paid two shillings to attend the event, with proceeds going to the Food For Britain cause. They clutched small sale booklets, with 'Shannon' etched in blue across the cover. Inside, photographs of Shannon's race finishes sat next to text on his pedigree, his race record giving a 'convincing testimony of his class and versatility'. 'Although Shannon has started in comparatively few races,' the spiel went, 'consensus of opinion is that he has proved one of the greatest horses Australia has produced.'

The horse arrived at Newmarket at 2 pm. Barney O'Brien had been working on him all morning, buffing his coat until it was brassier than a handrail at Town Hall, even be it the middle of winter. O'Brien had polished Shannon's feet, pulled his mane and brushed it until it hung, not a strand out of place, long down the off side of his neck. When it had come time to leave Bowral Street, the moment had not been lost on the old strapper. He had taken a deep breath, stifling the sadness that had welled at leaving his racing home. Henderson's stable lads came to give them a cheerio, showering Shannon with pats. O'Brien had led his friend out of his blue stable for the last time.

At the commotion and excitement at Newmarket, Shannon grew hot and bothered. Thousands of strange faces peered at him. For 40 minutes he was led in and out of his stable, paraded up and down for registered bidders. Juan Ysmael, president of the Philippines Racehorse Owners Association, was one of them. Ysmael was in Australia on a postwar purchasing mission to replenish Philippine racing stock. He had made several purchases, but conceded Shannon was out of his budget. Azzalin Romano suspected the same thing. Bernborough's dazzling former owner took a good look at Shannon as a *Sun* journalist scribbled nearby. 'Mr Romano was wearing a brown striped suit with brown hat and figured tie,' the reporter wrote. 'Shannon was wearing a blue and white bath towel.'

At 2.40 pm O'Brien called a halt to it, insisting he needed time to clean his horse up. As people flocked to the ring to get any available vantage, the strapper worked on Shannon's neck with a dry cloth, rubbing and polishing the anxiety out of his coat. By the time 3 pm ticked around, Shannon looked magnificent again.

Barney O'Brien led him through Newmarket towards the sale ring, following the sound of Reg Inglis hushing the crowd. As Inglis began to recite an introduction, Shannon was hustled through a thick throng of people into the ring. They fell so quickly across the path behind him that he broke into a startled trot, and then stopped in the ring, absorbing the few thousand that encircled him, cross-legged on the grass at his feet and swinging off the famous fig. There were bodies everywhere, cameras and amplifiers broadcasting the event live on national radio. He stood and looked at it all until a confident tug from O'Brien walked him on.

The horse looked sensational. His extraordinary forehand was there for all to see: a perfect shoulder setting, long and muscly to forelegs as straight as organ flutes. His neck was so curved and neat

he could have been a dressage horse, and though he was obviously
stressed he strode along beside O'Brien, unquestioning. Even when
Inglis's introduction droned on for 10 minutes, reciting Shannon's
pedigree, his record, pitching the champion as if he were new to
these shores, the horse walked on in his small circle, pausing only
every so often to have a good look at the business. Inglis was quick
to pay tribute to O'Brien.

The auctioneer boomed, 'never in history . . . well I won't
say never, but almost never has a similar transaction taken place.'
Inglis worked hard to propel the uniqueness of the occasion on the
crowd, and then he was ready for bids. 'He will be sold, gentlemen.'

Darby Munro sucked on a pipe near Ossie Porter, Bert Riddle
and Felix Finn in the rostrum with Reg Inglis. Just about every
racing identity in Sydney was buried in the crowd. Inglis opened
the floor and bookmaker William McDonald shot the first bid –
10,000 guineas. The auctioneer pointed his gavel at McDonald.
'I have 10,000.'

Immediately, a curious fellow near the podium chimed in
with 15,000. But Inglis didn't hear him. Maurice McCarten piped
up with 20,000 guineas.

'I have 20,000 now, 20,000 guineas.' A mumble of surprise
rippled through the ring at what seemed like a doubling of the
price. And then the mystery bidder called 25,000.

'Twenty-five thousand,' Inglis called. Then, cool as he liked,
Maurice Grogan yelled 26,000 for W. J. Smith. Excited silence fell
over proceedings.

'I've got 26,000 for Shannon.' Inglis's voice had climbed
higher. 'I've got 26,000 guineas, 26,000 for Shannon. He's the
greatest horse I've ever had the pleasure in my history of selling.
Gentlemen, any rich man'll live forever if he owns him! Twenty-
six thousand guineas. Once. He's a sire when he's done racing. I'll
take 500.'

The mystery bidder looked to the man beside him who
shook his head. They were out. Ossie Porter was mute with disbelief; the price had rocketed over him. William McDonald was

out, Maurice McCarten had already gone over his budget. Even Azzalin Romano, who had purchased Shannon's full brother some months before, wouldn't meet that money. Maurice Grogan's bid stood.

'Come on gentlemen, I've gotta give you a bit of time,' Reg Inglis yelled. 'Twenty-six thousand . . . Twenty-six thousand *once*! *Twice*!' He raised his gavel, took one last look around. 'Last time, gets you on the other side.' The crowd was silent.

'Done!'

He cracked the gavel on the podium and Peter Riddle's horse was sold, to W. J. Smith for the highest price ever paid at auction for an Australian thoroughbred.

Shannon slipped out of the ring and the crowd began to absorb the sale. It had lasted just 75 seconds. Bidding had reached 20,000 guineas in less than 20 seconds, while Inglis had held Grogan's bid of 26,000 (£27,300) for nearly a minute. William McDonald had been taking bets of 100/1 that the price would be closer to 30,000 guineas than his opening call of 10,000. Still, he maintained after the sale that he had been a serious buyer.

The mystery bidder became one of the most talked about elements of the sale. Who was this man? Darby Munro didn't recognise him. Reg Inglis knew him only as a bidder who had filed his interest at the office a few days before, and who had requested an inspection of Shannon at Bowral Street. No one in racing knew who he was, and in the following days he led the Sydney press on a wild goose chase.

He was, in fact, Lewin Wiles, a taxi driver from Neutral Bay. Reporters clamoured at his home on Clarke Road, his children fielding questions through the windows. Eventually, Wiles revealed to the Sydney *Herald* that he was bidding for a third party. 'I did not bid for myself,' he confessed. 'I'm a taxi driver. I could not have afforded to bid for a horse like Shannon.'

Knockout Smith could well afford it. Maurice Grogan had told his employer before the sale that he'd have to 'touch his kick' to get the horse, and Smith had instructed Grogan that he only stop bidding for Shannon when he, Smith, put his hat on. Smith didn't bring his hat to the sale that day, as good as telling his friend to buy the horse, no matter the price. 'I don't know how deep Mr Smith's pockets are, but I knew he'd take some bowling,' Grogan said. 'Shannon must be a good buy at the price paid today. But he's not a cheap horse at 26,000 guineas. That's big money for a horse in any country.'

Smith made his way from the sale ring towards Shannon's box, swamped with congratulatory pats and handshakes. By the time he reached his horse, he was annoyed by the scrum, though he worked hard to hide it. He had fielded questions from every angle: was he going to race Shannon in the Epsom, had he bought the horse for Bing Crosby? One old codger, introducing himself as a retired worker from the 'bots', asked for his autograph. When he finally reached his horse, Smith posed for photographs. Barney O'Brien had hosed Shannon off in the dock, and the horse stood dripping beside his new owner, Smith even taking the reins to stare at what so much money had got him. He assured O'Brien that the strapper would continue to look after Shannon, that racing's famous partnership would not be separated.

The immediate plans for Shannon told that the horse would move into the yard of Frank Dalton, one of Randwick's foremost big-string trainers. Dalton kept an elaborate set-up on Bradley Street, which ran behind Wansey Road on the east end of the racecourse, near the mile chute. At first, Dalton was very reluctant to accept Shannon. He thought he was on a hiding to nothing taking on such a famous animal. 'If I take him and he gets beat, they'll say I ruined him,' he told Smith. 'If he continues to win, I'll get no credit 'cos they'll say any mug could have trained him.' But Smith was used to getting his way, and Frank Dalton was his first-call trainer. So it was agreed: Shannon would go to Dalton. 'All I can say is that the horse will race in Australia this year,' Smith told the press after announcing Dalton trainer. 'After that, I have made no plans.'

Reg Inglis had continued selling after Shannon. Quarter

sheets, hoods, bits, halters, a saddle – more than 100 items from Peter Riddle's tack room – were auctioned for £139. Not an hour after the sale, Barney O'Brien led Jerry up the ramp of an idling horse float, loading for the short trip to Bradley Street. It had been a long, affecting day, and evening was just blanketing Randwick when the pair walked into Dalton's yard. Neither horse nor strapper knew much about the highway ahead. Comforting certainty had died with the Peter Riddle part of their lives.

32

'I would not like to guess what he can do'

Frank Dalton's stables had the feel of Bowral Street, a working yard crisp with the smell of dry hay and molasses. But it was a different place. It had a red brick stable house with pitched roof and sliding, barn-like doors. The apprentices and stable lads lived in the loft. There was a sand roll, pot plants and swept concrete, a tightly mowed patch of grass outside the stable block. It was a rich, orderly place, the kind of yard run by a no-nonsense, austere sort of fellow.

Frank Dalton was that man. He had a stiff upper lip, was straighter than straight and less raffish than many in the training ranks. He didn't say much, was cut from the cloth of old Australia when men were of few words. He had small, deep-set eyes and a face weathered and beaten like a coastal fence post. He would stroll about with a cigarette in his mouth, serious and succinct, as if he was troubled by something. In fact, his lot was pretty good. Dalton was one of the most established trainers at Randwick, boasting among his clients the likes of W. J. Smith and the starchy AJC chairman Alan Potter.

He lived across the road from his yard, in a rented flat at 15A Bradley Street. He'd been there since 1940 (though he had been training much longer than that, hacking up from the pony scene). When he had first moved into the little dead-end street behind Wansey Road, Dalton had only a handful of horses in his charge. By 1947 he had 20, with a collective worth of £45,000. When Shannon moved in on 20 August, that figure burst its banks. The Midstream horse was the most high-profile animal Frank Dalton had ever handled, and only the creases on his seasoned face disguised his nerves at how the six-year-old might settle in.

Shannon was moved into the Dalton routine as quickly as possible. Though he had been jittery the day of his arrival, had to be coaxed right into his new box, he had settled down like the even-tempered animal he had always been. Dalton, unfamiliar with the horse, had worried no end through the first night. The trainer slipped down to the yard well before the birds the following morning to check on his new horse, relieved then to find that Shannon had not only slept, he had licked up every oat and chaff morsel in his manger. The horse slid into the string on Monday morning, following his new stablemates onto the racecourse for early morning work. With Barney O'Brien up, the big team left Bradley Street towards Alison Road, across Wansey Road and onto the course through a gate that brought them close to the mile chute. Dalton asked only light work of Shannon in those first few days, a jaunty circuit of the course, an easy canter in even time (15 seconds to the furlong). Clockers watched and waited for news of the horse's spring program.

Smith and Dalton had conferred on this the night after the sale, agreeing only two things: Shannon would race in Australia that season, and he would not contest the Epsom. The horse had been given an epic 10 st 5 lbs for the big mile, and it made no sense to point him at that race. 'We have a very valuable horse to consider,' Dalton told the press, 'and in my opinion there is a risk in him in an Epsom Handicap with that weight, a risk that should not be taken.' The trainer suggested to Smith that Shannon should be kept within the weight-for-age ranks, and he was pleased that the owner concurred. When questioned about the betting implications of Shannon's withdrawal from the Epsom, Dalton was curt. 'Betting is not the consideration that worries Mr Smith or myself.'

On Friday morning, 22 August, as Shannon wound down in the scraping sheds at the track, Dalton held conference with Darby Munro and his stable jockey Jack Thompson, who had served his apprenticeship at Bradley Street and who had been loyal to Dalton's operation since 1936. Speculation had circulated that the Demon Darb would be dumped from Shannon in favour of

Thompson, but it seemed a poor idea to the trainer. Munro knew Shannon, rode him as coolly and softly as if he were his own, and he knew how to squeeze the best out of him. Munro had never ridden Shannon with spurs (Riddle didn't allow it), and Dalton had already gauged that the horse was intelligent and sensitive. A change of jockey might sour him, and Jack Thompson took it with good humour that Munro would be retained.

The horse settled and grew confident with every morning that passed. He had been spared any hard work since the King's Cup of 1946, so blowing away the cobwebs would take a while. A week after the sale, Dalton popped the question, asking Barney O'Brien to gallop Shannon from the half-mile to the winning post on Randwick's new stretch of surface, the 'screenings'.

The screenings had been laid over the tan track in February 1946. Made of blue metal shavings ground into a fine dust-like compound, the surface was laid over the full width of the tan to a depth of four inches. Graded, rolled and watered, it had proved spongy underfoot with plenty of give, eased concussion for fast work, and had first been a hit at Warwick Farm. The morning of Shannon's half-mile, it wove its magic. Setting off at an even pace, Shannon worked into a good clip approaching the half-mile. O'Brien opened him up passing that post, and Shannon swept full pelt through the first furlongs in 12 seconds. He clocked two in 23½, three in 35¼, and the total distance in 47¾, which was the fastest half-mile ever clocked on that track. His sectionals read 12 seconds, 11½ seconds, 12¼ seconds, and 12 seconds. It was a clattering gallop that had *Sun* clocker Jack Charles agog.

The trial set Dalton's, and Smith's, hopes on their merry way. Shannon would debut for them in the Warwick Stakes on 30 August, and the gallop told them the horse was as sharp as his old days. Munro, too, had expressed a similar opinion, climbing aboard the champion for a few hit-outs in the 10 days after the sale. Barney O'Brien was less enthusiastic. Peter Riddle had taken months to restore Shannon after his spells, patient, grinding work over weeks and weeks, and the strapper worried that Dalton had tried to do it in just 10 days. Though the papers bleated Shannon 'as good as ever', O'Brien didn't share their optimism.

The Warwick Stakes was a traditional debut race for horses in the new season, a weight-for-age event with allowances over a little further than seven furlongs. Shannon would run into some old foes: Victory Lad was nominated, as was the sensational Epsom winner Blue Legend. Both had races under their belts already, though at level weights they weren't given a chance against Shannon. Smith's new horse was 3/1 on in the betting, 11/2 Victory Lad. It was confident backing, given the horse had not raced in almost a year.

Around the paddock, people gazed at Shannon as he paraded for the Warwick Stakes. He cut a spiffy picture, neatly turned out and healthy, not much condition about him. When Darby Munro strode out, a small cheer broke over the crowd. He was kitted out in W. J. Smith's familiar colours, orange and white bars, black cap. Jockey up, Shannon looked a different horse. People knew him in Riddle's blue and black halves, and new silks were like a new haircut: they changed his identity. Yet to Munro, Shannon was the old Jerry from Bowral Street, and he trotted the six-year-old onto the course proper.

The false rail was out, accounting for the race's seven furlongs 19⅔ yards. When they jumped, outsiders Prince Consort and Shading leaped into a cracking lead. They blitzed the first two furlongs in 24 seconds, the three in 36¼, and the half-mile in a cool 47½. Munro made an odd decision to track them, leaving the rest of the field behind. For the first part of the race, therefore, Shannon did a lot of work, towing the more fancied runners along behind him.

Straightening for home, Shannon moved up on the tiring pacemakers. At the Leger, he took a run between them, inside Prince Consort and outside Shading on the rails. Searching for the old dash, Munro drew his whip and gave Shannon a short crack, but at the same time Prince Consort, wobbling on tired feet, veered in. For the first time in his career, Shannon was sour at being crowded, and he gave Munro the shock of his life when he swung his nose around to take a chunk out of Prince Consort's chest. The two horses collided, their jockeys scrambling to correct their courses. Munro dropped his whip in the scrimmage. On the outside, Victory Lad took full advantage of the scrum and he blasted past the pair into the lead. At the winning post he was a length ahead of Shannon, with Prince Consort a half-neck for third.

The Sydney racing scene was stunned. Only a few had seen Shannon throw the race away by savaging the other runner, and they didn't learn about it until J. B. Donohue, chief steward, inquired into the events. A few angry patrons hooted at Munro as he trotted back in. 'Wake up Munro!' But Shannon was wet with sweat, plain as day not fit enough to win a sprint in 1:25¼. It was exactly what Barney O'Brien had feared. The papers went to town. 'Shannon sensation: beaten in first run for his new owner.' That was the front-page headline for the *Sun* that afternoon, while every paper in the land digested the defeat well into the following week. In Adelaide, the *Mail* tried to be forgiving: 'It was not the first time the Warwick Stakes has caused a major upset, because Amounis beat Phar Lap in this event. Taking a line from that, there is still hope for Shannon to prove worth the big sum Mr Smith gave him for him.'

Frank Dalton didn't see it that way. 'He's not the first good horse to be beaten when not fully wound up,' he said. He added there was no need to panic. W. J. Smith laughed off suggestions that he might regret his fabulous purchase. 'It was just a question of a good horse not being quite fit enough.' Darby Munro, who knew Shannon too well, was baffled. The six-year-old had pinged from his number-five barrier very smartly, had raced right on the pace with his fresh racing legs. Usually a moderate beginner who summoned speed in the last bit, Shannon had run the Warwick Stakes upside down. Victory Lad had taken advantage of that, but Munro believed it was only a partial excuse. Shannon had been beaten on his merits.

Barney O'Brien was defensive for his friend, believing that the sale had had more of an effect on Shannon than had been realised. He felt the interruption to the horse's training was significant, as he was a bigger animal now, a full year older than his last preparation. He hadn't been galloped as much as was necessary for normal training. 'My job was to get Shannon to the sale ring without a mark or blemish on him,' O'Brien said. 'It was not my job to take risks by galloping him. But for all that I thought his class would carry him through Saturday's race.' In a way, O'Brien felt he had failed his horse.

Frank Dalton went back to basics after the race. He stifled his fears that he was handling Shannon incorrectly and, conferring with Darby Munro, he decided that fitness was the only issue. The bay was eating and sleeping well, seemed settled in his new surroundings, and even O'Brien piped up that Shannon could be a lazy horse. If Dalton wanted him ready for the AJC spring meeting the first week of October, the trainer would have to open the pipes in the mornings, which is exactly what he did.

On 3 September, a little after sunrise, Shannon set off for a circuit of the screenings. Clockers watched him canter at his leisure under his strapper, and after a full circle he picked up and shot away at the five pole. Sprinting wide, he rubbed off the outside fence at one point, but steamed through the distance in 1:00¾. It was an amazing time, bump and all, and O'Brien rode on a light rein into the finish. The strapper had hardly moved. The previous day Shannon had gone with Darby Munro over six furlongs in 1:16¼. It was the fastest time of the morning, and jumping off Darb had professed to Dalton, 'He won't be beaten again this spring.'

—

To the surprise of many, Shannon was declared for the Canterbury Stakes on 6 September, backing up seven days after the Warwick Stakes. It was a big call on Dalton's behalf, who believed that a race would improve the horse more than a long string of gallops into the Chelmsford Stakes, due to be run on 13 September. The Chelmsford had been the obvious next choice for the Midstream stallion, a weight-for-age event with penalties and allowances. But the weights were not favourable to Shannon. He had been allotted 9 st 11 lbs, while the boom three-year-old Temeraire, undefeated that season, had slipped in with 8 st 2 lbs. Dalton had no intention of running his horse three weeks in a row, so with the Canterbury start confirmed, he nominated for the Hill Stakes as the next port, which Shannon had won in 1945. It would occur a fortnight after the Canterbury race, and would be the horse's final prep before the AJC meeting.

Shannon had trialled at Canterbury racecourse, but he had never raced there. On Saturday morning, he stepped into a horse float and motored to the inner west Sydney track. It was a small course, under the governance of the STC. It was a plain place too, hardly as spectacular as Randwick and Rosehill. Its turns were tight and its straight narrow, and it suited horses against the fence. Over six furlongs, the Canterbury Stakes would jump from the chute, so Shannon would have a long, sweeping turn to swing through before the straight.

It was a dry, snappish September day. A healthy crowd showed up to watch the races, in part because Temeraire was contesting the Guineas. Only six horses paraded for Shannon's race, but the field was good. Victory Lad was on equal weights with Shannon, while Russia, who had won the 1946 Melbourne Cup under Darby Munro, was also in, though first-up. Deep Sea, under Eddie Fordyce, had a significant pull in the weights with 8 st to Shannon's 9 st 2 lbs, but most thought he would set the pace. Betting on a one-two basis, bookies had Shannon and Victory Lad all the way.

Shannon left the barriers first in a perfect start, pinging into the lead before Munro hit the brakes. He wasn't going to make the same mistake twice. He let Deep Sea steal around his outside to lead out of the chute, and Victory Lad settled third behind him. Down the back, the order didn't change as they swung into the long turn for home.

Deep Sea made a move as they straightened, carrying Shannon until they were four lengths clear of Victory Lad. At the Leger, Munro shook up his horse, and Shannon switched out, overhauling the leader with whimsical precision. With his nose well in front, he turned off, falling asleep for a moment in Munro's hands. But the jockey woke him with a sharp crack and Shannon burst away again. Crossing the line he was hard held by Munro, three-quarters of a length clear of Deep Sea, who had Victory Lad by a neck.

The win was efficient and painless and soft. Shannon didn't turn a hair, returning to scale a much harder animal than had gone out for the Warwick Stakes the week before. The time was 1:13½, two and a quarter seconds outside the distance record set by Beaulivre in 1940, but everyone was smiling. Shannon was back on top. The purse was worth £810. It brought the horse's winnings to £17,354 and 10 shillings, with 13 wins from 23 starts (six times second, only four times unplaced). Dalton was relieved, Smith vindicated, and the papers rolled out predictable spiel: 'Back on his pedestal', 'Shannon is back in the good books.'

Dalton was making headway with the Midstream horse. Shannon had been chased into the Canterbury meeting, but his tractability had come out on top. Many had suggested that he had grown sour from his stable change, which might have explained his crankiness in the Warwick Stakes. The truth was that Shannon was a six-year-old entire, within his rights to be distracted and brutish as stallions of his age often are. It was only good manners on the horse's part that had him still in heavy training at his age, and he had a tight season ahead of him if all went to plan. Shannon was due to run next in the Hill Stakes on 20 September, followed by the George Main and Craven Plate during the AJC meeting, and Dalton had also nominated for the Linlithgow at the VRC meeting on 6 November. But plans began to unravel.

Ten or so days after the Canterbury meeting, Shannon trotted off the course proper at Randwick after a searching six furlongs, clocking the best time of the morning. He took a tentative step under Barney O'Brien on the way to the scraping sheds, like he had hurt himself, and when the strapper inspected things he found Shannon had split his near-fore heel. Dalton called track veterinarian Roy Stewart for a closer look.

Stewart thought the wound shallow enough that it must have been caused at low speed, probably by treading on a nail or a sharp piece of stone on the way from the track. The object had driven between the frog and hoof wall, though it had fallen out by the time the men inspected the injury. Shannon was only a tad lame, and he didn't mind having the foot poked and prodded. Dalton called in his farrier to cut away some of the heel, and they fitted a bar shoe to take the horse's weight off it. It was a standard injury in thoroughbreds, and Dalton told the press he wasn't worried in the slightest. 'He's not a brittle-footed horse, and there was nothing in the condition of the track to cause the injury. It's just one of those things that can happen to a horse at any time.' Nevertheless, after inspecting Shannon with W. J. Smith the morning after, Dalton scratched from that weekend's Hill Stakes. 'There are plenty of races for him to contest during the spring,' he told the papers, 'and though it's only a precautionary act, unless I am completely satisfied with his condition he will not run at Rosehill.'

The scratching meant that Shannon would lay over until the George Main Stakes on 6 October. It was a long run between races – a month – but it couldn't be helped. O'Brien knew that when Shannon peaked in fitness, he held on to it, so the strapper put it on himself to keep the horse fit. For the first few days, the pair exercised at Bradley Street only, but by the Friday Shannon was ready to work. Over the following week he resumed galloping over Randwick, but Dalton thought that a race-day hit-out would sharpen him up. He lodged a request with the STC to gallop Shannon between races at Rosehill on 27 September. Permission granted, Sydney racing readied for an exciting exhibition at the west Sydney track.

The meeting was Hawkesbury Race Club's spring event, and Shannon's cameo put a few extra tickets through the turnstiles. It would occur at about 3.20 pm, between the Quality and Grand handicaps. When Shannon appeared in the paddock to warm up, patrons flocked from the betting enclosure to watch him. Some were even surprised when Jack Thompson, decked out in Knockout Smith's orange and white silks, stepped up to the springboard. Darby Munro was riding in Melbourne, so Dalton's number-one hoop took the reins.

The trainer watched closely as the pair trotted onto the course proper. Shannon had bar shoes on both fore feet and a small white boot over his injured heel. The bar shoes had been specifically designed for him; the bar running across the heel was much smaller than conventional bar shoes. He carried 7 st 9 lbs in his saddle, which was a featherweight for him. He was to begin from the seven furlongs, cantering until he passed the six where he was to go top speed. Dalton had instructed Thompson to make it count. 'Whether Shannon breaks the track record or not, the public will see a first-class exhibition of galloping,' the trainer said. 'If he can break the record, so much the better.'

Shannon felt fit and springy under Jack Thompson; he hadn't lost any of his hardness. Thompson was leading the jockeys' premiership that year (he had won it multiple times), but this was the first time he had sat on the champion. He was impressed. He pressed for a gallop from the six furlongs. They ran two or three horse-widths off the rail, and skipped through the first three furlongs in 35¾ seconds. Shannon was stretching out like a greyhound, the stride so easy for him it was like he did it in his sleep. Straightening for the winning post, with Rosehill cheering the spectacle, he clattered through the final three in 35½. At 1:11¼ for the full six, Shannon blitzed the track record by a quarter-second.

When the time was known, Rosehill patrons were surprised. Few had thought the horse was travelling that quickly, so easy was his action. When Thompson brought Shannon back in, he was wondrous as he jumped off. 'He's an amazing galloper,' he said to Dalton as he slipped the girth and dragged the saddle off. 'I would not like to guess what he can do.'

A few men in the judge's box had also timed the gallop, and their watches read an even quicker time. Jack Thompson recalled the effort. 'After I had turned into the straight I clicked my tongue to him and he bounded away so smartly that I had to grab hold of him before he went too fast.' Dalton was ecstatic at the trial, though few knew it, austere as ever in the enclosure. He followed the horse back to the stalls, checked the heel and found it was still in one piece. Shannon was some sort of remarkable, he thought, turning over these times with heavier shoes, an interrupted prep and half a hoof.

The champion rattled back to Bradley Street later that afternoon. He wouldn't race again until the George Main Stakes in two weeks' time, with the Craven Plate two days later. It was a stop-start preparation, one less than ideal for a horse at this level of the game. But the Dawson camp had a long spring ahead for Shannon, the trip to Melbourne would carry him well into November. There wasn't much chatter about it, the papers only casually mentioning that Shannon might clash with the Victorian champion Attley. It was like everyone knew something was afoot.

33

A matter of black and white

The game was different in the spring of 1947. Bernborough was gone, Flight retired. The great mare had gone out in the Autumn Stakes in April, and the turf was quieter without her, and less competitive. The weight-for-age ranks were slim, only a spattering of horses vying for top gun. Still, it was a surprise when it looked like Shannon might have a walkover in the George Main Stakes. No one was stepping up to take him on.

Acceptances for the race had to be in by Saturday night, and two of the assumed runners, Victory Lad and Puffham, had run in the Epsom on Derby Day. Neither had won it, Puffham scraping home last in the rich mile. The performances of both horses were abysmal enough that it was questionable if they should press on. But the George Main was a useful race for place money, so both declared. Three horses would go to post for the race. Shannon's old sparring partner, Victory Lad, would also take him on.

The two horses had been crossing paths since Shannon's very first outing when he went down to Victory Lad in the Breeders' Plate. The horse had not beaten him again until the Warwick Stakes, but he'd always been there, shadowing Shannon's career like a hungry deputy. Victory Lad had won more than £13,000 in prizemoney, racing and winning in Sydney, Brisbane and Melbourne. Like Shannon, he was a cheap graduate from the class of 1943, had paid himself off in jig time.

He came into the George Main in good enough form, commanding 7/2 in the betting. Shannon had disposed of him in the Canterbury, but Victory Lad's owner was an optimistic fellow. He bet on his horse every time he went around, and could never understand why he always got a good price. Nevertheless, the satcheleers didn't want to know. Shannon had run a record six furlongs at Rosebery on Saturday morning, and was 4/1 on to claim the George Main for the second year in a row. He had equal weight of 9 st 3 lbs with Victory Lad, while Puffham, a seven-year-old gelding, carried 9 st.

When the three horses entered the paddock, people clung to the rails to see Shannon. It was an uninteresting betting race, particularly as the Metropolitan was next, but racegoers loved the Randwick horse, cheered his every move. There were 61,000 of them packing the stands and the Flat, and Shannon strolled around in saddlecloth two until it was time for Darby Munro. The pair cantered to the mile chute like it was any old track gallop.

Down in the ring, punters were adjusting to the new betting boards and multicoloured umbrellas that had been set up for the 100 paddock bookmakers. They had been a long time coming, debuting on Derby Day. Now they were chalked with odds for the George Main. Their presence had drawn bets away from the total-isator, as paddock punters could now clearly see the prices from the fielders. Tote investments were down £40,000 that day, but Randwick's tote manager, Fred Wilkinson, disputed it was because of the betting boards. 'It's the time factor, and not bookmaker competition,' he said.

Due to the small field, much betting on the George Main occurred on the one-two basis. Shannon remained a prohibitive odds on. He had drawn the rail in the three-horse field, Puffham in the middle and Victory Lad on the outside. The track was firm, and Gaxieu sent them from the barrier stalls at 2.25 pm.

Victory Lad was slow away as Shannon and Puffham jumped clear. Munro took hold of Shannon leaving the chute, allowing the other horse to clip along down the back of the course. It was a fetching gallop, leaving the first two furlongs in 24½, the half-mile in 49½. Bowling along towards the final turn, Puffham led Shannon by a length, Victory Lad another two behind. As they straightened, Munro sent his mount around Puffham, and Shannon flicked his pacemaker as if he were a fly on his shoulder. He leaped to such an easy lead that Munro sat back on him with half a furlong to go. The winning post drew close, closer still, and Shannon wound down. Suddenly Victory Lad burst onto his flanks. Billy Briscoe had driven him furiously from the Leger, and for the split of a second, Munro was panicked. But the winning post came and they were over it. Shannon won the George Main by a half-neck.

The sigh of relief over Randwick caused a small southerly. Munro had got away with it, but only just. The stewards didn't call for the photo-finish camera, though several in the crowd did. Nevertheless, the Demon Darb was hauled into the dock. 'If I had hit him with the whip near the post he would have jumped away again and won by a length,' he told chief steward J. B. Donohue. 'I was amazed when Victory Lad swooped and got so close.' The stipes were not impressed, insisted that it was negligent riding of an odds-on favourite. They slapped a £20 fine on Munro, and warned him that next time they wouldn't be so kind.

In the enclosure, Smith looked on as his horse wound down. He had a curious expression on his face, a cocktail of relief and bemusement. 'I don't attach too much blame to Munro for that ride,' he said. 'Shannon has a big programme ahead of him and Munro was told not to use him up in the Main anymore than was necessary. I did get a shock when they came so close to defeat though, because obviously he would have won by a number of lengths had he been ridden out all the way in the straight.' The *Sun* had a similar view. Its trackman believed that Shannon, who had run the race in 1:36½, would have at least equalled his own mile record if he had been ridden out in the straight.

Without knowing the sectionals of the race, or hearing Munro's explanation to the stipes, many racegoers thought Shannon was below par. The horse was led off the course immediately after the race, Barney O'Brien cooling him off at Bradley Street instead of the stalls, leading to a wild rumour that he had broken down. It was only squashed when Frank Dalton assured the press that Shannon was fine, and the afternoon dailies did the rest. Later on, the owner and trainer conferred at the stables about

Shannon's trip to Melbourne. They agreed that, all going well after the Craven Plate, the champion would probably ship to the southern city on Sunday.

—

W. J. Smith had a lot of money to recoup on Shannon. The George Main and Canterbury wins, plus the showing in the Warwick Stakes, had returned him £2103 on a £27,000 price tag. Logic told the businessman that he wouldn't earn back his outlay via the racetrack, even if Shannon won all his starts into the autumn of 1948. The only way he could hope to balance the ledger was through stud fees.

At St Aubin's that season, Smith stood four stallions. Heading his roster was the exciting Manitoba, leading sire in Australia for season 1944–45. He was an imported horse, as demanded the cluttered ranks of the sire table. Even at 250 guineas a serve, as expensive as any stallion in the land, his book was full. In boxes nearby were Beau Son, a son of Beau Pere, and Derby winner Hua, both 120 guineas. Whipping in the list was The Jeep, an average son of Manitoba at 80 guineas.

There was room for Shannon at St Aubin's. He was the best horse going around in Australia, had revealed remarkable tractability and brilliance. He was faster than a bad cheque, too. The problem was that he was no guarantee as a sire, and there wouldn't be a shortage of Midstreams entering stud. Idle Words, too, had had two useful sons since Shannon, both full brothers to the champion. They would be attractive and cheaper options for local breeders.

The good stallions covered 20 to 40 mares in a season, and if Shannon entered St Aubin's at 250 guineas, he might return 10,000 guineas in his debut season. It was a big figure, one that could grow with progeny sales from Smith's own mares. All going right then, Shannon would recoup his price in three or four years. But to command a high fee at stud, and to keep it, he had to win big for Smith (who had opted to keep him racing) and prove an outstanding stallion down the line. If he did neither, he could slide into quick obscurity. For Smith, the horse's future was therefore a business decision, a matter of black and white. He would delay it as long as Shannon kept winning.

—

Wednesday's Craven Plate was the second, last race of Sydney's spring meeting, the traditional weight-for-age championship for Sydney horses. But every year it suffered in numbers, mostly because the good horses headed south after Derby Day, and 1947 was no different. Only five horses nominated for the race, by declarations only three stood. They were Russia, Columnist and Shannon.

Russia was the Melbourne Cup hero. He had come back to racing in Shannon's Canterbury Stakes, lugging home at the back of the field. But over six furlongs, that race had been a prep gallop for him, nothing more. At his next start he had won the Colin Stephen Stakes at Randwick (in a dead heat), bringing him nicely into the Craven Plate. He had trained for this race, his owner deciding back in August that he wouldn't try for the cup handicaps in Melbourne; he would keep him in the weight-for-age corral. Columnist, too, was on song. A five-year-old chestnut, he had won or placed in his previous three outings in Sydney. He was interestingly bred, by the French import Genetout, who W. J. Smith had brought to St Aubin's in 1938. He also edged Russia in the Craven betting, 9/2 against Russia's 8/1. Shannon edged them both at odds on.

It was a cool spring day over Randwick when the three horses cantered to the 10-furlong chute, a shade off 3.30 pm. A strong wind was blowing down the backstretch. Darby Munro was steely, the black cap of Smith's colours low over his eyes, Shannon shifting under him. It was Munro's third ride that day, none a winner yet. He had found the track holding after a shower of rain early in the morning, drying quickly with the wind that was whipping. Jack Thompson was nearby aboard Russia, George Weate on Columnist. The three stood quietly for Gaxieu, Columnist on the rails, Shannon sandwiched and Russia on the outside.

The tapes flew up, a cheer rose and the three horses lifted into a gallop. Columnist broke the line first, hugging his rails spot with Shannon on his flanks. Behind them, Russia sat back, allowing the pair to tow him into the backstretch. It was a clever move by his jockey. As the front horses ploughed on, they broke the headwind for the Melbourne Cup winner crouching behind them.

Shannon was going kindly, stretching out as he always did. He had found his stride, and as they leaned into the second turn he moved up on Columnist. At the half-mile he was on terms with the leader, but it hadn't come easy to him. Munro sensed an emptiness in Shannon, a failure to kick into those top gears he possessed. Darb was concerned, and drew his whip. He had never hit Shannon so early in a race, and though the horse lifted, it wasn't with any usual brilliance. He was scrubbing along as they bent into the straight, so Munro kept at him. Shannon slowly picked away at Columnist, and past the Leger he had pulled clear by a length. But Columnist was coming again, finding something inside the final furlong. The grandstands rose at the tussle.

Munro was riding for his worth, and Shannon held Columnist. But Russia had sat in the slipstream of the battle, and he came at the pair with fresh legs. He quickened around them, bursting into the middle of the track full of running. Shannon had nothing, nor Columnist. Russia plunged over the line a half-neck clear, and Shannon was beaten.

It would go down as one of Randwick's great competitions, but in the seconds after the Craven Plate, dumb shock spoke loudest. How had a stayer out-sped the fastest horse in the country, especially since that stayer had been running for place money? Russia's trainer, Frank McGrath Jr, had given his horse little more than hope of collecting third place, let alone flicking Shannon into second. Russia's owner, the sporting Gordon Leeds, gave Barney

O'Brien a slap on the shoulder before he left the enclosure. 'I knocked you Barney,' he said, 'but Shannon is not the first good one Russia has knocked.' O'Brien was gracious.

'There were no excuses Mr Leeds,' he replied. 'The best horse won, but the three of them put up a great effort.'

Munro couldn't explain it, had nothing to offer by way of excuses. Shannon had run empty. It happened, but it was a surprise to him that it had happened to this horse. He told the press there was no doubt Shannon was fit, but when a reporter asked him to comment on Shannon's condition against his condition in previous years under Peter Riddle, he refused to say anything. It was perhaps the greatest clue that Darby Munro believed the Dalton operation hadn't figured Shannon out.

Smith was very disappointed, his expression taut and serious in the paddock. A loss wasn't just a loss when it came to Shannon; it was an expensive dent in a plan to make back some money. He said little to the press after the race, hinting only that Shannon's Melbourne plans were now in doubt. In fact, Smith had no intention of pressing on with the six-year-old. He was far too good a businessman for that. Almost immediately, before he had even left the paddock that afternoon, the big man made a decision that changed Shannon's life.

'SHANNON TO LEAVE SOON FOR U.S.; NO MORE RACING HERE.' The front page of the *Sydney Morning Herald* splashed the news to the harbour city the following morning.

The decision was so quick that it stank of the bottom dollar. W. J. Smith announced he would be sending Shannon to America in less than a fortnight, to race, he said, in his own colours. It was hardly a surprise. In the past, Smith had paid big money for Beau Pere and Ajax, hawking both to the United States. There was no question of Dalton going with the horse, so unless Barney O'Brien took up a trainer's licence, Shannon would go into the barn of an American trainer. The *Herald* reported that O'Brien had been offered the chance to 'continue his association with Shannon', but the conditions of the association were cloudy. Did it mean O'Brien would train the horse, or continue to strap him on foreign shores? As the hours passed after the announcement, the whole thing became confusing.

Though Smith declared he would be racing Shannon in his name, he made no venture to Darby Munro to accompany the horse. The jockey told reporters that he would rush at any offer to ride the champion on US tracks, especially since he would not have to leave immediately. He could arrive in America just in time to pilot Shannon in the new year, but when Smith was asked about this, he was gruff. 'It's a private matter. I don't wish to discuss it.' The truth was that Smith wanted to sell his horse in America. It was why he needed neither a trainer nor a jockey. It was also why he declared that he had no definite race plans for Shannon, which seemed unlikely if he had really planned to race him in America. He thought Australians would be upset if they knew Shannon would be sold, remembering well that Phar Lap's loss in 1932 had been a sore episode in the country's history. Bernborough's ejection also had been taken hard in some circles. So even though Smith was no sentimentalist – bloodstock was a business, not a hobby – he kept his real plan to himself, telling only Dalton.

The trainer was a good confidant. He agreed with Smith that the time was opportune to ship Shannon. The US racing season would kick off in January, with the rich stakes beginning in February. Shannon would have to go immediately to make room for acclimatisation, never mind find a new trainer to settle in with, but Dalton was still disappointed. He revealed that his job had been to bring Shannon along gradually, at least for a Melbourne campaign, but he admitted he was only just 'getting' the horse. 'I understand him better every time we gallop him,' Dalton said, 'and I'm certain he would have raced better than he has ever raced if we'd brought him south. But I'm sure he will do more for the Australian thoroughbred by racing in America than he could here. He'll be a great advertisement.'

Around Sydney, people spoke like the horse might come home after Smith retired him. But it was a pipedream. Even if Smith had not planned to sell Shannon, it was almost impossible to bring a horse to Australia from the US. An interchange agreement existed between Australia and Britain, but it did not exist between Australia and America. In part, it was due to foot rot (a bacterial disease that affected hoofed animals, including horses). Any attempt to return Shannon to New South Wales would involve him shipping to England for six months of quarantine, after which time he could then sail for Australia. People speculated openly on the odds that Smith would do this, and most concluded that he wouldn't. It would be too hard, and too expensive.

Watching from the sidelines, veteran trainer Mick Polson thought Shannon would do all right in America. Polson had taken his star charge Winooka, a celebrated speedster, to the US in 1933. The campaign had ruined his horse. 'Winooka was what is known as a "pile driver",' he said, 'a horse with extravagant action. But Shannon is a "daisy cutter" and should relish the going there. I think he is the ideal type for American dirt tracks.' Polson added that Shannon should settle quickly, and fit for work almost immediately.

Aside from Polson, few were giving consideration to Shannon's suitability for the American dirt surfaces. It wasn't a matter of just landing the horse on US tracks and hoping for the best. The going on these courses was very fine, constituting a foundation of mostly clay and cinders, with two to three inches of light loam. Tracks were harrowed and watered before meetings, but the horse that could skip over the surface rather than cut into it would fare better. Shannon, economical in action as he was, would enjoy the American dirt more than a horse like Bernborough, but there were next to no examples to prove this. No Australian horse before him had been campaigned on American soil for an extended period, pitched to meet the top American horses for the top stakes races on their calendar. Phar Lap had died after his first outing, having raced in Mexico and not the US, and Winooka had failed on his tour. While there was no shortage of Australian horses in US stud farms, there were virtually no Australian horses in barns along the backstretches of American tracks, and certainly none like Shannon, who was aiming for elite company.

In the days that followed, Shannon was booked passage aboard the *Boogabilla*. It would sail from Sydney on 18 October, a Saturday. Dalton complained, saying it was hardly time to prepare the horse for a long sea voyage. If Smith listened, he didn't change his mind. The ageing, ardent Barney O'Brien turned down the offer to travel with Shannon. It broke his heart. 'I haven't seen much of my wife and children in the past 15 years,' he said. He had lived where the horses had lived, outside their boxes on the floor or in the loft above them, far from his warm bed at Glebe Point. He said he would take a short holiday and apply for a number one trainer's licence when he returned, but plans were brittle and salty to him. No Shannon. The kind strapper with the big ears didn't know what to do with himself in that final week. Three days to go. Two. 'This time tomorrow.' It was wrenching, right down to the moment at Bradley Street when O'Brien's hand left Shannon's bridle for the last time, and he was gone.

34

Passage

It had inched through Sydney Heads on 12 October, nose pointed for San Francisco. *Boogabilla* was a beauty, a near-new Swedish freighter on a single, grinding screw. It laid up at Glebe Island, tilting against its mooring and the harbour tides. It was clean grey steel in glassy waters, and it waited for 18 October, for wool and racehorses.

Shannon left Bradley Street before 9 am. The *Boogabilla* would sail at noon. It was a stiff day, hot as Hades as the horse walked off the float. The smells of Glebe Island were strong and strange to him, industrial and agricultural in a dirty cocktail. There were wheat silos and nearby abattoirs, and dust and grease and sweat. A small crowd gathered to watch Shannon take his final steps on Australian ground. He would travel with Colonus, 1942 Melbourne Cup winner (Colonus was heading to a San Jose stud farm). Wharf labourers, customs officials, and a few press-men hovered. W. J. Smith was there, and Lloyd Menck, owner of Colonus. The man who would see to Shannon during the crossing was present too, affable Billy Webb. He'd done this before. Webb had delivered Derby-winning Reading to California in a risky Pacific crossing in 1942.

Shannon stood under the *Boogabilla* hull in bandages and kneepads. It was too hot for rugs. He was lamb-like, only his twitching ears betrayed his nervousness. Webb took his bridle and led him a few steps along the wharf to the *Boogabilla* livestock hoist, a tiny horse stall that would be winched over the side of the ship onto deck. Shannon stepped into the contraption and stood as men fussed all around him, tying ropes around his neck, securing chains and fixing a padded strap to his head to protect his poll. Webb scratched the horse's cheek and told him to be calm, much like Barney O'Brien might. Moments later the men stepped away, someone hollered and Shannon was lifted off the wharf.

A small cheer rose from the crowd that watched him. 'Good on you Shannon, farewell boy.' The horse looked around at them as he slowly rose up the flanks of the *Boogabilla*, his withers twitching and sweat bubbling on his summer coat. His container was swung on to the top deck and it landed with a thump on the steel. Men got busy releasing the ropes and extracting Shannon, until he was out of his confines and headed on the short trip to his living quarters.

He would cross the Pacific in a makeshift stall, 10 feet by 10 feet on the open deck of the *Boogabilla*. It was well padded for a rough passage and deep with shavings. Unlike the previous accommodations for stars Phar Lap and Bernborough, there was no outside pen for Shannon to stretch his legs. One journalist remarked that the outfit 'fell far short of the box in which Bernborough travelled'. Though it was expected the *Boogabilla* would take 18 days to cross the Pacific, Smith had arranged for 24 days of fodder to accompany his horse. He packed minimal water. Though horsemen believed that thoroughbreds were sensitive to their water, often refusing to drink it if it wasn't what they were used to (and in the case of Phar Lap and Bernborough, months of water had travelled with them), Smith insisted that Shannon would survive off supplies brought on board during sailing.

Billy Webb walked around the two boxes when Shannon had been settled next to Colonus, checking the stall doors, the bedding. He threw summer sheets over the horses, though they were sweating in the hot confines of the stalls. Sacks of grain and chaff slouched against the walls, bales of lucerne and rakes, pitchforks and brooms. Shannon was ready. The stock inspector had passed him, the certificate already on its way to California. A light physic had been done in the previous few days to cool his system. As the *Boogabilla* began to ready for sailing, W. J. Smith looked in on his horse briefly, then hurried ashore. He would catch a plane on 29 October to meet Shannon in San Francisco.

The ship began to drop its moorings, and shuddered as it edged away from port. A long blast bellowed from the whistle as *Boogabilla* slipped its berth. It inched away from Glebe Island, turning around in deeper water, then powered slowly under the Harbour Bridge. Circular Quay to starboard, Woolloomooloo and Garden Island in brilliant sunshine, they slipped away. As Midstream had come in 1938, so Shannon crept gracefully out of Sydney Harbour. The whiff of ghost gums and bush scrub grew faint as the salt and sea breezes moved in. Out of the heads, the freighter leaned to port and *Boogabilla* carried Shannon into the Pacific Ocean.

PART II

35

San Francisco

San Francisco rose over the bow of the *Boogabilla* on 3 November, smoky and sprawling. It was almost winter. The cliffs of the Marin Peninsula perched to the north, the bay area to the south, in between the Golden Gate Bridge. *Boogabilla* slipped under it, ushering its cargo to the Americas. It tilted south around Alcatraz Island, and nudged into the port that hugged the corner of San Francisco Bay. It was two days ahead of schedule.

Shannon had been at sea for 17 days, over two weeks standing on narrow legs in a small box. He was fresh. The crossing had been smooth, glass-like. Neither Shannon nor Colonus had given Billy Webb any trouble. Shannon, in particular, had been dozy and comfortable. He gained 50 pounds during the sailing (when most horses were dropping tonnage with stress), and he was round and healthy when he walked out into the San Francisco winter afternoon.

He felt the cold immediately. Underneath his rug, Shannon's thin coat was expecting a summer dry as sticks. Instead, the American air was brittle and chilly. In pads and bandages, he was led into the hoist stall and swung over the side of the *Boogabilla*, and he touched the San Francisco wharf a few minutes later. So a small crowd in Sydney had sent him on his way, another greeted Shannon as he stepped out of the stall and on to America. They were W. J. Smith, local reporters, and a small battalion of Californian breeders curious about the new horse from Australia.

Smith said little when he saw Shannon, though pleased that the horse looked robust. The men chattered as Webb loaded Shannon on a waiting van, curious wharf workers peeking inside. 'I hope this one has better luck than Phar Lap,' one of them said. The van door closed, and Shannon was chugged away through the streets of San Francisco.

The float carried the Australian horse south, away from the tram-clad downtown arteries and towards San Bruno Mountain, South San Francisco, and eventually San Bruno. Shannon would board at Tanforan racetrack for a night. The following morning, Webb would deliver him to San Mateo, to the backstretch barns of Bay Meadows racecourse and trainer Willie Molter. This had not been Smith's decision, because before the *Boogabilla* had even nudged into American waters, Smith had done what many Australians had suspected he would.

He had sold Shannon.

The buyer was Harry Curland, a wealthy Californian who lived in Beverly Hills. Smith had gotten to know Curland during his business visits over the years, and the two shared an entrepreneurial ambition and a love for thoroughbred racing. Curland had an enormous catering business in California, held the concessions for both Santa Anita racetrack and Hollywood Park, along with smaller contracts at Bay Meadows, Golden Gate and Tanforan. He had also fed the 1932 Olympics in Los Angeles. Much as Smith had done, Curland had risen from little. At the turn into 1900, he had arrived in sunny California from New York, just eight years old. One of his earliest jobs had been at the old 'Lucky' Baldwin track, the later site of Santa Anita. Peddling *Racing Starter* inside the admission gates, Curland had been fascinated by how much folks ate and drank during a day at the races. His young mind had gone wild with ambition. He took up a cart at the Hippodrome Theatre on Main Street, downtown Los Angeles, selling candy and ice-cream during movie intermissions. That was 1916. By 1922, he had 48 theatres on the Pacific Coast. But the advent of the 'talkies' brought a plummet in fortune, and Curland had to look elsewhere to make a buck. He went back to the seed of his idea: the racetrack. When modern Santa Anita opened in 1934, Curland secured the catering rights, and the rest of California racing fell into tow.

For a few years, the man who was known as the 'hot-dog king' grew rich without dabbling in horses. But it was impossible to work amid the colour and excitement of West Coast racing without joining in the fun. In 1936, Curland paid $10,000 for the two-year-old Sweepalot, his first horse, a colt by the winner Sweep All. Whether it was luck or foresight, few knew. Sweepalot proved one of the nattiest gallopers of his time, a multiple stakes winner and a fabulous introduction to the dizzying heights of ownership. Before long, Curland's wife Rae was involved, and the string grew from one to two and three, quickly 16 or 17.

Rae Curland was pert and breezy, two years younger than her husband. The pair had married in 1911 or so when they were still teenagers. Almost 40 years on, their partnership was equal and affectionate. Rae Curland admitted her husband's business genius, which included management of their team of racehorses. But every single animal was in her name. She and her daughter owned the string, while her husband made the wheels turn. 'Harry manages our stable, and as a manager he has a lot to say,' Rae said. 'Confidentially though, he doesn't get to say much. Two women can outtalk him anytime.'

The Curlands were at home in California racing, cherry-picking yearlings to bring along or plunging big dollars for a proven galloper. They sent most of their team to Willie Molter. They had made a racing profit every year bar one, and when Harry Curland proffered his formula for success, it sounded a lot like hot dogs and hamburgers. 'Get the best meat obtainable at the best price, and concentrate on quality,' he said. But when it came to Shannon, it seemed the best price wasn't a priority. Before W. J. Smith had boarded his trans-Pacific flight from Sydney on 29 October, Harry Curland had handed over $100,000 for the Midstream horse.

In Australian currency, the sale was worth about £33,000, or £5700 more than the price Smith had paid for Shannon. The horse had won him £2503 in prizemoney, bringing Smith's gross profit to just over £8200. Even less shipping expenses and training costs, Shannon had returned a tidy sum in a short space of time. But Smith didn't say a word about the sale to the Australian papers as he had boarded his flight to California. Instead, he had made fools of them, telling the press he was thinking of choosing a set of green and gold silks in America for Shannon to race in. Even when news of the sale leaked into the Los Angeles office of Australian Associated Press (AAP), promptly sending a journalist in search of Smith for comment, he refused to reveal anything.

'Was Shannon sold before you left Australia, Mr Smith?' enquired the AAP reporter.

Smith was hostile. 'There's no point in answering that question.'

Harry Curland didn't have a problem with talking to the papers. 'I've bought Shannon as a gift for my wife,' he explained. 'We intend to race him for at least a season, and then retire him to stud. If he shows good form he could be raced longer.' Curland's intention was to use Shannon as a cornerstone stallion in a breeding operation he was planning. As for the horse's racing career, Curland wanted Shannon off the blocks almost immediately. He had pencilled in a first start in the seven-furlong San Carlos Handicap at Santa Anita on 1 January, with two or three further starts before a tilt at the $100,000 Santa Anita Handicap in late February. It was obvious immediately: as had been the case in Smith's ownership, in Curland's ownership Shannon would be racing to recoup his price tag.

The US press was doubly interested in the Australian horse that was now in local ownership. Dr Charles Strub, known across the California seaboard as Doc Strub, a former dentist turned owner of the Santa Anita track at Arcadia, Los Angeles, was pressing his manager of publicity to use Shannon. Fred Purner, promotions man, got in touch with Braven Dyer at the *Los Angeles Times*. 'How's about giving a thought to Santa Anita and the greatest thoroughbred to reach these shores in many years?' he said. He was talking about Shannon's proposed tilt at the Santa Anita Handicap. Dyer had jumped in his car and headed north-east through Los Angeles city to the Arcadia racecourse, running into W. J. Smith while there. Smith was taking a look at the Santa Anita starting gates with an idea to recommending their duplication in Sydney, but he stopped to regale the *Times* journalist with stories of Shannon's feats, so much so that Dyer wrote on 10 November that Shannon had flat run out of opposition in Australia. Smith had stoked the fire. 'He's the greatest horse I ever saw. I'm sure he'll make a big hit at Santa Anita.'

On 12 November, Smith lodged a request for registration of Shannon with The Jockey Club, the New York-based body that presided over racing in America. This process wasn't new to Smith, he'd done it a few times already. He shipped the paperwork from California, and presumed the normal channels would operate. He couldn't have guessed the mess that lay on the road ahead.

The Jockey Club had been founded in New York in 1894, set up out of a necessity to organise what was then a chaotic, fragmented state of racing across the country. Official status was given to the club to issue licences for running-race tracks, and that such tracks would operate meetings under regulations prescribed by The Jockey Club. The governance of the club, much like the AJC that oversaw New South Wales, was confined to the eastern racing states, those that sat on the Atlantic seaboard. As laws were passed in various other states, the jurisdiction of The Jockey Club was weakened. In California, for example, the sport fell under the governance of the California Horse Racing Board, founded in 1933. However, The Jockey Club remained the ethical and moral power of American racing, and specific to W. J. Smith's application, it was the keeper of the American Stud Book.

As in Australia, The Jockey Club had in effect a complex, exhaustive web of checks and crosschecks when it came to the registration of thoroughbreds. Smith had brought with him all of Shannon's Australian papers, including his Certificate of Registration from the AJC registrar and evidence of pedigree, which the New York club pored over. Smith and Harry Curland believed it would be a simple matter of paper pushing, as had always been the case with horses formerly registered with the AJC and VRC. They were stunned, therefore, on 13 November, when The Jockey Club declared it would not register the horse prima facie.

The club told Curland by telephone that a flaw had been

detected in Shannon's pedigree. It insisted to Curland that the matter was in abeyance, and not definite. A problem had arisen with one branch of Shannon's ancestry and, until this problem was fully investigated, the Australian horse could not be registered with the American Stud Book. The Jockey Club advised that Curland seek a special permit to race Shannon while the matter was investigated. Such a permit could be obtained under racing rules that allowed a horse ineligible for registry to race if it had been recognised by racing authorities in its native land (in this case, the AJC). W. J. Smith went to ground, and Harry Curland went into a panic.

'I don't understand it,' he said. 'I'd thought that a horse that had raced in the last six months, and one that had been identified, would be eligible for registration here.' Without even waiting for a definite ruling from New York, Curland cancelled his purchase of Shannon. On 18 November, he gave the horse's papers back to Smith, a decision he stated was mutual. Smith was in a fury over the debacle, refused to answer any telephone calls from Australia or take interviews from the AAP reporters in Los Angeles. He said only that he would depart soon for New York with a supply of Australian Stud Books, but before he did even that, he called on the brains of Los Angeles attorney Neil S. McCarthy.

McCarthy was a big player in California, the personal attorney of Louis B. Mayer and the MGM operation, as well as Mayer's bloodstock adviser, so he was well versed in racing lore. He had had many horses at the top of the sport himself. McCarthy took the Shannon case and went straight to the source, sought a report from the keeper of the Australian Stud Book, Albert Lodden Yuille. As Harry Curland withdrew, McCarthy stepped up, declaring his confidence that Shannon would be cleared to not only race, but also stand stud.

Curland begged to differ. He insisted that Smith had no chance of clearing Shannon for stallion duties. 'There's little doubt that Shannon will be allowed to race here,' he bleated, 'but a cloud in his pedigree has devalued him as a sire. A horse with no stud future is certainly not worth $100,000.' Both the American and Australian press were all over the issue, and Curland kept going. 'Even if he is cleared, I'm not interested in buying anymore. There are too many strings attached. It's a shame because my trainer, Willie Molter, is crazy about him, thinks he's a very good horse. But bad publicity will prevent any owner obtaining high stud fees for Shannon. I don't believe he'd bring more than $20,000 if he was auctioned today.'

Neil McCarthy didn't buy that, knew racing red tape better than Curland. He thought the caterer had bowed out too easily. Saying Shannon was tainted publicly was ill informed. McCarthy didn't think Shannon's reputation had been soiled an iota. The horse was getting column inches from California to Canada, and if the pedigree puzzle could be ironed out with The Jockey Club, they'd have a very famous horse on their hands, a thoroughbred cleared to race and breed in the United States, a horse that all of America knew about. So while Curland headed for the hills, McCarthy threw his hat into the ring. By the middle of December he revealed he was negotiating with W. J. Smith to buy Shannon outright.

36

The case of the Spaewifes

Shannon's pedigree crisis was too troubling for most men, but Neil Steere McCarthy wasn't most men. He was something of a genius, a man whose manner was kind and approachable, his mind a steel trap. With small, set eyes beneath thin and silver hair, swept back, McCarthy was handsome and vigorous, and in the American winter of 1947, he was 59 years old.

He was more of a horseman than his exterior let on. Clad in pressed shirts and bold ties, he practised law at 510 West 6th Street, but he lived at opulent 9481 Sunset Boulevard in Beverly Hills. It was a palace, a small Versailles in the Beaux Arts style, all arches and pediment doorways and frontage to the exclusive Sunset Strip. It sat in the foothills of the Santa Monica mountains. To the south lay Culver City and MGM studios; a short way east, Hollywood. It was the catchment of the filthy rich and famous, the sort of people who had made McCarthy wealthy.

He had long been the attorney for Louis B. Mayer and his MGM operation, along with neighbouring Paramount Pictures. Mayer was famously temperamental, prone to outbursts of random churlishness, but Neil McCarthy knew how to handle that. He and Mayer were a smooth operation, photographed often together at society functions or the races. They were almost friends. The attorney drafted contracts for so many of Hollywood's golden greats – Ava Gardner, Ginger Rogers, Katharine Hepburn and Fred Astaire – and represented many more. Outside of Mayer, McCarthy's portfolio included the film producer Cecil B. DeMille, Amadeo Giannini and his new Bank of America, the Chrysler Corporation and, more famously, the surly Howard Hughes.

McCarthy possessed a boatload of patience, which was how he handled volatile bigwigs like Mayer and Hughes. But more than this, he was a gifted attorney, owned a natural aptitude for law and, as the American Blue Book California Lawyers stated in 1928, had 'splendid energy and initiative'. He had graduated from the University of Michigan in 1910, admitted to the bar that year and took up sticks in Los Angeles. For a few years he practised with the firm Jones, Smith and McCarthy as partner, but he went solo quickly, setting up at West 6th Street. No one remembered how he migrated from probate and corporation matters to representing Hollywood, but by World War II his standing was such that he was pushing the divorces of Mrs Cornelius Vanderbilt Jr and Mrs James Roosevelt, wife of the president's son. McCarthy was a name on every top society party, knocking elbows with the rich, famous and outrageous on a daily basis.

Intelligent, learned, Neil McCarthy was a natural leader. He knew how to speak in large crowds, and he demonstrated this in May 1947 during a heated labour dispute between California owners and trainers (of which he was a member) and a representative of the American Federation of Labor (AFL), which was pressing for better pay, bonuses and rewards for grooms. McCarthy felt the AFL was in a corner, and he called a standing vote to reject the grooms' proposals. 'If they want to strike, let them strike!' McCarthy yelled, and before the meeting had properly been adjourned, he led the owners out the door.

McCarthy was not native to glittering Hollywood. He was the grandson of Irish immigrants, the son of Boston-born John McCarthy and Mary Enright, native of Kerry, Ireland. His parents had moved to Phoenix, Arizona, sometime in the mid- to late-1800s, and Neil Steere McCarthy had been born there on 6 May 1888. Because his father was a farrier, he had been exposed to horses from infancy. By the age of four he had his own pony, and he learned to identify local horses as if people. That was a time, he said, when Arizona was 'still predominantly horse country'. By age 14, McCarthy possessed what he later claimed might have been the best quarter horse in the state, and when he moved to Michigan to study law, he drove stagecoaches at Yellowstone National Park between semesters. 'I guess I was born with an Irishman's instinctive love for horses,' he said. It stuck to him, even when he moved into choked, hazy, urban Los Angeles around 1911.

McCarthy had played polo for years when he reached the city of angels. As he climbed the social rungs of Hollywood, he joined the elite, expensive Midwick Country Club in the San Gabriel Valley, which opened its doors in 1913 to the rich, ultra-conservative residents of west Los Angeles and Pasadena. It was the sort of place where big Buicks and Cadillac 62s littered the parking lot, where Bing Crosby and Walt Disney knocked about the golf course or tennis courts. Among them, Neil McCarthy was in polo breeches, riding number-two position in the Pacific Coast Open Championships, and representing Midwick in tournaments all the way through the 1930s. He became such a staple at the exclusive Polo Lounge in Beverly Hills that they named a salad in his honour.

The saddle taught him to walk straight and tall, as it did most men. McCarthy was 5 ft 9½ in, with a fair, Irish complexion, a high forehead and blue eyes. Hollywood and its merciless business didn't alter the softness in his face, but that might have been because of his horses. He had been racing thoroughbreds since the 1920s and, he said, 'They keep me going. Breeding them, racing, buying and selling them; they get me out in the open, keep me active.' Later on in life, he would admit that if it weren't for the horses he wouldn't be alive. He had happened on thoroughbreds by breeding polo ponies, whose fleetness was improved by racing stock. His first prominent racehorse was Lion, an English-bred colt by Ampelion, shipped into the US in 1915. McCarthy owned the horse in partnership initially, standing him in Phoenix as a stallion. Eventually he bought Lion outright, and moved him to California.

He raced horses from Tijuana and old Exposition Park to the top tracks on the west coast, associated his name with racehorses like Outbid, Buckhorn Creek and Augury. In 1939 he had Today, a natty little horse that was something of a giant killer. It was

Today who famously downed Seabiscuit by two lengths in the Los Angeles Handicap in track record time. McCarthy also spawned a little breeding operation. He owned 400 acres in the picturesque Moorpark region, a rural hamlet with rolling vales about 50 miles north-west of Los Angeles. By 1947 he had Moonlight Run at stud, an imported three-quarter brother to the English Derby-winning Hyperion, and Sierra Nevada, by Gainsborough. It was said that McCarthy's broodmare band, though not huge, was the equal of any in California.

The attorney held his horses in high affection, particularly those he bred. He would say, 'When you buy a horse and see him win, that's one thing. When you have bred a winner, it's almost like having a child or grandchild achieve great success. You couldn't be more proud.' McCarthy never had a large racing stable, dotting a few horses here and there in Santa Anita barns or Hollywood Park, usually no more than 10. If he went to the races, it was often because he was expected to, and he rarely bet. He dug such pleasure out of his animals that friends wondered if his bloodstock pursuits were business or pleasure. 'Let's say it's a hobby,' he said, 'one that must pay its own way. You have to use business methods to make it succeed.' Success, as a result, didn't elude him. In 1941, Neil McCarthy was 24th on the American winning list of owners. He slowed down when the US entered the war, almost completely sidelining racing, but in 1947, as Shannon's file with all its complications landed on his desk at West 6th Street, McCarthy was ready to leap back in.

The Australian horse fascinated him. From a breeder's perspective, Shannon was rolled gold. He was by a fashionable, and wildly successful, sire line in England (Blandford), by a sire who had barnstormed the local ranks in Australia (Midstream would top the sire's list for season 1947–48, and again in 1950–51 and 1951–52). Idle Words, also, had proved an attractive broodmare. Her progeny were topping the yearling sales each season (thanks to Shannon). McCarthy also knew that Shannon was a speedball, held a mile record for Australia that was only just short of

Equipoise's record for the American dirt. Shannon had records hanging off him like Christmas decorations. McCarthy believed that he was the most brilliant horse to arrive in the US of recent years, certainly better than Winooka in 1933, and more attractive a stud prospect than Ajax and Bernborough because Shannon had, unlike those two, an opportunity to prove himself in America before heading for the covering shed. W. J. Smith wanted out, and McCarthy did the sums.

If he paid the same price for Shannon as had Harry Curland, McCarthy could return his costs with one or two major wins. For example, the Santa Anita Handicap, the 'Hundred Grander', was worth $102,500 to the winner in 1948. In prizemoney, Shannon could be in profit figures if he hit the dirt running. Then there was stud value. McCarthy didn't plan to stand Shannon at his Moorpark establishment; he had bigger things in mind. Back in February, he had paid $135,000 for the exceptional mare and one-time Horse of the Year Busher. He had sold her a few months later to Maine Chance Farm for an overnight profit of $15,000. McCarthy knew how to sell a horse. For years he had served as Louis B. Mayer's bloodstock adviser, and he knew the stud masters of the Bluegrass now as if old friends, Leslie Combs II in particular. The irascible, brilliant Combs was the master of Spendthrift Farm, where Beau Pere had gone, Bernborough too. McCarthy had effected the sale of both horses to that farm. If he was going to pay $100,000 for Shannon, a horse that wasn't yet registered with a chance of never getting registered, McCarthy had to have plans up his sleeve.

On 17 December he revealed he was negotiating with W. J. Smith to buy Shannon for himself. The horse was good to race, Smith having obtained a special permit under Rule 59 from The Jockey Club. That application had been shipped to New York, with relevant papers from the AJC, and passed unanimously by stewards on 11 December. But for weeks, McCarthy and Smith grappled over clauses in the sale contract that would null the purchase if it transpired that Shannon could not be registered for stud purposes with The Jockey Club. The press, both local and Australian, angled for comment on this, but McCarthy remained mum. Smith, who had left San Francisco in mid-November, arrived by airplane again in the second week of January to close the deal. Over the dinner table the night of 12 January, a Monday in mild Los Angeles, he sold Shannon for the second time, for $87,000.

The parties kept the sale arrangements private, McCarthy revealing only that he 'planned to race Shannon for an indefinite period and then retire him to stud'. When Smith was asked for comment on the sale, he was charming as ever. 'If McCarthy has made a statement, that's enough. It's a private business, just like any other. And no, I don't wish to discuss the terms.' Little else was revealed about the sale except that Shannon, who had been in the care of Bay Meadows trainer Willie Molter for almost three months, would stay with him, McCarthy believing that a change of stable would unsettle the horse so soon after his arrival.

The morning after the sale, veteran Australian breeder Ernest Shaw, who lived in Los Angeles, contacted W. J. Smith at his San Mateo lodgings. Shaw had a long association with Smith, had handled Beau Pere during his tenure at St Aubin's and travelled with that horse when he had exported to Louis B. Mayer's ownership in 1941. Shaw had stayed on in the US to set up Mayer's impressive Perris Farm in Orange County, eventually getting American citizenship and settling in Beverly Hills (in a few years he would be put in charge of all Mayer horses in training). By January 1948, he had worked with a long list of Australian imports in California: Beau Pere, Reading at Ryana Ranch, and recently Colonus in San Jose, all at stud. Shaw was a sensitive horseman in tune with Australian thoroughbreds and their difficulties adjusting to American conditions. He thought he might do well handling Shannon, and had enticed a prominent California owner, Walter McCarty, to buy the horse. McCarty had consented to paying the full $100,000 for Shannon, and Ernest Shaw had made his offer, fatefully, about six hours too late. He was shattered to learn the horse had been sold to Neil S. McCarthy the night before. He held off saying anything public about his interest, in part because he held concerns already for Shannon's campaign. Shaw thought the horse was in training too soon, that Shannon should have been spelled after coming off the *Boogabilla* on 3 November. He believed that standing a horse in a stall for three weeks lost all its racing form, and he didn't think that rushing lightly raced Shannon would amount to much when it came time to race him on US dirt. His fears would come back to him later in 1948.

W. J. Smith, having sold his famous horse, washed his hands of the episode. He boarded a flight to Sydney a week after the sale and didn't come back, raising the ire of the stewards at The Jockey Club. Marshall Cassidy, executive secretary and assistant treasurer of the club, was annoyed that Smith hadn't appeared in New York at any stage to consult with him or his colleagues about Shannon's registration. He revealed further that Smith had ignored a cable message from The Jockey Club advising him back in October not to ship Shannon to California until the club had given its consent. Smith hit back, claiming The Jockey Club had sent a letter, not a cable, and anyway, 'If Shannon is not registered then America's loss will be some other country's gain.' Neil McCarthy's handling of the situation was far more diplomatic, the lawyer knowing well how to handle the east coast racing body (and how to dazzle them with legal argument), so with Smith's exit in mid-January it fell to Shannon's swish, smart new owner to argue things out.

—

The problem was such.

In Shannon's immediate pedigree there was a mare called Peptamint, a New Zealand hen who was the dam of Idle Words (making her Shannon's granddam). Peptamint was by an Australian sire called Finland, a very respectable stakes winner in Australia (VRC St Leger and Sires' Produce Stakes) before his exportation to New Zealand in 1901 for stallion duties. Finland was a remarkable producer, getting a score of winning stock in the

Dominion through the early 1900s, but he was out of the mare Fishwife, and this was where Shannon's problems began.

Fishwife threw seven generations back to a mare called Spaewife, a horse that had arrived in Australia by ship at some time and that eons of stud-bookkeepers had been trying to iden-tify ever since. Fishwife herself was a smart mare, bred in 1884 and the winner of the VRC Standish Handicap (Finland was one of three stakes winners she foaled), but her lineage to Spaewife clouded everything. Since the dawn of the Australian Stud Book in 1878, Spaewife had been given so many fanciful pedigrees that she might never have existed at all. She had been confused with a horse called Fortune Teller in Volume II of the Australian book, 1882. It stated, 'the particulars as regards her [Fortune Teller's] sire, colour, name and date of shipment correspond so closely with those of Spaewife that her [Spaewife's] identity seems nearly established.' The fact that the book used the word 'nearly' was a hint that no one was really sure. But then, 19 years later, evidence emerged that Fortune Teller had died on the voyage from England in 1826, and the Australian Stud Book was back to square one.

That was in 1901, and that year, in Volume VII, the book published in its 'Errata and Addenda' pages a transcript of the New Zealand Stud Book which stated Spaewife's pedigree as 'chestnut mare Spaewife (imp.) by Soothsayer, dam by Selim'. The problem was that this pedigree had been tacked on to another mare, a horse called Cutty Sark who for years had been masquerading under a family tree that in fact belonged to Spaewife. So in its 1901 edi-tion, the Australian Stud Book declared, 'It is evident, therefore, that Fortune Teller and Spaewife were not identical, and that the latter was instead the unnamed chestnut mare, foaled in 1822, got by Soothsayer from a mare by Selim from Ringtail, by Buzzard, sold in England to go to Australia in the same year as Fortune Teller, and heretofore supposed to be Cutty Sark.' Of Cutty Sark, the book said, 'There is little chance of [her] true pedigree ever being discovered.'

By 1901, therefore, the Australian Stud Book was satisfied that

Spaewife was an English-bred mare, foaled in 1822 by the excellent stallion Soothsayer (who had got an English Derby winner and a 2000 Guineas winner) and out of a mare by the stallion Selim, who herself was out of Ringtail by the stallion Buzzard. But the pedigree was never established beyond reasonable doubt and this was where the trouble was.

The General Stud Book of England was the father of all books, the forbearer of thoroughbred records and the model by which all other stud books were crafted. At the end of 1947, at the time when Neil McCarthy was presenting Shannon to New York for registration, the English book was governed by a controversial rule, passed in May 1913, known as the Jersey Act (after senior steward Lord Jersey). It stated, 'No horse or mare can, after this date, be considered as eligible for admission unless it can be traced without flaw, on both sire's and dam's side of its pedigree, to horses and mares themselves already accepted in the earlier volumes of the book.' That meant that from Volume XXII of the General Stud Book, every single thoroughbred contained within its pages had unquestionable heritage back to the General Stud Book.

The Jersey Act, overnight, repelled an invasion of brilliant American horses to the English racing scene. Because of anti-gambling laws in the US, many owners had been sending their horses to England to race, and their success had put English racing out of joint. The Jockey Club in England, perhaps loosely, had decided that because the American book required only five generations of proven bloodlines, and because events like the Civil War had destroyed much record-keeping in America, the American thoroughbred could not be classified as 'pure'. Because of the Act, therefore, US heroes like Man O' War and Gallant Fox were inadmissible, and any descendant of the champion sire Lexington. The Act didn't prevent American horses from racing in England, but it did render them useless to breeding as they, and consequently their offspring, were considered half-breds. And it wasn't only America that was affected; French thoroughbreds were also suddenly ineligible, writing famous stallions like Djebel, sire of an enormous number of classic winners in England, off the page.

Spaewife's progeny were certainly barred. The mare herself pre-dated the Jersey Act, so she could be found within the early editions of the General Stud Book. But the cloudiness in her pedigree meant that all of her progeny were barred, including Fishwife, Finland and Shannon, and the omission applied to Cutty Sark also (and hundreds of other colonial mares). It was an extraordinary situation, because some of Australia's outstanding racehorses, including The Barb (Cutty Sark was his great-great-granddam), were officially 'not thoroughbreds' in the eyes of the General Stud Book. While Australian breeding had not sung off about it, the American Stud Book had been complaining, loudly, for years about the draconian Jersey Act – only it went and applied a similarly iron fist to Shannon when it refused his registration in November 1947.

Rule 64 of the American book stated, 'Only those horses are eligible for registry which authentically trace, in all of their lines, to animals recorded in the American Stud Book or in a recognised Stud Book of another country.' As such, the rule permitted any Australian racehorse to be registered because the Australian Stud Book was the recognised book of that country. Commenting on this, turf authority Joe H. Palmer stated in *The Blood-Horse*, 'The rather obvious intention of the men who wrote Rule 64 was . . . to register any horse if, on due examination, he proved to be a racehorse.' Nevertheless, in November 1947 The Jockey Club took Shannon's application for registry, laid his pedigree out on a table at their offices on 250 Park Avenue, and spotted Spaewife 11 generations removed. Her presence rendered Shannon's lineage 'flawed', and the American Stud Book immediately turned him over for investigation. 'This should not be interpreted as a refusal,' said Marshall Cassidy. The club, he said, needed more time to look at the application and to hear evidence from the then prospective owner, Neil McCarthy.

The Jockey Club's great problem was that it had been seeing Spaewifes before its eyes for years. Spaewife, to them, had four possible pedigrees: by Soothsayer out of Cutty Sark; by Ben Ledi out of that Soothsayer–Cutty Sark combination; by Soothsayer out of Streamlet; by Soothsayer out of the Selim mare. The latter pedigree was the one the Australian Stud Book had adopted in 1901, but this wasn't good enough for the American book. Without even realising it, The Jockey Club in New York had ruled its own Jersey Act.

Turf authorities across America were disgusted. Joe Palmer wrote that he knew The Jockey Club members were sensible, fair-minded people, but 'Why the devil does their concerted action so frequently suggest sanctified dodos?' Palmer went even further, suggesting that it would be a 'joyous day' for him if Shannon's owner 'applied to the courts for an injunction requiring The Jockey Club to register Shannon under their own rules'. He reminded his readers that for a great many years, it had been a sound policy of the American book to work with the French and Australian books for mutual recognition of horses, believing this would undermine the relevance of England's Jersey Act, a rule they had been complaining about for years. *The Blood-Horse* commentator Joe Estes believed similarly. Honing in on The Jockey Club's use of the word 'defect', he said, 'What is a defect in a pedigree? It is a failure to make a clear connection with an ancestor in the General Stud Book of England. That is the English definition, now reaffirmed as the American definition.'

Estes was a formidable opinion in the Shannon debacle. He was a prominent bloodstock commentator, editor of the industry-leading publication, *The Blood-Horse*, but he had entered that company a number of years ago with a then radical attitude to breeding thoroughbreds. He had labelled Bruce Lowe an 'all-time hocus-pocus champion in thoroughbred breeding'. 'The most important item in appraising the stud prospects of a young horse is his racing class,' he wrote in 1939. 'The racing class and breeding records of his sire and dam are also worthy of consideration, but beyond that the pedigree will tell you nothing worth remembering.' This opinion pre-dated Shannon's problem by almost a decade, but it was the root of Estes's criticism now: Shannon's flaw, if that's what it was, was so far back in his pedigree that it was of no genetic importance.

The facts were absurd. In 12 generations, Shannon possessed 4096 ancestors. Neil McCarthy could identify 4094 of them, the missing two being the parents of Spaewife. That mare, in the 11th remove, represented one-half of one-tenth of one per cent in Shannon's family tree, which was tough luck, Estes pointed out, because Spaewife had a great many high-class offspring. 'The British seem to think that it really makes a difference whether some ancestor 175 years back had his pedigree printed somewhere,' he said. The absurdity of the situation badgered him. Shannon had been barred because of his great-great-great-great-great-great-great-granddam's great-granddam.

The Jockey Club was well aware of the frustrations that rebounded across America after Shannon's initial refusal. Even the popular *New Yorker* had covered the matter, describing Shannon as 'that Australian fellow there's been such a pother over'. But the club stewards held firm, declaring that inclusion in one country's stud book does not automatically qualify a horse for entry into the American book. In Australia, people were baffled. Bert Riddle said he had not the faintest idea as to where Shannon's pedigree might be questioned, and Albert Lodden Yuille, keeper of the Australian book, told the papers there was nothing in Shannon's pedigree to prevent his admission to the American version. He said the Australian Stud Book was, and always had been, meticulously compiled, and if there were assumptions in the US that any and every horse was allowed into it, they were misaligned. For example, good gallopers Katanga and Beaulivre had been rejected from admission recently, Beaulivre's being in the New Zealand book making no difference.

The fiasco was becoming an international incident, Australians wounded and defensive over what they perceived as a slight on their stud book. Shannon, their champion racehorse and a horse with impeccable breeding according to their judgement, was flawed in the eyes of the Americans. Marshall Cassidy, reports reaching him from the Australian press, went into damage control. He refuted claims that Shannon's case was a slur on Australian bloodlines. 'Such a suggestion is absurd. All newspaper comment [in Australia] seems to be based upon the fact that Shannon has been refused registration, and nothing could be more inaccurate. There has been no refusal. The case merely has been held over until more information reaches us.' Cassidy added, 'We are very happy that Australia recognises our stud book. However, that does not place us under any obligation to accept Australia's.' In New York, the *Morning Telegraph* agreed. 'Australians are surprised by our refusal to admit their crack racer to our stud book. But we have just as much right to protect our stud book as have the English to keep theirs "pure". More power to our Jockey Club for its vigilance in keeping our book free of possible taint.'

Shannon was having a far-reaching effect on international horseracing. Never in the history of Australian or American racing had a horse so divided opinions at the highest levels. Everyone was throwing his two cents in, and the spiral effect was that other Australian horses in line for American sale suddenly were not. Columnist, the horse that had tussled with Shannon in the Craven Plate, was one of them. He threw back to Cutty Sark through Wallace (who was a great-great-grandson of The Barb) and, because Cutty Sark had no pedigree, Columnist's flaw was more awful than Shannon's. Cashing in on the controversy, the owners of Victory Lad put their horse up for sale in America, placing a banner ad in *The Blood-Horse* with the heading, 'There's no Flaw in his pedigree.'

—

Neil McCarthy put his head down and tackled his problem quietly. He was made of stern stuff, had bought an expensive horse with a monster problem, but he wouldn't have done it if he hadn't thought he could squeeze Shannon through. One of the first things he did was request comment from Albert Lodden Yuille in Sydney, and Yuille penned a letter of evidence to the lawyer. It read: 'Volume VII of the Australian Stud Book [1901] was compiled by my late father. Although I was only in my teens at that time, I was aware of his painstaking efforts and I am absolutely certain that he and his committee would not have made the amendment in Volume VII [in the Errata and Addenda pages] unless conclusive evidence had been placed before them. At that time they would have had access to documents held by the sons and grandsons of early settlers and racing men in Australia.' It wasn't overwhelming with physical evidence, but Yuille's letter was an endorsement of the Australian Stud Book's record by its highest authority and, as such, it carried weight.

McCarthy filed it for later use. He would have to go to New York to plead his horse's corner, and he would take the letter with him. He spent the first few weeks of 1948 on the floor of his office, laying out pedigrees and cross-referencing the earliest editions of the Australian Stud Book. He was on the telephone to Sydney at all hours, to the AJC and the stud book, and to the New Zealand Stud Book for its records. He also sought out the General Stud Book in England, and as if the situation could not have got any more confusing, it did.

The General Stud Book had two Spaewifes. The first was legitimate: a chestnut foaled in 1823 by Soothsayer out of (an equally legitimate) Cutty Sark. This Cutty Sark had a flawless breeding record from 1817 until 1833, and had never been exported to New South Wales. Her Spaewife foal also possessed a complete English record, a breeding account from 1830 to 1842. It was impossible, therefore, that this Spaewife could be in Shannon's pedigree. The second Spaewife was a different matter. McCarthy was arguing she was the mare by Soothsayer out of the Selim mare, who was out of Ringtail. She didn't possess an entry in the General Stud Book, but she was mentioned. Ringtail was recorded in Volume III as foaling a filly in 1814 by Selim (the Selim mare), and in the notes under Ringtail's pedigree, the General Stud Book stated of this

1814 filly: 'This mare or a sister had in 1822 ch.f. by Soothsayer which was sent to N.S. Wales in [1825] and there called Spaewife.'

Written in black and white, therefore, was the mysterious Spaewife. She had existed, had been recorded as being foaled in England in 1822 and exported to Australia in 1825. Her ancestors all traced to the English book.

E. A. Lamb, a resident of Bowral, country New South Wales, confirmed this. In a letter to the *Sunday Herald*, he explained that his grandfather, Captain John Lamb, had been the man behind the importation of Spaewife and Cutty Sark so long ago. He wrote, 'My grandfather imported these two mares with the stallion Peter Finn. The story I have always heard is that when staying with his friend, Sir William Maxwell, in Ayrshire, he admired two of his (Maxwell's) blood fillies, and I understand one or both were first foals. In those days there was a prejudice against first foals and they were often given away, sometimes even killed. Sir William presented the two fillies to my grandfather, and I understand they were by Soothsayer. He no doubt called one Spaewife after a favourite mare of Sir William's, hence the confusion.'

Sir William Maxwell owned the official Spaewife who appeared in the General Stud Book, so Lamb's story was coherent. The Australian Spaewife now had a mention in the English book and a story that corroborated her export, but the problem was that even the General Stud Book was unsure of anything further, didn't know if she was out of the 1814 Ringtail filly or a sister to her. The General Stud Book had only one record of a possible sister: a Sancho mare who was a half-sister, bred from Ringtail in 1809 and who possessed her own complete breeding record in Volume III. In the year 1822, when Shannon's Spaewife was recorded as being foaled, this Sancho mare had a colt by Don Cossack, and she had a covering record on either side of 1822, from 1813 all the way to 1828. It was therefore impossible that she was the dam of Spaewife, making it almost certain that the Selim mare was the correct pedigree. So, while McCarthy had it there in front of him that Shannon's Spaewife did exist, had been exported and was legitimately thoroughbred in all removes, there was lingering confusion about her in the English Stud Book and it was probably enough to make the New York stewards decide against Shannon's application. The attorney knew early that it would come down to catching The Jockey Club on a good day, and to brass argument.

The moment arose on a wintry Thursday morning in New York, 29 January 1948, at 250 Park Avenue. The heavies of The Jockey Club were waiting: chairman William Woodward, vice chairman George D. Widener, secretary–treasurer Joseph Davis, along with Robert Fairbairn, Ogden Phipps, Donald P. Ross and Alfred Vanderbilt. Confident, an air of California brilliance about him, Neil S. McCarthy acted like it was any other day in the office, wrangling the delicate particulars of the Howard Hughes empire, the Chrysler Corporation or MGM Studios. He presented his letter from the Keeper of the Australian Stud Book, saying, 'It seems to me that the Australian stud authorities can be depended upon and the comments of Mr Yuille are pertinent.' McCarthy described the Spaewife shipped to Australia in 1825, cited her mention in the English book, and added, 'She is the mare that is called Spaewife in the Australian Stud Book and is not intended or represented to be identical with the mare Spaewife in the General Stud Book.' In addition, he produced an article from an AJC racing calendar, as well as the documentary evidence from the English and Australian books to support his argument. He advised the club that if confusion existed around the Spaewife in Shannon's pedigree, it was because of the errors that had been attributed to her in the early versions of the Australian Stud Book when shipping records were lost, confused or unreliable. More confusion had occurred because she shared a name with another mare of the same era, but since 1901Australians had been almost certain of her lineage.

McCarthy was presenting reason to The Jockey Club, sensibility and an explanation as to why Spaewife had so confounded everyone for 123 years. The job of the stewards was to assess his argument, to be satisfied that Shannon was thoroughbred in all removes, and with the letter from Australia and the records from the General Stud Book, it was hard to discount that Shannon was 'pure' all the way to his 12th generation. In fact, without the Jersey Act he might have qualified for the English book. The Jockey Club chewed the matter over. There was still a flaw with Spaewife insofar as the General Stud Book cited her as the progeny of two possible mares. But both mares were thoroughbred, so even if the pedigree was unidentifiable, it was certainly pure blood. Therefore, the club had little recourse in the path of McCarthy's argument.

The Jockey Club passed a vote: Shannon's application for registration was approved, and he was admitted to the American Stud Book on 29 January 1948.

The club released a statement. 'The stewards are today instructing the Registry Office to register the horse Shannon, recently imported from Australia. The application for registration, as originally made, complied with the requirements of The Jockey Club except that there was a possible flaw in the eleventh generation. Those charged with the responsibility for the keeping of the stud book cannot accept performance as a substitute for pedigree and definite defects should not be disregarded, even when they go so far back. However, in this case it has been decided, after careful study, that the horse may be properly registered as being of thoroughbred blood.'

Breeders in Australia scoffed at the news. 'We could have told them that.' Marshall Cassidy had plenty to say. 'The fact that a country as careful about bloodlines as Australia has accepted Shannon is prima facie evidence that the horse is O.K. It's just a pity there's been such a hullabaloo over him.' Reporter James Roach, writing in the *New York Times,* said, 'Few horsemen had expected that happy decision.' In *The Blood-Horse*, Joe Estes spoke for many Americans. 'Horsemen were pleased to learn of the decision; they would have felt, vicariously, like heels if the horse had been declared ineligible.' He added that The Jockey Club was probably relieved that it had found an excuse to admit Shannon, 'but it must have been a narrow squeak'.

Estes took exception to The Jockey Club refusing to release

any particulars about their decision, only that they had made it. He wanted to know what the stewards had pinned their decision on, conjecture or evidence. He wondered if they had accepted the last guess of the Australian Stud Book about the true identity of Spaewife, and 'if such is the case, a precedent has been established'. He said this because in the past, the American Stud Book had accepted no conjectures on pedigree except those made in the United States or England. 'The Jockey Club presumably knows the basis on which it accepted the pedigree of Shannon. Undoubtedly, that registration was in keeping with its policies. Therefore it should be able to state the pedigree of Spaewife as officially accepted, the stud book evidence leading up to the acceptance, and the policy under which further acceptances may be made.' But no such information was released by The Jockey Club. Shannon was registered, and that was that.

Estes had a right to be upset. The Shannon fiasco had been fantastic, in that definition that made it almost unbelievable. The Jockey Club's announcement that Shannon had been accepted for registration was cryptic, giving neither the agreed pedigree of Spaewife, or indeed a mention of Spaewife. It also used the phrase 'in this case', as if in the next case, registration might be refused. Commenting on this, 'Chiron', a Victorian journalist with the *Argus* newspaper, said, 'There are many more horses in the American Stud Book, particularly in the early volumes, with more flaws in their pedigree than Shannon.' Many Australians found the whole situation ridiculous, given that America's stud book had roots as chaotic as Australia's.

The story of Shannon's refusal and subsequent acceptance went around the world, and drew argument on the mutual recognition of stud books. In Australia, the *Sunday Times* commented, 'When our horses go abroad, if their pedigrees are not acceptable to the stud books of other countries, what is the good of having a breeding control such as that exercised by the Keeper of the Stud Book?' It was a valid point. There was no uniformity between any of the stud books of the breeding world. Commenting on this,

New Zealand turf expert 'Blair Athol' said that the 'continuance of these inconsistent, illogical and fatuous regulations have led to a different definition in each country of what constitutes a thoroughbred'. His words were prophetic. Before the year ended, the English Jockey Club called a conference of world authorities on breeding and pedigrees. Albert Lodden Yuille went along, putting the Shannon case on the table as an example of how the current system wasn't working. A few months later, the cockeyed doctrine that was the Jersey Act was repealed.

Neil McCarthy headed home to California with a registered racehorse, job done. His thoroughbred was now Shannon II (to avoid confusion with a different horse of the same name already in America). It had been a long and laborious process since November, one that had made headlines around the world, rendered him a household name in Australian racing. He was credited with 'one of the finest bits of research ever attempted'. But McCarthy was of such ilk that rather than feeling weary from it all, he was invigorated, excited even. He possessed the most talked about racehorse on the American continent.

37

Willie 'The Kid' Molter

The breeze that blew off San Francisco Bay carried west, over the flat hinterlands of San Mateo to the backstretch of Bay Meadows racetrack. Well before dawn, trainer Willie Molter was moving around in it, wending his way down El Camino Real to his barn, a rustic, dusty collection of boxes on the east fringe of the racecourse. He would park his motor car, walk out into the early morning and run into his animals: two goats and a dog, a rooster and two ducks, 10 cats and 40 thoroughbreds in training, more or less.

By 4 November 1947, Shannon was one of them, rugged, deep in straw and staring out at his new trainer. Molter liked the horse right away, enjoyed his graceful temperament and tractability. Though a six-year-old entire by the northern hemisphere calendar (he would be seven on 1 January), Shannon was neither distracted nor sour, got about eating and sleeping as soon as he arrived. But the shuffle of the Bay Meadows backstretch was strange to him. The barns sat in neat, ordered rows, one after the other, the boxes under timber awnings and homely straw strewn everywhere, bridles and blankets dangling. Molter would emerge in the mornings, stride along the shed row and scratch the Australian horse on the neck. The pair was quickly friends.

Molter was 36 years old that year, born in 1911 to German parents in Fredericksburg, Texas. It was a small place, only 3500 people, with German-settled shopfronts on broad, tidy streets. It was also the hometown of Max Hirsch, famous Belmont trainer. A small, lithe teenager, Molter followed Hirsch's lead, took to race riding by the age of 12, hammering quarter horses around jerkwater tracks in dusty Reno, Emeryville and Butte. He gradually migrated to thoroughbreds. At one stage he was a force at Tijuana, and wound his way north of the border to Vancouver's Hastings Park (later Exhibition Park). It was a rough-and-tumble joint, a track so tight (a half-mile around) that sore horses ran onto the outside rail. Jocks were brazen as brass at this place, but they had to be. Johnny Longden learned something there, passing through it in 1928 only a year into his career. It was also where he and Molter struck a long friendship. Unlike Longden, who was just 4 ft 11 in, Willie Molter outgrew his silks, and in 1937 he took to training.

He was a sympathetic handler. Horses liked him. For a time, he held up in the barns of other trainers, first Jack P. Atkin, for whom he had ridden, and later Frank Rust. He and Rust formed the Edgemont Stable partnership in the late 1930s, but Molter took tack on his own. When he took out his sole licence, he owned backstretch secrets from west Canada down to the ding-busting Agua Caliente. Molter saddled his first winner there on 3 March 1935, a Sunday at Tijuana. He had two winners that day, but it would be more than a decade before he got a stakes winner. That came on 1 September 1945, with High Resolve in the San Diego Handicap at Del Mar. Four days later, the horse won another, and before 1946 rolled in, Molter had won five stakes races. He was leading trainer by winners that year, and by the time Shannon arrived at the trainer's Bay Meadows barn on 4 November 1947, Molter was on his way to that title again.

The slight Texan, nicknamed 'The Kid', was apple-cheeked, sorrel-haired and taciturn. He never used two words if one would do. A standard owner–trainer conversation in the Molter barn went: 'How do you like my horse today, Willie?'

'I like him a little.'

'He's a good bet to win?'

'He might be.'

Molter's owners ranged from people like the Curlands to Louis B. Mayer's second-stringers, their horses useful stakes animals down the West Coast, but hardly superstars. The trainer admitted that the hardest part of his job was handling the owners, whom he thought overestimated horses and demanded higher classes. 'I prefer to put them in races they can win,' he said. Molter was the best in the business at that. If there was a formula to accruing winners, he didn't know it, saying only that there were two ways to win races. 'One of them is to know your horse,' he said. 'The other is to know the condition book.'

The condition book was published every fortnight, and dispersed at the racing secretary's office of the tracks where meetings were due. It was the bible of the business, a roster of all the races coming up in that fortnight, and those races were written around the types of horses stabled at the track during that time. For example, if there were an abundance of maiden horses in the barns, the condition book would advertise a greater number of maiden events. There were always listed and stakes races included in the book, for it was the job of the racing secretary to create competitions for every class of horse. When the book came out, it disappeared down the backstretch like hairlines. Molter was one of its most ardent fans. He would sit in his director's chair in the shed row, hat pushed back, dog Billy at his feet, poring through the book and marking pages. He had horses to fit almost every type of race, and he ran them constantly. Once a horse was fit, Molter didn't believe in keeping it in its box. It was a west American attitude that Molter would stand by all his life, but rather than assuming his horses were overworked, they were in fact fitter for the regime. Battle-hardened, they maintained their form through racing rather than trackwork.

They went kindly for Molter, the trainer possessing a manner that settled horses. There was kindliness about him, and modesty that belied his success. He never lost his wick with a horse, rarely complained about a race, a track or a rival. His barn was civilised and friendly, almost farmyard-like. On any day, his teenage daughter Norma Jean pottered about. She was devoted to her father (Molter was divorced). The trainer 'dated' with his daughter on many of racing's social occasions, and Norma Jean tagged along to major race meetings. In 1947, when her father became the first trainer in California to fly a horse (On Trust) to the Kentucky Derby, she went along for the flight.

At that time, Willie Molter raced his charges solely in California. He was smart with money, cut down on travelling expenses by supporting the West Coast meetings from Del Mar, Hollywood Park and Santa Anita to Tanforan, Golden Gate Fields and Bay Meadows. He cleared $40,000 in 1946, a fortune. Molter charged $10 a day for each horse in his barn, and took 10 per cent of winnings. But he didn't skimp on jockeys; it cost the same to use Johnny Longden as it did a halfwit apprentice with no experience, so Longden rode all of Molter's first-choice horses. Other riders for the barn included big names Johnny Adams and Jack Westrope. The trainer gave a winning hoop $35, $15 for a losing ride. The trainer also believed in finding the best grooms, paid them top wages for their loyalty. And he thought that an excellent track rider, or exercise boy, was more important than a jockey. Molter learned more about his string from his morning riders than he did on any race day.

At the time of Shannon's arrival, the big gun in the Molter barn was On Trust, the three-year-old son of boom sire Alibhai. He was the best three-year-old Molter had handled, a big chestnut who had snatched the Santa Anita Derby that March. He had lost the Kentucky Derby by two lengths, running a respectable fourth to Jet Pilot, on terms all the way. Molter thought he would improve with age, as the Alibhais often did, and he was right. On Trust was almost a four-year-old when Shannon moved in, but the pair would get to know each other very well, very quickly.

Molter's first impressions of the Australian horse were of a tidy, compact thoroughbred, all smooth lines and long mane, an elegance about him. Shannon wasn't big, a shade over 16.1 hands high, but his shoulder was impressive, long and sloped. He was also deeper through the girth than the average American horse. But his temperament spoke louder than his looks, for he was hardly off the *Boogabilla* when he settled into Molter's rhythm. He slept well in the deep straw of his new box, drank the American water he found in his trough, the strange oats in his manger. He gave no trouble, and it endeared him to his new trainer immediately.

For his first few days on the backstretch, Shannon strolled around, growing acquainted with the place, its hundreds of horses coming and going, the hot-walkers. At any point, Shannon looked over his box door at Molter's ducks or cats squabbling and playing, and it settled him. The barns were alive with activity all day. Bay Meadows wasn't an old track, its first meeting occurred on 3 November 1934, but it was a pretty course, all palm trees and Spanish curves, an oasis feel to it. The track itself was a one-mile oval, with a six-furlong chute on the far stretch. It was clay loam underfoot, the straight only a furlong and a half from the home turn. It wasn't at all like broad, spacious Randwick. There were automatic starting gates (far more advanced than those in Australia) and a totalisator board. The grandstand housed 7500 people, the clubhouse another 2000. Created out of the ground by California's racing visionary Bill Kyne, it was the first track in North America to use the totalisator and the photo-finish camera.

Shannon stepped on to it for the first time early on the morning of 6 November 1947, a wintry Thursday over San Francisco. Temperatures were barely above freezing, about 44 degrees (7° C) locally. In his thin Australian summer coat, Shannon walked (rugged) under his exercise boy onto the track, shivering. Willie Molter tracked his every move, watched him loosen up as he picked up into a trot. After a circuit of the course the horse was led back in, trembling violently. Plenty of reporters trailed the session, curious about the import. Molter told them he wasn't concerned about Shannon's shivering. 'There's nothing wrong with him that rest won't cure,' he said. 'Everybody at the barn is just gratified that he is eating and sleeping normally.'

The horse was tired and cold, only days off an exhausting stint at sea. He was thin in the coat and adjusting to new food, and there wasn't a familiar face in sight. Molter knew all of this, and gave the Midstream stallion time to find his reserves. He gradually pulled Shannon up from walking and trotting exercises to light canters in the early mornings, and allowed him space to bury his toes in the track dirt. The surface was far different from any turf course, requiring a different stride, different action. The turns were also much sharper than Randwick or Rosehill. Shannon would learn them, but how long that would take was anyone's guess.

It went this way for a few weeks, right up until 18 November when Harry Curland pulled out of Shannon. Molter thought he might lose the horse, but W. J. Smith, in San Mateo at that time, advised the trainer that he would continue to manage the horse, assisted by Smith and David Davis, who had brought Phar Lap to Agua Caliente in 1932. Davis hadn't returned to Australia after his famous horse's very famous death, preferring to set up shop in California. He had dabbled in the importation of Australian and New Zealand horses ever since the Phar Lap years, with little success, but he thought he knew a thing or two about what it took to acclimatise them. In his opinion, Shannon should be raced right away. Form, Davis thought, held in an imported thoroughbred for at least three to four months after arrival. It would prove disastrous advice.

Molter was not about to make decisions for Shannon based on anyone's urgings. As the horse began light gallops in the mornings, the trainer professed he was 'very satisfied with the way Shannon was shaping up', but he wasn't going to rush things. Harry Curland had wanted the horse fit for the San Carlos Handicap on 1 January at Santa Anita, but after Curland's exit, Molter took things slowly with his new horse. Shannon's debut, he said, 'will not be for some months as we plan on going all-out for the Santa Anita Handicap on 28 February'. The tilt at the rich 'Hundred Grander' had been the plan before Shannon had left Sydney, and it didn't change, even when Neil S. McCarthy breezed into Bay Meadows in early December, the prospective new owner of the superstar.

—

The American racing calendar was very different from anything in Australia, organised into an ordered, clever set of racing weeks at alternate racetracks. In California in 1948, the season began on 1 January at Santa Anita Park, and the picturesque Arcadia track, resplendent in the foothills of the San Gabriel range, would play out its biggest events of the year until 6 March. After that, racing headed north, to Bay Meadows from 13 March to 8 May. From the middle of May until 24 July, Hollywood Park in Los Angeles had its turn. That meeting was one of the grandest of the year, hosting the rich Hollywood Gold Cup on 17 July, a $100,000 purse. After that, the sport went to Del Mar, then north again to Golden Gate Fields in San Francisco, and eventually Tanforan late in the year. It was a well-oiled regime that suited trainers. California was an enormous state, and the distances between tracks so significant that basing horses at a single barn and shipping them to meetings was impossible. Under this system, trainers took teams of horses to racetracks and left them there for weeks, boarding them wherever the meetings were going on. For this reason, stable accommodation at California's major tracks was massive: Santa Anita boasted 1833 boxes, Hollywood Park 1400, while Tanforan could squeeze in 1600 horses.

Willie Molter prepared his team for the Arcadia meeting. Shannon, travelling with the three-year-old On Trust, as well as the stakes horses Prevaricator and Burning Dream, stepped into a van on 16 December, rattling the 300-odd miles south to the Los Angeles hinterland. Santa Anita was a beautiful racecourse, the mountains tumbling towards the backstretch like a spectacular painted canvas. Even in winter, without the haze that rolled off the range onto the infield, the track was a vision. For the first time in months, Shannon lifted his nose into air that was free of the smell of saltwater. He settled into his quarters, in the track stables that sat on the south-west fringes of the course, beside the grandstand. The barns were even busier than Bay Meadows, many horses arriving for the first meet of the year.

There was plenty of interest in Molter's charge. Shannon had been galloping for a week or two, turning over his opposition back home. The week before, Molter had sent him around Bay Meadows with Burning Dream, who was no slouch. That horse had won the San Francisco County Handicap on 22 November and was in fighting fettle. The pair galloped steadily for the first part of the trial until Burning Dream broke away at the five-pole. He clattered away as they arced into the turn, and Shannon sat coolly, lengths behind. Coming into the straight, the Australian horse picked up, motoring over the Bay Meadows dirt towards Burning Dream. He picked off his rival before he passed the winning post, and was going away when he did. Clockers spoke at length of the episode, of the import who had run over the seasoned stakes winner that morning. The trial followed Shannon all the way to Santa Anita, and commenting in the Los Angeles paper *Examiner*, turf editor Maurice Bernard said that the horse had 'brought with him some tall tales about his speed'. Bernard said Shannon wasn't 'a picture horse, but his record is tremendous'.

After a few days at Santa Anita, the horse was breezing with the rest of Molter's team. Clockers, journalists, fellow trainers . . . they lined the rails to watch the Australian clip. Shannon didn't disappoint. On 21 December, he ran what looked like a lazy three furlongs in a smart 35 seconds, his action so easy that watchers had to check their timepieces. Nevertheless, Molter wasn't convinced the horse was race-ready. He admitted Shannon was getting stronger every day, dropping the condition he had put on during his voyage and adjusting to cooler climes, different food. But Molter didn't expect to start him in competition until the end of January, probably in an easy mile race that would pop up in the condition book.

It was foresight on the trainer's behalf, for Santa Anita fell into a winter heatwave that no one was expecting. Temperatures broke 86°F (30° C) in the first fortnight of 1948, and a virus swept through the barns, running many horses down. Shannon began coughing, and Molter kept him off the track for several days. The trainer wasn't concerned, as the horse didn't have a fever and he was eating well, but Shannon's system was awry and Molter took no chances. About the same time, the weights for the Santa Anita Handicap emerged, and the Australian received 9 st. It was only 4 lbs less than the top weighted horse, the sensational Armed. Webb Everett, the Santa Anita handicapper, had made his judgement off Shannon's Australian form, which probably wasn't fair, given the vastly different circumstances Shannon would be racing in. Nevertheless, the horse was installed 8/1 in the betting for the February event.

Crisp and clear over Arcadia on 21 January, five weeks from the 'Hundred Grander', Shannon stepped on to the Santa Anita dirt for a workout. Molter perched on the rail, his hat pushed back, squinting into the rising sun. It was warm. His horse trotted away from the straight and around the bend towards the six-pole. Shannon would sprint out of the backstretch for the drill. Molter clicked his stopwatch when Shannon sprang away, as did a posse of gawking onlookers. Shannon gathered himself down the backstretch, leaning into the first half-mile in 46⅖, and breezed into the straight all power and easy energy. He stopped the clock at 1:12⅕ for the six, blowing only a little. The Texan was thrilled. He put the horse back in the barn and dug up the Santa Anita condition book.

Shannon was ready.

38

Too quick out of the bend, the straight too short

There it was, the sixth race on the card on 24 January, a seven-furlong spurt around Santa Anita. It didn't have a name, but by declarations it had a smart field. Seven horses would go to post, but interest across California fell on Australian Shannon.

The bay left Molter's barn in the mid-afternoon, race day. It was mild, and the sun was out as Shannon warmed up in front of the stalls. He was relaxed, strolling along on a loose lead behind Molter's assistant trainer, Clyde Turk. The tiny redhead, once a jockey, shadowed Molter's top horses, and he was buttoned up in a smart shirt, pleated pinstripe trousers, Cuban heels. Locals lined the rails to look at the pair. 'Do you like him Clyde?' they chirped, flicking between the pages of their race books, cocking an ear to track announcer Joe Hernandez. Turk grinned back at them. He would be a solo trainer within years.

Santa Anita was busy and colourful, bursting with winter bloom and west coast energy. Perhaps it was the Sierra Madre that rolled off the backstretch, or the easy Los Angeles swagger, but the racecourse was the idol of Pacific horseracing, the richest track in the world. In the hands of its captain, Doc Strub, it had made money since its very first meeting in 1934, and it operated like no other place in California. It had its own fire department, printing presses and police. In 1947, it turned over $140 million during its 55 days of racing, trucking vans in and out with $2 million, $3 million in change at a time. Doc Strub was unabashed about its efficiency. 'We park 30,000 cars in an afternoon. No other place in the world does a parking job so great,' he said. He was also famously confident. 'I could run anything,' he once quipped. 'I've always had a very vivid imagination.'

On 24 January 1948, Santa Anita was popping with colour. There were camellia bushes taller than men, and pansies lining the paddock gardens. The infield was a carpet of burnt yellows and reds, while the warm weather had woken the laurels, pepper and orange trees early. With its art deco clubhouse and English-like gardens, Santa Anita was old-world and new in exotic, extroverted California.

Shannon's race would jump at 4.02 pm, and by 3 pm he was in the stalls getting ready. Molter opted to run him in a simple snaffle with D-rings, but he put a sheepskin noseband on the horse, hoping it would help Shannon concentrate around the turns. Molter looked at the horse's feet one more time. He had pried off Shannon's heavier bar shoes and replaced them with light aluminium plates, standard for American tracks. But when the shoes had come off Molter had been concerned at the deep holes, many more than he had expected, that punctured the walls of Shannon's hooves. The farrier had filed the holes, and the team hoped they wouldn't weaken Shannon's action, but no one was sure they wouldn't.

The Australian had 8 st 5 lbs (117 lbs) on his back, and jockey Noel 'Spec' Richardson was engaged (Johnny Longden, though Molter's first call, had opted to ride the fancied Plover). Spec Richardson was a veteran from Idaho, a seasoned, ballsy hoop who had seen it all. He would forever be marked by the Seabiscuit–Ligaroti match race of 1938: riding Ligaroti, who hadn't a realistic chance of towing Seabiscuit home, Richardson had snagged his rival's saddlecloth, then his jockey George Woolf, dragging Seabiscuit back to a crunching photo finish. The stewards wiped both riders out for the stunt, in days when old-fashioned chicanery was on the run from the telefilm tower. These days, ageing Spec Richardson was better behaved, one of the wizened rags of the California scene. In the minutes before he swung onto Shannon, he was told to go easy. Molter didn't want his import knocked about on his first appearance.

The Midstream horse walked out of the paddock and through

the tunnel that led to the Santa Anita dirt. Richardson perched on his back in McCarthy's silks: green and blue quarters, green and blue cap. When Shannon emerged, thousands of racegoers drifted across the apron to stare at him, Braven Dyer among them. 'He is a nice-looking horse,' Dyer wrote of Shannon, 'along the lines of Seabiscuit, but he doesn't impress as being another Phar Lap.' Across the racecourse, people wondered if Shannon might run like him. The horse had to walk to the seven-furlong chute for his race (unlike Australia, America didn't ask for preliminary gallops). As Shannon picked his way to the start, he grew tetchy and hot under Spec Richardson, his feet so much lighter than he was used to, the crowds so much larger, the space different. Baulking at the narrow confines of the automatic starting gate, he was one of the last horses to load. He was in postposition four, staring anticlockwise for the very first time in his life down the Santa Anita backstretch.

Before the gates pinged, an atom of a second was silent. Willie Molter was in the stands, Neil McCarthy in his owner's box squinting across the infield. Neither had any clue how their horse would race, but conceded Shannon had adversity in every corner: new feed, new water, a new jockey. He was first-up in four months, had gained weight, dropped it and bounced into work with a thin summer coat. He had never jumped from an automatic stall, had never run over the American dirt, had never raced in aluminium shoes. He had also never run anticlockwise. The Australian horse was up against it when his metal gate clanged open at a half-second past 4.02 pm and he threw his forelegs onto the Santa Anita seven.

Windfields, the east-coaster, burst from Shannon's outside into an early sprint, cutting across to the rail and hauling the field of seven through the first quarter-mile in 22⅖. It was incredibly fast for an inexperienced Shannon, who had sat all his life off the Australian style, settling early and building up for the dash home. Spec Richardson hustled him to keep up, so Shannon spurted after the leading division, ripping along behind Windfields and Plover on the rail. As they came out of the backstretch they turned the half-mile over in 45⅖.

The Santa Anita track was an oval, a constant curve out of the back to the straight, and Richardson leaned on his left rein all the way, keeping Shannon in. But the Australian found the bend too sharp at the speed he was travelling, and he tried to go wide, looking for space to put his stride. His jockey held him in, and Shannon slipped back to fourth, then fifth, fumbling. Out of the bend he looked out of contention. He hit the straight almost at the back of the pack, but in straight running he found his feet and went after the leaders as he always had. He quickened so easily that he powered onto the Argentine horse Endeavour II, and Richardson snatched him up to avoid a collision. When he came again, he ran out of straight. The Santa Anita home stretch was only a furlong and a half long, and Windfields was over the line before Shannon had reached top speed. He ran under the wire third on Endeavour's flanks, two and bit lengths off the winner. They cracked 1:22⅖ for the seven.

Spec Richardson stood up in the irons and slowed his mount down. Shannon had gone around the clubhouse turn at full speed, was one of the last to pull up. The jock hadn't given him a punishing ride, didn't throttle him in the straight. If he had, Shannon probably would have run past Endeavour for second, but Molter had been clear about preserving him. Shannon's coat was wet and brassy when Richardson jumped off and weighed in, the jockey scurrying for his next ride in the San Felipe Stakes. He paused to talk to the press boys. 'He put up a nice race, looks like being a good horse,' he said. 'There are no excuses for him not winning, except that I was blocked at one stage when Endeavour drifted out. I had to snatch Shannon out to keep him from running up on that horse's heels.' Then he was gone.

No excuses for him not winning. It was a silly comment from the jockey, suggesting that Richardson didn't appreciate how difficult it was for Shannon to overcome the conditions. The greatest obstacle, atop the new shoes, direction and surface, was that American races went like the clappers from the jump. Sectionals on US tracks often ran 10 and 11 seconds to the furlong from start to finish in sprint races, with jockeys driving their mounts out of the gate into the lead, and squeezing them to stay in front all the way to the judge. For 25 races in Australia, Shannon had learned to relax then race for home. Had Richardson expected the horse to learn otherwise within his first American effort? Neil McCarthy said only that it was a 'satisfactory' effort, and Molter said nothing at all. But privately, the trainer was surprised that Shannon had run so well. He had predicted that Shannon's showing would depend on how he handled the starting gate, if he would adapt to it, jump away on terms. In the end, it wasn't the starting gate that undid the horse: it was the turn.

Shannon took place money of $600 for the run. There were 47,000 patrons at Santa Anita that afternoon, and they had invested 12 per cent of the tote pool on the Australian horse. They murmured about the result, unsure if Shannon had figured things, if he had fumbled in the turn or tired in the straight. But it was pretty clear to Jack McDonald, sporting editor of San Francisco's *Call-Bulletin*. He thought Shannon had run a terrific race in the circumstances. He said, 'Only one things [sic] sours me on Shannon, and that is a recent quotation from an Australian horseman that Shannon is almost as good as Winooka. There must be some mistake here. Winooka was a dud. Shannon is a lot better a horse than Winooka and his pop and mom put together. He may not be as great a horse as Phar Lap, but what Australian horse ever was?'

—

The debut had gone according to plan, neither electrifying nor taxing for Shannon. Molter interpreted it as introductory, a race that brought the horse along into racing condition, chiselled away the cobwebs after a long lay-off. The plan for Shannon remained the Santa Anita Handicap on 28 February, which was four weeks away, and Molter had a cloudy map in his head of how they would get there. He planned to squeeze the horse into at least another two races before the big one, including the San Antonio Handicap on Valentine's Day. It meant Shannon would back up almost every week.

Molter scanned the condition book for a possible next start. In particular, he was looking for an 'overnight' race, one in which a horse could be entered the day before a race was due off. They were popular at this time of year at Santa Anita, as many of the big guns worked their way up into stakes company. Molter spotted one on 3 February, a seven-furlong race once again out of the chute. He pencilled it in for Shannon, and by final declarations there were six entries. Among them was the imposing Irish import Mafosta, a former champion two-year-old, now six, for Montrose Stable.

Mafosta had 8 st 10 lbs in the 3 February race, and Johnny Longden had opted to pilot. The horse was a slick customer when he was in top form, but he was winding up and probably wasn't yet at his best. Bymeabond, a former Santa Anita Derby winner, shared top weight with him. Among the others, Amble In was a winner of the Longacres Mile and Happy Issue had clinched the Hollywood Gold Cup in 1944. Apart from Shannon on 8 st 3 lbs, there was the lightweight Plumper on 7 st 12 lbs. For a mid-week race, it wasn't a shabby one, and Molter thought it was well within Shannon's grasp. Racegoers thought so too; they backed the horse into odds on.

Shannon jumped slowly from the inside stall, and Spec Richardson bustled him to keep the rail. He was fifth to leave the gates, and after a furlong down the backstretch he was ahead of only Happy Issue. Bymeabond was tearing through the first quarter in 22⅖, with Mafosta giving him headaches all the way. Leaning into the turn, Shannon moved up to fourth to threaten Plumper. At the half-mile they had gone 45½, and Richardson urged Shannon to follow Plumper as that horse closed in on the leaders. Plumper sprinted around the fighting pair upfront, and by the straight he had surged ahead with Mafosta. Shannon, who had hung wide again on the turn, gathered himself and passed Bymeabond. But the leaders were too quick out of the bend, the straight too short to make an impression. When Plumper flashed under the wire in 1:23⅖, Shannon was four lengths down the track, third again.

Richardson kept driving Shannon on, and past the judge he went another furlong before he let up on the horse. He rode out a full mile, and in the towers, the stewards were on their feet. Unless sanctioned, a post-race workout was strictly forbidden. Before Spec Richardson had trotted Shannon off the track, the Santa Anita officials were waiting. They had already lodged a complaint with Willie Molter, who denied he had instructed his jockey to gallop on for the mile, and Richardson himself denied doing it. 'I was cooling him off,' he said. Looking askance at that, the stewards declared no penalty would be imposed, but they were agitated. They warned that any post-race workout in future would be approved and programmed on the card. Molter and his jockey left the stewards' room like reluctant schoolboys.

Across Santa Anita, there were mumbles about Shannon's mediocre showing, mostly from punters who had taken the horse at odds on. But American race crowds were not like their Sydney cousins: they grumbled politely, tossing their spent tickets in the air, shrugging and moving to the tote machine for the next event. The newspapers were not so well mannered. Paul Lowry took to the *Los Angeles Times* in a spouting editorial: 'All Shannon did was burn the public's money,' he said. 'None of the horses he has faced so far are the real speed burners at the track. Horses like With Pleasure and Brookfield would tie him in knots.' Lowry suggested that the American public had been oversold on Shannon's virtues.

Neil McCarthy was furious, hit back at the *Times* reporter. 'What do these writers expect of a horse that has raced only twice on a different type of track in a different direction, with different shoes and different feed in his belly?' He rebutted a rumour that the film genius Harry Warner, of Warner Bros, had withdrawn an offer of $125,000 for Shannon after his third-place run that day. 'I have never talked any deal over with Warner and I have no plans to do so.' The Hollywood attorney was learning quickly about the prickly end of the racing game.

He wasn't disappointed with Shannon. McCarthy was a patient man, and this horse had demanded patience from all men since his arrival. McCarthy saw Shannon as a puzzle that he had to put together. After the race, he wondered if the horse wasn't acclimatised. Dave Davis' suggestion to race Shannon immediately hadn't gone to plan, hadn't returned the results Davis expected. It was silly to think the model that had worked for Phar Lap 16 years before would work for Shannon; Phar Lap had raced in Mexico, not Santa Anita, and Shannon was an altogether different horse, a speed horse. Doubts hovered in McCarthy's head about aiming for the Santa Anita Handicap. 'He's a really good horse,' he told the local press, 'but I think he might need more time to become acclimatised. I still hope to get him up for that race, but he may not come around to himself until the summer, when he'll race at Hollywood Park.' Conferring with Willie Molter about this, McCarthy suggested that the Santa Anita conditions book was unfair to foreign horses. Molter didn't think so, though he had never trained a seven-year-old import from the southern hemisphere. He was learning as much as Shannon as they went along, and he was the first to admit it.

Eleven days later, Shannon stripped for the San Antonio Handicap on Valentine's Day. It was his first stakes race in America, and he was up to his eyes in it. Among the field of 18 horses were the best California could cough up, thoroughbreds like his stablemate On Trust, and Olhaverry, who had won the Santa Anita Handicap in 1947. Talon was there, a mottled grey who had won the Los Angeles Handicap on 27 January and was pre-post favourite for the Hundred Grander. Also present was Autocrat, winner of the San Carlos on New Year's Day, and Terry Bargello, winner of the Santa Catalina a month before. Traditionally a rod for the Santa Anita Handicap, the San Antonio was a stiff test for Shannon in a big field over the mile and a quarter course. Molter was nervous about it, considered switching Spec Richardson to another horse. In the end, the veteran hoop kept the ride, and he was proffered little instruction before he walked Shannon out of the tunnel onto the dirt.

It was a very warm day in Arcadia, and the nine-furlong San Antonio would jump at 4.50 pm. There was a haze over the infield, the San Gabriel range looked purple and fuzzy. Shannon was edgy when he arrived behind the starting gates; the huge crowds in the grandstand were right beside him. The field would jump from the home stretch, so the bustle of the apron was only feet away. As he slid into gate 16, only two horses on his outside, Shannon shifted from toe to toe. He had 8 st 5 lbs in his saddle, against On Trust with 9 st. He was favourably weighted for the race, but he was badly drawn. He was also coupled in the betting with his stable-mate On Trust (which meant that anyone who backed him backed On Trust also), so it was impossible to measure how much support the Australian had on the tote. Most guessed it was minimal.

His gate clattered back and he sprang away, eighth to leave the stalls. Sprinting past the judge for the first time, he had moved into fourth on the outside behind Bymeabond, Brabancon and V-Boy. They dashed into the clubhouse turn, turning over the first quarter in 22⅘, and Shannon leaned into the backstretch with the leaders. He was on terms as they straightened, and Spec Richardson sat quietly, allowing the horse to run his own race. Shannon was galloping handily, his stride improving as they skipped down the back. But the trouble began at the long turn for home. Shannon couldn't keep his speed around the tight bend, grappling with changing leads, and he drifted out, opening up a space on his nearside that immediately swelled with horses. He lost a length when On Trust bumped him out further, then another, and Talon surged up, then Autocrat. Richardson drew the whip and asked his horse to go on, but Shannon found little. He was scratchy and awkward over the surface, had no time to find his rhythm before Talon raced under the wire and won the race. The field was strung out behind him like butchers' sausages, with Shannon in the chasing pack finishing eighth.

Talon's victory was impressive, the six-year-old earning his oats as favourite for the Hundred Grander, but it took a backseat to Shannon's loss. Commenting in the *Examiner*, Maurice Bernard said the Australian would have to show miraculous improvement to be any force in the Handicap. 'Shannon is undoubtedly a better horse than he has shown here [in America], and we probably won't see him at his best until the summer at Hollywood Park.' Headlines covering the feature were dismal: 'Shannon Fails Again', 'Shannon Outclassed', 'Shannon's Humiliation.' They went all the way to Australia on the evening wires. At Santa Anita, racegoers decided the import was nothing more than hot air, an also-ran for the big handicap on 28 February. It was pretty simple to them: Australia's champion had been oversold.

—

A long way across the Pacific, in the enclosure at Melbourne's Caulfield racecourse, Darby Munro stood with Ossie Porter before the Futurity Stakes. It was a week after the San Antonio Handicap, and the Demon Darb was thinking about his old friend Shannon. Glib, he turned to Porter and said, 'You've been lucky with your high-priced buys Ossie, but you were luckier still missing Shannon. I don't think he'll win a race in America.'

39

The Hundred Grander

Shannon was falling out of the newspapers. As the days inched towards the Hundred Grander, the California press devoted less and less space to the faltering Australian. He was another import losing its way, a horse that had arrived with fanfare and reputation built on the stopwatch, but had lost it all somewhere on Santa Anita's final bend. Australians didn't understand it, took to questioning the trainer, then the jockey. It was impossible their champion was no such thing. Spec Richardson must have been getting it wrong.

In Sydney, Darby Munro followed reports that Shannon was being ridden too soft. Australian writers even suggested the horse was missing Munro's vigour, that if Richardson had been more aggressive with him, their San Antonio result would have been much better. It was probably not true, for Talon had been streets ahead of the chasing bunch, but Australians didn't know that. They rapped on Munro's door for his opinion. Shannon's old pilot didn't repeat what he had said to Ossie Porter, instead made a trans-Pacific offer to fly to America for the Hundred Grander. Munro didn't think he could get it wrong with Shannon, because he never had before, and it mattered little to him that surfaces, sectionals and style were vastly different on American tracks.

The Australian papers went giddy at the idea of horse and jockey reuniting, and they carried the story across the country, from the city dailies to tiny country weeklies in remote Queensland. It had the US press askance. 'One finds it difficult to believe that Shannon's connections would support such a proposal,' New York's *Morning Telegraph* said. It was right. Neil McCarthy wired to Australia that he was appreciative of Munro's offer, though he would have to decline it. He said, 'It isn't the jockey that's wrong.

It's the fact that the horse isn't in condition and cannot get into condition as long as certain restrictions prevent his entry in practice races.'

It was becoming a bugbear for McCarthy. For weeks, he and Molter had been cruising the condition book for prep races, easy mile events that could improve Shannon's fitness, sharpen him up for stakes company. But time and again the restrictions imposed on entries opted Shannon out. A good example arrived the week before the San Antonio. McCarthy had wanted to enter the horse in an overnight event on 10 February, but the conditions limited entries to horses who had not won a race outside the US, Canada or Mexico in 1947. In other words, Shannon, who had been winning across Sydney in 1947, was ineligible. McCarthy slammed the conditions as 'terribly unfair and unsportsmanlike', and bemoaned them to the local press. 'How is Shannon ever to get in top shape unless we are permitted to run him?' He conceded that Shannon had not been ready for the calibre of the San Antonio, but McCarthy had had little other choice as a run-in to the Hundred Grander.

Fred Purner was the publicity director at Santa Anita, Doc Strub's right-hand man. He slammed McCarthy as a 'perpetual complainer', saying the attorney was familiar with the Santa Anita condition book and knew exactly why certain conditions were imposed. He reiterated that under California racing law, each day of racing required a California-bred field only, and that myriad other terms existed that everyone, not just foreign horses, had to live with. McCarthy wouldn't be put down. 'Shannon has been prevented from starting in many races because of his Australian victories in 1947. They might do well to revise conditions of the racing book to give foreign horses a less difficult task.'

Santa Anita was allergic to negative press, so Purner put the issue to bed. He said the racing authorities would take a good look at McCarthy's complaint, and would consider revising the condition book pertaining to foreign horses. McCarthy was satisfied, but he was still left with a displaced racehorse. With just over a week to go before the Santa Anita Handicap, he wondered if he should run the horse at all.

Willie Molter didn't think he should. The Texan wasn't convinced that Shannon was ready for the Hundred Grander. Molter wasn't worried about the distance; the mile and a quarter of the handicap, America's championship distance, would be no problem for Shannon. Molter was concerned about the competition. The Santa Anita Handicap was, arguably, the stiffest event of its kind in America, every year the slickest horses vying for its rich purse. It was one of nine $100,000 events on the American calendar, but it was the best. In that year's field there would be stablemate On Trust, who was flying, as well as Talon, Autocrat, Double Jay and Olhaverry. Each was at their top, and Molter feared that flinging Shannon among them, when he was anything but on terms with them, would humiliate him.

One other thing pressed on Molter's mind: Shannon's handicap weight. Webb Everett had given Shannon 9 st for the big race back in December, which hadn't bothered the trainer. But that was before Shannon had let everyone know he was struggling to grip his new American environment. As race day neared, it looked likely the Australian would carry top weight in the Santa Anita Handicap, four pounds more than Talon, three more than On Trust. Endeavour II, the Argentinian import, was closest to Shannon on 8 st 12 lbs. It was a remarkable situation, because on his form Shannon was nowhere near worthy of his impost, and if it weren't the Hundred Grander, Molter would have scratched him right away. But McCarthy was making the final decision about the race, and he was erring on the side of running.

In the two weeks between the San Antonio and the big one, Shannon was set a fetching schedule. On 18 February, he went with On Trust over the full handicap course of a mile and a quarter, clocking 24 seconds for the first quarter-mile, 47⅘ for the half, 1:37⅕ for the mile, and the full measure in 2:04⅗. A day or so later, Shannon worked seven furlongs alone, going under the wire in 1:38⅕. He pulled up full of running. If clockers didn't know of his average form so far, they would have installed him as favourite for the Handicap. He was galloping so easily, so dazzlingly, in the mornings that he was almost a different horse. Molter told McCarthy that on these trials, Shannon was doing well, so McCarthy decided not to race the horse again before the Santa Anita. He had planned to start Shannon in the Washington Handicap on 23 February, five days before the feature event, but he scratched the day before. As a final hit-out, Molter scheduled a gallop between On Trust and Shannon on 21 February, between races. Johnny Longden was aboard On Trust, and Spec Richardson took Shannon's reins. The pair set off on a smart gallop as Santa Anita racegoers clung to the rails to watch them. They covered a mile in 1:37⅖, and the Handicap distance of 10 furlongs in 2:04⅘. In a photo finish, On Trust had a nostril in front. It was a sparkling trial for Shannon, in particular because his stablemate was at the top of his game. Though the locals decided that On Trust had more in the tank at the finish, Shannon came home in good fettle.

—

28 February, the gates into Santa Anita swung open at 10.30 am. Some 62,000 racegoers began a buoyant march into the Arcadia track. It was a dull, cool day over Los Angeles, trench coats and umbrellas the order, but by the first race at 12.30 pm, patrons slugged cold beer and lemonade, and Harry Curland's hot dogs and hamburgers, and they hardly noticed the weather. The track was unaffected by the day's drizzle, so the Santa Anita surface was 'fast'. The Handicap was the seventh race of eight, the feature event of the year due off at 4.50 pm.

Shannon arrived at the stalls in the early afternoon. He was feeling the cold, and Molter's boys kept him rugged right up to saddling time. They brushed his thin coat, straightened his long mane and slipped Spec Richardson's saddle onto his back. Under the leather there was 9 lbs of lead. When the horse walked into the parade area with On Trust, the crowds were thick around the rail. People stared at Shannon, not because he was a fancied contestant for the Hundred Grander, but because he was a headline horse and had been in the news for months. Spec Richardson stood in the centre of the paddock with his arms folded, McCarthy and Molter flanked him either side. Molter dangled his binoculars in his right hand, and McCarthy, in a pale striped overcoat, stuffed his hands into his pockets to keep warm. Molter ran over final-moment tactics with the jockey, telling him to stay with On Trust. Shannon had drawn barrier nine for the race, and the trainer wanted the horse on the leaders before the turn out of the clubhouse. McCarthy wished the jockey luck as Richardson strode away from them to climb aboard Shannon.

The horses headed for the tunnel, a much smaller field than the Handicap usually had. There were 14 entrants, down from 22 the year before. Club officials had doubled the entrance fee in 1948, and Paul Lowry commented in the *Los Angeles Times* that the race was missing those owners that used to run their horses just to say they had had a starter in the Santa Anita Handicap. Nevertheless, the competition was fierce. Talon was the on-course favourite with everyone, the best route-running horse in the field. On Trust was second choice, though he was coupled with Shannon in the betting. In Sydney, locals had flocked to bookmakers in support of the Australian runner, but Californians had shown no such loyalty. They were cheering for On Trust, who would be on pace all the way. Autocrat, though seven years old, was prominent in figures, and the only blight on the field was the defection of the defending winner Olhaverry. He had been reshod in the days leading up to the race, but the farrier had fitted the new plates too tight and the horse had gone lame.

The enormous crowds mumbled as the horses circled behind the starting gates. Shannon looked rough; he was sweating down his neck, between his hind legs and under his saddle. He was also twitching around the withers, a very nervous horse. William Mills, the Santa Anita starter, shuffled them into gate order. Terry

Bargello went in on the rails with Talon next, then On Trust. Shannon gave a little trouble going into nine, with Class Day on his outside. On the extreme outside was Flashco, and they were ready to jump at 4.53 pm.

A spirited cheer rose over the Arcadia racecourse when the gates slammed open, and the Hundred Grander was on its way. Shannon was eighth to leave the stalls, and as On Trust hugged the rails down the straight for the first time, he was well back in ninth position. Spec Richardson scrubbed him to improve his gallop, but Shannon had been crowded from the outside horses coming in, and he had nowhere to go. Chasing On Trust was impossible. Out the clubhouse turn, Shannon was impossibly placed. He was 11th through the first half-mile, 12th after six furlongs, and only Talon and Terry Bargello were behind him. Leaning out of the back-stretch, Talon moved into a gear and shot past him, and Shannon scrambled away at the back of the field. By the time he reached the straight, the race was almost over. Talon had swept around the field to win the Santa Anita by a nose, edging out On Trust in a photo finish, and Spec Richardson was hammering Shannon to beat Terry Bargello at the back. The bay horse was a shadow of his brilliant self, spent as he pawed his way over the final lengths of the race. Terry Bargello beat him by a neck, and Shannon ran dead last in the Hundred Grander.

McCarthy watched his little horse slow down to a walk after the winning post, and he knew he had made a mistake in start-ing him. There was no way Shannon was ready for this level of competition in America. Nevertheless, he was angry. 'He ran the worst possible kind of race,' he would say. 'He lacked confidence in the turn and over the last three furlongs he didn't even try.' Across Australia the following day, newspapers carried the headline that McCarthy would sell Shannon if he had 'the right type of offer'. They quoted the attorney as saying Shannon had been poorly ridden, but that Darby Munro wouldn't have done any better.

Any other man would have thrown in the towel, decided that Shannon was worthless, a dud. But McCarthy had watched

Shannon dazzle the clockers in the early mornings, and he knew there was breathtaking speed there. It just couldn't get out on race days. McCarthy had to figure this out, and as he calmed down after the race, his mind was turning the problem over. He went in search of Molter. The Texan was doubly heartbroken. On Trust had been pipped by a cruel margin, and at the other end of the field Shannon had scrambled home. Both horses were fine when they returned to the barn, but the Australian was exhausted, and everyone noticed. Maurice Bernard told his Los Angeles readership, 'Shannon is not himself here yet. They have been rushing him.'

Ernest Shaw hated to say it, but he'd seen this coming from the minute W. J. Smith had told him he'd missed out on Shannon. The ex-pat trainer was devastated for the Australian horse, and he found it maddening that Molter had imposed an American rhythm onto Shannon when, in fact, he should have trained the horse to his Australian pattern of running. 'Jockeys here hustle their mounts out of the gate,' he said, 'and race them along furiously in the early going, trusting the horse to have something left for the final furlong. Shannon is used to reserving his greatest effort for the final run.' Shaw was right. In his four starts to date, Spec Richardson had pushed, or tried to push, Shannon onto the speed right away. The first half-mile of American races was usually run in 46 and a bit seconds, while in Australia they were run in about 48 seconds. But the last half-mile of an Australian race was run at a much faster clip than in America. In other words, Shannon, racing one way for five years, was suddenly being forced to race upside down without any proper instruction on how to do so. 'It is absolutely vital for the jockey to give the horse the kind of race he has been trained to run,' Shaw said. 'Shannon was raced too soon and too often.' It was fool's material, and Molter and McCarthy had learned it the hard way.

The owner and trainer had not looked at Shannon's history with Peter Riddle. The wily, kind Bowral Street trainer had raced Shannon sparingly, his last two seasons with the horse bearing only five starts apiece. Aside from this, Riddle had known Shannon performed best when he had fresh legs. The horse's first-up record after long lay-offs was spectacular: first in the Campbelltown, and first in the Campbelltown. Peter Riddle had known exactly what it took to keep his stallion on the job of winning races, with precise management controlling every ounce of Shannon's brilliance. Trackwork was never taxing, the horse was rested in open paddocks regularly. As a result, he had turned into the Shannon that every Australian knew. But not for a second had McCarthy or Molter credited the late trainer for Shannon's record, and it was a mistake.

Willie Molter was California's leading trainer, no idiot when it came to horses. He understood them, could ply them this way and that because of his patience and talent. His errors with Shannon, therefore, were out of form. It was partly his inexperience in handling an international, but so much of Shannon's failure also fell on Harry Curland. It had been Curland who had insisted Shannon be pointed at the Hundred Grander before he was even off the boat, and it was two months later that McCarthy had stepped in, two months too late to preserve Shannon. Molter confessed that he was baffled by the Australian. 'He is the finest horse I think I have ever trained,' he said. 'He does things with such ease in the mornings as to convince me he is one of the truly great horses of modern times. But he just does not seem to convert his zip of a morning into winning races of an afternoon.' As much as McCarthy, Molter was determined to solve this puzzle.

The two men met after the Santa Anita to figure things out. McCarthy was distressed, for he had been criticised the length of California for starting his tired, unfit racehorse in the biggest race of the year. In addition, the Australian press was reporting that he wanted rid of the horse. In fact, nothing was further from the truth. McCarthy had worked painfully over many months to clear Shannon's road in America, and he was hardly going to back out of it after less than a month. In addition, he didn't part with horses easily (he had dozens of retired horses on his Moorpark pastures, animals that had long passed their use but that he was too fond of to get rid of). So in the aftermath of the Santa Anita failure, McCarthy did right by Shannon. He scratched the horse from all engagements, even though the Bay Meadows meeting was due to kick off on 13 March. He said Shannon would be rested, then brought along slowly for summer racing. Molter was relieved. 'By the time the Hollywood Park meeting comes around in July, I think you will see a different horse altogether,' he said.

And so it was that Shannon left Santa Anita on 1 March, in some sort of public disgrace. He was a tired horse, sore and cold after three strenuous months. Peter Riddle would have been turning in his fresh grave.

40

'Champion money burner of the United States'

March climbed into April in San Francisco with the speed of a watched pot. The cool nip of winter persisted in the early mornings, settling on the horses as they blew and snorted their way over Bay Meadows racetrack. Shannon had begun to feel it less, his thin southern skin growing thick to the chills, his constitution adapting slowly, like the seasons. He was getting over his tiredness in the warm, working environment of Molter's barn.

He would wake in the mornings long before the birds, to the rattle of rakes and buckets. The exercise boys would turn up, clanking saddles and girth buckles, chattering about this horse, that horse, the night before. They would rub Shannon off, tack him up and lead him out. They would walk him from the barns onto the backstretch. Sometimes Johnny Longden would jump on, sometimes Clyde Turk, but they all had been teaching Shannon how to gallop their way. They would drop the stirrup on the inside lead, encouraging the horse to shift his weight onto the near side around the turns. At first, they took it slow, building up his confidence on the corners. He slowly got the hang of it until he wasn't losing two, three and four lengths on the final turn, until he wasn't finding the lean into the straight so sharp. Gradually, they asked him to go faster. They taught him how to wake up coming out of the backstretch, to go and win his race well before he felt the straight under his feet. He was starting to race like an American.

He was starting to look like one too. Shannon had lightened up in the back end a lot, his waist much more greyhound-like than it had ever been. He was an angular horse now, seemed taller. Some of the American press had even taken to calling him 'the big bay'. Reporters on the west coast racing scene followed him with interest, curious to learn if the Australian would ever come good on his promises. The *Morning Telegraph* reported in mid-March that he was on the track regularly, was 'eating freely and, so far as the human eye can detect, is the picture of health'. Molter agreed with them. Shannon was in excellent nick on the outside, but the Texan wasn't so sure the horse was adjusted on the inside, and so he hesitated to say when Shannon would race again. Into April, this caused a few headaches for Neil McCarthy who thought the Hollywood Park summer meeting, due to commence on 18 May, was coming up quickly. He wanted Shannon to race a few times at Bay Meadows before he was vanned south to Los Angeles again, but Molter was adamant: the horse would not leave the barn unless everything was right. Rumours sprinkled around the backstretch that Molter and McCarthy were at loggerheads. One of Molter's staff commented, 'One of the charms of being an owner is seeing your horse run. But trainers look on this whole business from a different viewpoint. We thought Shannon had got over his tough sea voyage long ago, but it seems now we might have been wrong.'

The Bay Meadows meeting was due to close on 8 May, and McCarthy had nominated Shannon for the San Mateo Handicap on 24 April and the Bay Meadows Handicap on 1 May. These were highlights of the meeting, and the latter was Shannon's target race, but Molter had no fast plan on how to get there. On 17 April he scratched the horse from a six-furlong sprint, largely because he was worried about the penalty Shannon would incur if he won it, and then he scratched from the San Mateo also. The California press grumbled about the toing and froing, and Molter told them, 'It isn't that Shannon is not ready. We think he is, but we made up our minds that the track (for the sprint) was just not right for a newcomer to American racing after heavy rain.' He had noticed in the mornings that Shannon didn't enjoy sloppy going, so they elected to run the horse on 20 April instead, in an ordinary sprint race called the Marina Purse. It would be a soft debut for Shannon, only four others going to post and none was outstanding. Johnny Longden agreed to ride.

Race day was summery over Bay Meadows. The horses broke smartly in the Marina Purse, and Barbastel, on Shannon's outside, dashed into an early lead under Jack Westrope. Longden urged Shannon into a chasing position, and after two furlongs he was on Barbastel's flanks. The pair charged down the backstretch together, but Longden let Shannon settle a little, and Barbastel opened a length and a half on the pair. Going around the bend, the leader was still going like the clappers. He ran 22⅖ for the first quarter, 45⅖ for the second, and entering the straight he was a length and a half the better of Shannon. Longden sat low and rode furiously, and Shannon charged into the space in the middle. He closed quickly, so quickly that the Bay Meadows racegoers were on their feet. Barbastel and Shannon had gone five lengths clear of the rest of the field, and the Australian was motoring onto his rival. When they ran under the wire few could separate them, and a stride after the post Shannon had flown past Barbastel. As Longden stood up in his irons around the clubhouse, the judge called a photo finish. Barbastel won by a short neck.

Willie Molter thought it was an excellent race, for he was looking for things that no one else was. Shannon had raced on the pace, handled the turn and, with another yard in it, he would have won. He was also carrying 10 lbs more than Barbastel, so there was nothing to grunt at. At 1:10⅖ for the six, they had equalled the best time for the distance all year, and when Shannon trotted back in he was jaunty, pleased with himself. Longden slid off. 'He's a nice horse,' he said to Molter. 'He would have won in another stride.' But no one else saw it as did the trainer and jockey. Jack McDonald told his *Call-Bulletin* readers that Shannon was 'well on his way towards earning the title of champion money burner of the United States'. 'Is he another Winooka? The Australian champion might have sent the bookmakers in his own country to the poorhouse, but the bookmakers here could throw a champagne cocktail party for the horse and still be in front.'

McDonald was right. Shannon's competition in the Marina Purse was average. Barbastel was a six-year-old without a decent win to his name that season, and Shannon, in Australian form, would have sewn up the race without even warming up. The American press insisted that he should be winning already. They expected him to be on terms with On Trust and Mafosta, the leading horses on the west coast, because that is what they had been promised. Shannon had arrived in America in November, had started racing in January, and four months down the line he hadn't won a race. Even the cheap overnighters had proved beyond him. But Molter's suspicion was that Shannon was getting there, and in the meanwhile he just had to ignore the papers. It was almost impossible, and even more so after 1 May.

Ten horses lined up that late afternoon for the $50,000 Bay Meadows Handicap. It was a nine-furlong race, and Mafosta was top weight with 9 st. Shannon had only 8 st 4 lbs, and with Longden aboard the fancied Mafosta, Molter had given the ride to the hustling Willie Bailey. They moved into the stalls at 5.38 pm, an overcast and cool Saturday evening, and Shannon stood in gate eight. On his inside was a horse called Why Alibi with jockey Herb Lindberg, and on his outside the runners Miss Doreen and Amble In. When the stalls clattered open, Shannon jumped on terms and Bailey pushed him towards the front early. He ran over the track with Miss Doreen towards the rail, but he had gone only a few strides when Harry Lindberg rode Why Alibi hard into his path. Bailey took a sharp pull of Shannon to avoid a collision, getting a bump anyway, but Miss Doreen wasn't so lucky. As Shannon fell back, Why Alibi slammed into the mare and nearly knocked her off her feet. Lindberg charged off to the front of the field, and Bailey tried to rebalance Shannon into the clubhouse turn. They were eighth towards the back, trapped wide and looking hopeless. Down the backstretch, Shannon motored towards the front until he was fourth wide out. Bailey rode for a hole on the rail as they swept around the bend, but it closed before he got there. Once again, he pulled Shannon out of rhythm and the Australian horse slid back to fifth, sixth, seventh. Mafosta surged past the post six lengths up the track, and that was that.

The imported English stallion Midstream, photographed at Kia Ora Stud in September 1954 with stud groom Jack Keown. *(Fairfax Syndication)*

Lot 79 in the William Inglis & Son catalogue for the 1943 yearling sales, the Midstream colt out of Idle Words.

Trainer Peter Riddle, photographed in good health in the early 1930s.
(Courtesy of Mardi Henderson)

Shannon and strapper Barney O'Brien warm up before trackwork the morning
of 28 September 1945, a week before their first Epsom Handicap.
(Norman Brown/Fairfax)

One of the most famous of racing's front pages – the *Sun* headlines Shannon's
sensational Epsom Handicap loss of 5 October 1946.
(State Library of New South Wales)

Shannon wins the George Main Stakes at Randwick on 7 October 1946, defeating Flight by six lengths in Australasian record-breaking time.

Shannon's King's Cup victory over Flight (second) and Russia (third) on 12 October 1946 dispelled long-standing doubt about his ability to stay a mile and a half.

Darby Munro, in Peter Riddle's silks, unsaddles Shannon in the Randwick enclosure after the King's Cup victory. *(Frank Burke/Fairfax)*

Shannon's race books: (L–R) 1944 Sires' Produce Stakes; 1945 AJC Derby; 1946 Campbelltown Handicap; 1948 Sunset Handicap.

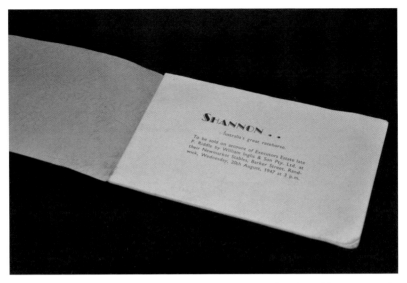

The sale booklet distributed by William Inglis & Son for the public auction of Shannon on Wednesday, 20 August 1947.

Shannon, led by Barney O'Brien, eyes nearly 4000 people that squeezed into Newmarket to witness his public sale. *(E. C. Bowen/Fairfax)*

W. J. 'Knockout' Smith meets his expensive purchase, Shannon, at trainer Frank Dalton's yard after the sale. *(E. C. Bowen/Fairfax)*

Shannon and Darby Munro step out for the Campbelltown Handicap on 30 August 1947 in W. J. Smith's colours for the first time. *(Gordon Short/Fairfax)*

Dashing Hollywood attorney Neil McCarthy, photographed on the
polo field at the Midwick Country Club, Los Angeles, in January 1934.

Neil McCarthy, pictured many years later in July 1951, with film magnate
Louis B. Mayer and his wife at the Keeneland yearling sales.

Almost a different horse after many months in America, the much lighter
Shannon photographed with jockey Johnny Adams in May 1948.

Jockey Johnny Longden drives Shannon to his first win in America, a track-record-breaking 12-length victory in the San Francisco County Handicap at Bay Meadows on 8 May 1948. (*Hollywood Park*)

Shannon, under Johnny Adams, storms over Mafosta and On Trust
to win the Argonaut Handicap at Hollywood Park on 31 May 1948.
(Hollywood Park)

A fortnight later, Shannon, with Adams up, stands in the winner's enclosure
after his greatest American victory – the rich Hollywood Gold Cup on
17 July 1948. *(Hollywood Park)*

Shannon steps off the Santa Fe Express in Lexington, Kentucky, on 20 December 1948 after a long rail passage from California. *(Keeneland-Meadors)*

Later the same afternoon, Shannon arrives at Spendthrift to begin stud duties. *(Keeneland-Meadors)*

This advertisement, making much of Shannon's record-holding career, appeared in *The Blood-Horse* magazine on 25 December 1948, only two weeks after the horse's shock retirement. *(The Blood-Horse)*

A conformation shot of Shannon just after his retirement from racing in late 1948. *(Keeneland-Meadors)*

A much different Shannon photographed at Spendthrift Farm after several seasons at stud. *(Keeneland-Meadors)*

At Spendthrift Farm on 17 September 1949, Shannon gets a pat from Azzalin Romano, Australian owner of Bernborough, while (L–R) Spendthrift master Leslie Combs II, Myron Fox and Baron D'Osten watch on. *(Keeneland-Meadors)*

Shannon is paraded outside the Spendthrift stallion barn for a group of visiting officials from the United Nations, 11 November 1951. *(Keeneland-Meadors)*

TURF
MONTHLY
★ *December, 1958*

AUSTRALIA'S PREMIER
RACING MAGAZINE

2'6

Registered at the G.P.O., Sydney, for transmission through the post as a periodical.

HOW
TO PICK
**LONG-PRICED
WINNERS**
— Page 4
★

This *Turf Monthly* cover from December 1958, showing Shannon with his Spendthrift groom Booker Payne, is one of the last known photographs taken of the horse before his death in May 1955.

Bailey weighed out cussing under his breath, along with Johnny Adams who had been aboard Miss Doreen. They were furious with Herb Lindberg, who had booted Why Alibi home into fourth. Bailey complained long and hard to Molter as he pulled his saddle off Shannon, telling the Texan he had no chance at the start of the race. But the stewards had seen it all, and before the yelling began in the jocks' room, they were calling for the film of the race. In 1948, that would take a day or so. In the meanwhile, the Shannon camp bemoaned the interference, and the AAP reporters scribbled into their notebooks. 'Shannon Robbed', 'Unlucky Run For Shannon', they wrote, getting ready to wire the words to Sydney. Prescott Sullivan, also in the press box readying his report for San Francisco's *Examiner*, took a peek at the AAP copy. He laughed, and in the paper the following week he took direct aim at Shannon.

'One question seems definitely answered by last Saturday's race. Shannon, the noble steed from Australia, took on a bit more than he could handle when he invaded these shores. The race marked his sixth start and his sixth failure since he came to America. Shannon had no excuse on last Saturday's showing. He has been here long enough to learn the ropes if he is ever to learn them. The way the race was run on Saturday it could not even be said he had the worst of racing luck. This will not show on the official charts, but between calls at the far turn, a few bounds from the end of the stretch, and the horse from down under was second and in a challenging position on the rail. He had plenty of room and before him was the shortest route home. Shannon had only to step out and prove his greatness. Instead he folded up, dropping steadily backward until one could safely start tearing up tote tickets on him.

'Australia will probably never get the true story unless it is read here. In the press box after the race we copped a peek at the lead one of the boys had prepared for the Associated Press (AAP) servicing newspapers throughout the Antipodes. It began with something about how Shannon was "defeated but not disgraced", and went on to make all sorts of apologies for the horse. Shannon is a revered figure in Australia and it was perhaps well to couch his failure in gentle language without, however, sparing Australian readers the simple truth. The only reason Shannon ran seventh in the race was that there were six better horses. Why not let Australia know? We have no kinsfolk down there and no friends that we know of either. But it makes our old hearts bleed to think of those poor Australians losing their money on Shannon, race after race, because they have not been told their champion is over-matched here. We write these words in the sincere hope that they will help improve this country's relations with Australia which, from a sporting standpoint, have long been strained.

'Australia has never quite forgiven us because Les Darcy – great Australian middleweight boxer – was branded a slacker in his own country, and chanced to die here some 30 years ago of an illness which might have taken his life anyway had he not stirred from Sydney. Much less has Australia forgiven us for the death of the mighty Phar Lap of more recent date. But let not Australia blame America for what has happened to Shannon. Granted the Yankee rascals did murder poor Darcy and slip a lethal dose of arsenic into Phar Lap's oat bin – no one has molested Shannon. The fact is that on Saturday many hundreds of Americans, having bet thousands of dollars on him, were praying for his success. When the barrier went up he was third choice in the race. Thus Shannon carried the well wishes of a large portion of the crowd. Had anyone dared draw a pistol on Shannon, two-dollar bettors would have torn the culprit limb from limb. No, Shannon did not lack for friends. All he lacked was speed and staying power enough to beat six other horses. Australian papers, please copy.'

Sullivan's words were carried across Australia's press, and Sydney's racing fraternity was outraged. Friends of Peter Riddle despaired, recalling so many times the late trainer had refused offers from America. It was as if he had known how draconian it might get for his beloved horse. And while Sullivan's editorial went down Australia's throat like a square peg, Neil McCarthy wondered just what race the *Examiner* journalist had been watching. The race charts showed Shannon in second spot at no stage during running, citing him fourth at best, and that was at the six-furlong pole. In addition, the stewards had got their race footage and were not happy. Herb Lindberg had ridden Why Alibi right into Shannon's path, had violated the racing room of the Australian and Miss Doreen, and deliberately endangered the horses and their riders. The *Call-Bulletin* said, 'Films show clearly that Lindberg forced Shannon's rider to take up sharply at the start, thus losing all chance. Shannon was severely bumped and nearly knocked off his pins.' Stewards whipped into action. They suspended Lindberg for the rest of the meeting, and encouraged the California Horse Racing Board to continue the term into the Hollywood Park schedule. San Francisco's *Chronicle* newspaper commented, 'Lindberg's suspension authenticates jockey Willie Bayley's claim about his Aussie mount Shannon.' The *Call-Bulletin* added, 'What about it now that the movies have told their tale? What price Shannon and Johnny Longden next Saturday?'

There came no apology from Prescott Sullivan, who sat on his heels in downtown San Francisco, waiting for Shannon's next defeat.

—

Mafosta was the outstanding horse of the Bay Meadows meeting, and with the Handicap in his pocket he departed for Hollywood Park. In seven weeks of racing he had won five feature races in as many starts, a staggering achievement, and $72,420, not including his winnings from Santa Anita. He was the thesis of what American racing was all about, an iron little horse racing solidly since 1 January. But he was on his way south to Los Angeles, and the Bay Meadows meeting would draw to a close without him. There were only a handful of races left for the racecourse on the bay, but one of them had Shannon's name on it. It was the San Francisco County Handicap on 8 May.

The race was a mile and three-sixteenths, or nine and a half furlongs. It was a $10,000 added stakes race, had attracted a field of six smart horses. Faucon had run Mafosta to a neck in the Bay Meadows the week before, while Suncap held the Santa Anita speed record for six furlongs. Please Me was also in, and he owned the mile record for Hollywood Park, while the remaining pair were Why Alibi and Bymeabond. Faucon was the fancied runner, and Shannon was next carrying 8 st 2 lbs. One Bay Meadows racegoer remarked of the race, 'It's Australian redemption day. If Shannon doesn't pull it off this time, he never will because Mafosta's not here.' Without On Trust or Mafosta, Johnny Longden had agreed to ride the Australian horse, and he donned McCarthy's blue and green silks for the seventh on the card.

Almost 24,000 people climbed into Bay Meadows that day, and it was suppertime when they watched the six horses load for the County Handicap. At 5.43 pm the gates clattered back, and Shannon was almost last to leave the stalls. When he loped past the judge for the first time only Please Me was behind him, but Johnny Longden sat tight, waiting for the backstretch. Up front, Bymeabond turned over the first quarter-mile in 23 seconds, the half in 46⅕, so they weren't burning time. But entering the back Longden shook up his mount and Shannon closed. He was third in a few bounds, second passing the six-furlong pole. As they leaned into the turn he had run up to Bymeabond's offside and then ran right away from him. Longden hunched low into the Australian's mane and let him gallop. Shannon breezed past the mile post nearly two lengths clear of the field. Out of the bend he was six clear, and Longden kept riding. Another length, then another and another, and Shannon was flying down the Bay Meadows straight alone. Ten lengths clear, 11, then 12. He tore over the line in 1:55⅗, stripping Seabiscuit's 11-year-old track record by a fifth of a second.

Neil McCarthy couldn't believe his eyes as he watched his embattled horse heave Johnny Longden around the clubhouse turn, pulling up. The attorney was speechless. Shannon had withered his opposition in a 12-length cakewalk, had run just like the Australians had said he could. Relief spilled from McCarthy as he headed to the winner's circle, and again when he spoke to the press boys. 'All these months in which we have seen Shannon run with discouraging results have ended in the victory I knew he had in him,' he said. 'This is a great horse.' In the crowd, punters were buoyed by the victory. Shannon was second choice in the betting, paying $2.05 for the win, though he had been as wide as 6/1 with bookmakers. But the energy of the victory had excited them because Shannon had been written off in almost all the papers. People had been rooting for the horse for no reason other than he had been given a hard time.

Hy Schneider, one of the better professional handicappers at metropolitan tracks, was impressed. He had seen everything from Man O' War to Equipoise and Seabiscuit. He said, 'Neil McCarthy, who bought Shannon at a price which some thought exorbitant for a horse of his recent showing, is to be congratulated on his fore-sight in introducing this fine Australian horse to American tracks when everyone else seemed discouraged. McCarthy asked to give him a little time, and Shannon has had that time, and he proved himself the overwhelming horse McCarthy knew he was.' Paul Lowry, one of Shannon's consistent critics, applauded the victory with a disclaimer: 'Shannon has finally come around and appears to be getting acclimatised to American tracks and customs,' he said. 'But he certainly is not the weight packer the track handicap-per thought he was in his first races at Santa Anita. He is no 128 lb (9 st 2 lbs) horse, such as he was called on to be in the Santa Anita Handicap. Shannon came over here with too many hopes pinned on him for immediate victories, and his speed in this race demon-strated his real talents as a pace setter. But I doubt seriously if he is, or ever will be, in the top class of such thoroughbreds as Coaltown and Citation.'

The comparison was redundant, and Lowry should have known better. Coaltown and Citation were three-year-olds, the freak youngsters of 1948. Citation would clinch the elusive Triple

Crown that year, plunging into legend because he didn't know how to lose a race. It was ridiculous to hope that seven-year-old Shannon could emulate him, in the process undoing everything he had learned in his Australian life.

Neil McCarthy didn't care what they wrote. He was overwhelmed by Shannon's victory, impressed his horse had finally found his running shoes and used them to demolish a speed record that had stood for years. 'Shannon has had all the bad luck a horse could have,' he said. 'He still has not learned to take the turns properly. Right now he is losing two to three lengths on the bend, but this will be corrected by experience. He seems to have the faculty of recovering quickly from a jar during a race, and believe me that is a valuable asset.' People wanted to know what his plans for the Hollywood Park meeting were, and he said little. 'This sweet little horse is going to do wonders. Tell the folks in Australia this is a horse they can really be proud of.'

For the first time, Shannon stood in the winner's circle of an American racetrack with a thick garland of flowers over his withers. The Australian vice-consul looked on, saying, 'Now you know why we are all so interested in Shannon.' Johnny Longden slid off, delighted. 'He is a fine, fine horse, and if he keeps on like this it will take a lot to beat him at Hollywood Park. I would welcome the chance to ride him again, against any opposition.' It was the second win for the Molter-Longden combination that day. They had got On Trust home in the sixth.

In the press box, Prescott Sullivan wasn't saying much, knowing well he had to backflip for his *Examiner* readers. It was less than a week since his assassination of Shannon, but no one could have guessed what he would write. It had Australians in disbelief. 'Without this column's assistance,' Sullivan said, 'Shannon would not have roused himself out of a walk. With it, he broke the great Seabiscuit's record for a mile and three-sixteenths, and proved himself the terrific racehorse he was cracked up to be when he left Australia. How did I help? I worked a bit of psychology on the noble animal. Obviously what Shannon needed was a good rousing, so I let him have it. Now, Shannon cannot talk, but he can read. He was plenty sore at what we wrote, and resolved to show us – which he certainly did.

'The record is clear. Shannon runs better when someone calls him a bum.'

41

Hollywood

Shannon's float rocked and rattled the long road south to Los Angeles. He was getting used to the mileage, dozing most of the way with On Trust, Prevaricator and the youngster Okey Smokey. He had some mileage under his belt. Shannon had been crawling the California coast since November: San Francisco to Los Angeles and back again, now back to Los Angeles. This time he was on his way to Neil McCarthy's playground, to the fold of America's rich and wildly famous – Hollywood Park.

The 'track of lakes and flowers' sat in the district of Inglewood, on 315 acres of what was once a deep and messy bean field. Century Boulevard ran down one side, Crenshawe and Prairie the others. The place was glitzy, polished, as debonair as Fred Astaire. Its clubhouse and grandstands were dazzling white art deco, decorated with mature palms and thick creepers falling from window boxes. There were six lakes in the infield, an indoor amphitheatre for parading horses, and an ethos for flamboyancy that went around the world. It had opened in 1938 with all the fanfare that came with movie-star investment. On any feature day at 'Hollypark', Bing Crosby slugged highballs with Harry Warner, Walt Disney or Spencer Tracey.

It was Neil McCarthy's kind of place, a sanctum for the Hollywood lawyer. He knew almost everyone who was anyone at Hollywood Park, and he loved its shameless glamour. The track, more than Santa Anita, represented what Los Angeles was all about, and the attorney didn't hide his allegiance. When his horse arrived on the Inglewood backstretch on 10 May, McCarthy said, 'I won't be looking for any such condition book nonsense as Shannon had to endure at Santa Anita. There are real sportsmen at Hollywood Park.' The barns had the same local feel as the other tracks, long lines of identical sheds with hot-walkers here and there, bales of loose straw, and goats, cats and dogs trotting about. But Hollywood Park was close to the bustling Los Angeles, only 11 miles away, and it was often choked by smog. On brassy summer days, a hazy film would settle on the infield. The track itself was a one-mile oval, chutes at the seven and 10 furlongs, and was sandy loam underfoot. The straight was just over a furlong and a half long, almost identical to the Arcadia and San Mateo courses, so there was nothing at Hollywood Park that would surprise Shannon, especially not the sprays that came after his arrival. Nominated first-up for the Angelino Purse on 25 May, Paul Lowry said of Shannon, 'If he is ever going to show anything against good horses, this is the day, the time and the place.'

After his slashing win in the County Handicap, Shannon sat on American winnings of $10,480. He had started seven times in California for a single victory, a second and two thirds. He had been out of the money only three times, though that wasn't quite good enough for the locals. Overall, the horse had raced 32 times since his debut in October 1943, but in less than five months in America Shannon had raced more times than he had in a year in Australia. And he was nowhere near done. Before the season rolled to a close in December, McCarthy planned to race Shannon on the east coast, perhaps tackle the International Gold Cup at Empire City in October. First to hand, though, was the summer meeting at Los Angeles, where Shannon could expect five or six starts in as many weeks.

Willie Molter gave the horse a look at the track as soon as they arrived. Shannon trotted a circuit on the bit, looking about him. He wasn't a flighty horse, didn't carry his emotions on the cuff. Molter was learning that Shannon would always go willingly, was always affable to handle, but he was a thinker. He processed things, felt them. The Australian settled into life at Hollywood Park. In early May there were 500 horses in the various barns. Charlie Howard had the largest string, about 45 by the first day of racing on 18 May, and owners from Belmont, Saratoga and other east centres were represented. The Inglewood meeting was, in many respects, the coveted event of the west coast, more so than Santa Anita.

The first stakes target for Shannon was the Argonaut Handicap of eight and a half furlongs on 31 May, a $50,000 feature. All the big hitters were nominated, including Mafosta, On Trust and the speedster With Pleasure. Molter wouldn't send Shannon into the Argonaut without a warm-up, so the Angelino Purse would come first on 25 May. After these two, they were aiming for the coveted Hollywood Gold Cup, with a smattering of races in between. The Gold Cup was the race everyone wanted to win. Occurring on 17 July, it was the championship of summer racing, a mile-and-a-quarter event with a $100,000 purse. Neil McCarthy was leaving Shannon in the trainer's hands, for he would be crossing the Atlantic by then. McCarthy was bound for London with the American Olympic team.

The Angelino Purse crept up on 25 May, a breezy spring afternoon over Los Angeles. It wasn't warm, only 64°F (18°C) over the city, but the track was magnificent, neatly graded and fast. The club had introduced a new electronic timer to its races, modelled off a military device that calibrated and tested the speed of artillery shells. The timer at Hollywood Park allowed horses to be timed at any stage in a race, and not just the quarter-mile poles. It was a ravishing addition to the meeting.

Shannon stepped out for his race at 4.45 pm, carrying 8 st to Mafosta's 8 st 6 lbs. Olhaverry was also in, the former Santa Anita Handicap winner, but Johnny Longden had opted to ride Shannon after their 12-length spin at Bay Meadows. But a repeat wasn't to be in the one-mile Angelino Purse. Breaking fourth at the jump, America's champion rider hustled Shannon for early speed because Mafosta went like a scalded cat up front. He was 10 lengths ahead when Shannon ran into the straight, and there were another two legless horses in between. Shannon galloped past the post in fourth position, a bewildered Olhaverry another three and a half lengths behind. The trailer, an unfortunate horse called Double F. F., was another 20 lengths in arrears.

It was a ridiculous race, won at the jump by the wily Mafosta. Longden had punched and pushed at Shannon the entire circuit, urgent to close on the lead. Longden was an immense rider, a gifted jockey, but he wasn't a good fit for Shannon. He didn't allow the horse to settle and spring, instead squeezing him right from the start, which the horse resented. When he jumped off, 2 lbs overweight, Longden said to McCarthy and Molter that he couldn't explain the loss. 'He just didn't have it in him,' he said, shrugging. Before he even hung up his silks in the jocks' room, he determined to switch to On Trust for the Argonaut.

The usual drivel poured out of the newspapers after the race. Commenting in the *Los Angeles Times*, Paul Lowry said, 'Shannon is just an Australian champion. All that can be said of him is that if he is a $100,000 buy, Harry Curland was lucky to get out of the original deal.' Lowry added that a 'fast watch' had recorded Shannon's track record at Bay Meadows, which was false, and added that 'the mediocre field he defeated was certainly nothing in the Australian's favour'. 'I'll never pick Shannon to win another race around here,' he quipped.

The negative press was ceaseless; it went on and on like Chinese whispers until the Australian papers were quoting McCarthy 'disgusted with Shannon'. They said he was 'sick about it all', growing frustrated and impatient with the horse's 'lack of perseverance'. When McCarthy learned about them, he was dismayed. He cabled to W. J. Smith right away: 'Understand Australian papers quote me as disgusted Shannon. Disappointed last race. Confident eventually will redeem himself.'

The truth was that McCarthy had fallen in love with his little horse. 'I have owned a lot of horses in the many years I've been in racing,' he said, 'but I have never had so much interest, or confidence, in a horse as I have in Shannon.'

—

Four days after the loss, it was Memorial Day in America. It was a holiday Monday, the day of the Argonaut, and parking stewards at Hollywood Park had their hands full. Motor cars choked the long driveway from Century Boulevard, filling all 22,000 parking spaces at the track. It had never occurred before, club officials learning very early in the day that they would have a record crowd.

By racing, 71,789 people crammed the racecourse, nearly 10,000 more than had ever poured into Hollywood Park. From the terraces, the view was an ocean of hats and heads, and John Maluvius, the club secretary, lit a cigar in delight. People clamoured for a view of the track as the early races scampered home, wolfing Harry Curland's cheap food and drink, or slinking upstairs to the better eateries. Anyone who was someone took their own boxes, clinking champagne and cocktails right up to the running of the Argonaut. The atmosphere sizzled when the runners appeared in the amphitheatre a little after 5 pm.

Longden had defected to the fancied On Trust, so McCarthy had had to dig around for a jockey to pilot Shannon. Next to none stepped forward, but Johnny Adams did, the 4 ft 8 in 'Iola Mite' from Kansas, three-time leading rider in America. Adams was a chunky, barrel-chested fellow, his face full of expression. He wasn't a stylish jockey, wasn't rigorous like Longden or hustling like Willie Bailey. But McCarthy saw something in Adams that might fit him for Shannon: the jock rode with a famously long rein, and always seemed to know how to move with his horse. Of Adams, it was said he never came too late or early, something that he explained was down to understanding his mount. McCarthy suspected that with that sort of intelligence in his saddle, Shannon might unfurl.

McCarthy took the jockey aside before mounting, told Adams all about the horse's aversion to American turns. He asked Adams to talk to Shannon approaching the bend out of the backstretch, anything that would coax the horse's concentration away from the turn and back to the rider. Adams nodded. He was a sympathetic horseman, understood that Shannon must be an unusual thoroughbred. As he climbed aboard the horse at 5.15 pm, he had the mindset to learn all about this neat Australian.

In the betting, Shannon was coupled with On Trust, and as he slipped onto the dirt track he advertised saddlecloth 1A. Of the eight horses going to post, he was the featherweight with 8 st. On Trust had 9 st, Mafosta 8 st 12 lbs, and With Pleasure, the speedster that Paul Lowry had said would 'tie Shannon in knots', had 8 st 13 lbs. Shannon had already met the rest of the field in various contests – Olhaverry, Stepfather, Flashco and the smart Autocrat – but his chief opposition was the first two. Not a single tipster in California gave him a chance of defeating On Trust and Mafosta.

Neil McCarthy settled into the terraces to watch the race. He was nervous, didn't know what to expect from his horse. 'I'm keeping my fingers crossed,' he said cheerily, but it was hard work being cheerful as the seconds ticked towards the jump. Down the straight, the horses began to load one by one. Shannon was on the rails, With Pleasure on his outside. Then came Flashco, On Trust, Autocrat and Olhaverry. Mafosta was next and Stepfather had drawn the widest marble. They shifted nervously for a few long seconds, then thwack. The gates sprang open and they were off.

An almighty cheer welled over Hollywood Park, sending the Argonaut horses down the straight for the first time. With Pleasure had jumped like a startled deer, but Mafosta had snatched the lead past the judge and was running away like he always did, clipping the first two furlongs in 22⅖. Johnny Adams let Shannon bowl along in the slipstream, putting him to sleep in fourth position. Out of the clubhouse turn Mafosta was four lengths in front of With Pleasure, another one and a half to On Trust, then another three back to Shannon. Adams wasn't concerned. He listened to Shannon's rhythm, let the horse tell him how to run this race.

Shannon followed the white rail into the backstretch. His stride was smooth and even . . . one-two-three-four, one-two-three-four. His neck stretched and bobbed with his perfect forelegs. He was enjoying Adams' long rein, his quiet hand and still balance down the back straight. As the turn approached, Adams muttered to the horse. 'Easy now boy, don't bother about this turn up here.' Shannon's ears flicked back and forth, tuning in to his rider's voice. It was working. He didn't break stride as he followed the rail around the bend. Adams clicked to him then, nudging him forward towards On Trust. 'Let's go now boy, time to win.' Shannon responded, accelerating into the straight with a professional's turn of foot. It was withering, carried him up to On Trust in a few bounds and away from that horse as if he were standing still. In another few strides he flicked With Pleasure, and bore down on Mafosta with reckless abandon. Adams kept riding, his face buried in the long black mane, and Shannon kept running. Alongside Mafosta, then past him. He was going away. As the Hollywood crowd roared itself dry, Shannon swept under the wire by a length and a quarter. First in the Argonaut Handicap.

Neil McCarthy was on his feet, along with everyone in the terraces, the clubhouse and down the grandstands. It was a thrilling victory, and when Johnny Adams ambled into the winning enclosure, he was smiling from ear to ear. He had ridden a perfect race. When the garland fell over Shannon's neck and the formalities were over, Adams slid off and unbuckled his saddle, turning to the press. 'I didn't ride him as you would one of our horses,' he said. 'Instead, I tried to ride him just as he felt under me. He's a lot different from an American horse, but he certainly is a nice one to ride. He was very easy to control and responds when you ask him. I hope I'll be able to ride him in the rest of his races here.'

McCarthy hoped so too. He thought Shannon was a different horse in Adams' hands. 'He fits him to a tee. Adams let Shannon do the running and the thinking, merely sitting against him early. Shannon knows what he is doing, and when given that sort of a ride he will give his best.' Shannon finally had a jockey who appreciated him. Johnny Longden had known the horse was fast, but he'd had no patience to alter his riding routine to extract it. Hy Schneider confirmed what everyone was thinking after the Argonaut: 'They have finally got a jockey that fits Shannon. It appears that Longden was not the man to ride this Australian whiz.' The ex-pat Ernest Shaw agreed. 'Shannon will never run well when asked to go flat-out in the early stages. Johnny Adams, who allowed Shannon to run the way he wanted to, proved that. Johnny Longden, a fine rider for American horses, is not the right jockey for Shannon.'

The Argonaut was worth $32,400 to Shannon, hauling his American earnings to $43,480, exactly half of what McCarthy had paid for him (and more than he had earned in five seasons of racing in Australia). The eight and a half furlongs had been clipped in 1:42⅖, four-fifths of a second outside the course record, but scrutiny revealed Shannon had run an outstanding race. He had been 12 lengths behind Mafosta down the backstretch, and still four and a bit adrift entering the straight. Johnny Adams didn't know how fast Shannon was travelling to close so quickly in the stretch, to take less than a furlong to run down nearly five lengths, but it must have been quick. At the *Daily News*, turf writer Bob Hebert said, 'There may have been a flaw in Shannon's pedigree, but there is certainly nothing wrong with his speed.'

Others were not so gracious about the victory. Paul Lowry told his readers that Shannon had carried nothing on his back, and then reminded them that the horse had run 'dead last' in the Santa Anita Handicap. Lowry didn't want a bar of the horse, even when he was winning. But he was in good company. 'Shannon commands new respect, but he has not shown himself as the really great horse reports from Australia led us to believe,' said the *Morning Telegraph*. The *Herald Express* in Los Angeles was one of the only papers to tune the other way. 'The Argonaut victory certainly stamps Shannon as the horse to beat in the Hollywood Gold Cup on 17 July.'

Suddenly, victory in the Gold Cup seemed possible to Neil McCarthy, though he had hardly the time to entertain it. He was packing up for London right after the Argonaut, but he first made sure that Johnny Adams would stay aboard his horse for the rest of the Hollywood meeting (Adams was the first-call rider for the Charles Howard stable). McCarthy told the press, 'Adams seemed to ride the horse perfectly, and Shannon ran the type of race that I felt all along he was capable of. He was a great horse in Australia, and looks as though he might do something here.' Adams agreed to stay on Shannon, and the partnership was sealed.

Willie Molter didn't say much publicly about the victory. He had been as shocked as anyone that Shannon had run so brilliantly, though he knew the horse had it in him. But the Texan was worried about On Trust. Longden had jumped off the four-year-old saying he didn't seem quite himself, and Molter had escorted both charges back to the barn to watch them cool off. On Trust was tired, but Shannon was fresh as summer rain, something like the horse of old.

Shannon didn't hit the track for a number of days after the Argonaut, Molter deciding that he ran best with rest. On 8 June he emerged for a workout on the dirt, breezing six furlongs in easy time. Talking to the press boys that morning, Molter said they were aiming for the American Handicap on 5 July before the Gold Cup, but would entertain a start before then. It came in the shape of the Riverside County Handicap on 17 June, a mile race with $10,000 of added prizemoney.

On race day, Mafosta and With Pleasure broke in a charge to reincarnate the Angelino Purse. Shannon was last from the stalls, and by the time he carried Johnny Adams around the far turn, Mafosta was tearing along up front. Down the backstretch, Shannon cleaned up the back of the field with long, relaxed bounds, but into the straight Mafosta and With Pleasure were 10 lengths up the track. Shannon flashed under the wire in third place, and he had worse luck in the American Handicap. Breaking sixth of eight in that race on 5 July, he was trapped wide at the back of the pack as On Trust blazed along with the lead. Shannon got no closer than fifth, rolling past the judge in sixth spot. The only grace was that he defeated Mafosta by eight and a half lengths, and even On Trust had faded to a poor third. The races reflected poorly on Shannon's Gold Cup chances, even with average efforts from Mafosta and On Trust. As McCarthy prepared to embark on the S. S. *America* for the Olympic Games, he didn't bother to read the papers. He knew exactly what they'd be saying.

About this time, Sydney hoop George Moore arrived in California. He was on holiday, bouncing back from a broken collarbone that Puffham had given him at Canterbury. The wiry little jockey came to Hollywood Park to visit his old friend Shannon, and he gave the horse an affectionate scratch when he found him at Willie Molter's barn. McCarthy made a special effort to meet Australia's leading jockey, and the two talked each other into the late afternoon, about Shannon's old life in Australia, about horseracing and plans that Moore might have to ride in America. McCarthy offered to get the paperwork in order for the Australian to ride in the state, and the newspapers got a hold of the story in Australia and went to work. Suddenly, Moore was trying to replace Johnny Adams for the Hollywood Gold Cup, had got his mother to post his riding gear from Sydney. The stories were fantastic, and even Molter had to deny them. In fact, Moore had no intention of piloting Shannon in any of his races, least of all the Gold Cup. He met with Paul Zimmerman, sports editor at the *Los Angeles Times*, in mid-June, and they discussed Shannon at length. Moore told the writer about his seven-furlong jaunt on the horse in the Theo Marks at Rosehill in 1946. 'He picked up his 9 st 5 lbs, 131 lbs to you and you,' Moore said, 'and he broke the track record over the Rosehill course by a full second and a half from a standing start.' He added that he hadn't been surprised to hear of Shannon's early defeats in California. 'He runs all his best races when he comes from far out of it instead of being kept close to the place as he had been here on occasion,' Moore explained to Zimmerman. 'If you let him run easily at the start, the way he likes, he'll almost always come home for you.'

Moore said that Shannon had made the front page of every newspaper in Australia the day he won the Argonaut. 'There's been nothing like it since we sent Phar Lap here to win the Agua Caliente Handicap,' he said. The two men bantered over the merits of Australian race riding, and Moore made a strong case for the settle and sprint style that Americans found so unusual in Shannon. Zimmerman wrote in the *Times*, 'There's logic to it. I don't recall any horse getting paid a purse for his efforts up at the top of the home stretch. Our nags are full of early run and late arrival.'

The Sydney jockey was in the stands for the Riverside and American handicaps, and he knew that if this was Shannon at his American best, it wasn't the Shannon of old. 'I don't think it was his best though, because he seemed to be racing under difficulties,' Moore said. 'In the Riverside Handicap he was off his stride at the first turn and never hit it again.' McCarthy agreed with Moore, adding the horse was still 'a little embarrassed at the turns. If he is in his stride when they hit them, he seems to be able to stay in and run well all the way'. Privately, George Moore didn't think Shannon looked as well in California as he had in Sydney, that his condition wasn't as hard and his guns weren't firing on all cylinders. No wonder, he thought, when the jocks all ride lopsided. Moore didn't approve at all of the American riders leaning on the inside leather.

He would be there for the Hollywood Gold Cup on 17 July, and it rolled around quickly in summery, hazy Los Angeles. Nine horses would go to post for the feature, for the glittering gold trophy that lured man and movie star.

42

For gold and glory

It was 17 July 1948, and the stalls behind Hollywood Park were the centre of the world. Nine horses stood tethered, waiting for the ninth running of the Gold Cup. They were Molter's three and the ragtag Olhaverry, and Autocrat, Pay Me, Challenging, Stepfather and Capt. Flagg. It was a million-dollar line-up, the accumulated winnings of all runners tumbled well over the million mark. With only the injured Talon and the tired Mafosta missing, the field was sharp as truth.

On Trust was entered as the winningest horse ever bred in California. His tally stood at $384,120, which was ninth on the world's all-time leaders list and within a whisker of overtaking Seabiscuit. Hollywood Park had handed the four-year-old 9 st 2 lbs, a good horse's weight and one that Johnny Longden couldn't afford to muck around with. On Trust was giving at least 12 lbs to every other runner (Shannon had 8 st 4 lbs), but it was within him and he would go off favourite. His stablemate Prevaricator, owned by the same outfit, had 8 st 3 lbs and was coupled with On Trust, along with Shannon.

Stepfather was the second choice in the race, a four-year-old by the imported Beau Pere. He was an interesting horse, bred by Louis B. Mayer and sold to Harry Warner, of Warner Bros, for a hefty $200,000. He had won the American Handicap on 5 July, when Shannon had run backwards into sixth, and his stable expected a good showing with his favourable weight. Autocrat was also in shape for victory, having run Stepfather to a neck in the American, and he looked even better with only 8 st 1 lb. Olhaverry, at an enticing $4.35 in the betting, was one of the fastest horses in the field, had as much chance as any with the same weight. Of Shannon, Paul Lowry commented, 'He is such an in and outer that his chances are not any too well fancied.'

The Australian horse was calm in the pre-race stalls, turning his bit on his tongue, peering out over his sheepskin noseband. His long mane was curried and tidy, his coat buffed, saddlecloth 1A over his back. Molter notched the girth up a hole or two, laid the skin flat inside Shannon's elbows. Then he ushered the horse after On Trust towards the amphitheatre.

Hollywood Park was packed tight, though less so than Argonaut day. People shuffled and clambered to catch a look at the runners, others at the stars in the middle. Harry Warner and his wife were there, and Charles and Marcela Howard, along with the wealthy businessman Earl Stice (On Trust and Prevaricator) and Raoul Espinosa, former president of the Panama Jockey Club and owner of Olhaverry. In the private boxes up high, society from Pasadena to Santa Barbara, Texas and New York partied hard. Anyone who was someone had converged on Inglewood for California's great race.

The Shannon camp was thin. With Neil McCarthy on a liner over the Atlantic, only his daughter Rosemary represented his horse. Formally Mrs John Bullis, she was a popular face in Los Angeles, would be the *LA Times* Woman of the Year in 1951. She shared her father's table that day with the du Blois Wack family of the elite suburb Hope Ranch, and they ate and drank their way to the seventh race. Rosemary had no expectations of Shannon; his last two runs, she thought, had surely sullied his chances in this one. Nevertheless, she put a little something on him because it would have pleased her father.

At 5.15 pm, the horses jogged out of the amphitheatre and onto the track to the cheers of 47,690 racegoers. On Trust led them out, followed by Shannon. There were yellow marigolds and roses everywhere, lining the lakes of the infield, clinging to gilded chicken wire on the pillars and fences of the apron. Not even the famous haze that had settled over the course could dampen the hues of the occasion. The horses circled behind the starting stalls, and Johnny Adams moved Shannon up to barrier three. On Trust moved into two, while Olhaverry stood on the rails, and in succession Capt. Flagg, Pay Me, Stepfather, Prevaricator and Challenging moved up. Autocrat, with Jack Westrope aboard, shuffled into the outside stall last of all.

Adams pulled his goggles down and crouched low over Shannon's withers. He wanted to ride the race as he had the Argonaut, allowing Shannon to do all the thinking. There would be no Mafosta to run down today, and while On Trust was the one to watch up front, Molter had thrown Prevaricator in to ensure that no horse would get too far in front, On Trust included. But with a pull in the weights as Shannon had, Adams guessed he could settle out of the stalls and wake up out of the backstretch, after which Shannon would do the rest. The jockey readied for the jump.

The clock hands ticked to 5.25 pm – racing! Hollywood Park roared for its race of the year. Challenging, on the outside, broke the line first, and clattered away to take charge on the rails. Shannon jumped fourth, and passing the judge for the first time Adams had settled him one off the rails behind the pace-setters On Trust and Pay Me. They clipped the first quarter in 23 seconds flat, and they left the clubhouse behind with a rousing cheer from the grandstands.

Shannon drummed along steadily, his forelegs reaching into the dirt one by one, his back end following in beautiful succession. Adams crouched high in the irons, gave Shannon his head to run as he pleased. Into the far turn the Australian was sixth, about seven lengths off the pace, but his stride was smooth like water, and he was full of running. As the turn approached, Adams woke him up with a flick of his hands, a message that Shannon knew like words. Go forward, it said, and forward he went, lunging towards the horses in front until he was third without drawing a breath. Adams was amazed, and at the three-quarter pole he rode for home. Shannon cruised up to On Trust, who had wrestled the lead from the fading Challenging, and the pair clattered into the straight side by side. On Trust on the rails, Shannon on his flank – they left the field by three lengths. Longden was driving and whistling at On Trust before Adams had even moved, and when they straightened Shannon poked his nose in front. Johnny Adams crouched lower and pulled the trigger, and Shannon shot away like a bullet springing from its gun barrel. He went out by a length, then another, and On Trust was all at sea to stay with him. Shannon sprinted under the wire in the Hollywood Gold Cup, ravishing in ravishing victory.

Rosemary Bullis almost burst with excitement in the terrace, and so too Willie Molter, who had one-two in the city's premier race when On Trust had kept on for second. He slapped Clyde Turk on the back, shook hands with just about everyone, and hurried to the winner's enclosure to wait for Shannon. Thousands of people cheered him there, and cheered their coupled result, getting $1.15 about Molter's three-pronged assault, or $4.30 on the pari-mutuel, and they also called to Johnny Adams as he came back in. The jock was beaming, and he was still smiling when Marcela Howard presented the trophy to Rosemary and the blanket of roses fell over Shannon's shoulders. Only Molter's smile was broader, and everyone at Hollywood Park stared at the Australian import, soaking up his story, its ups and downs and furious headlines. Shannon was a popular winner that day.

The victory was worth $67,600 to him, kicking his winnings up to $112,280, far clear of what McCarthy had paid for him. Harry Curland couldn't believe his bad luck, was watching up in the terrace as the Australian blistered home in 2:01 $\frac{3}{5}$. The time might have been quicker, and it disguised how fast Shannon was travelling in the last two furlongs, but the track was 'hopped up' and it probably slowed things down. Nevertheless, nothing could be taken from the style of Shannon's victory, and even Paul Lowry admitted that. He said, 'While owner Neil McCarthy was on the high seas with the American Olympic team, Shannon II was electrifying a crowd of 47,690 with a cyclonic rush that left his eight rivals down the track in the $100,000 battle for gold and glory.' He added, 'Shannon was a different horse.'

Neil McCarthy had kept his watch on California time, and as his cruise liner skirted the bottom of Ireland, he telephoned Hollywood Park steward Wendall Cassidy. When Cassidy told him his horse had won the big one, McCarthy hollered, 'I can't believe it! The whole American Olympic team had been barracking for me.'

It would remain one of McCarthy's greatest regrets: that he had not been there to cheer Shannon home.

The horse's greatest critics were mostly mute in the wake of his immense win, one or two of them drabbling about his hot and cold form, others bleating about his unknown ability to carry weight. But few people paid attention. Shannon had backed up the Argonaut win, and his victory had been anything but accidental. He was second top-weight, had come from behind in a great rush that had gathered up California's top younger horse, and he had gone on by two lengths. It had been a decisive victory. In Australia, the papers splashed the story across front pages, back pages and sports pages. Shannon had run the mile and a quarter almost half a second faster than any horse had ever done in Australia. In Perth, the *Daily News* carried an unusual take on the story: 'Shannon's rich win in America has made him the first horse to seriously challenge Phar Lap as the greatest Australasian stakes winner.' On conversions, Shannon was just £13,335 short of bypassing the Red Terror.

Across Australia, almost everyone was proud of the horse, including a Queensland editor who held a candle for Prescott Sullivan. 'To many, the chief merit of Shannon's success was the one in the eye it gave to that Californian turf writer who roasted him so devastatingly a few weeks back.'

43

The lightning strip

In the summer of 1948, everyone in America was watching Citation's gradual push westward. The three-year-old was like a cosmic creation, something dreamed up by the racing gods fat on lotus leaves. He had won everything, collected the Triple Crown and then moved on to Arlington Park. A mile at Churchill Downs, two miles at Belmont Park – it was all the same to the iron bay by Bull Lea.

His record was downright frightening. Through 1947, Citation had raced nine times as a two-year-old, amassing eight wins and a second on the heels of his slick stablemate Bewitch. Since debuting as a three-year-old in February, the Calumet colt had notched up 11 starts for 10 victories, losing only a six-furlong sprint at Havre de Grace when his jockey took the blame. That had been in April, after which Citation had rolled over the Kentucky Derby, Preakness and Belmont fields, the Jersey Stakes in between and the Stars and Stripes Handicap in Chicago. He was also a long way off done for the season.

When people looked at him, they saw a plain sort of horse with a simple, handsome head and a high tail, nicely coupled but not flashy. He wasn't brassy red like Man O' War, or shimmering chocolate like War Admiral. There was nothing about Citation that made a man gasp, until he started to move. Then he was like rubber bands all put together, stretching and pinging across America's dirt with hysterical ease, his rider's feet on the dashboard. Men would watch him, tip their hats back and shake their heads in disbelief.

Eddie Arcaro was Citation's jockey in 1948. He said of the horse, 'God, he was built beautifully, strong and muscular but very agile. He was no showman, and no glitter. He just cocked his head, like he was bowing before a king or queen, then went about his business of being a racehorse.' Arcaro said that where Citation might have been lacking in charisma, in fact he was just well mannered. The horse's trainer, Calumet's H. A. 'Jimmy' Jones, couldn't recall a youngster as tough as him. 'He's as strong as a bull.' And it wasn't like there hadn't been scope to measure the horse's mettle: midway through his three-year-old season, Citation had already clocked up 20 lifetime starts.

It was inevitable the colt would push west in the winter, to the warmer climes of California and its winter meetings. His owner, the irascible but brilliant Warren Wright, was determined the horse would be racing's first million-dollar-winning thoroughbred, and so they would follow the purses; Belmont in early October, probably Empire City, possibly Pimlico. California tracks wanted a slice of the superstar, and as early as August they were trying to make it so. Santa Anita didn't have to try very hard, knowing well its January meeting would attract the camp, but Tanforan put in a bid early. Talk was that Wright had friends with financial interests in the track, and he was thinking about shipping Citation to south San Francisco to help them out. If he did, the colt would run into California's hottest tickets – Mafosta, On Trust and famous Shannon.

Neil McCarthy knew it was coming, knew the Calumet wagon was rolling west towards him. He didn't presume that his horse could beat Citation, for Citation was made of something else, something that couldn't be measured or bottled. And Shannon was seven years old, not three; it would have to be a terrific seven-year-old to meet a younger comet like this one. McCarthy, though, never took his eyes off the fact that Shannon was on his way to stud, likely at the end of 1948. If he kept on the path he was going, notching up high-profile wins like the Gold Cup, a loss to Citation would be not just humiliating, but an expensive dent in Shannon's sire record. So, like every owner on the west coast of America that year, McCarthy had no ambitions to run into the east coast wonder.

From London, the attorney agreed to let Molter enter Shannon in the Sunset Handicap a week after the Gold Cup at Hollywood Park. The Texan suspected that Shannon's running style, sitting off the pace and coming to the front with a rush, would enjoy the longer courses, so he opted the horse for a mile and five furlongs, which was a furlong longer than any race Shannon had ever run. It stunned Sydney racing men, who had confabbed for years over Shannon's stamina issues. Running him in the Sunset was like running him in the Metropolitan, which Peter Riddle never would have done. But Molter was insistent, and it was probably his misunderstanding of Shannon's pace. The Midstream horse was a miler, a brilliant one, with the scope to squeeze out another half mile. But a staying track? It didn't sit with his record in either country, and it was a blunder by Molter.

Johnny Adams broke Shannon quickly in the Sunset and sent him off after On Trust. The pair had 8 st 12 lbs and 9 st respectively, and they juggled the lead all the way down the backstretch, leaning into the turn together. They were boxing on in the straight where Shannon just had the upper hand, but they were tiring, and Drumbeat, carrying only 7 st 2 lbs, raced wide to poach the lead. He kicked to a three-length win as Shannon and On Trust fought for second, but the distance had quenched Shannon's turn of foot. He faded by three-quarters of a length to take third, six lengths clear of the nearest horse.

In the aftermath of the race, Adams blamed the weight. 'He ran a good race, and we were never in trouble,' the jockey said. 'Apparently Shannon didn't like all that weight.' Hardly anyone stepped up to blame the distance, which was well beyond Shannon's liking. Nevertheless, the horse earned $7500 for third prize, crowning him the money-winner of the Hollywood meeting with $109,300 in earnings. Overall, he had netted $119,780 for Neil McCarthy, and the attorney cabled from London that he wanted the horse rested. If it were up to Molter, he would have kept Shannon going, onwards to the Del Mar meeting due to commence on 27 July. But it wasn't up to him. McCarthy held the reins in their arrangement, and he had learned his lesson at Santa Anita. Shannon would not be over-raced.

So, on 25 July, the day after the Sunset Handicap, the Molter barn packed up and vanned south towards San Diego, to Del Mar racecourse overlooking the Pacific Ocean. On Trust went, with Prevaricator and Okey Smokey and a dozen or so of Molter's other charges. Though Shannon would not race, he shipped south with the team and took it easy as Neil McCarthy made his way home from the Games.

—

Into September, as the autumn began to change the colour of California, Shannon relaxed at Del Mar. He loafed around the barn, slept and ate, and Molter kept him just in trim with long, slow gallops in the mornings. The horse looked well, was brighter the last few months, had drawn buckets of confidence from his victories at Hollywood Park. He had also acclimatised; his coat adjusted to the northern hemisphere season and, like every other horse at that time of year, he was shimmering. To Molter, though, Shannon was still something of a puzzle, for the Texan was yet to find him as push-button as On Trust, or as simple as Prevaricator. Shannon required careful handling. In later years, Molter would say that every horse was different, that he couldn't train them all the same, and perhaps it was Shannon who taught him that early.

Molter didn't reveal any plans for the horse's autumn campaign, for he was waiting on advice from Neil McCarthy. The attorney arrived in California the first week of September, just as Molter was preparing his team for Golden Gate Fields. Shipping out of Del Mar, they trucked the long highway north to San Francisco again, onwards to the northern suburb of Albany and the track that jutted onto San Francisco Bay. Golden Gate Fields was one of California's youngest courses, opened in 1941 (though shut down during the war years), but one of its most dazzling.

Aside from its decorated infield and escarpments to the east, to the west it eyeballed the Golden Gate Bridge.

Between 14 September and 30 October, the track would host 41 days of autumn racing. McCarthy announced that Shannon's target was the $75,000 Golden Gate Handicap on 23 October. It was the featured stake of the meeting, and at early declarations, 25 horses were nominated, including Triplicate, the defending winner who belonged to Fred Astaire. But before then, Shannon would have to run in other events, and Molter planned to start him in the San Francisco Handicap on 18 September. McCarthy didn't think the horse was ready, 'He's been idle since Hollywood Park,' he said. 'I don't want to run him so soon [after arriving in San Francisco].' He scratched the horse on the eve of the race.

Trainer and owner gave Shannon another week to settle into Golden Gate Fields. The track, like all the others, was a one-mile oval, two chutes, and sandy loam. But it had been resurfaced since its wartime occupation, and somehow it felt lighter and faster, and in the mornings Shannon skirted over it like a two-year-old running for the first time. He was fresh. Molter didn't ask much of him in the beginning, but gradually turned the screws until the horse was clipping along with the heavily raced On Trust. So far as the eye could see, there was little between the pair, but Molter suspected that Shannon's lazy lay-off would catch up with him in his first race back. McCarthy had pencilled his horse in for the six-furlong Walnut Creek Handicap on 24 September.

Only six horses would go postward that Friday afternoon, but one of them was Mafosta, and he was the plum ride for Johnny Adams, who opted for the Irish import over Shannon. McCarthy had another horse in the event, a five-year-old by War Admiral called Be Sure Now, and they were Molter's two-pronged entry. For this reason, the trainer boosted Johnny Longden into the saddle, and Jack Westrope was called in for Be Sure Now. The pair was odds on when they stepped onto the dirt for the sprint, largely off the back of Shannon's Hollywood record, but also because Longden was in the irons. The odds to $1 were only 80 cents.

The crowd was thin at Golden Gate Fields when the six horses burst from the stalls. Be Sure Now took charge early, and down the backstretch he towed everyone else, turning the first two furlongs over in 22⅗. Longden was riding like Johnny Adams, had left Shannon almost last in fifth spot. But around the bend he called on the horse, and Shannon moved up into fourth, then third entering the straight. Mafosta was driving to reach the lead. Inside the last furlong, the Irish horse was a neck in front of the lightly weighted Tape Buster, and Shannon closed to within a length but got no closer. Mafosta slipped past the winning post in 1:10 flat for the six, with Shannon a smidgeon unfit in third.

Longden was cheesed off when he climbed down, for Shannon was frustratingly hot and cold with him. There were probably fitness excuses, which Molter alluded to when the trainer grumbled that Shannon should not have been rested for as long as he had been. 'I think he's the type of horse that goes well with constant racing,' he said. McCarthy didn't agree, and it certainly didn't concur with Shannon's Australian pattern. Nevertheless, Longden hung up his silks that afternoon and was sure he probably wouldn't ride McCarthy's horse again.

Mafosta looked to be back to his brilliant best, and with Johnny Adams committed to that horse, McCarthy fished around for a new pilot for Shannon. He approached Jack Westrope with the offer, for Westrope was a regular rider for McCarthy, and he wasn't contracted to any stable at that time. 'The Rope', as turf men dubbed him, accepted.

Thirty-year-old Jackie Westrope was the train wreck that jockeys were known for. Boozing, bingeing since he'd hit the circuit in 1933, he was a confessed alcoholic on the road to a messy divorce. He'd been patched up so many times from riding falls that he'd lost count of body parts that didn't work and, unlike affable Johnny Adams, he was mouthy and fractious. He'd learned to ply his trade in the days before motion picture monitoring, and as such he was something of a scallywag. Westrope could hook another jockey on the home turn, or shut them out of a run on the rails. When he got caught, which was often, he argued viciously, holding grudges for days. He'd been escorted from Santa Anita, and barred from Tanforan, and he never seemed to learn his lesson. In later years, when he was disqualified from first prize for interference in the Santa Anita Handicap, he would say, 'For 10 grand, I ain't giving nobody room.'

He had an elfin smile and a freckled face, but Westrope was wily and everyone knew it. The turf writer Red Smith said of him, 'Don't let the grin fool you. He was aggressively militant and full of resentments.' Ambrose Campbell, an old friend of Westrope's, went a step further. 'He was a thieving rascal.' Flamboyant, Westrope could walk into a restaurant after a big stakes win, shout the bar then tear the place down. He was jailed for being drunk and disorderly after an all-night binge at La Jolla one year, and when he, Johnny Longden and Eddie Arcaro got together, people shuddered. Westrope was devilish, a disaster in the wings, but he was at the top of the game for a reason.

There were few riders that could handle hot horses as he could. Dino Romoli, a veteran starter on west coast tracks, declared that no horse ever intimidated Westrope. 'If Jack couldn't ride him, no one else wanted to,' he said. Largely, it was because Westrope was fearless. But while aggressive and bullish on the ground, Westrope was not so in the saddle. He didn't punish horses if he thought they were spent, and his skilled, sympathetic hand had landed him big wins with horses like Stagehand, Cravat and With Pleasure. He had also coined the 'acey deucy' seat, by which he rode with his left iron much longer than his right. At first, it was to alleviate a crooked knee that had been busted in a fall. But it was found among jockeys to be a tasty cure for leaning horses into a tight bend, and before Westrope knew it, many other riders had adopted it.

By the time McCarthy came calling, Westrope was slipping, the drinking and the injuries taking their long toll. He had set a record of wins in his very first year in the saddle, hitting the 25 per cent mark, but these days he wasn't hitting 15 per cent. He was a long way behind Longden and Arcaro. The tragedy was blood deep, as Westrope's brother William, also a jockey and known around the circuit as 'Wootsie', had been killed in a race fall at Agua Caliente in 1932. It was as if Jack Westrope was riding towards the same reckless fate.

McCarthy liked him, didn't mind his boorish attitude or his lifestyle. The attorney was hardened Hollywood and had seen it all; the only thing that mattered to him was that Westrope fitted Shannon. The jock had ridden against the Australian horse in many outings, and much had been said and written of Shannon's come-from-behind patterns, his preference to settle then swoop in the straight. Westrope thought he could manage it, and on the last day of September he flew from his riding engagements in the east to San Francisco. Shannon was nominated for the Golden Gate Mile Handicap on 2 October, and Westrope would pilot.

The pair had 8 st 10 lbs for the race, only Mafosta carried more with 9 st. The field was deeper this time too, with Prevaricator and Hemet Squaw, as well as Autocrat, Stepfather and Fred Astaire's Triplicate. It wasn't a rich stake, only $15,000, but it was the Saturday feature on the card. When they went to post for the mile, it was 5.18 pm on a nippy, autumn evening.

Shannon leaped slowly from the widest stall as Mafosta bounded into the box seat. He was fifth going away from the clubhouse, and into the far turn Westrope settled him sixth. They stayed there down the backstretch as the leader rattled off the quarters: $22\frac{4}{5}$, $45\frac{3}{5}$, 1:$09\frac{3}{5}$ for the six. They were motoring, and when Westrope called on Shannon, the Australian powered to life. He was in top gear going around the final turn, but Prevaricator and Hemet Squaw, who were harrying Mafosta for the lead, carried him right off the course, and he was wide out into the straight. The four horses belted towards the winning post in a line, and Prevaricator, given a peach of a ride from Longden, flashed home first by a head to Hemet Squaw. Shannon was less than a length third, holding Mafosta and Johnny Adams by a neck. The time was a new mile record for Golden Gate Fields: 1:$34\frac{2}{5}$, equalling the American benchmark.

The result was so close that a photo finish was called, with only a length between the first four. As Jack Westrope eased up, he thought he might have won if he hadn't been carried so wide into the straight. He'd had nearly four lengths to collect going for home. Nevertheless, the run had impressed the jockey, the Australian horse demonstrating the turn of foot that everyone had been talking about. It wasn't sharp enough to win that day, but Westrope thought there were excuses. Another quarter of a mile, the result would have been different.

The local press weren't making any excuses for Shannon, labelling him the 'hot and cold horse from Australia'. 'Shannon runs a smooth race on his good days, but in the form chart he jumps up and down like a kangaroo. His flip flops are hard to explain because his Australian record showed him to be a very consistent animal down under.' It was a reasonable argument. Shannon's Sydney record from 1945 onward was almost flawless, and a few people wondered if Molter was playing games with the handicapper. Shannon had won the rich Argonaut, floundered in his next two runs, then came good again for the Gold Cup. But Willie Molter had never dabbled in that sort of cunning, and Shannon's last four runs were hardly disgraceful: first, third, third and third. He hadn't been out of the money since his sixth place in the American Handicap on 5 July.

Neil McCarthy wasn't complaining. Shannon's earnings rested on $121,780, a respectable profit on his purchase price. McCarthy had long learned to turn a deaf ear to the bleating of the newspaper beat. So he remained optimistic, not at all put off by Shannon's third place in the Mile, especially when Mafosta had managed fourth. They would head to the Forty-Niners Handicap next on 16 October, which Molter regarded as a dress rehearsal one week before the big one.

The Forty-Niners was named after San Francisco's football team, and it was a popular race for name alone. It was also a prep run for the rich Golden Gate Handicap, which was where most of its field was headed in 1948. Over nine furlongs, the race had attracted the usual top suspects in California racing: Mafosta, Autocrat, Stepfather and Triplicate, as well as Molter's famous trio, On Trust, Shannon and Prevaricator. On Trust was top weight with 9 st, Mafosta next and Shannon had 8 st 12 lbs. After that, the weight spread down to 7 st 4 lbs. Johnny Longden had opted for On Trust, and most of the betting money had followed him. Molter's three, bracketed once again, were 55 cents in the dollar, Mafosta as wide as $5.15.

It was a very warm afternoon when Shannon arrived at the track, surprisingly hot for October in San Francisco. The Forty-Niners was seventh on the card, and as the horses trotted on to the track, a splendid blue evening stretched over them and onto the bay. The crowd was a good one, over 22,000, and the form watchers were there, the clockers and the press corps all lining the rails with their watches. The horses reached the stalls at a tick before 5.20 pm.

Shannon went into the extreme outside of the nine horses, Mafosta and On Trust into the rail seats. When the gates pinged, Johnny Longden drove On Trust straight to the front, and Mafosta sat on him all the way into the first turn. Shannon had no option but to run wide without cover, and entering the first turn he was four horses deep in the leading group – fifth at the quarter pole, fifth at the half, and Westrope gave up worrying about it. He let the Australian cruise down the backstretch at his own clip, and covering so much more ground Shannon bounded along on a loose rein. Into the far turn he picked up by himself, sensing the chase was afoot. He skirted around the leaders, heading Stepfather, then Prevaricator, and On Trust was fading under Johnny Longden. Only Mafosta was fighting on the rails. Westrope gathered his horse as they hit the straight, and he sent Shannon into open running.

The Australian charged away when Westrope flicked the switch, kicking so quickly that the jockey was almost left behind. Shannon surged past Mafosta, went out by a length and then a bit more, and then he was running down the clock. He clattered through the last few yards until he blew over the line in 1:47 ⅗ , smashing the track record for Golden Gate Fields, and equalling the world record for nine furlongs.

Flying.

—

The clocks didn't lie. The world (and American) nine-furlong record had stood across America since 1936 when Indian Broom set it at Tanforan, but Shannon's effort was wildly more impressive because he carried 8 st 12 lbs against Indian Broom's 6 st 10 lbs. Across San Francisco, clockers looked hard at their watches, and all the doubts that had wrangled about Shannon's integrity crumbled away. At this level of competition, no one could argue with the watch.

Shannon fever was catching in California. Australians peeled out of pockets of San Francisco to cheer the Sydney horse, sending telegrams and letters to Neil McCarthy and Willie Molter. It made McCarthy cartwheel with delight. All his patience, all his faith in Shannon, had paid off.

The horse was hot talk in the days between the Forty-Niners and the Golden Gate Handicap, but a littering of negative press persisted. 'This Down Under champion blows hot and cold,' one reporter remarked, 'and next time out means anything.' The papers doggedly stuck to their criticism. They didn't understand Shannon, and none took a step back to blame the trainer or the owner. Simply, many of them disliked the horse.

Thankfully, Shannon couldn't read, and in the days after the Forty-Niners he was brilliant in his morning work. Jack Westrope swung a leg over in the mornings, and the pair worked six furlongs with On Trust, most of the time the stablemate getting the upper hand. But regular clockers wouldn't be fooled. Shannon did only what was asked of him before breakfast. He was mature about his speed, knew he had it but didn't flaunt it unless he was asked to.

It was something Peter Riddle had enjoyed about the horse, and Willie Molter had learned to work with it. Shannon required a different training manual from the rest of the barn. But the Texan was looking forward to the big handicap on Saturday, for his three best horses were nominated, and the *Los Angeles Times* carried the obvious headline on the morning of the race: 'Molter Trio Favoured at Golden Gate.'

The $75,000 handicap was northern California's richest turf prize, and it was a showpiece for the racetrack on the bay. San Francisco tarted up for its running, and 30,000 racegoers streamed into the course that day. Autumn had firmly arrived, nudging warm summery days into memory, so when the 13 horses for the Golden Gate Handicap paraded before the stands in early evening, it was almost chilly. Molter's trio was favourite, both On Trust and Shannon considered the logical winners of the event. For days, people had bantered over the merits of the two horses, most arriving on On Trust because of his consistency. Johnny Longden said his mount was ready for 'some real running', and even Westrope had to admit, as sharp as Shannon had proved in the Forty-Niners, On Trust was very good.

'The Rope' sat high aboard Shannon as they moved to the starting gates. They had again drawn the outside marble, would jump from 13 while On Trust, yet again, had drawn the rails. Shannon had 8 st 12 lbs to tote, as he had in the Forty-Niners, while On Trust had 9 st 2 lbs. Jackie Westrope stared down the stretch as he waited for the line to complete, and Shannon was still underneath him. The jockey had no plan for the race; he would let Shannon figure it out. Thwack! The gates sprang open at 5.33 pm.

The horses exploded from their stalls like a wave rushing to shallow shore, and they found their feet down the stretch for the first time, going full pelt at 23 seconds for the first quarter. Shannon crossed the track to sit sixth out of the straight, but he was widest again, three deep without cover. Westrope allowed him to bowl along, and down the backstretch Shannon was the balanced, metrical machine of old, didn't notice the extra ground.

The jock had only to push the button. Out of the stretch, On Trust picked up the lead from Mafosta. Shannon crept forward around horses, and Westrope slowly let him go. The bay lengthened his stride, throwing his forelegs further and deeper into the dirt, went around Triskelion, See-Tee-See, and eyeballed Mafosta. Johnny Adams had all his sails open on Mafosta, but the Irish import had nothing. Westrope clicked to Shannon and Mafosta was gone, falling into their slipstream. They ran the mile in 1:35 flat.

Shannon picked off On Trust before he even reached the straight, and then he set sail for the winning post. He was out by three lengths turning for home, and an almighty roar swelled over Golden Gate Fields as the Australian superstar leaped into history. Shannon raced over the line two lengths clear of the field in 1:59⅘, the first horse in America to crack two minutes for a mile and a quarter.

A new American record.

Another world record equalled.

Shannon whizzed around the far turn as Jackie Westrope eased him up. The jockey couldn't believe the time when he saw it on the boards – less than two minutes. Phew. See-Tee-See and Stepfather had left On Trust struggling for fourth, while Mafosta had dropped like a stone to finish second-last. Over 19 lengths covered the field. The cheers that followed the Australian horse as he came back in were monumental. Shannon was a famous story now. The stretch run had been a spectacle, and in the terraces Neil McCarthy was on his feet, clapping as loud as any. Two runs in a week for his little horse, for two world-record ties, an American record and a track record on San Francisco's lightning strip – dazzling for any horse, but spectacular for the one who had overcome so much. Shannon had torn down that Golden Gate straight as if it were made of Mexican jumping beans.

When McCarthy stood in the winner's circle that San Francisco evening, the money was far from his mind. The Golden Gate Handicap had netted him $61,000, pushing Shannon's earnings into a marvellous $194,510 (sending him right over Phar Lap as the greatest money-earner in Australian history), but McCarthy preferred to absorb the wonder of his horse come good. He was extremely proud of Shannon, fostered some pride for investing in the animal and defending him when the road was rocky. 'I need only say,' he said, 'that after last Saturday's victory in the Forty-Niners, and today's miraculous race, this is a complete vindication of Shannon and I hope that his critics are at last satisfied.'

The horse had all sorts of nicknames before the day was out. United Press called him 'the powerful Australian cannonball'. They wrote, 'The seven-year-old bullet from Down Under put on a kick in the straight that few have seen the equal of.' Jackie Westrope couldn't argue with that. 'He certainly ran like a race-horse,' he dryly told the press. 'He was in the clear all the way, and when he moved up to third at the three-quarter mark, he was just breezing. He could have gone to the front any time. When I did ask him to really move, he responded right away.'

The jockey was conservative. Like Molter, Westrope rarely used two words when one would do, especially when he found himself in front of a posse of journalists. But he was starting to appreciate the big deal that was this Australian horse, and before he snuck off that night to paint the town red, he told Molter he would stay with Shannon as they rolled towards the end of 1948.

The excitement of the racing week simmered down, but the significance of Shannon's Golden Gate efforts settled in. Form experts did some reading, and they were astonished. On the table of world racing records to date, Shannon appeared no less than three times. He was there for his mile in the George Main of 1946, and also for his two San Francisco runs. Put simply, Shannon held a share of the world-record times for eight furlongs, nine furlongs and 10 furlongs. It wasn't a crowded club. For nine furlongs, only Indian Broom shared the limelight with him, and for 10 furlongs there was only Saint Andrews. That horse had set his benchmark at Brighton, England, in 1939, but he had been assisted by a downhill slope most of the way. The only question mark regarding Shannon's entries was his Randwick mile, which he had clocked in 1:34½. It was the fastest time in Australia for the distance, but Equipoise and Prevaricator stood at 1:34⅖, which most Americans believed was faster. It was. But Australian watches split to quarters, not fifths, and this discrepancy brought about a difference in opinion as to whether Shannon deserved parity with the American speed figures. Either way, when the American Racing Manual published its table in 1949, Shannon appeared with Equipoise and Prevaricator as a world record holder for a mile.

44

'The white hope of the west coast'

In Australia, the newspapers would hit street corners early in the morning with a soft thud, as they did on Saturday 13 November 1948. That particular morning, in the sports leaves or on the back pages, a small cable article ran from the AAP in San Francisco: 'Shannon finished third in the Marchbank Handicap at Tanforan. The race was won by Please Me, with Tropical Sea second.' The 20 words gave little more than a result: no margins, no details of any sort. Australians wondered: in the wake of the vivid Golden Gate headlines, had Shannon lost a race?

He had. The Molter barn had rolled out of Albany the last week of October and south to Tanforan racecourse, 14 miles from downtown San Francisco. The meeting would start on 2 November, would run for six weeks, and Molter was pitching Shannon at two big races: the $25,000 San Francisco Handicap on 25 November, and the richer Tanforan Handicap on 11 December. But the horse had to run in something in between, and so he had lined up for the Marchbank on 11 November, toting 9 st 1 lb, 11 lbs more than any other runner. Westrope had brought him wide around the five-horse field, and Shannon had clattered into the straight in front. But he'd been going very fast, and his weight told in the dying strides. The speedy Please Me, carrying 7 st 11 lbs, and Tropical Sea, carrying 7 st 8 lbs, collared him on the wire. Shannon had lost by less than a length. They had equalled the Tanforan track record.

Molter took no stock in the loss. 'I have no excuses for it,' he said, 'but I don't feel that Shannon disgraced himself. Please Me holds the Hollywood Park mile record, and Shannon needed the race badly. His few weeks lay-off after the Golden Gate did him no good.' The trainer added that he'd come to the conclusion the horse needed to be racing a lot. 'A temperamental horse like Shannon should be running often,' he said.

That was 13 November, and three days later Tanforan came to a standstill when Citation arrived. Tired and crabbish after a long train journey west from Pimlico, the superstar three-year-old moved into his lodgings with an entourage of humans – his trainers Ben and Jimmy Jones, grooms, and his exercise rider Freeman McMillan. 'He laid down a few times for short periods coming west,' McMillan reported, 'But at no time did he really get a real restful sleep. We're going to allow him to rest and sleep all day today, and then put him on the track tomorrow morning.' Every turf scribe in San Francisco declared they would be there when the Triple Crown colt stepped out for the first time.

He had been entered, as expected, in the rich Tanforan Handicap on 11 December, as had Shannon and On Trust. Privately, his crew thought it was ludicrous. By the time his Tanforan campaign was over (he would run twice), Citation would have had 20 starts in less than 11 months, winning 19. 'Those two races at Tanforan,' his jockey Eddie Arcaro would recall years later, 'were races that should never have been.' Elmer Polzin, of the *Chicago Herald-American*, was telling anyone that would listen: 'Putting Citation in a boxcar and shipping him thousands of miles from Maryland to California after so strenuous a campaign was criminal and inexcusable.' There were also grumblings about the state of the track, a few reckoning it rock solid when it was dry, a swamp when it was wet. But it wasn't going to stop Warren Wright. Citation was running and that was that.

As promised, Citation stepped onto the dirt the following morning, doing little more than a light, slow stretch with Freeman McMillan, but everyone was in tow to watch. Racing's headline looked superb. He was fit, race-hard and sound. His arrival had spiked interest across all of California, and he was doing what superstars do best – hustling attention, sending the publicity department into overdrive. Tanforan was preparing for record crowds, had its guys all over the big handicap on 11 December. And as much as people were watching Citation, Citation's people were watching Shannon.

The Australian went out for a gallop between races on Saturday 18 November, clocking 1:12⅖ for six furlongs and 1:39⅖ for a mile. It wasn't a blazing trial, for Molter was brushing away the Marchbank loss and as such was tuning Shannon, but the horse did it effortlessly, pulled up fresh as summer's grass. The Calumet camp stood together by the rails, Freeman McMillan taking a good long look at Shannon. 'It was good work on a track like this,' he said. 'He seemed to do it effortlessly.' Molter was very satisfied with a week to go before the San Francisco Handicap – 'If he can keep it up,' he quipped.

It had been a long year. Shannon had been in the United States for 12 months, and he was coming onto his 19th race start. In Sydney, he had started 25 times in five years, so he had covered almost as much turf in 11 American months as he had in five Australian years. But like children's clay, Shannon had moulded under Molter's pressing hands, and he was still flying so late in the year. It was a credit to the horse's constitution that he was neither sour nor unsound at seven years of age, and he would have had excuses to be both.

Across California, the horse had fans now, none more qualified than Jackie Westrope. The jock had cancelled his vacation to ride Shannon at the Tanforan meeting. Talking to Oscar Otis of the *Daily Racing Form* about the Shannon–Citation match on 11 December, Westrope said, 'I think Shannon has a better chance to beat Citation than any other horse in training in this country. Citation is truly great, but Shannon is also that kind of a horse. If they meet we might not win, but Citation will know he's been in a horse race.'

Otis was impressed, and told his readers, 'Westrope's appraisal of Shannon is keenly interesting because he is not only a canny soul concerning a horse, but also because he is ultra-conservative.' It boded well for Shannon. Here was his button-lipped American rider stating that no horse was better equipped to face off Citation than the speedy Australian, and in case anyone needed reminding of how extraordinary Citation was (no one did), he was in the same vernacular bucket as Man O' War.

Westrope's confidence came, in part, from the Molter barn. The Texan trainer had been defending Shannon since January, but in the lead-up to the San Francisco Handicap on 25 November, he was at it again, mostly because of the Marchbank loss. He told the papers, 'Whatever has happened in the past, Shannon is the white hope of the west coast against Citation.' With that, Molter sent the sensational bay out to race.

———

Lifetime start number 44. Shannon stepped onto the Tanforan dirt for the San Francisco Handicap. There were 10 horses going to post, including On Trust, Stepfather, See-Tee-See, and the Marchbank pair of Please Me and Tropical Sea. Shannon was top weight with 9 st 1 lb, giving a pound to On Trust, 8 lbs to See-Tee-See and 14 lbs to Please Me. Over nine furlongs, the race was worth $25,000 in added prizemoney, and $16,800 to the winner. Shannon had drawn the middle in gate five, On Trust widest in 10.

Neil McCarthy sat in the terrace, staring out. There was much riding on the outcome of this race. The Calumet camp was nearby thinking the same thing, and even they knew this field was not to be sneezed at. Please Me, See-Tee-See and Happy Issue, all running, possessed Tanforan records from six furlongs to a mile and 1/16. But the real weapon was Shannon, and everyone knew it. Bracketed with On Trust, the Australian was only 55 cents to $1 on the boards.

Westrope and Shannon shuffled into their stall. It was a familiar view: the jock staring out over Shannon's long, neat mane, the Tanforan home stretch laid out in front of them like a speedway. The Australian stood quietly as horses moved in around him, and

Westrope waited for the clang of iron gates. It came at 4.14 pm.

Shannon stood stock still for a split of a second when the stalls crashed open, so he was almost last leaving the line. A swarm of rushing horses crossed to the rail in front of him, and Westrope left him wide without cover as they ran past the judge for the first time. Out of the straight, Johnny Longden was wrestling for the lead aboard On Trust, and they went through the first quarter in 23 ⅗, leaning towards the half in 47 ⅕. Shannon was seventh as they clattered down the backstretch.

Punters were uneasy when they saw how far back the favourite was. Neil McCarthy, too, wondered what the heck Westrope was doing. Arcing into the far turn, On Trust was eight lengths ahead of Shannon, and the attorney was on his feet in temper. Wake him up. Westrope roused Shannon at the three-quarter pole, and the bay loosened, began to speed around the outside of the field. His response was lightning fast, and he picked off Tropical Sea and Class Day. Entering the straight he was fourth, with the speedsters On Trust, Stepfather and See-Tee-See racing for home. Driving, Westrope rode hands and heels at them down the middle of the track, and a tremendous roar followed him as he flew over the top of them. The jock had timed the run to perfection. Shannon's handsome head burst into the lead as he blew past Stepfather, and then he was over the line.

There were 17,000 people at Tanforan that day, and they hollered the roof off the grandstand as Shannon rocketed home in the San Francisco Handicap. The time read 1:50 ⅘, a new track record.

Though Citation's camp said nothing publicly, it was game on for the Tanforan Handicap. The Australian seven-year-old would be Citation's stiffest test in a long while, a mature speedster with a racing brain and a turn of foot that withered the leaves from trees. He could stalk the pace, sprint over the top of everyone in the straight. Right then, Shannon was the exploding hero of California racing.

Tanforan's publicity boys were popping with excitement at

the duel of the year: Citation versus Shannon, east versus west in a spangled handicap over a mile and a quarter. They expected 40,000 people if the marketing machine did its job, but Shannon had already done half the work. The wires were abuzz with the horse's victory. 'The big horse from Down Under responded [to Westrope] with a charge that saw him figuratively flying past the leaders,' reported the *Los Angeles Times* on the San Francisco Handicap. 'The run down the stretch was a thriller.' No one could fault the victory, as narrow as the margin was, because Westrope had left his mount with a hell of a lot of work to do into the straight. 'It's the greatest he's ever run,' McCarthy said of Shannon after the race, and he criticised Westrope for letting the horse get so far behind. The truth was that Shannon had run true and straight for Westrope, and under his ride, the horse had hit his straps and won the race. It hadn't been a perfect ride, but Shannon had absorbed Westrope's shortcomings.

The American west coast waited for 11 December as a child waits on Christmas, but behind the scenes McCarthy was fielding a heavy proposition from Leslie Combs II. Combs, the master of Spendthrift Farm, Kentucky, was in California for a dispersal sale, and pressing on McCarthy to part with Shannon. He'd been at it for months, had on board around 20 parties to form a stallion syndicate to install Shannon at Spendthrift. But McCarthy hadn't felt it was right to retire Shannon earlier in the year, largely due to the horse climbing slowly into his running shoes, but also because the attorney understood sire value as much as the next man. Until Golden Gate Fields, Shannon hadn't been a lucrative stallion investment. It was a different story now.

Combs proposed the following: a Shannon syndication comprising 30 shares. Each share cost $10,000, valuing the Australian horse at a staggering $300,000. With McCarthy retaining two shares, there were 24 spots already filled. Among the 18 eventual shareholders were Harry Warner, the du Pont Weir family, Lou Doherty (from a society family), J. S. Phipps, Peter Widener (grandson of P. A. B. Widener, of Philadelphia), and Combs himself, along with his uncle Brownell. Whipping in the group was crinkle-eyed, silver-haired Texan Clifford Mooers, owner of Walnut Springs Stud in the Bluegrass. Mooers was connected, vocal, and he didn't like to lose, so it was an endorsement that he was in the syndicate at all. With six shares remaining available in Shannon, Combs had 22 applications, and the Spendthrift master was coolly elated when McCarthy telephoned him after the San Francisco victory.

The attorney wanted to sell, but he had two conditions: McCarthy reserved the right to withdraw Shannon from the Citation match-up if the weights were unfavourable, and if Shannon did race, any prizemoney would go to McCarthy, not the syndicate. Combs agreed, and the paperwork was rustled together. But McCarthy put the transaction on ice until the weights for the Tanforan Handicap came out in the last week of November, and it proved a long few days.

Everyone wanted to know which horse would get top impost – the three-year-old Citation or the seven-year-old Shannon. Santa Anita handicapper Webb Everett placed a bet with a friend of his that the younger horse would certainly get the heavier weight. At stake: dinner for four with champagne. On the scale, Citation was due 8 st 8 lbs for that time of year, Shannon 9 st, but no one thought Citation would get off that easily. It was as *The Blood-Horse* said, 'No allowances will be given for newspaper clippings.'

Barry Whitehead, racing secretary for Tanforan, released the weights on 30 November. He allotted Citation 8 st 11 lbs, three over scale, and Shannon 9 st 1 lb, one over scale. Webb Everett had lost his bet, and Neil McCarthy was filthy. Without any public statement, he telephoned Combs and told him Shannon was out. American racing went into meltdown.

Tanforan officials rushed about as the bottom fell out of their big match race. Eugene Mori, track president, telephoned both McCarthy and Leslie Combs II, pleading with them to change their minds. McCarthy said, 'I told Eugene Mori that it was his own fault Shannon was not racing. Had we been given a reasonable weight, we certainly would have started.' Combs put his hands in the air. 'We had no idea of getting into any controversy over the matter,' he said, 'but we bought Shannon for stud. We have no interest in racing him. He has a fine record, and we want to preserve it. And personally, I wouldn't want to run him against Citation in any kind of race.' Paul Lowry decided that that was a confession on the syndicate's behalf that Shannon was a far inferior animal to Citation, and other newspapers across California took a similar thread: 'Turfmen Critical As Aussie Ducks Citation.' Said the *Chronicle*, 'By taking a run-out there would seem to be a lot of room for doubt that Shannon is anything like the champion he is supposed to be.' It was a ludicrous statement.

Clifford Mooers stepped into the hysteria, saying he could see why McCarthy had opted not to race. 'I must say, I believe Citation to be a 10 lbs better horse than Shannon,' he said. 'Sure, I think Shannon is a grand horse. But at the same time I think Citation is the greatest horse in the world.' Combs was diplomatic, reiterated, 'This is strictly business with us.'

Turf men from Kentucky to California implored the syndicate to change its mind. They went so far as to telephone the Australian Consul-General in San Francisco, Lieutenant-General E. K. Smart. 'I have no intention of making any statement on this matter,' Smart replied. The Northern California Turf Writers Association took its own tack. They wrote a strong letter, sending it to McCarthy, Combs, Harry Warner and Clifford Mooers. It read: 'The organisation views with extreme regret the decision to deprive western turf patrons of the opportunity to witness what otherwise would have been the greatest thoroughbred race in western history, and one of the great races of modern times. Turf enthusiasts everywhere will be bitterly disappointed if Shannon II, with his splendid record, is compelled by his owners to avoid meeting with a three-year-old who, by the scale of weight-for-age, is actually conceding Shannon 2 lbs. We seriously urge your reconsideration in the light of sportsmanship and the best interests of racing.'

Neil McCarthy was the wrong man to affront in this manner.

Sportsmanship, so the Association had brought up, was a hefty accusation, and knowing well that the public would weigh the Shannon scratching on the strength of that one word, the attorney based his public response on it: 'Under the circumstances, the only sporting thing to do was to withdraw Shannon from a race in which he had no chance to win. Had I started him, he would have been heavily backed in Australia, as he always is. The decision to withdraw him was mine alone, and in selling Shannon I retained two rights: one was to declare him from the race if I thought the weight excessive, and the other was to retain what money he won in the Tanforan Handicap. In determining to withdraw him, I forfeited a certain $10,000, for he surely would have been second.

'Shannon has come along the hard way. He was maligned because he failed to run to his best immediately after his arrival in this country. The horse made good, and I owe something to him. I am not going to have him humiliated. I have always felt that the scale of weights is unfair, and that a thoroughbred reaches his peak at the end of this three-year-old year. The late Col. E. R. Bradley shared this belief. We all know that Citation is no ordinary three-year-old, and he should not be weighted as such. While the decision to withdraw him from the race was mine, the responsibility was Tanforan's.'

Speaking to *The Blood-Horse* correspondent Robert Hebert, McCarthy said that he had turned down an offer from trainer Bill Finnegan after the Hollywood Gold Cup. Finnegan had wanted to ship Shannon east for the International Gold Cup at Belmont Park, but despite rich pickings in the east, McCarthy had preferred to race in his home state. 'I have always supported California racing,' he told Hebert, 'but in this instance, I cannot.'

The critics halted in their tracks after McCarthy's capable public defensive, Paul Lowry included. 'The Australian champion had absolutely nothing to gain in running to certain defeat at the hands of Citation. At the age of seven, Shannon is over the hump as a racehorse. In less than a month he will be eight, which is considered well past the racing peak, and he came up the hard way in the United States. While his removal from the Tanforan Handicap wrecks the build-up for that event, on the other hand Shannon's glory cannot be dimmed by a smashing defeat on the eve of his retirement.'

Willie Molter, as was his way, said the least of anyone about it all. 'No one is more disappointed than I am over the failure of a truly great thoroughbred to get the one big chance of his life,' the trainer commented. 'The horse has been deprived of his right to challenge Citation. Shannon's true ability will be a matter of doubt now forever in turf history.'

—

Shannon had run his last race, and chalked in black and white by the close of 1948, his statistics were phenomenal. With American winnings of $212,810, only one horse had won more than him that long year – Citation. With 20,254 thoroughbreds racing across the United States in 1948, horses of the like of Coaltown, Stymie, Better Self, On Trust, Blue Peter, Talon and Mafosta, Shannon led all of them bar one.

No horse anywhere possessed more world records than the fleet Australian. He shared the world's mile record, nine-furlong record and 10-furlong record, as well as individual records at Randwick, Rosehill, Rosebery, Bay Meadows, Golden Gate Fields and Tanforan. Johnny Longden had stated in the jockeys' room at Santa Anita that he'd never been astride a faster horse. He wasn't kidding.

Sydney's export had climbed to the highest echelon of American racing, and not even Australians understood how acclaimed were his triumphs in America. Shannon was rated equal fourth (with Phalanx) on the American scale of the Best Racehorses for 1948, handicapped 125 lbs behind only Citation (134 lbs), Stymie (127 lbs) and Assault (126 lbs). These three horses would withstand the passing of time. While Shannon didn't race against any of them, his Californian opposition had been formidable enough. Mafosta, claimed the *Daily Racing Form*, was 'undoubtedly one of the fastest thoroughbreds the American turf has seen in years', while On Trust was the leading four-year-old in the country.

At a glance, Shannon's American record was pinched by heavy defeats. The *American Racing Manual* commented in its review of 1948, 'Starting 19 times, Shannon won only half a dozen races, and he was often beaten by horses who were giving him weight.' This was true. In 19 starts, Shannon had six victories, but his record deserved better scrutiny. He had run second once, and third a total of seven times, which meant he had been unplaced only five times. It could not be forgotten that within these 19 starts lay terrible difficulties; Shannon had never run on dirt, never started from automatic stalls, never run in American plates or eaten American oats, had never run on bends as tight as Santa Anita or Bay Meadows, had never run anticlockwise, and never sprinted 22-second sectionals at the front of a race. Out of the money only four times (his fourth place in the Angelino Purse netted him $600), Shannon owned a very gallant record in the northern hemisphere.

He led his age division in 1948, and the accolades kept coming. In Horse of the Year honours, Shannon was named 'Best Of The Year' in the four-year-olds and up category. Shannon was also crowned Champion Handicap Horse in a poll by *Turf and Sport Digest*, and later in December the weights were released for the Santa Anita Handicap. Shannon was top weight. 'This is a tribute to him', said the *Morning Telegraph*. All this from the horse Harry Curland had given away, the horse Darby Munro had said wouldn't win a race in America.

Few could remember a more sensational equine story. Robert Hebert said in *The Blood-Horse*, 'When Shannon II was imported to this country, the Australian hero was the centre of what is generally termed a storm of controversy. Now that he is retiring from racing, things are no different. Shannon is, for better or worse, still in big, black headlines in the newspapers.' Even *TIME* magazine was acquainted with the champion: 'Shannon is a seven-year-old bay stallion, Australian by birth and friendly as an overgrown puppy. Unlike Citation, everything about him is controversial.' Neil McCarthy had never owned a horse that had attracted so much individual opinion, or one to whom he was so attached. He hadn't bred Shannon, hadn't taught him to be brilliant, but McCarthy was the man behind the horse. His perseverance alone, careful and faithful, was responsible for making Shannon a star in 1948.

He told Willie Molter to unwind the champion, and on 8 December Shannon trucked out of Tanforan and south to Santa Anita. He travelled with McCarthy's other charge, Be Sure Now, following the rest of Molter's string southward. When Shannon stepped off the van in Arcadia, the familiar whiffs of the purple San Gabriel mountains filled his belly, and he began to slow down under an easy regime of soft canters. On 11 December he knew nothing of Citation's slashing victory in the Tanforan Handicap, or the poor crowd that stepped out to witness it. Veterinarians came and went from his stall, verifying his fertility so that his sale might be finalised. It went through on 13 December, and less than a week later, Shannon was ready to leave Santa Anita. Willie Molter gave him a long, touching scratch when the time came to part. The trainer would have other champions in his barn in later years, horses like Determine and Round Table, but none would bring Molter the heel and spur turbulence that Shannon had.

Sunday afternoon, 19 December, the horse breathed in the palms and haze of Los Angeles for the last time when he left Santa Anita. It would be a long rail trip east, and rugged, bandaged, Shannon kicked the California dirt off his shoes and boarded a boxcar for the Bluegrass.

45

Iron Works Pike

The Bluegrass country was still and bare that Christmas week, the black oak and hickory trees naked and choked by quiet winter. Soft frosts sat on the fences that crawled over hundreds of miles of bluffs and pasture, settling on thoroughbreds swollen with foals, including those who idled along the Iron Works Pike. They were Spendthrift mares; some belonging to the farm, others to Louis B. Mayer, Harry Warner or Elizabeth Arden Graham. Under the grey veil of chilly December, they picked at the sleeping fields, waiting for spring.

Spendthrift was 1070 acres of farm and grazing land, grown by Leslie Combs II from a modest plot of 127 acres in 1937. He remembered the day he moved in. 'Everybody said I was a damn fool to come in here. They said, you got Walmac on that side, the Whitneys over there and the Wideners down here. How the hell you gonna buy any land?' It didn't stop Combs. Within a decade he had 10 times the property he started with, and was breaking commercial breeding records up and down the United States.

Spendthrift house was postcard Kentucky, a columned colonial mansion that sat in the snow in winter, gleamed in the spring rains. It threw back to 1804, but with the Combses it was propelled into the glitzy fold of the new rich – film stars, movie executives, ambitious industrialists, they all wanted a slice of southern hospitality. The house became the epicentre of expensive parties, Cadillacs burying the driveway. Combs knew just how to leak his guests of their money. Rumour had it he would spread grain along the fences outside the dining room. Staring out at the romantic scene of grazing thoroughbreds, how could a man not buy a horse?

Combs was a brilliant, capable captain of Spendthrift Farm, a 'garrulous showman with a faux Southern gentleman surface charm, a foul-mouthed bully when that suited the situation better'. He was a gambler, investor, and high-roller at any point of the day, and he was eccentric. He had a fear of tornadoes, built a bunker on the farm just in case, and slept with a machine gun under his bed, like some sort of character from an Al Capone novella. Very odd and very complex, with more layers than the bedrock under his farm, Combs was nevertheless adored by his clients. They called him 'Cuzin' Leslie', and they trusted his breeding acumen. In turn, Combs picked stakes winner after stakes winner for them.

His success was mostly brilliance, but part geology. The Bluegrass was the thoroughbred country of America, the priceless bowl of rich pastureland in which racehorses seemed to grow like weeds. It had everything to do with the phosphate compounds that lay in the limestone under the dirt. As far back as 1876, scientists had been fascinated by it. Locals didn't know about the science, but they knew about the benefits. 'It makes fine whisky, cattle, trotters and runners, and gives strength to our men and symmetry and beauty to our women,' so said a local paper in 1889. The grass that grew in the region, the famous *Poa pratensis*, was the shimmery 'blue' variety from which the region derived its name. Settling right in the middle of it, Spendthrift was dictionary Bluegrass.

Late in 1948, the farm had eight stallions in its barn and one empty, spacious cedar stable. It had been Beau Pere's box, and it was swept now and lined deep with straw. Next door was Bernborough, down the row Alibhai and Jet Pilot. They waited on another famous Australian. On 20 December, they waited on Shannon.

His Santa Fe boxcar crept east from Los Angeles with the slow, blissful rhythm of a Sunday evening. Through Arizona, New Mexico and the top of Texas, it sloped north to Arkansas and Tennessee, easing into its siding in Lexington, Kentucky, late on Monday afternoon. Shannon had travelled with two of McCarthy's mares, Brora and Avillion, each with a booking to the stallion, and as the steam whistled from under the belly of the tired train, the doors swung open on Shannon. He poked his nose over the compartment wall at the old fellow who came in to clip his lead rope, and when the Spendthrift groom strode up the gangway, he found the stallion so affable that he led him out by head collar, no bit needed.

Shannon stepped off the express car to a small party of Spendthrift men, among them was farm manager, cool Hugh Sharphorn. Finally on firm ground, the stallion stood with his head in the air and took a long sniff. It was freezing in Kentucky, his welcoming party in gloves and double-breast woollen coats, shoulders up against the temperature. The horse was led away from the platform, and Shannon strode out with remarkable calm. He was loaded into the Spendthrift van and driven through Fayette County to 884 Iron Works Pike.

The van plugged up the long driveway, leaning right to the stables. It backed up to a loading ramp near the yearling boxes, and Sharphorn climbed out, lowered the door to let Shannon out. The stallion walked into the late afternoon, pausing on the ramp to look around him. Sharphorn ran his hand through Shannon's tail as he took in the famous horse. Already, he saw a sensible, easy-going thoroughbred. All the way to the barn the stallion paused to look about, breathing in the thick, cold fresh air, the farm smells of lucerne and chaff and the quiet. There were no hot-walkers, no saddles slung over doorways or liniments and cocktails burning the breeze. After such a long time, Shannon was home.

The Spendthrift staff liked the horse right away. There was Clem Brooks and also Tom Harbut, who had worked on the farm for a few years, had sidled in to a part-time groom position after war service and who would remain at Spendthrift until his retirement. Harbut was the son of Will Harbut, famous attendant to Man O' War, and he took charge of Shannon after his arrival, settled him in to his new lodgings. After a day or so, he let Shannon meet Bernborough. Harbut walked the horse outside and over to Bernborough, who had his head out the window of his stable. The horses nosed for a brief moment before they were separated, and the occasion was not lost on Harbut. Finally, Australia's two great heroes had met. It wasn't the circumstances that everyone had yearned for years ago, no silks or grandstands or gusty pumping jockeys, but Shannon and Bernborough had come face to face. A decade after Midstream and Emborough had sailed into Sydney together, their most famous sons were side by side.

Those first few months, Shannon let down from an angular, over-raced thoroughbred into a round, magnificently set stallion. The change was astonishing. His neck arced into a crest, his hindquarters caught up with his shoulders. He was elegance and masculinity in place of the 'rather light, a little thin-waisted horse, reminding one of a gelding rather than a stallion'. His kind expression grew nobility, and even as he began sire duties in January 1949, he was never mean or overbearing as many mature stallions could be. His later groom, Booker Payne, couldn't recall a sweeter horse. Shannon began covering at the top-shelf fee of $2500 (Bernborough was $1500), and only the established Alibhai held a higher position on the Spendthrift roster at $5000 a serve. Shannon's book was full, helped along by glowing national recommendations: 'He is a beautifully moving individual, and there is no denying that he possesses a world of speed.'

The seasons were good to Shannon, sighing slowly from winter into spring, oily summer into crimson autumn. The Bluegrass showed off its wares in pristine summer pastures bursting with new growth, and oaks tumbling over the roads, bright red cardinals posing on starch-white fences. It was a paradise that Shannon had earned, and he was a splendid part of it right up to the spring of 1955. On 14 May that year, only 14 years old, he took an awkward step in his field and shattered a bone over his near hock. When Payne found him, he was standing quietly with his hind leg dangling, and inspections showed that nothing could be done. The horse that had ripped over the turf and dirt at breakneck speeds had succumbed to a wrong step at rest. Magnificent, affable Shannon was destroyed that day.

Famous thoroughbreds find their resting places under trees or granite headstones, or bronze monuments in their likeness. But Shannon was laid in a hole at Spendthrift Farm, covered over and never seen again. There is no headstone or statue, no plaque, no trace of the horse that turned the stopwatch upside down. Shannon's monument is made of memory.

Notes

PART 1
1: 1938
p. 3   'wharf 3': *Sydney Morning Herald*, 15 February 1938, p. 16.

2: Sire
p. 4   'a warm, balmy English summer':
        www.london-weather.eu/category.46.html.
p. 4   'stood over in his front knees': Thoroughbred Heritage
        www.tbheritage.com/Portraits/Blandford.html.
p. 4   'three-time champion sire': Thoroughbred Heritage
        www.tbheritage.com/HistoricSires/LeadingSires/GBLeadSires.
        html.
p. 4   'excelled over the 10-furlong average': Thoroughbred Heritage
        www.tbheritage.com/Portraits/Blandford.html.
p. 4   'trainer Thomas . . . Leader': Weatherby's pedigree details for
        Midstream (by email).
p. 5   Midstream's race record: Weatherby's race details (by email).
p. 6   'Get me the best looking Blandford that you can': *Sydney Morning
        Herald*, 8 December 1937, p. 21.
p. 7   'a Gainsborough colt called Emborough': *Sydney Morning Herald*,
        22 December 1937, p. 18.
p. 7   'could he bring a horse in for Maguire': Ibid.
p. 7   'Clarence Hailey joined some of Europe's big-gun breeders':
        Nottingham Evening Post, 9 December 1937, p. 1.
p. 7   'Federico Tesio': *Nottingham Evening Post*, 7 December 1937, p. 1.
p. 8   'brief stop in Melbourne': *Argus*, 12 February 1938, p. 5.
p. 8   'it was £5300 later': *Argus*, 9 December 1937, p. 21; *Sydney
        Morning Herald*, 20 September 1938, p. 6.
p. 8   '10 sons of Blandford in Australasia': Ibid.

3: Kia Ora
p. 10   '102 broodmares': *Sydney Morning Herald*, 29 November 1938,
        p. 5s.
p. 10   'Mint, was a half-sister to the producer of the 1000 Guineas
        winner Brown Betty': Pring, *Analysis of Champion Racehorses*,
        pp. 380–383.
p. 10   'Mint, was a half-sister': 1941 Sydney Thoroughbred Yearlings
        Catalogue.

p. 10   'on Tuesday 3 April': *Examiner*, 4 April 1934, p. 2.

p. 10   'an honest 110 guineas': *West Australian*, 4 April 1934, p. 4.

p. 10   'Miller had 23 youngsters': *Sydney Morning Herald*, 4 April 1934, p. 17; 8 May 1934, p. 12.

p. 11   'affected by strangles': *Sydney Morning Herald*, 8 May 1934, p. 12.

p. 11   Idle Words' owner and trainer details for 1938: *Sunday Telegraph*, 29 September 1945, p. 15.

p. 11   'for the small fee of 75 guineas': Inglis, *Horsesense*, p. 24; 'Mighty NSW horse ended life in Kentucky pasture': *Daily Mirror*, 23 January 1967, p. 7; *Sunday Telegraph*, 29 September 1945, p. 15.

p. 12   'nearly 2000 acres in all': Kass, Terry, *History of Kia Ora Stud Scone*, p 10.

p. 12   £15,040: Ibid., p. 9.

p. 12   'and many city and suburban cold stores': Bill Whittaker, 'Racing Recollections – Kia Ora Stud – breeding establishment extraordinaire', *Bloodhorse Review*, August 2006, p. 74.

p. 13   'draft of only three': *Sydney Morning Herald*, 26 July 1937, p. 13.

p. 13   'under the persuasion of his good friend Richard Wootton': Whittaker, op. cit.

p. 13   'Of 1880 acres': Kass, op. cit., p. 10.

p. 13   'By 1928, Kia Ora was sending 103 yearlings': Inglis, *Horsesense*, p. 173.

p. 13   'Miller almost always made back': Ibid., p. 173.

p. 13   'Rivalry with his neighbours': Ibid., p. 177.

p. 14   'always speaking through the middle man': Ibid., p. 175.

p. 14   'Kia Ora had a crew of 24': 'Stud Farm: Birthplace of Many Champion Australian Racehorses in the Past 30 Years', *PIX* magazine, vol. 16, no. 8, 3 November 1945, p. 17.

p. 15   'eight mare and foal paddocks': Ibid.

p. 15   'foaling paddock and 18 foaling pens': Ibid.

p. 15   'just room enough for two horses': author's visit to Kia Ora Stud, 26 February 2012.

p. 15   'the Kia Ora stallions were stabled to avoid the heat and flies': 'Stud Farm', *PIX* magazine, op. cit., p. 19.

p. 16   '29 September 1941': 1941 Sydney Thoroughbred Yearlings Catalogue.

p. 16   'cleanse and disinfect the youngster': 'Stud Farm', *PIX* magazine, op. cit., p. 17.

p. 16   'colt had a low-set appearance': Comment by Bert Riddle, undisclosed source.

A note on Bert and Peter Riddle: Clive Inglis, in his 1950 publication, *Horsesense*, states that Bert Riddle did not inform his brother Peter about the yearling Shannon. He offers an alternative history. During the research for this book, several inaccuracies were picked up in Inglis's version of Shannon's story in Horsesense, so the author has run with trusted sources in the writing of Shannon's sale to Peter Riddle.

4: War and horse-trading

p. 17   '19 youngsters by Midstream': 1943 Sydney Thoroughbred Yearlings Catalogue

p. 17   'they had to walk three miles': Bill Whittaker, 'Racing Recollections – Kia Ora Stud – breeding establishment extraordinaire', *Bloodhorse Review*, August 2006, p. 72.

p. 19   'dispersed around Australia': *Sydney Morning Herald*, 26 March 1943, p. 8.

5: Peter Riddle

p. 21   'He dressed well': Interview with Mardi Henderson, at home in Sydney, 26 April 2012.

p. 21   '1938-model Chrysler Royal sedan': Peter Riddle's will, 1947.

p. 22   'born at Kaarimba, Victoria': Peter Riddle's birth certificate, Births, Deaths and Marriages, Department of Justice, Victoria.

p. 22   'found himself there on the gold trail': Ken Dyer, 'The Riddle Dynasty', *Harness Racing International*, May/June 2005, p. 50.

p. 22   'In 1897 his father paid 100 guineas': Ibid.

p. 22   'dragging Nellie from a stool by her hair': *Western Mail*, 18 February 1898, p. 19.

p. 22   'On 3 February 1897, Catherine was on a bender': *Sydney Morning Herald*, 16 February 1898, p. 4.

p. 23   'Woman or Fiend': *South Australian Register*, 16 February 1898, p. 6.

p. 23   'Cruelty to a Husband': *Sunbury News and Bulla and Melton Advertiser*, 19 February 1898, p. 2.

p. 24   'Sydney driver championship seven times': Championship list supplied by John Peck, Harness Racing Victoria.

p. 24   'married in February 1922': Riddle's marriage certificate, Births, Deaths and Marriages, New South Wales.

p. 25   'A few of the country's leading flat trainers': *Argus*, 11 November 1947, p. 200.

p. 25   'the poor health of the sport': Brown, op. cit., p. xx.

p. 25   'lingering back weakness': Telephone interview with Mardi Henderson, 11 June 2012.

p. 25   'won his last trotting race': Dyer, op. cit., p. 55; 'already held a permit from the AJC to train a single thoroughbred': AJC Racing Calendar, 1 February 1927, p. 13.

p. 25   gaining a trainer's licence from the VRC in 1980: Rod Nicholson, *The Track: Australian Racing's Hall of Fame*, News Custom Publishing, Melbourne, 2005. p xx.

p. 25   'In August 1928 it was granted': AJC Racing Calendar, 1 August 1928.

p. 27   'AJC officials disqualified Riddle and Byers for 12 months': *Canberra Times*, 20 March 1931, p. 3.

p. 27   'Turf Sensation: Three Men Sent Out': Ibid.

p. 27   'Three Disqualified: Prince Elmo Case': *Sydney Morning Herald*, 20 March 1931, p. 14.

p. 28   'Riddle horses one-two in mid-week meetings': *Sydney Morning Herald*, 27 May 1935, p. 12.

p. 28   Divorce particulars: Riddle vs Riddle: *Sydney Morning Herald*, 18 October 1940, p. 3.

p. 28   'gossip pages of the tabloid newspapers': 'Trainer's Wife Preferred the Butcher Boy': *Mirror*, 2 November 1940, p. 17.

p. 28   'his father's death in 1933': http://npollock.id.au/history/smeaton.html.

p. 28   'June married in 1942': Telephone conversation with Mardi Henderson, 11 June 2012.

p. 28   'he worried what people thought of this situation': Interview with Mardi Henderson, at home in Sydney, 26 April 2012.

p. 29   'coronary sclerosis': Peter Riddle's death certificate.

p. 29   'He was suffering from arteriosclerosis': Interview notes, Dr Meghan Newcombe, 7 June 2012.

p. 29   'from the 8 family of Bruce Lowe's figures': 1943 Sydney Thoroughbred Yearlings Catalogue.

6: The small fellow with the big brain

p. 31   'they planted themselves cross-legged on the grass': Film footage of yearling sales Sydney 1940–45, British Pathé, www.britishpathe.com/video/yearlings-bring-amazing-prices-aka-stud-sales/query/auctions.

p. 33   Yearling prices as recorded: *Sydney Morning Herald*, 21 April 1943, p. 10.

7: The little Irish horse

p. 34   'box number seven': *Australian Women's Weekly*, 3 June 1959, p. 3.

p. 34   'leading rider in the western districts': *Daily Telegraph*,

29 September 1945, p. 20.

p. 35 'He's a good judge of horses': *Daily Telegraph*, 29 September 1945, p. 20.

p. 35 'promising Glade yearling became Beltana': Australian Stud Book, vol. XX (1944), p. 287.

p. 35 'filly by Le Grand Duc became Gipsy Lady': Ibid., p. 286.

p. 35 'became Randolph': Ibid., p. 361.

p. 36 'By July, Peter Riddle was training the colt': *Sydney Sportsman*, 8 July 1943, p. 1.

p. 36 'ex-Queenslander, now Sydney hoop, Fred Shean': 'Lillye on Legends: Fred Shean (Part One)', AJC Racing Calendar, February 1993.

p. 37 'Shannon and Shean sprinted two furlongs': *Sydney Sportsman*, 26 August 1943, p. 12.

p. 37 'Shean got three furlongs': *Sydney Sportsman*, 9 September 1943, p. 12.

p. 37 'The formula for sectionals in horseracing': Ellis, *The Science of Turf Investment*.

p. 37 'Shannon lined up for a public two-year-old jump-out': *Sydney Sportsman*, 16 September 1943, pp. 1, 3.

p. 38 '"raciest two-year-old" he had seen': *Sunday Telegraph*, 3 October 1943, p. 10.

p. 38 'the little Irish horse': *Barrier Miner*, 28 September 1945, p. 6.

p. 38 'Shannon won a two-year-old trial': Sydney Sportsman, 23 September 1943, p. 12.

p. 38 'Shannon . . . will prove one of the smartest youngsters of the season': *Sydney Sportsman*, 16 September 1943, p. 1.

p. 39 'though Majesty appears to overshadow': *Sydney Sportsman*, 7 October 1943, p. 12.

8: The Sydney Turf Club

p. 40 'recipes that required neither butter nor eggs': *Daily Telegraph*, 6 September 1943, p. 10.

p. 40 'Mutton and lamb supplies': *Daily Telegraph*, 9 October 1943, p. 5.

p. 40 'the Milk Board had issued warnings': Ibid.

p. 40 'Items like silk stockings': Ibid.

p. 40 Prime Minister Curtin quotes: Ibid.

p. 40 'Record betting': Ibid.

p. 41 'All we want is fine weather': *Sydney Sportsman*, 16 September 1943, p. 1.

p. 41 'helmed the AJC as secretary since 1932': Painter and Waterhouse, *The Principal Club*, p. 149.

p. 41 'Racing is an outlet': *Sydney Sportsman*, 16 September 1943, p. 1.

p. 42 'Its objective was to establish a genuine non-proprietary racing association': Richard Boulter, *Forty Years On: The Sydney Turf Club*, Macarthur Press, Sydney, 1984, p. 13.

p. 42 '£50,000 a year to operate': *Sydney Sportsman*, 12 August 1943, p. 1.

p. 42 'promoted a score of cricitism': Ibid.

p. 43 'His appointment recognised the natural link': Boulter, op. cit., p. 35.

9: 'It was bad luck'

p. 44 '65 race-day trams': *Daily Telegraph*, 9 October 1943, p. 5.

p. 44 'in the tens of thousands': Ibid.

p. 44 'racing had begun there in May 1860': Barrie, *Turf Cavalcade*, p. 54.

p. 45 '100 feet wide at its narrowest point': *Town and Country Journal*, 25 September 1886, p. 36.

p. 45 'Beer was limited': *Daily Telegraph*, 9 October 1943, p. 5.

p. 45 'rain bucketing': Accumulated weather readings for Observatory Hill, Sydney, 28 October 1943, Station 66062, Bureau of Meteorology.

p. 46 'Shannon was trading at 7/2 against': *The Australasian Turf Register*, 1944, p. 57.

p. 46 'AJC timekeeper William Kerr': *Sydney Morning Herald*, 21 July 1954, p. 13.

p. 46 'Peter Riddle told me he can keep the horse fit': *Sunday Telegraph*, 10 October 1943, p. 9.

p. 46 '£1137 to the winner': *The Australasian Turf Register*, 1944, p. 57.

p. 48 'five-furlong Randwick record': *J. J. Miller's Sporting Annual*, 1944, p. 32.

p. 49 '16 lots after Shannon': 1941 Sydney Thoroughbred Yearlings Catalogue.

p. 49 'one of the biggest shocks': Ibid; *Sunday Telegraph*, 10 October 1943, p. 10.

p. 49 'I knew Majesty would have to be': Ibid., p. 9.

p. 49 'As fast as Victory Lad finished': *Truth*, 10 October 1943, p. 3.

p. 49 'It was bad luck': *Sunday Telegraph*, 10 October 1943, p. 9.

p. 49 'a bag of offers': *Sydney Sportsman*, 14 October 1943, p. 1.

10: The glamour horse of south-east Queensland

p. 51 'dispersed to the Bach brothers Jack and Frank': Hobson, *Racing's All-Time Greats*.

p. 51	'glamour horse of sunshine racing': *Sydney Sportsman*, 17 June 1943, p. 1.
p. 52	'At 1.55 pm': *Courier-Mail*, 28 April 1943, p. 5.
p. 53	'Roberts produced a £25 betting slip': Ibid.
p. 53	'credited with being Queensland's best horse': *Worker*, 6 September 1943, p. 9.

11: 'One up with plenty to play'

p. 54	'26¼ for two furlongs': *Sydney Sportsman*, 21 October 1943, p. 3.
p. 54	'36½ for three': *Daily Telegraph*, 22 October 1943, p. 10.
p. 55	'37 flat, hard held': *Daily Telegraph*, 22 October 1943, p. 11.
p. 55	'heavy wager was placed on Billy Cook': *Daily Telegraph*, 23 October 1943, p. 15.
p. 56	'fastest five furlongs ever clocked': *J. J. Miller's Sporting Annual*, 1944; *Sunday Telegraph*, 24 October 1943, p. 10.
p. 56	'crowd of 55,500': *West Australian*, 25 October 1943, p. 4.
p. 56	'unofficial estimates on Cup Day': *Truth*, 14 November 1943, p. 10.
p. 57	'women fainted on their feet': Ibid.
p. 57	'refugees were pouring into the city every month': web.wm.edu/so/monitor/issues/15-1/2-kepple.pdf
p. 57	'Tagged as "reffos"': Elliott, Sumner Locke, *Edens Lost*, Penguin: Melbourne, 1986.
p. 57	'he had his own rainbows': Interview with Mardi Henderson, at home in Sydney, 26 April 2012.
p. 57	'Riddle worried constantly: Ibid.
p. 58	'Sydney weather took a turn': Accumulated weather readings for Observatory Hill, Sydney, 28 October 1943, Station 66062, Bureau of Meteorology.
p. 59	'track was drying out by the running of the Two-Year-Old Stakes': *Sunday Telegraph*, 21 November 1943, p. 15.
p. 59	'even Riddle was surprised': Ibid., p. 10.
p. 60	'the easiest £557': *The Australasian Turf Register* 1944, p. 107.
p. 60	'I don't know how they're going to beat him next Saturday': *Sunday Telegraph*, 21 November 1943, p. 15.
p. 60	'I thought my colt was certain': Ibid.
p. 60	'Riddle wasn't known for exciting outbursts': Interview with Mardi Henderson, at home in Sydney, 26 April 2012.
p. 60	'his mount was well beaten before the turn': *Sunday Telegraph*, 21 November 1943, p. 10.
p. 61	'After today's performance I am convinced that he will win': Ibid., p. 9.
p. 61	'receiving offers for Shannon since 15 October': Ibid.

p. 61   'pay his rent in a semi-detached brick cottage': based on the annual rent of a brick, semi-detached cottage in Division Street, Coogee, in October 1943, from *Sydney Morning Herald*, 30 October 1943, p. 15.

p. 62   'drilled three furlongs without shoes': *Sydney Sportsman*, 25 November 1943, p. 12.

p. 62   'cruised over a soft track': Daily Telegraph, 26 November 1943, p. 11.

p. 62   'Shannon will be odds on': *Sydney Sportsman*, 25 November 1943, p. 2.

p. 63   'arms folded and head cocked': *Truth*, 28 November 1943, p. 3.

p. 63   'three minutes after post time': Ibid., p. 5.

p. 64   'Majesty went with me all right': Ibid., p. 2.

p. 65   'politely scoffed at the suggestion': *Sunday Telegraph*, 28 November 1943, p. 9.

p. 65   'as good a two-year-old as he had ever ridden': Ibid.

p. 65   'that horse was a game ol' bastard': 'Lillye on Legends: Fred Shean (Part One)', AJC Racing Calendar, February 1993.

12: 'I think Bravo is the better of the pair'

p. 67   'much more weight on Shannon's back': *Daily Telegraph*, 29 November 1943, p. 12.

p. 68   'Riddle scratched Shannon from the Voluntary Aids' Handicap': *Canberra Times*, 7 December 1943, p. 4.

p. 69   'If both Riddle's colts were trotted out': *Truth*, 19 December 1943, p. 2.

p. 69   'Before today I didn't think': *Sunday Telegraph*, 19 December 1943, p. 1.

p. 69   'it is hard to guess whether he or Shannon': *Daily Telegraph*, 20 December 1943, p. 12.

p. 70   'he didn't plan for the colts to meet': Ibid.

p. 70   'Bravo is not as good as they thought': *Canberra Times*, 28 December 1943, p. 4.

13: A short neck or four lengths

p. 71   'Riddle had heart disease': 'Medical effects of heart disease', Wallace Mason Yater, *Fundamentals of Internal Medicine*, D. Appleton-Century Company, Inc., New York, 1944.

p. 71   'No one noticed it more': Interview with Mardi Henderson, at home in Sydney, 26 April 2012.

p. 71   'expecting the hardest year': *Daily Telegraph*, 28 December 1943, p. 6.

p. 72 'the cornered German people will struggle bitterly to the end':
       Daily Telegraph, 27 December 1943, p. 6.

p. 72 'from long habit': *Australian Women's Weekly*, 1 January 1944,
       p. 10.

p. 72 'apples had hit a ceiling price': *Sydney Morning Herald*, 1 January
       1944, p. 6.

p. 73 'He was a lovely horse to look at': Description based on a photo-
       graph from *The Sun*, 1943, supplied by Daryll Cook.

p. 73 'half-miles in 50¼ seconds': *Sydney Sportsman*, 2 March 1944,
       p. 12.

p. 74 'Australian Comforts Fund': Samuel H. Bowden, *The History
       of the Australian Comforts Fund*, Scotow and Presswell, Sydney,
       1922.

p. 74 '45,000 racegoers paid their way': *Mornington Bulletin*, 20 March
       1944, p. 2.

p. 75 'the stewards swept in on him': *Sunday Telegraph*, 29 March 1944,
       p. 15.

p. 75 'I was about to go around two horses': Ibid.

p. 76 'He jumped well, settling third': *Sunday Telegraph*, 2 April 1944,
       p. 15.

p. 77 'a horse had a neutral zone': Ellis, *The Science of Turf Investment*.

14: The 1944 Sires' Produce Stakes

p. 79 '82,400 people': *The Sun*, 8 April 1944, p. 6.

p. 79 'handing over 1/3 to get in': Racebook, AJC St Leger Day, 8 April
       1944.

p. 79 'If the punt were good': story as told by Graham Caves to the
       author, email, 15 September 2012.

p. 79 'Shannon paying 2/1 against': *The Australasian Turf Register*,
       1944, p. 289.

p. 80 'he carried number two saddlecloth': Racebook, AJC St Leger
       Day, 8 April 1944.

p. 80 'chaotic start at 2 pm on the tick': *Sunday Telegraph*, 9 April
       1944, p. 20.

p. 81 'bolted under the judge's string': Ibid, p. 13.

p. 83 'Shannon wouldn't run in it': *Sydney Sportsman*, 13 April 1944,
       p. 1.

p. 83 'Shannon was not as sharp as he had been in the autumn': *Sunday
       Telegraph*, 9 April 1944, p. 20.

15: The Abbeville Affair

p. 84 'McGrowdie confessed to Porter': *Truth*, 13 August 1944, p. 3.

p. 84 'The morning after the race': *Daily Telegraph*, 12 August 1944, p. 16.

p. 85 'Aub Fulford, a champion bare-knuckle fighter': *Townsville Daily Bulletin*, 31 July 1944, p. 5.

p. 85 'called in for a preliminary hearing': *Sydney Morning Herald*, 8 August 1944, p. 6; *Daily Telegraph*, 8 August 1944, p. 16.

p. 85 'mystified as to why he had been called in': *Daily Telegraph*, 8 August 1944, p. 16.

p. 85 'he suspected he was being asked for evidence': *Daily Telegraph*, 9 August 1944, p. 16.

p. 85 'no idea who had put Shean up to it': *Truth*, 20 August 1944, p. 4.

p. 85 'delivering a message': *Truth*, 13 August 1944, p. 3.

p. 85 'I've been offered £600 to stop Hall Stand': Ibid.

p. 85 'This offer applies to you too': *Daily Telegraph*, 12 August 1944, p. 16.

p. 85 'the monies would be handed over': Ibid.

p. 85 'had been laid a fortune to win the race': *Truth*, 13 August 1944, p. 3.

p. 86 'enduring two hours': *Singleton Argus*, 9 August 1944, p. 2.

p. 86 'Shean confessed that it was Andy Knox': *Sydney Morning Herald*, 18 August 1944, p. 10.

p. 86 'No business Andy': *Daily Telegraphy*, 12 August 1944, p. 16.

p. 86 'Knox muscled up to McGrowdie': *Daily Telegraph*, 9 August 1944, p. 16.

p. 86 'riding at the top level': *Sydney Morning Herald*, 18 August 1944, p. 10.

p. 86 'wondering if the Newcastle Jockey Club': *Advocate*, 19 August 1944, p. 3.

p. 86 'I couldn't believe my ears': *Daily Telegraph*, 9 August 1944, p. 16.

p. 86 'I may appeal in an attempt to clear my name': Ibid.

p. 87 'What an invidious position I was in': *Truth*, 20 August 1944, p. 4.

p. 87 'My only request': Ibid.

p. 87 'impounded the betting books': *Daily Telegraph*, 12 August 1944, p. 16.

p. 87 'Precise's owner': *Canberra Times*, 15 August 1944, p. 4.

p. 87 'carbon copies were so bad': *Daily Telegraph*, 16 August 1944, p. 16.

p. 87 'his risks . . . were no more than £3000': Ibid.

p. 88 'Knox first to give evidence': *Morning Bulletin*, 18 August 1944, p. 4.

p. 88 'the penalty was not justified': *Daily Telegraph*, 17 August 1944, p. 16.

p. 88   'Charlie McLoughlin testified': *Daily Telegraph*, 18 August 1944, p. 16.
p. 88   'Andy Knox was ejected for 10 staggering years': Ibid.
p. 89   'slamming a rolled-up newspaper': Ibid.
p. 89   'I couldn't cross-question them fully': Ibid.
p. 89   'railroaded by the jockeys I thought pals': Ibid.
p. 89   'these admissions got me into trouble': Ibid.
p. 89   'wife had been ill with worry': Ibid.
p. 90   'Knox's offence was very serious': Ibid.
p. 90   'ex-Queensland hoop George Moore': *Daily Telegraph*, 14 August 1944, p. 12.

16: The Demon Darb

p. 91   '5 ft 2¾ in, weighed 8 st 12 lbs': *Daily Telegraph*, 24 July 1944, p. 9.
p. 91   'swarthy colour to his complexion': Clan Munro Australia www.clanmunroaustralia.org/PDFFiles/CMAAU%20-%20 ANCESTORS.pdf
p. 91   'had things that most people didn't have': Interview with Daryll Cook by telephone, 24 September 2012.
p. 91   'drank, smoked, ran red lights': Ibid.
p. 91   'Take whatever's in my pockets, kid': Ibid.
p. 92   'ran ragged around the yard': *Daily Telegraph*, 24 July 1944, p. 8.
p. 92   missing sheets in the linen press: Ibid.
p. 92   'the nickname came from little Munro's handshake': As told to Daryll Cook c.1959 by Jim Munro. Interview with Daryll Cook by telephone, 24 September 2012.
p. 92   'hitch a racing saddle to a rail fence': Interview with Daryll Cook by telephone, 24 September 2012.
p. 92   'Eric Connolly noticed him': *Daily Telegraph*, 24 July 1944, p. 8.
p. 92   'Darby learned to walk like Connolly, dress like him': Interview with Daryll Cook by telephone, 24 September 2012.
p. 93   'No jockey in Sydney was more vilified': *Sydney Sportsman*, 9 December 1943, p. 1.
p. 93   'refused to get a silent number': 'What Makes Demon Darb tick?', *Sport*, June 1956, p. 9.
p. 94   'raised his hat to them': *Daily Telegraph*, 24 July 1944, p. 8.
p. 94   'Rogilla the greatest weight-for-age': *Argus*, 7 February 1949, p. 18.
p. 94   'Ajax a "fake"': Ibid.
p. 94   'testify greatness': Ibid.
p. 94   'Jim always thought they were after Darb': Interview with Daryll Cook by telephone, 24 September 2012.

p. 94   'arrive at the boxing on Friday night': Interview with Daryll Cook by telephone, 24 September 2012.

p. 94   'rarely ate breakfast': *Daily Telegraph*, 24 July 1944, p. 9.

p. 95   'that the minimum riding weight': Ibid.

p. 95   'so inebriated he was still drunk when he began riding': Interview with Daryll Cook by telephone, 24 September 2012.

p. 95   'relations between her and his daughter were strained': Interview with Mardi Henderson, at home in Sydney, 26 April 2012.

p. 95   'half-miles in 52 seconds': *Sydney Sportsman*, 3 August 1944, p. 12.

p. 96   'acquired his jockey's license in Brisbane in 1938': *Courier-Mail*, 20 December 1938, p. 12.

p. 96   'nine minutes after the advertised start time': *Sydney Sportsman*, 31 August 1944, p. 11.

p. 96   'broke his ankle, then came down with an infection': *Daily Telegraph*, 24 July 1944, p. 9.

p. 97   'consider staying aboard for the AJC Derby': *Daily Telegraph*, 31 August 1944, p. 16.

17: Pipedreams of fortune and glory

p. 100   'It was a mammoth performance': *Sydney Sportsman*, 31 August 1944, p. 2.

p. 100   'Scaur Fel had been scratched': *Truth*, 3 September 1944, p. 3.

p. 100   'the AJC had watered'; *Sunday Telegraph*, 3 September 1944, p. 20.

p. 100   'confident their colt was the goods': *Truth*, 3 September 1944, p. 2.

p. 100   'biggest betting drifts': *Sunday Telegraph*, 3 September 1944, p. 20.

p. 101   'four minutes over start time': *Sydney Sportsman*, 7 September 1944, p. 11.

p. 102   'wouldn't be held to a ride': *Sunday Telegraph*, 3 September 1944, p. 9.

p. 102   'they've come with fighter escorts': *Daily Telegraph*, 7 September 1944, p. 16.

p. 102   'the track looked like a bowling green': Ibid.

p. 102   'ban on race-day trains': *Daily Telegraph*, 30 August 1944, p. 16.

p. 103   'meeting would resume at Rosehill': *Daily Telegraph*, 6 September 1944, p. 16.

p. 103   'he's a little on the light side': *Daily Telegraph*, 5 September 1944, p. 12.

p. 103   'rescinded his ban on transport': *Daily Telegraph*, 9 September 1944, p. 16.

p. 103   'benefit the breeding': *Truth*, 24 September 1944, p. 3.

p. 103   'six furlongs at Rosebery': *Sydney Sportsman*, 21 September 1944, p. 1.

p. 103   'the colt would have demolished the Rosebury course records': *Daily Telegraph*, 22 September 1944, p. 16.

p. 104   'I think he's too small': *Daily Telegraph*, 18 September 1944, p. 12.

p. 104   'The *Telegraph* was so certain': *Daily Telegraph*, 23 September 1944, p. 16.

p. 105   'Munro was sure he was going down': *Sunday Telegraph*, 24 September 1944, p. 11.

p. 105   '14 minutes after the advertised start time': *Truth*, 24 September 1944, p. 9.

p. 106   'sore and tied up': Ibid.

p. 106   'racing plates was twisted': Ibid.; *Sydney Morning Herald*, 23 September 1944, p. 6.

p. 106   'Neither the racing public nor breeders': *Daily Telegraph*, 6 October 1944, p. 14.

p. 106   '£50,000 of public betting money': *Morning Bulletin*, 28 September 1944, p. 7.

p. 106   'I could see by the way Shannon was travelling': *Sunday Telegraph*, 24 September 1944, p. 11.

p. 107   'the colt had recovered well': *Sunday Telegraph*, 24 September 1944, p. 11.

18: The AJC Derby

p. 108   'bounced back from the Guineas': *Sunday Sun*, 1 October 1944, p. 1.

p. 108   'a bit of a stir by opting for light exercise only': *Sun*, 3 October 1944, p. 10.

p. 108   'trainers discussed this': Ibid.

p. 109   'foments and poultices': *Sun*, 4 October 1944, p. 8.

p. 109   'He feels thoroughly sound': *Daily Telegraph*, 4 October 1944, p. 10.

p. 109   '£1000 cash bet': *Daily Telegraph*, 5 October 1944, p. 20.

p. 109   'train down from Kia Ora the night before': Ibid.

p. 109   'red and tender': *Sunday Sun*, 7 October 1944, p. 8.

p. 109   'He'll need a good hit-out tomorrow': *Daily Telegraph*, 7 October 1944, p. 20.

(A newspaper strike in Sydney reduced all daily papers to one composite edition of the *Sydney Morning Herald* from 7–19 October 1944.)

p. 110   Details of Rosebery trackwork: *Sydney Morning Herald* composite edition, 11 October 1944, p. 4.

p. 110   'scratch Shannon from the VRC event': Ibid.

p. 110   Details of Rosebery trackwork: *Sydney Morning Herald* composite edition, 13 October 1944, p. 6.

p. 110   'doesn't matter how good Tea Rose is': *Sydney Morning Herald* composite edition, 12 October 1944, p. 6.

p. 111   Details of Rosebery trackwork: *Sydney Morning Herald* composite edition, 11 October 1944, p. 4.

p. 112   '30 degrees in the shade': Accumulated weather readings for Observatory Hill, Sydney, 14 October 1944, Station 66062, Bureau of Meteorology.

p. 112   'warm-up canter': *Sydney Morning Herald* composite edition, 14 October 1944, p. 6.

p. 112   'lifted his foot': *Sydney Morning Herald* composite edition, 15 October 1944, p. 9.

p. 113   'race-day anaesthetic': *Sydney Morning Herald* composite edition, 11 October 1944, p. 4.

p. 113   'The condition . . . wouldn't affect his ability': *Sydney Morning Herald* composite edition, 16 October 1944, p. 6.

p. 113   'radio perched on his bedside table': Ibid.

p. 114   'first filly since 1898': *Mercury*, 16 October 1944, p. 15.

19: Fellow citizens, the war is over

p. 116   'bright, chilly morning over Sydney': Accumulated weather readings for Observatory Hill, Sydney, 15 August 1945, Station 66062, Bureau of Meteorology.

p. 116   'a little after 9 am': *Sydney Morning Herald*, 16 August 1945, p. 1.

p. 116   'Fellow citizens, the war is over': Australia's War 1939–1945, www.ww2australia.gov.au/vevp/index.html.

p. 116   'street bands appeared out of nowhere': *Sydney Morning Herald*, 16 August 1945, p. 6.

p. 116   'strewn paper': Ibid., p. 5.

p. 117   '300,000 people': Ibid.

p. 117   'a million people clung to downtown Sydney': Ibid.

p. 117   'the Roosevelt . . . remained open for business': Ibid., p. 10.

p. 117   'Anzac Memorial in Hyde Park': Ibid., p. 3.

p. 117   'a giant shift had taken place': 'The World Seems to be on the Move', *Argus*, 14 July 1945, p. 25.

p. 118   'the most mobilised of Allied nations': *Australia is Like This*, c. 1944, Australian War Memorial film archive, ID F01303.

p. 118   '40,000 would not make it back': Australia's War 1939–1945, www.ww2australia.gov.au/vevp/index.html

p. 118   'converting a wartime economy': *Sydney Morning Herald*,
16 August 1945, p. 2.

p. 118   'the need for unity and unselfishness is not less': Ibid.

p. 119   'International Olympic Committee began planning the next
Games': Ibid., p. 12.

p. 119   'Sydney–London flights': *West Australian*, 4 April 1946, p. 8.

p. 119   'the Queensland government': *Cairns Post*, 22 August 1945, p. 3.

p. 119   'It is unthinkable': comment by C. M. Barker, General Manager
of Dairy Farmers' Co-operative Milk Co., *Sydney Morning
Herald*, 26 April 1945, p. 4.

p. 119   'Trainers and owners will work out their own salvation': *Central
Queensland Herald*, 17 May 1945, p. 10.

p. 119   AJC ban details: *Sydney Morning Herald*, 26 June 1945, p. 3.

p. 120   'had there been the extreme shortage': *Sydney Sportsman*,
5 September 1945, p. 1.

p. 120   'best years in the history of the nation's turf': *Sun*, 16 May 1945.

20: Eyes on the Epsom

p. 121   'Munro has asked the trainer about his plans for Shannon':
Sunday Sun & Guardian, Sporting Section, 9 September 1945,
p. 3.

p. 121   'If he runs in the Epsom, I'm your jockey': *Morning Bulletin*,
10 September 1945, p. 7.

p. 122   'the neck of a chicken': *Sunday Telegraph*, 2 September 1945,
p. 14.

p. 122   'sweetest horse I have ever handled': *Sunday Telegraph*,
2 September 1945, p. 14.

p. 122   Descriptions of Shannon playing with O'Brien: *PIX* magazine,
11 October 1947, pp. 3–5.

p. 123   'fed five times a day': Ibid., p. 4.

p. 123   'letting him eat whenever he wants to': *Sunday Telegraph*,
2 September 1945, p. 14.

p. 123   'nothing disturbed him': *Sunday Telegraph*, 2 September 1945,
p. 14.

p. 123   'penchant for laziness': *PIX* magazine, op. cit., p. 5.

p. 123   'Shannon often ate and drank sitting down': Quote from Barney
O'Brien, Ibid., p. 4.

p. 123   'liked the company': Ibid., p. 5.

p. 123   'painted light blue': *Sunday Telegraph*, 2 September 1945, p. 14.

p. 123   Alsatian dog Rico: Ibid.

p. 124   'when the bandages came out': *PIX* magazine, op cit., p. 4.

p. 124   'three furlongs in 28½ seconds': *Sydney Sportsman*, 26 July 1945,
p. 14.

p. 124   'play-bucked Jack Thompson': *Sydney Sportsman*, 2 August 1945, p. 11.

p. 125   'scrap the Epsom altogether': *Daily Telegraph*, 27 August 1945, p. 20.

p. 125   'something persisted in Peter Riddle': Ibid.

p. 125   'second line of favouritism': *Sydney Sportsman*, 14 August 1945, p. 1.

p. 125   Descriptions of Sleepy Fox: *Sunday Telegraph*, 2 September 1945, p. 14.

p. 126   'a few pounds on an each-way result': *Sunday Telegraph*, 26 August 1945, p. 13.

p. 126   'four minutes after the scheduled race time': *Sydney Sportsman*, 29 August 1945, p. 12.

p. 126   'a few days of rain': *Daily Telegraph*, 25 August 1945, p. 20.

p. 127   'Metrop likely mission for Shannon': *Daily Telegraph*, 27 August 1945, p. 20.

p. 127   'Riddle had to admit': *Daily Telegraph*, 3 September 1945, p. 16.

p. 128   'Metropolitan doubles for £60,000': *Daily Telegraph*, 4 September 1945, p. 16.

p. 128   'gifts and winning percentages': *Morning Bulletin*, 10 September 1945, p. 7.

p. 128   'Fred Shean . . . had also stepped out': *Sun*, 4 September 1945, p. 10.

p. 128   'Abbeville ban was about to expire': 'Shean, Moore to ride at Randwick', *Sun*, 6 September 1945, p. 12.

p. 128   'Munro went with Shannon': *Sun*, 5 September 1945, p. 12.

21: 'The best Epsom trials the turf has ever seen'

p. 129   Flight's measurements: A. Pritchard Morris, *Flight: A Story of Courage*, Sydney, 1947.

p. 129   'ambling along so commonly': Ibid.

p. 130   Scots College colours: *Sunday Telegraph*, 3 April 1944, p. 20.

p. 130   Flight was named in his honour: Ibid.

p. 130   'insisted on returning to the yard': Morris, op. cit.

p. 130   'an untamed shrew': Cliff Graves, 'Racehorses are only human, after all', *Sunday Times* magazine (Perth), 18 September 1949, p. 9.

p. 130   'Shannon, Tahmoor and Victory Lad': *Sydney Sportsman*, 5 September 1945, p. 6.

p. 131   'Munro considered her a moral beaten': Morris, op. cit. p. 22.

p. 131   'the colt didn't have opposition': *Sun*, 7 September 1945, p. 12.

p. 131   Shannon's Victoria Park trial: *Daily Telegraph*, 7 September 1945, p. 18; 8 September 1945, p. 18.

p. 131 'he's a good thing for Saturday': *Daily Telegraph*, 7 September 1945, p. 18.

p. 131 'finance their liabilities': *Daily Telegraph*, 8 September 1945, p. 20.

p. 131 'radio station 2UW': *Sydney Morning Herald*, 30 August 1947, p. 4.

p. 131 'Where the report originated': *Sunday Telegraph*, 9 September 1945, p. 14.

p. 132 'the most patient punter': Ibid.

p. 132 'An enormous plunge of £50,000': *Sunday Telegraph*, 9 September 1945, p. 14.

p. 132 'start from the extreme outside spot': *Daily Telegraph*, 11 September 1945.

p. 134 '47¾ for the final half-mile': *Sunday Telegraph*, 9 September 1945, p. 14.

p. 134 'covered in sweat': *Sun*, 8 September 1945, p. 3.

p. 134 'two-inch skin gash': *Sunday Telegraph*, 9 September 1945, p. 1.

p. 134 Munro's explanation of Flight interference: *Sunday Telegraph*, 9 September 1945, p. 13: *Sunday Sun and Guardian*, 9 September 1945, p. 3.

p. 134 'every opportunity of beating him': *Sun*, 8 September 1945, p. 3.

p. 135 'some people think Shannon isn't tough': *Daily Telegraph*, 11 September 1945.

p. 135 'didn't plan on running Shannon again until the Epsom': *Daily Telegraph*, 11 September 1945.

p. 135 Shannon's plans: *Sun*, 14 September 1945, p. 17.

p. 136 Flight's scratching from Epsom: *Sydney Sportsman*, 12 September 1945, p. 1.

p. 136 'may as well have a gallop in a race': *Sun*, 14 September 1945, p. 17.

p. 136 Munro picked up ride: *Sunday Sun and Guardian*, 16 September 1945, p. 3.

p. 136 '30,000 people': *Sunday Telegraph*, 16 September 1945, p. 13.

p. 137 'jaunty as he trotted back to scale': *Sun*, 15 September 1945, p. 3.

p. 137 Sectionals for the Hill Stakes: *Sunday Telegraph*, 16 September 1945, p. 14.

p. 137 'Shannon was easing up': Ibid., p. 13.

p. 138 'shortest-price favourite since 1933': *Daily Telegraph*, 24 September 1945, p. 15.

p. 138 'They have not the means to pay': *Sunday Telegraph*, 16 September 1945, p. 14.

p. 138 'hosing dock': Ibid., p. 15.

p. 138 'The best Epsom trials the turf has ever seen': Ibid.

22: The hardest of races

p. 139   '6d to a book's 1s': *Sunday Telegraph*, 23 September 1945, p. 15.
p. 139   '78,000': *Sunday Telegraph*, 30 September 1945, p. 13.
p. 139   'hottest public favourite in over a decade': *Daily Telegraph*, 24 September 1945, p. 15.
p. 140   'a record sum into the tote coffers': *Sunday Telegraph*, 30 September 1945, p. 13.
p. 141   'withdrawn their horses': *Daily Telegraph*, 28 September 1945, p. 24.
p. 141   Barrier and weight details: AJC Derby Day race card, 29 September 1945.
p. 141   '2.56 pm to the tick': *Sun*, 30 September 1945, p. 8.
p. 141   'Munro was getting desperate': *Sunday Sun and Guardian*, 30 September 1945, p. 2.
p. 142   'Peter Riddle thought so too': Ibid.
p. 142   'lost at least four lengths': Ibid.
p. 142   'Immediate had tired': Ibid.
p. 143   'half the width of the track separated them': Ibid.
p. 143   'Outside the jockeys' room': Press were allowed into the jockeys' room only after the stewards had released the riders after the last race. Mid-card interviews were conducted at the jockeys' room door as riders went in and out.
p. 143   'bolter's chance of winning': *Sunday Sun and Guardian*, 30 September 1945, p. 2.
p. 144   'Shannon was so wide out': *Sunday Telegraph*, 30 September 1945, p. 14.
p. 144   Dudley Smith comments: Ibid.
p. 144   'the best horse he had ridden': *Sunday Telegraph*, 30 September 1945, p. 14.
p. 145   'slept outside the stable': *Daily Telegraph*, 29 September 1945, p. 20.

23: The horse will tell me

p. 146   'Bert Warburton': H. G. Warburton, death notice *Argus*, 23 June 1947, p. 9.
p. 146   'Shannon looks a better mile-and-a-quarter horse': H. G. Warburton, *Sun*, 4 October 1945, p. 12.
p. 147   'Shannon to cop Craven shekels': *Sydney Sportsman*, 3 October 1945, p. 1.
p. 147   'William Kerr . . . didn't think Shannon would last': *Daily Telegraph*, 4 October 1945, p. 28.
p. 147   'half-mile in 50 seconds flat': *Daily Telegraph*, 5 October 1945, p. 17.

p. 147   'the hardest task for an Epsom winner': *Daily Telegraph*,
4 October 1945, p. 28.

p. 147   Flight trackwork details: *Daily Telegraph*, 6 October 1945, p. 24.

p. 148   'She adds interest': *Sydney Sportsman*, 3 October 1945, p. 1.

p. 148   'scratched Modulation': *Sun*, 6 October 1945, p. 8.

p. 148   'I leave the matter entirely to Peter': *Daily Telegraph*, 5 October
1945, p. 17.

p. 148   Craven Plate sectionals: *Sun*, 6 October 1945, p. 8.

p. 149   'What happened in the Metrop?': *Sunday Telegraph*, 7 October
1945, p. 18.

p. 149   'It was no disgrace': Ibid.

p. 150   'a huge crowd milled': *Sunday Sun*, 7 October 1945, p. 1.

24: The Bernborough surge

p. 151   'sold for 2600 guineas': *Daily Telegraph*, 6 October 1945, p. 24.

p. 152   Bernborough's measurements: 'That Horse Bernborough', *Daily
Telegraph Sports Book* 1946, p. 21.

p. 152   'Mulley worried constantly': Hickie, *Gentlemen of the Australian
Turf*, p. 182.

p. 152   'I was worn out and tired': Mulley speaking to the *Sun* newspaper. Ibid., p. 180.

p. 153   'when his brother sold Bravo': *Courier-Mail* Sporting Supplement,
15 September 1946, p. 2.

p. 153   'used up for the benefit of the government': *Argus*, 25 February
1947, p. 3.

p. 153   'back for the next spring and a new financial year': *Singleton
Argus*, 6 September 1946, p. 1.

p. 153   'limit Shannon to four or five races a season': *Daily News*,
25 February 1947, p. 13.

p. 153   'personal reasons': *Argus*, 25 February 1947, p. 3.

p. 154   Romano's ambitions for Bernborough: *West Australian*, 6 August
1946, p. 4.

25: Little, if anything, inferior to Bernborough

p. 155   Temperature readings for August 1946: Accumulated weather
readings for Observatory Hill, Sydney, August 1946, Station
66062, Bureau of Meteorology.

p. 155   'hottest August day and night on record': *Sydney Morning Herald*,
13 August 1946, p. 1.

p. 155   'all-time dry spell': *Sydney Morning Herald*, 8 August 1946, p. 1.

p. 155   '100 times the force of gravity on his feet':
Thoroughbred Owners and Breeders Association,
www.toba.org/owner-education/essentials-side-view.aspx

p. 155 'threw right back to Blandford': National Horse Racing Museum, Newmarket, UK, www.horseracinghistory.co.uk/hrho/action/viewImage?id=868.

p. 156 Victoria Park trackwork: *Sun*, 22 August 1946, p. 20.

p. 156 'Shannon rarely wanted to anyway': Peter Riddle's comment that Shannon was lazy, *Sunday Telegraph*, 7 October 1945, p. 18.

p. 156 'the Epsom weights were released': *Sun*, 26 August 1946, p. 12.

p. 157 'Mr Wilson is a fair handicapper': *Daily Telegraph*, 27 August 1946, p. 24.

p. 157 'Wilson thinks him a 2 lbs better horse': *Daily Telegraph*, 29 August 1946, p. 31.

p. 158 'It might be too severe first-up': *Daily Telegraph*, 27 August 1946, p. 24.

p. 158 'Plans are being made': *Daily Telegraph*, 29 August 1946, p. 32.

p. 158 'six furlongs in an easy 1:19½': *Sun*, 29 August 1946, p. 20.

p. 159 Darby Munro's thoughts on starting stalls: *West Australian*, 19 March 1946, p. 3.

p. 159 Stall incidents at Rosehill: *Barrier Miner*, 1 October 1946, p. 4.

p. 159 'Shannon's class should carry him through': *Sun*, 30 August 1946, p. 14.

p. 160 Bert Warburton's comment 'little, if anything, inferior to Bernborough': Ibid.

p. 160 Randwick attendance figures: *Sun*, 1 September 1946, p. 1.

p. 161 'started at 4/1 in the morning': *Sunday Telegraph*, 1 September 1946, p. 18.

p. 161 '2.38 pm': *Sun*, 31 August 1946, p. 8.

p. 161 'I had a perfect run': *Sunday Sun and Guardian*, 1 September 1946, p. 2.

p. 161 'a perfect Epsom trial': Ibid.

p. 162 Riddle collapses at Randwick: *Townsville Daily Bulletin*, 2 September 1946, p. 5.

p. 162 'postponed rest and treatment': Ibid.

p. 162 'greeted an old friend there': *Sun*, 2 September 1946, p. 14.

p. 162 Dr C. J. Walters: *Sun*, 2 September 1946, p. 14; *Sydney Morning Herald*, 14 October 1936, p. 14.

p. 162 'Shannon is the best miler': *Sunday Telegraph*, 1 September 1946, p. 18.

p. 162 'Peter Riddle improved slowly': *Daily Telegraph*, 2 September 1946, p. 23.

p. 163 'Public exasperated': *Sunday Sun*, 8 September 1946, p. 1; *Daily Telegraph*, 8 September 1946, p. 32; *Sun*, 2 September 1946, p. 14; *Daily Telegraph*, 5 September 1946, p. 32; *Daily Telegraph*, 3 September 1946, p. 24.

p. 163   Details of Jimmy Duncan's death: *Sun*, 14 September 1946, p. 1; *Townsville Daily Bulletin*, 16 September 1946, p. 4.

p. 164   Munro's condition in week after fall: *Daily Telegraph*, 16 September 1946, p. 24.

p. 165   'stand by for the Epsom also': *Sun*, 16 September 1946, p. 14.

p. 166   'the first stakes race to be recorded': *Daily Telegraph*, 21 September 1946, p. 27; *Sun*, 19 September 1946, p. 22.

p. 166   'an official sheet of acceptances': *Sun*, 19 September 1946, p. 22.

p. 166   'Moore would advise connections of Young Veilmond': *Sunday Sun*, 22 September 1946, p. 1.

p. 167   'After riding Shannon today': Ibid.

p. 167   'Shattering from an Epsom viewpoint': Ibid.

p. 167   'had not ridden a greater miler than Shannon': Ibid.

p. 167   'I don't think Shannon will race again before the Epsom': *Sunday Telegraph* (Sports Section), 22 September 1946, p. 1.

p. 167   'Peter Riddle managed to get out of hospital': *Sun*, 6 October 1946, p. 14.

26: Those crazy press blokes

p. 168   'one red apple, two red apple': Interview with Hugh Bowman, Queen's Park 2009.

p. 169   'I thought we trainers were fools': *Daily Telegraph*, 16 September 1946, p. 29.

p. 169   Victoria Park trackwork: *Sun*, 24 September 1946, p. 24.

p. 169   'Shannon's dazzling speed over five': Ibid.

p. 170   'extend Bernborough over a mile': *Daily Telegraph*, 4 October 1946, p. 23.

p. 170   'No horse could have trained on more perfectly': *Sun*, 4 October 1946, p. 14.

p. 170   'Randwick oasis': Ibid.

27: The 1946 Epsom Handicap

p. 171   'long look out the window': Munro's flat on Wansey Road overlooked Randwick, his sitting room in particular (from photographic evidence).

p. 171   'turned down rides': *Daily Telegraph*, 5 October 1946, p. 23.

p. 171   Munro's bribery: Accounts of this incident were written about by Darby Munro and published in the *Argus* on 17 January 1949, p. 18.

p. 173   Tom Powell's comments on Shannon: *Daily Telegraph*, 5 October 1946, p. 23.

p. 174   '66,400 patrons': *Sun*, 5 October 1946, p. 1.

p. 174   Randwick 'back to jungle law': *Sunday Sun and Guardian*, 6 October 1946, p. 1.

p. 174   'Well son, only an accident can beat you': *Argus*, 17 January 1949, p. 18.

p. 175   'Lachie Melville': Lachie Melville, from Steve Cairns, 'London to a Brick On: A Salute to Australian Race Calling', *The Australian Bloodhorse Review*, Sydney, 1994.

p. 175   'the greatest and gamest punter': Hickie, *Gentlemen of the Australian Turf*, p. 106.

p. 175   'sound judge of horse': *Courier-Mail*, 5 August 1952, p. 7.

p. 176   'hunched low and quiet over his neck': *Sunday Sun and Guardian*, 6 October 1946, p. 1.

p. 176   'cursing wildly into the wind': *Sunday Sun and Guardian*, 6 October 1946, p. 1.

p. 176   'There was Buckley's chance': *Argus*, 17 January 1949, p. 18.

p. 177   '10 lengths off the tail of the field': Ascertained from race footage of the 1946 Epsom Handicap.

p. 177   'Shannon shot through on the rails': *Argus*, 17 January 1949, p. 18.

p. 178   'the greatest effort he would ever know': Ibid.

p. 178   'Albert Davidson': *Mirror*, 2 November 1946, p. 12.

p. 178   'arrested him for using indecent language': *Sunday Sun and Guardian*, 6 October 1946, p. 1.

p. 178   'I'll fix him this time': *Sunday Sun and Guardian*, 6 October 1946, p. 1.

p. 179   Jack Gaxieu's background: '28 Starters!', *Sporting Life*, December 1947, p. 15; 'Wait for me, Sir!', *Sporting Life*, August 1947, pp. 45, 62.

p. 179   'I became confused when Scotch Gift upset the field': *Sunday Telegraph*, 6 October 1946, p. 1.

p. 179   Stewards' report into the incident, as published Ibid., p. 2.

p. 180   'The people are wrong in blaming me for this defeat': Ibid., p. 1.

p. 180   'furious that the true facts of the event were not released': Ibid.

p. 180   'It might have been a fluke beating Shannon': Ibid., p. 18.

p. 180   Turf editorial: 'The Epsom start was an occasion . . .': *Sydney Morning Herald*, 7 October 1946, p. 7.

p. 181   'Oh, it's just one of those things': Ibid.

p. 181   J. B. Donohue's comments: Ibid.

p. 181   Alan Potter's comments: Ibid.

p. 181   'How are you going to throw this one, Darb?': *Sunday Telegraph*, 6 October 1946, p. 2.

p. 182   Turf editorial criticising the AJC: *Daily Telegraph*, 7 October 1946, p. 8.

p. 182   'wondered why he had bothered': *Sunday Sun and Guardian*, 6 October 1946, p. 1.

p. 183   'the fastest mile ever recorded at Randwick': Bill Whittaker, 'Fastest mile ever deserved a better result', *Sydney Morning Herald*, 1 October 1984, supplied by Mardi Henderson; and Bill Whittaker, featured on the documentary *That's Racing*, produced by Graham McNeice. Visual Entertainment Group, 2000. This latter statement by Whittaker is supported by official records. At the time of publication (November 2013), no metropolitan racetrack in Australia had recorded a faster mile than Shannon's unofficial Epsom time of 1:32½. But because Bob Skelton was not the official AJC timekeeper, his clocking of the 1946 Epsom remains 'unofficial'. Conservative estimates of the day, which are also unofficial, cited Shannon's effort at 1:33½, which would still have broken the Australasian mile record by 1¼ seconds. Because the identities of clockers behind that estimate were not made available, and in light of Bob Skelton's long background in timing racehorses expertly, I believe the Skelton time to be more accurate.

p. 183   '50-yard disadvantage': Discrepancies exist about the official distance by which Shannon was left at the post in the 1946 Epsom (e.g. 'half a furlong', '50 yards', etc.). While it is believed he was left 12 lengths at barrier rise, because Shannon and Munro had trot up to the barrier line, stop and then set off after the field, the margin was far, far greater by the time the pair was galloping.

28: Mr Wonderful

p. 184   'fresh as summer rain': *Daily Telegraph*, 7 October 1946, p. 1.

p. 184   'The jockey had been advised by his physician': Ibid.

p. 185   'Darby Munro had not been rewarded with a win': *Sunday Telegraph*, 6 October 1946, p. 2.

p. 185   'opting out of all other offers': *Courier-Mail*, 8 October 1946, p. 6.

p. 185   'an ovation of cheers and claps': Ibid.; *Sydney Morning Herald*, 8 October 1946, p. 8.

p. 186   'the first half-mile in 47 seconds': *Sun*, 7 October 1946, p. 10.

p. 186   Sectionals for the George Main Stakes: *Daily Telegraph*, 8 October 1946, p. 24.

p. 186   'three-quarters of a second off the Randwick record': Ibid., p. 23.

p. 186   'Pushed right out': Ibid., p. 24.

p. 187   'a quick wave': *Courier-Mail*, 8 October 1946, p. 6.

p. 187   'Of course I'm happy': Ibid., p. 6.

p. 187   'He'll dismiss that tank he came to the races in': *Daily Telegraph*, 8 October 1946, p. 1.

p. 188   'I was determined to ride Shannon today': Ibid., p. 23.

p. 188   'Riddle conceded that his horse was fit enough': Ibid., p. 23.

p. 188   'I have until tomorrow week to nominate him': Ibid.

p. 188   'laid up with a broken leg': *Sydney Morning Herald*, 8 October 1946, p. 8.

p. 189   'thin April afternoon': *Mornington Bulletin*, 25 April 1927, p. 7.

p. 190   'It will be purely experimental': *Daily Telegraph*, 9 October 1946, p. 23.

p. 190   'they expected their horse to win': Ibid.

p. 190   '*Telegraph* picked Flight': *Daily Telegraph*, 12 October 1946, p. 32.

p. 190   '*Sportsman* opted for Good Idea': *Sydney Sportsman*, 9 October 1946, p. 1.

p. 191   King's Cup sectionals: *Sun*, 12 October 1946, p. 10.

p. 192   'already won': Ibid.

p. 192   'hottest October evening in years': *Sunday Sun and Guardian*, 13 October 1946, p. 1; *Daily Telegraph*, 14 October 1946, p. 3; accumulated weather readings for Observatory Hill, Sydney, 12–13 October 1946, Station 66062, Bureau of Meteorology.

29: Two horses, no race

p. 193   Conditions of the match race: *Sun*, 13 October 1946, p. 14.

p. 193   Fred Pilbrow's approaches to Azzalin Romano: 'The great match race that never was', *Turf Monthly*, July 1969, pp. 6–10.

p. 193   'quick to railroad the plan': *Sun*, 13 October 1946, p. 14.

p. 193   'Bernborough has already travelled 3000 miles': *Sun*, 15 October 1946, p. 14.

p. 194   'wouldn't hesitate to let Shannon gallop it out with Bernborough': *Daily Telegraph*, 15 October 1946, p. 24.

p. 194   'never race in a handicap again': *Cairns Post*, 29 October 1946, p. 2.

30: All the rest and residue

p. 196   'Modulation through the sale ring': *Examiner*, 16 April 1947, p. 10.

p. 196   'only Shannon . . . stood': *Sydney Morning Herald*, 8 May 1947, p. 8.

p. 196   'decided not to race through the autumn': *Daily News*, 25 February 1947, p. 14.

p. 196   'I'd be lost without one to train': *Sydney Morning Herald*, 8 May 1947, p. 8.

p. 196   J. Burke Clements lease offer: *Windsor Daily Star*, 13 December 1946, p. 34.

p. 197   Clements lease details and Riddle comment: *Argus*, 13 December 1946, p. 14.

p. 197   'Harry Plant gave it a go': *Sydney Morning Herald*, 8 May 1947, p. 8.

p. 197   'In America I saw many good horses': *Daily News*, 9 May 1947, p. 15.

p. 197   Harry Plant's offer for Shannon: *Courier-Mail*, 17 July 1947, p. 7.

p. 197   'Shannon was nominated for the Doomben 10,000': *Sydney Morning Herald*, 27 May 1947, p. 8.

p. 197   'I could have left him in longer': *Singleton Argus*, 18 June 1947, p. 1.

p. 198   'a wintry Saturday': Accumulated weather readings for Observatory Hill, Sydney, 12–13 October 1946, Station 66062, Bureau of Meteorology.

p. 198   'settled into his lounge to read': *Barrier Miner*, 30 June 1947, p. 8.

p. 198   Riddle's death details: Obtained from Death Certificate: Births, Deaths and Marriages, New South Wales.

p. 198   'followed Riddle's coffin from Kinsela Chapels': Family death announcement, *Sydney Morning Herald*, 30 June 1947, p. 16.

p. 198   'Shannon might end in USA': *Sydney Morning Herald*, 1 July 1947, p. 8.

p. 199   'Shannon's King's Cup': Interview with Mardi Henderson, at home in Sydney, 26 April 2012.

p. 199   'It wasn't until early August': *Sydney Morning Herald*, 9 August 1947, p. 14.

p. 199   'confessed that it was a difficult decision to arrive upon': Ibid.

p. 200   'There was never a chance of Shannon being sold': Ibid.

p. 200   Reg Inglis comments: *Sydney Morning Herald*, 9 August 1947, p. 14.

p. 200   'the only occasion . . . where a single thoroughbred would be sold': *Sydney Morning Herald*, 19 August 1947, p. 10.

p. 200   'Odds are being freely offered': *Singleton Argus*, 11 August 1947, p. 2.

p. 201   'transferred to the charge of trainer William Henderson': *Sydney Morning Herald*, 9 July 1947, p. 10.

31: 'Any rich man . . .'

p. 202   '4000 racing folk and curious public': *Daily Telegraph*, 21 August 1947, p. 3

p. 202   'average Sams skiving from the glassworks': Ibid.

p. 202   'I don't care how high I have to bid': Ibid., p. 20.

p. 202   Background to Ossie Porter: Hickie, *Gentlemen of the Australian Turf*, pp. 165–9.

p. 203   'He even named the races': *Daily Telegraph*, 19 August 1947, p. 20.

p. 203   'Knockout' Smith's nickname: *Sydney Morning Herald*, 24 January 1945, p. 7.

p. 203   William John Smith: Australian Dictionary of Biography, http://adb.anu.edu.au/biography/smith-william-john-bill-8492.

p. 203   'He was not book-learned': *Western Mail*, 4 February 1947, p. 5.

p. 204   Smith's habits: As recounted by Kate Fraser, granddaughter of W. J. Smith, telephone interview, 10 December 2012.

p. 204   'Well, 'e's never allowed a glassworker': *Sydney Morning Herald*, 24 January 1945, p. 7.

p. 204   'plunged into the racing game in 1917': As recounted by Kate Fraser, granddaughter of W. J. Smith, telephone interview, 10 December 2012.

p. 204   'In 1931 he had formed a partnership': *Argus*, 21 August 1947, p. 20.

p. 204   Descriptions of St Aubin's Stud: *Sydney Morning Herald*, 15 March 1939, p. 11.

p. 204   'Beau Pere': *Courier-Mail*, 4 March 1941, p. 8.

p. 205   'about $100,000': *Canberra Times*, 29 August 1947, p. 4.

p. 205   'bookies were giving 6/4 about Smith': Daily Telegraph, 21 August 1947, p. 3.

p. 205   'blank cheque to buy Shannon': *Sydney Morning Herald*, 21 August 1947, p. 8.

p. 205   'Food For Britain cause': *Sunday Sun and Guardian* Sports Section, 14 August 1947, p. 1.

p. 205   'convincing testimony of his class and versatility': Shannon sale booklet, produced by William Inglis & Son, August 1947.

p. 206   'showering Shannon with pats': *Sun*, 20 August 1947, p. 16.

p. 206   Inspectors of Shannon: Ibid., p. 1.

p. 206   Juan Ysmael: *Sydney Morning Herald*, 18 August 1947, p. 10.

p. 206   'time to clean his horse up': *Sun*, 20 August 1947, p. 16.

p. 207   'tribute to O'Brien': Ibid.

p. 207   Riddle and Finn in the rostrum with Reg Inglis: *Daily Telegraph*, 20 August 1947, p. 32.

p. 207   Description and transcript of auction: Cinesound Production, British Pathé. Film ID 2393.08.

p. 207   'Darby Munro sucked on a pipe': *Daily Telegraph*, 21 August 1947, p. 3.

p. 207   'Inglis didn't hear him': *Sydney Morning Herald*, 25 August 1947, p. 8.

p. 207   'the mystery bidder looked to the man beside him': *Sydney Morning Herald*, 25 August 1947, p. 8.

p. 208   'Bidding had reached 20,000 guineas': *Daily Telegraph*, 21 August 1947, p. 3.

p. 208   'William McDonald had been taking bets of 100/1': Ibid.

p. 208   'inspection of Shannon at Bowral Street': *Sydney Morning Herald*, 25 August 1947, p. 8.

p. 208   '"touch his kick" to get the horse': *Daily Telegraph*, 21 August 1947, p. 3.

p. 209   'stop bidding for Shannon when he . . . put his hat on': As recounted by Kate Fraser, granddaughter of W. J. Smith, telephone interview, 10 December 2012.

p. 209   'had he bought the horse for Bing Crosby?': *Daily Telegraph*, 21 August 1947, p. 3.

p. 209   'asked for his autograph': Ibid.

p. 209   'Dalton was very reluctant to accept Shannon': As retold by Billy Dalton, son of Frank Dalton. Telephone interview on 6 December 2012 with ex-Randwick identity John Holmes, who was present when Billy Dalton told this story many years ago at the Duke of Gloucester Hotel, Randwick.

p. 209   'will race in Australia this year': *Northern Miner*, 21 August 1947, p. 1.

p. 210   Particulars of Peter Riddle's gear sold: Probate package of late Peter Riddle, including his last will and testament. Inglis evaluation declaration from 25 August 1947.

p. 210   'Not an hour after the sale': *Northern Miner*, op. cit.

32: 'I would not like to guess what he can do'

p. 211   'stable lads lived in the loft': Recollection by John Holmes, telephone interview, 6 December 2012.

p. 211   'pot plants': Recollection by jockey Jack Thompson, recorded interview in 1984 with Neil Bennetts, National Library of Australia, Bib ID 1760763.

p. 211   'he didn't say much': Recollection by Max Presnell, telephone interview, 11 December 2012.

p. 211   'a face weathered and beaten like a coastal fence post': Recollection by John Holmes, telephone interview, 6 December 2012; recollection by Max Presnell, telephone interview, 11 December 2012.

p. 211   'By 1947 he had 20': *Mirror*, 6 September 1947, p. 17.

p. 212   'Dalton . . . had worried no end': *Sunday Sun and Guardian* Sports Section, 24 August 1947, p. 1.

p. 212 'We have a very valuable horse': *Sydney Morning Herald*, 22 August 1947, p. 1.

p. 212 'Dalton held conference': *Sunday Sun and Guardian* Sports Section, 24 August 1947, p. 1.

p. 213 'Munro had never ridden Shannon': *Sydney Morning Herald*, 9 October 1947, p. 8.

p. 213 'the "screenings"': *Sydney Morning Herald*, 28 February 1946, p. 8.

p. 213 Shannon's record half-mile on the screenings: *Sun*, 28 August 1947, p. 24; *Sydney Morning Herald*, 29 August 1947, p. 10.

p. 213 'It was a clattering gallop': *Sun*, 28 August 1947, p. 24.

p. 214 Sectionals for the Warwick Stakes: *Cairns Post*, 1 September 1947, p. 2.

p. 214 'shock of his life': *Mail*, 30 August 1947, p. 24.

p. 215 'a few angry patrons': *Sun*, 30 August 1947, p. 1.

p. 215 'Wake up Munro!': *Sunday Sun and Guardian* Sports Section, 31 August 1947, p. 1.

p. 215 'Shannon sensation: beaten': *Sun*, 30 August 1947, p. 1.

p. 215 'the *Mail* tried to be forgiving': *Mail*, 30 August 1947, p. 24.

p. 215 'He's not the first good horse': *Sunday Sun and Guardian* Sports Section, 31 August 1947, p. 1.

p. 215 'a good horse not being quite fit enough': *Barrier Miner*, 1 September 1947, p. 8.

p. 215 'Shannon had been beaten on his merits': Ibid.

p. 216 'My job': *Sydney Morning Herald*, 1 September 1947, p. 10.

p. 216 Details of screenings: *Sun*, 4 September 1947, p. 24.

p. 216 'he won't be beaten again': *Daily News*, 3 September 1947, p. 12.

p. 217 'Shannon and Victory Lad all the way': *Sun*, 5 September 1947, Race Guide.

p. 218 'Back on his pedestal': *Central Queensland Herald*, 18 September 1947, p. 18.

p. 218 'Shannon is back in the good books': *Chronicle*, 11 September 1947, p. 41.

p. 219 'fitted a bar shoe': *Sydney Morning Herald*, 17 September 1947, p. 8.

p. 219 'he wasn't worried in the slightest': *Morning Bulletin*, 19 September 1947, p. 6.

p. 219 'There are plenty of races': *Sydney Morning Herald*, 17 September 1947, p. 8.

p. 220 'patrons flocked': *Sydney Morning Herald*, 30 September 1947, p. 10.

p. 220 'bar shoes on both fore feet': *Daily Mail*, 27 September 1947, p. 21.

p. 220   'bar shoes had been specifically designed': *Sydney Morning Herald*, 29 September 1947, p. 8.

p. 220   'He carried 7 st 9 lbs': *Sunday Sun and Guardian*, 28 September 1947, p. 12.

p. 220   'Whether Shannon breaks the trade record': *Sydney Morning Herald*, 26 September 1947, p. 10.

p. 220   'two or three horse-widths off the rail': *Sun*, 27 September 1947, p. 8.

p. 220   exhibition sectionals: *Daily Mail*, 27 September 1947, p. 21.

p. 220   'He's an amazing galloper': *Sydney Morning Herald*, 29 September 1947, p. 8.

p. 221   'an even quicker time': *Sun*, 27 September 1947, p. 8.

p. 221   'After I had turned into the straight': *Sydney Morning Herald*, 29 September 1947, p. 8.

p. 221   'casually mentioning that Shannon': *Sun*, 16 September 1947, p. 14.

33: A matter of black and white

p. 222   'Shannon might have a walkover': *Sydney Morning Herald* Racing Supplement, 6 October 1947, p. 3.

p. 222   'over £13,000 in prizemoney': *Sydney Morning Herald*, 10 April 1947, p. 8.

p. 222   'could never understand why': Ibid.

p. 222   'run a record six furlongs at Rosebery': *Sun*, 4 October 1947, p. 6; *Argus*, 6 October 1947, p. 20.

p. 223   'new betting boards and multicoloured umbrellas': *Argus*, 17 July 1947, p. 10.

p. 223   Tote figures down: *Sydney Morning Herald*, 7 October 1947, p. 10.

p. 223   'It's the time factor': Ibid.

p. 223   George Main sectionals: *Sun*, 6 October 1947, p. 10.

p. 224   'If I had hit him with the whip': *Sydney Morning Herald*, 7 October 1947, p. 10.

p. 224   'I don't attach too much blame': Ibid.

p. 224   'would have at least equalled': *Sun*, 6 October 1947, p. 10.

p. 224   'wild rumour': *Sydney Morning Herald*, 7 October 1947, p. 10.

p. 226   'his owner deciding back in August': *Courier-Mail*, 14 August 1947, p. 9.

p. 227   'Shannon's loss to Russia': *Sun*, 9 October 1947, p. 24.

p. 227   'Frank McGrath Jr': *Sydney Morning Herald*, 9 October 1947, p. 8.

p. 228   Gordon Leeds and Barney O'Brien conversation: *Sydney Morning Herald*, 9 October 1947, p. 8.

p. 228   'he refused to say anything': *Sydney Morning Herald*, 10 October 1947, p. 10.

p. 228   'the horse's Melbourne plans were now in doubt': *Sun*, 8 October 1947, p. 1.

p. 228   'Shannon to leave soon': *Sydney Morning Herald*, 9 October 1947, p. 1.

p. 228   'Smith had paid big money': Gwyn Jones, 'A jockey eases up too soon', *The Blood-Horse*, 25 October 1947, pp. 206–7.

p. 228   'continue his association with Shannon': *Sydney Morning Herald*, 9 October 1947, p. 1.

p. 229   'no venture to Darby Munro': *Sun*, 9 October 1947, p. 24.

p. 230   'People speculated openly': *Sun*, 10 October 1947, p. 12.

p. 230   'the ideal type': *Sydney Morning Herald*, 11 October 1947, p. 8.

p. 231   'Dalton complained': Ibid.

p. 231   'I haven't seen much': *Sydney Morning Herald*, 10 October 1947, p. 10; Gwyn Jones, 'A jockey eases up too soon', *The Blood-Horse*, 25 October 1947, pp. 206–7.

p. 231   'the moment at Bradley Street': Barney O'Brien was in Melbourne the day Shannon sailed for San Francisco; *Townsville Daily Bulletin*, 20 October 1947, p. 4.

34: Passage

p. 232   'inched through Sydney Heads': *Sydney Morning Herald*, 10 October 1947, p. 11.

p. 232   *Boogabilla* details: *Advertiser*, 6 September 1947, p. 20; *Cairns Post*, 7 September 1950, p. 5.

p. 232   'a risky Pacific crossing in 1942': *Army News* Supplement, 2 February 1942, p. 1.

p. 232   'lamb-like': *Sun*, 18 October 1947, p. 1.

p. 233   'a makeshift stall': *Kalgoorlie Miner*, 20 October 1947, p. 6.

p. 233   'far short of the box': *Sun*, 18 October 1947, p. 1.

p. 233   '24 days of fodder': *Sydney Morning Herald*, 16 October 1947, p. 10.

p. 233   'Shannon would survive': *Sydney Morning Herald*, 17 October 1947, p. 10.

p. 233   'The stock inspector': *Sydney Morning Herald*, 16 October 1947, p. 10.

p. 233   'A light physic had been done': *Sydney Morning Herald*, 10 October 1947, p. 11.

p. 233   'Smith looked in': *Townsville Daily Bulletin*, 20 October 1947, p. 4.

p. 233   'He would catch a plane': *West Australian*, 20 October 1947, p. 3.

p. 234   'a long blast bellowed': International maritime rules state a vessel must sound one prolonged blast from the ship's whistle when leaving a dock or berth.

PART II
35: San Francisco

p. 237   'over two weeks standing': George McCann, 'The Shannon Error', *A.M.* magazine, August 1948, p. 40.

p. 237   'gained 50 lbs': *Los Angeles Times*, 10 November 1947, p. 12; *Morning Bulletin*, 29 January 1948, p. 6.

p. 237   'I hope this one has better luck': *Daily News*, 4 November 1947, p. 1.

p. 238   'fed the 1932 Olympics in Los Angeles': *Merced Sun-Star*, 21 March 1978, p. 6.

p. 238   'At the turn into 1900': *Los Angeles Times*, 21 March 1978.

p. 238   Harry Curland's story: *Los Angeles Times*, 7 March 1954, p. 11.

p. 238   'Hippodrome Theatre on Main Street': https://sites.google.com/site/downtownlosangelestheatres/hippodrome

p. 239   'two women can outtalk': *Los Angeles Times*, 7 March 1954, p. 11.

p. 240   'set of green and gold silks': *Sydney Morning Herald*, 6 November 1947, p. 10.

p. 240   'There's no point in answering that question': Ibid.

p. 240   'I've bought Shannon as a gift for my wife': *Argus*, 3 November 1947, p. 5; *Morning Bulletin*, 7 November 1947, p. 11.

p. 240   Curland's race plans for Shannon: *Argus*, 3 November 1947, p. 5.

p. 240   'Doc Strub': 'Doc's Gold Mine', *TIME*, 31 January 1949, http://www.time.com/time/magazine/article/0,9171,794537,00.html.

p. 240   'How's about giving a thought': *Los Angeles Times*, 10 November 1947, p. 12.

p. 240   'taking a look at the Santa Anita': *Cairns Post*, 10 November 1947, p. 2.

p. 241   'He's the greatest horse I ever saw': *Los Angeles Times*, 10 November 1947, p. 12.

p. 241   'On 12 November, Smith lodged a request': *Sydney Morning Herald*, 21 November 1947, p. 12.

p. 241   The Jockey Club: 'The Jockey Club: Its History, Its Powers, and Its Functions', *The Blood-Horse*, 1 November 1947, pp. 264–8; Montgomery, 'The Thoroughbred in America: The Jockey Club', *The Thoroughbred*, pp. 173–176.

p. 241   'California Horse Racing Board': Phipps, *Bill Kyne of Bay Meadows*.

p. 242 'the matter was in abeyance': *Sydney Morning Herald*, 21 November 1947, p. 12.

p. 242 'a special permit to race': *Sydney Morning Herald*, 24 November 1947, p. 8.

p. 242 'I'd thought a horse that had raced': *Townsville Daily Bulletin*, 21 November 1947, p. 5.

p. 242 'he gave the horse's papers back': *New York Times*, 19 November 1947, p. 5.

p. 242 'sought a report from the keeper of the Australian Stud Book': *Sydney Morning Herald*, 11 July 1950, p. 10.

p. 242 'There's little doubt that Shannon will be allowed': *Sydney Morning Herald*, 24 November 1947, p. 8.

p. 242 'a horse with no stud future': *Townsville Daily Bulletin*, 21 November 1947, p. 5.

p. 243 'too many strings attached', 'Willie Molter, is crazy about him': *Sydney Morning Herald*, 21 November 1947, p. 12.

p. 243 'I don't believe he'd bring': *Daily News*, 13 December 1947, p. 31.

p. 243 'California to Canada': *Montreal Gazette*, 19 November 1947, p. 17.

p. 243 'he was negotiating with W. J. Smith': *Daily News*, 17 December 1947, p. 21.

36: The case of the Spaewifes

p. 244 '510 West 6th Street': Ancestry.com. US City Directories, 1821–1989 (Beta) [database on-line]. Provo, UT, USA: Ancestry.com Operations, Inc., 2011.

p. 244 '9481 Sunset Boulevard': *Los Angeles Times*, 7 April 1959; Gross, *Unreal Estate*; www.uglyangel.net/2010/01/oranges-and-pome-granates-in-beverly.html. McCarthy is recorded (unofficially) as purchasing 9481 Sunset Blvd sometime in 1949 from Dolly Green, his lover (Michael Gross states in his book that no record of the sale was made). Before that, McCarthy had lived at an undisclosed address in Bel Air after moving out of the home that he had shared with his wife at 465 South Muirfield Road in 1945. In the City Directory of 1948, he is listed as still abiding at South Muirfield, though this is not correct. Because his purchase of 9481 Sunset Blvd coincided with the Shannon era, it is given here as his address.

p. 244 'Paramount Pictures': Obituary Neil S. McCarthy, *New York Times*, 28 July 1972.

p. 244 'surly Howard Hughes': Gross, op. cit., p. 192; *Los Angeles Times*, 5 June 1960, p. E17; Obituary Neil S. McCarthy, *New York Times*, 28 July 1972.

p. 245 'splendid energy and initiative': James H. Boswell, *1938 American Blue Book California Lawyers*, p. 151.

p. 245 'his standing was such': Gross, *Unreal Estate*, p. 193.

p. 245 AFL-grooms debate: Robert Hebert, 'Grooms' Salary, Bonus Demands Angrily Refused by Owners', *The Blood-Horse*, 24 May 1947, p. 395.

p. 245 'grandson of Irish immigrants': Gross, op. cit., p. 188.

p. 245 '6 May 1888': Ancestry.com. US Passport Applications, 1795-1925 [database on-line]. Provo, UT, USA: Ancestry.com Operations, Inc., 2007.

p. 245 'his father was a farrier': Gross, op. cit., p. 188.

p. 245 'still predominantly horse country': *Los Angeles Times*, 5 June 1960, p. E17.

p. 245 'born with an Irishman's instinctive love for horses': Ibid.

p. 246 Neil S. McCarthy and polo: Horace A. Laffaye, *Polo in the United States*, McFarland. Google eBook, 2011.

p. 246 'opened its doors in 1913': *Los Angeles Times*, 19 April 2006; http://articles.latimes.com/2006/apr/19/local/me-a2anniversary19.

p. 246 'number-two position': Laffaye, op. cit., pp. 140–1.

p. 246 'they keep me going': *Los Angeles Times*, 5 June 1960, p. E17.

p. 246 'first prominent racehorse was Lion': Welch, *Who's Who in Thoroughbred Racing*, p. 190.

p. 247 'downed Seabiscuit by more than two lengths': Hillenbrand, *Seabiscuit*, pp. 287–8.

p. 247 '400 acres in the picturesque Moorpark region': *Los Angeles Times*, 5 June 1960, p. E17.

p. 247 Moonlight Run and Sierra Nevada: Welch, op. cit., p. 190.

p. 247 'the equal of any in California': Ibid.

p. 247 'when you buy a horse and see him win': *Los Angeles Times*, 5 June 1960, p. E17.

p. 247 'twenty-fourth on the American winning list': Referenced by Allan Carter of New York Racing Association Hall of Fame, Saratoga Springs, visit 10 August 2012.

p. 248 'Busher': *Thoroughbred Champions*, pp. 128–9.

p. 248 'negotiating with W. J. Smith to buy Shannon': *Daily News*, 17 December 1947, p. 21.

p. 248 'special permit under Rule 59': Minutes of the meeting of 11 December 1948 at 250 Park Avenue, NY, courtesy of Bob Curran, VP Corporate Communications, The Jockey Club, NY.

p. 249 'McCarthy remained mum': *Morning Bulletin*, quoting the *Morning Telegraph* (New York), 15 January 1948, p. 7.

p. 249 'over the dinner table': *Sydney Morning Herald*, 15 January 1948, p. 8.

p. 249   'for $87,000': 'Highest-priced Foreign Thoroughbreds', *The American Racing Manual*, 1948, p. 598-A.

p. 249   'race Shannon for an indefinite period': *Sydney Morning Herald*, 15 January 1948, p. 8.

p. 249   'It's a private business': *Canberra Times*, 15 January 1948, p. 6.

p. 249   'in charge of all Mayer horses in training': *Examiner*, 13 December 1948, p. 27.

p. 249   Details on Ernest Shaw's bid for Shannon: Article forwarded by Graham Caves, Sydney racing historian: George McCann, 'The Shannon Error', *A.M.* magazine, August 1948, p. 49.

p. 250   'Marshall Cassidy, executive secretary': Email confirmation by Shannon K. Luce, Communications Coordinator of The Jockey Club, 29 December 2012.

p. 250   'annoyed that Smith hadn't appeared': *Sydney Morning Herald*, 13 December 1947, p. 9.

p. 250   'America's loss will be some other country's gain': Ibid.

p. 251   'the particulars as regards her . . . sire, name, colour': Australian Stud Book, vol. I, 1878.

p. 251   'in its 1901 edition, the Australian Stud Book declared': Australian Stud Book, vol. VII, 1901, p. 489.

p. 251   'little chance of [her] true pedigree ever being discovered': Ibid.

p. 252   The Jersey Act: 'The Jersey Act', *American Racing Manual*, 1949, pp. 1004–5; Roger Mortimer, Richard Onslow and Peter Willett, *A Biographical Encyclopedia of British Flat Racing*, Macdonald and Jane's, London, 1978; *Horse Racing's Top 100 Moments*, pp. 124–5.

p. 253   'this should not be interpreted as a refusal': *Sydney Morning Herald*, 10 January 1948, p. 8.

p. 253   'seeing Spaewifes before its eyes': J. A. Estes, 'The Spaewife Story Is Fantastic; Why Doesn't Someone Tell It?', *The Blood-Horse*, 10 July 1948, pp. 98, 123.

p. 253   'four possible pedigrees': J. A. Estes, 'Now Shannon Has A Pedigree, But We Don't Know What It Is', *The Blood-Horse*, 7 February 1948, pp. 364–5.

p. 254   'why the devil does their concerted action': Joe H. Palmer, 'Shannon and the Rule Book: Do We Need A Lawsuit?', *The Blood-Horse*, 13 December 1947, p. 716.

p. 254   'what is a defect in a pedigree?': J. A. Estes, 'Now Shannon Has A Pedigree', op. cit.

p. 254   'The most important item in appraising the stud prospects': J. A. Estes, *The Blood-Horse*, 26 August 1939, p. 316.

p. 255   'The British seem to think': 'Mr Smith Gets Purity Explained To Him', *The Blood-Horse*, 29 November 1947, p. 587.

p. 255 'that Australian fellow there's been such a pother over': Class C Surprise, 'The Race Track', *New Yorker*, 7 February 1948, pp. 74–5.

p. 255 'faintest idea as to where Shannon's pedigree might be questioned': *Sydney Morning Herald*, 20 November 1947, p. 10.

p. 255 'nothing in Shannon's pedigree': Ibid.

p. 256 'Such a suggestion is absurd': *Argus*, 19 December 1947, p. 24.

p. 256 '*Morning Telegraph* agreed': *Morning Telegraph*, 18 December 1947, quoted in *Argus*, 19 December 1947, p. 24.

p. 256 Columnist problem: *West Australian*, 18 December 1947, p. 4.

p. 256 Victory Lad advertisement: *The Blood-Horse*, 7 February 1948, p. 354.

p. 257 Albert Lodden Yuille's letter: As quoted in editorial by Oscar Otis, *Daily Racing Form*, 22 June 1948, p. 2.

p.257 'The General Stud Book had two Spaewifes': Telephone call to Rob Marriott, pedigree researcher at Weatherby's UK, 4 January 2013.

p. 257 'The first was legitimate': General Stud Book, vol. IV, p. 57.

p. 258 'this mare or sister had in 1822 a ch.f. by Soothsayer': General Stud Book, vol. III, p. 166.

p. 258 E. A. Lamb's letter to the *Sunday Herald*: Supplied undated by Michael Ford, Keeper of the Australian Stud Book.

p. 258 Half-sister Sancho mare out of Ringtail: General Stud Book, vol. III, p. 173.

p. 259 'it seems to me': Oscar Otis, 'Between Races', *Daily Racing Form*, 22 June 1948, p. 2.

p. 260 Statement by The Jockey Club on 29 January 1948: *New York Times*, 30 January 1948.

p. 260 'the horse is O.K.': Comments by Marshall Cassidy. *Sydney Morning Herald*, 31 January 1948, p. 10.

p. 260 'few horsemen had expected that happy decision': *New York Times*, 30 January 1948.

p. 260 'Horsemen were pleased to learn of the decision': J. A. Estes, 'Pedigree Points', *The Blood-Horse*, 7 February 1948, p. 364.

p. 261 'if such is the case': Ibid.

p. 261 'The Jockey Club presumably knows': J. A. Estes, 'Pedigree Points', *The Blood-Horse*, 10 July 1948, pp. 98, 123.

p. 261 'more flaws in their pedigree than Shannon': Chiron, *Argus*, 21 November 1947, p. 22.

p. 261 'when our horses go abroad': *Sunday Times*, 30 November 1947, p. 4S

p. 262 'these inconsistent, illogical and fatuous regulations': *New*

Zealand Farmer, 11 December 1947 as reprinted in *The Blood-Horse*, 7 February 1948, pp. 361, 365.

p. 262   'Albert Lodden Yuille went along': *Morning Bulletin*, 13 October 1948, p. 4.

p. 262   'the Jersey Act was repealed': Mortimer, Onslow and Willett, *A Biographical Encyclopedia*.

p. 262   'finest bits of research': J. A. Estes, 'The Spaewife Story Is Fantastic', *The Blood-Horse*, 10 July 1948, p. 98.

37: Willie 'The Kid' Molter

p. 263   'El Camino Real': Year: 1940; Census Place: Burlingame, San Mateo, California; Roll: T627_332; Page: 9B; Enumeration District: 41-89. Ancestry.com.

p. 263   'run into his animals': 'Winning Willie', *TIME*, 2 December 1946, http://www.time.com/time/magazine/article/0,9171,887299,00.html.

p. 263   'scratch the Australian horse on the neck': *Los Angeles Times*, 31 May 1948, p. 9.

p. 263   'born in 1911': Molter consistently overplayed his age. In the 1940 American census, he records himself as being 33 years old (possibly to avoid being called up for service). If this were true, he would have been born around 1907. However, the press of Shannon's era quoted him as being 36 years old.

p. 263   'German parents': Year: 1930; Census Place: San Bruno, San Mateo, California; Roll: 216; Page: 2B; Enumeration District: 16; Image: 486.0; FHL microfilm: 2339951. Ancestry.com.

p. 263   'race riding by the age of 12': Uncited article by Susan McCabe, supplied by Allan Carter, chief librarian, National Museum of Racing and Hall of Fame, Saratoga Springs, NY.

p. 264   'Johnny Longden learned something there': Pat Ryan, 'Johnny Comes Riding Home', *Sports Illustrated*, 20 September 1965, http://sportsillustrated.cnn.com/vault/article/magazine/MAG1077700/index.htm..

p. 264   '4 ft 11 in': *TIME*, May 1952, http://life.time.com/culture/johnny-longden-a-great-jockeys-life/#1.

p. 264   Molter's training history: Robert Hebert, 'Molter's Law: Know your Horses and Study the Condition Book', *The Blood-Horse*, 18 October 1947, pp. 134, 136.

p. 264   'two winners that day': Dick Nash, 'The Stakes Career of Bill Molter', August 1960. From an uncited document supplied by Allan Carter, chief librarian, National Museum of Racing and Hall of Fame, Saratoga Springs, NY.

p. 264   'apple-cheeked': Hebert ,'Molter's Law', op. cit., p. 134.

p. 264 'a standard owner–trainer conversation': 'Winning Willie', op. cit.

p. 264 'the Curlands': Hebert, 'Molter's Law', op. cit., p. 134.

p. 264 'Louis B. Mayer's second stringers': 'Winning Willie', op. cit.

p. 265 'One of them is to know your horse': Hebert, 'Molter's Law', p. 134.

p. 265 'dog Billy at his feet': photographic evidence from Hebert, 'Molter's Law', p. 134; *Los Angeles Times*, 31 May 1948, p. 9.

p. 265 'west American attitude': Oscar Otis, 'Between Races', *Daily Racing Form*, May 1954, pp. 40, 44.

p. 265 'a kindliness': 'In Memoriam . . . William Molter', uncited document, 1 May 1960, supplied by Allan Carter, chief librarian, National Museum of Racing and Hall of Fame, Saratoga Springs, NY.

p. 265 'modesty': Hebert, 'Molter's Law', p. 134.

p. 266 '$40,000 in 1946': 'Winning Willie', op. cit.

p. 266 Molter's fees and charges: Ibid.

p. 266 'best three-year-old Molter had handled': Hebert, 'Molter's Law', op. cit., p. 134. Other sources: Jeane Hoffman, 'Molter is Gone, but his Family Can't Stay Away from the Track', *Los Angeles Times*, 23 June 1961, p. C4; 'Racing Figures Pay Last Tribute to Molter', *Los Angeles Times*, 5 April 1960, p. C1; *Los Angeles Times*, 3 April 1960, p. H1.

p. 266 'compact thoroughbred': *Montreal Gazette*, 26 February 1948, p. 18.

p. 266 'slept well', etc.: *Cairns Post*, 8 November 1947, p. 5.

p. 267 'endeared him to his new trainer': *Sydney Morning Herald*, 21 November 1947, p. 12.

p. 267 'it settled him': 'Winning Willie', op. cit.

p. 267 Bay Meadows descriptions: *American Racing Manual*, 1949, p. 566; Phipps, *Bill Kyne of Bay Meadows*.

p. 267 'There's nothing wrong with him': *Cairns Post*, 8 November 1947, p. 5.

p. 268 'Form . . . held for at least three to four months': *Morning Bulletin*, 29 January 1948, p. 6.

p. 268 'very satisfied with the way Shannon was shaping up': *Argus*, 8 November 1947, p. 47.

p. 268 'we plan on going all-out': *Cairns Post*, 8 November 1947, p. 5.

p. 269 Stable accommodation figures: From 'Track Diagrams, Records, Best Times', Part XIII, *American Racing Manual*, 1949, pp. 557–674.

p. 270 Trial with Burning Dream: *Argus*, 18 December 1947, p. 24.

p. 270 'tall tales about his speed': Ibid.

p. 270 Shannon's three-furlong sprint at Santa Anita: AAP report,

Courier-Mail, 22 December 1947, p. 5.

p. 270   'Santa Anita fell into a winter heatwave': Temperature recordings supplied by Jan Null, Meteorologist Golden Gate Weather Services, Station ID USC00047785, San Gabriel Fire Department.

p. 270   'Shannon began coughing': As reported in *Morning Telegraph*, New York; AAP report, *Morning Bulletin*, 31 December 1947, p. 8.

p. 270   'Webb Everett, the Santa Anita handicapper': *American Racing Manual*, 1949, p. 556.

p. 270   '8/1 in the betting': AAP report, *Northern Miner*, 30 December 1947, p. 2.

p. 270   Sectionals for 21 January workout: 'Shannon Drills Well, Ready for First Start', *Los Angeles Times*, 22 January 1948, p. A12.

38: Too quick out of the bend, the straight too short

p. 272   'Molter's assistant trainer': Robert Hebert, 'Molter's Law: Know your Horses and Study the Condition Book', *The Blood-Horse*, 18 October 1947, p. 136.

p. 272   'We park 30,000 cars': Garry Morris, 'Santa Anita—The World's Richest Racecourse', *Sunday Times*, 23 November 1947, p. 15S.

p. 272   'I could run anything': Ibid.

p. 273   'Molter had been concerned at the deep holes': *Sydney Morning Herald*, 26 January 1948, p. 6.

p. 273   Seabiscuit–Ligaroti match race: Bill Christine, 'Jockeying for Position', *Los Angeles Times*, 12 August 1988; Hillenbrand, *Seabiscuit*.

p. 274   'a half-second past 4.02 pm': *Daily Racing Form*, Chart Book.

p. 275   Santa Anita sectionals: Ibid.

p. 275   'He put up a nice race': *Sydney Morning Herald*, 26 January 1948, p. 6.

p. 275   'went like the clappers': Ellis, *The Science of Turf Investment*.

p. 276   '"satisfactory" effort': *Sydney Morning Herald*, 26 January 1948, p. 6.

p. 276   'how he handled the starting gate': *Sunday Times*, 25 January 1948, p. 11.

p. 276   '12 per cent of the tote pool': *Argus*, 26 January 1948, p. 12.

p. 276   'sours me on Shannon': *Northern Miner*, 2 February 1948, p. 2.

p. 278   'I was cooling him off': *Townsville Daily Bulletin*, 6 February 1948, p. 4.

p. 279   'All Shannon did': AAP report, *Los Angeles Times*; *Townsville Daily Bulletin*, 6 February 1948, p. 4.

p. 279   'He wasn't disappointed with Shannon': AAP report, *Sydney*

Morning Herald, 5 February 1948, p. 8.

p. 279   'Doubts hovered in McCarthy's head': *Barrier Miner*, 12 February 1948, p. 4.

p. 279   'He's a really good horse': AAP report, op. cit.

p. 279   'unfair to foreign horses': AAP report, *Advocate*, 16 February 1948, p. 3; *Sunday Times*, 15 February 1948, p. 3.

p. 280   'a very warm day in Arcadia': Temperature recordings supplied by Jan Null, Meteorologist Golden Gate Weather Services, Station ID USC00047785, San Gabriel Fire Department.

p. 280   San Antonio race description: *Daily Racing Form*, Chart Book.

p. 281   'Shannon Fails Again': *Sydney Morning Herald*, 19 February 1948, p. 36.

p. 281   'Shannon Outclassed': *Daily News*, 16 February 1948, p. 9.

p. 281   'Shannon's Humiliation': *Sydney Morning Herald*, 14 February 1948, p. 7.

p. 281   'luckier still missing Shannon': *Western Mail*, 4 March 1948, p. 19.

39: The Hundred Grander

p. 282   Shannon's Santa Anita Handicap bid: Newbury, 'Mission for Shannon', *Western Mail*, 26 February 1948, p. 21.

p. 282   'getting it wrong': *Barrier Miner*, 30 January 1948, p. 8.

p. 282   'ridden too soft': *Advocate*, 20 February 1948, p. 5.

p. 282   'One finds it difficult to believe': AAP report, *Advocate*, 8 January 1948, p. 3.

p. 282   'It isn't the jockey that's wrong': *Sunday Times*, 22 February 1948, p. 10.

p. 283   'terribly unfair and unsportsmanlike': *Sunday Times*, 15 February 1948, p. 3.

p. 283   'allergic to negative press': Garry Morris, 'Santa Anita—The World's Richest Racecourse', *Sunday Times*, 23 November 1947, p. 15S.

p. 284   'if he should run the horse at all': *Advocate*, 20 February 1948, p. 5.

p. 284   18 February workout: *Montreal Gazette*, 26 February 1948, p. 17.

p. 285   Scratched from Washington Handicap: *Herald*, 26 February 1948, p. 18.

p. 285   Race-day trial with On Trust: *Sunday Times*, 22 February 1948, p. 10.

p. 285   'dull, cool day over Los Angeles': Temperature recordings supplied by Jan Null, Meteorologist Golden Gate Weather Services, Station ID USC00047785, San Gabriel Fire Department.

p. 285   62,000 racegoers, track 'fast': *Daily Racing Form*, Chart
Book; Paul Zimmerman, 'Talon Noses Out On Trust To Win
$100,000 Race', *Los Angeles Times*, 29 February 1948, p. 1.

p. 285   'day's drizzle': Zimmerman, 'Talon Noses Out On Trust'; *Sydney
Morning Herald*, 1 March 1948, p. 7.

p. 286   'flanked him either side': Photograph, *Sunday Times*, 21 March
1948, p. 3.

p. 286   'stay with On Trust': *Sydney Morning Herald*, 2 March 1948, p. 7.

p. 286   'owners that used to run their horses': Paul Lowry, 'Handicap
Hopes Stretch Legs in Mile Today', *Los Angeles Times*,
23 February 1948, p. A9.

p. 286   'In Sydney, locals had flocked': *Sydney Morning Herald*, 1 March
1948, p. 7.

p. 286   Defection of Olhaverry: Paul Lowry, 'Olhaverry Injures Feet, Out
of Handicap', *Los Angeles Times*, 27 February 1948, p. A9.

p. 286   'Shannon looked rough': *Argus*, 1 March 1948, p. 12.

p. 287   '4.53 pm': *Daily Racing Form*, Chart Book.

p. 287   'worst possible kind of race': *Sydney Morning Herald*, 2 March
1948, p. 7.

p. 287   'the right type of offer': Ibid.

p. 288   'They have been rushing him': *Sydney Morning Herald*, 1 March
1948, p. 7.

p. 288   Ernest Shaw's criticisms: Article forwarded by Graham Caves,
Sydney racing historian: George McCann, 'The Shannon Error',
A.M. magazine, August 1948, p. 49.

p. 288   American vs Australian styles: Ellis, *The Science of Turf
Investment*.

p. 289   Molter's comments: AAP report, *Morning Telegraph*, 19 March
1948.

p. 289   'criticised the length of California': Los Angeles correspondent of
Argus, 1 March 1948, p. 12.

p. 290   'different horse altogether': *West Australian*, 19 March 1948, p. 19.

p. 290   'Peter Riddle would have been': This sentence is not literal. Peter
Riddle was cremated at Botany Cemetery in June 1947.

40: 'Champion money burner of the United States'
p. 291   'lightened up in the back end': Photographic evidence.

p. 291   'the big bay': *Los Angeles Times*, 9 May 1948, p. 21.

p. 292   'was eating freely': *Morning Telegraph* New York, as reported in
Daily Bulletin, 19 March 1948, p. 2.

p. 292   'Molter and McCarthy were at loggerheads': *Sydney Morning
Herald*, 26 April 1948, p. 6.

p. 292   'one of the charms of being an owner': Ibid; *West Australian*,
          26 April 1948, p. 16.
p. 292   'it isn't that Shannon is not ready': *West Australian*, 19 April 1948,
          p. 16.
p. 293   'He would have won in another stride': *Courier-Mail*, 22 April
          1948, p. 5.
p. 293   Jack McDonald's comments: *Call-Bulletin*, as quoted in *West
          Australian*, 23 April 1948, p. 18.
p. 295   'Shannon Robbed': *Examiner*, 8 May 1948, p. 14.
p. 295   'Unlucky Run for Shannon': *Northern Miner*, 2 May 1948, p. 2.
p. 295   Prescott Sullivan's editorial on Shannon: Run across the
          Australian press from an editorial that appeared in the San
          Francisco *Examiner*, week of 2 May 1948. Reproduced with kind
          permission from Stephen Buel, editor-in-chief, *Examiner*.
p. 297   'films show clearly': *Examiner*, 8 May 1948, p. 14.
p. 297   'They suspended Lindberg': 'Lindberg Set Down', *Daily Racing
          Form*, 6 May 1948, p. 3; 'Lindberg's suspension authenticates
          jockey Willie Bayley's claim', *Chronicle*, San Francisco, 6 May
          1948, p. 6.
p. 297   Mafosta: *Daily Racing Form*, 4 May 1948, p. 32.
p. 298   'Australian redemption day': *Morning Bulletin*, 6 May 1948, p. 6.
p. 299   'the victory I knew he had in him': AAP report, *Daily Bulletin*,
          11 May 1948, p. 3.
p. 299   Hy Schneider, professional handicapper: *New York Post*,
          22 February 1935, p. 15.
p. 299   'Neil McCarthy . . . is to be congratulated': AAP report, *Daily
          Bulletin*, 11 May 1948, p. 3.
p. 299   'Shannon has finally come around': *Los Angeles Times*, 2 May
          1948; 'Shannon II Cracks Seabiscuit Track Mark', *Los Angeles
          Times*, 9 May 1948, p. 21.
p. 300   Neil McCarthy's comments on Shannon 'sweet little horse': AAP
          report, *Daily Bulletin*, 11 May 1948, p. 3.
p. 300   'now you know why we are all so interested': *Singleton Argus*,
          10 May 1948, p. 1.
p. 300   'Without this column's assistance': Prescott Sullivan's editorial,
          San Francisco *Examiner*, reproduced in 'Shannon's Win Makes
          Mr Sullivan Climb Down Gracefully', *Argus*, 11 May 1948, p. 12.

41: Hollywood
p. 302   'track of lakes and flowers': *Australian Women's Weekly*, 21 August
          1957, p. 13.
p. 302   '315 acres of what was once a deep and messy bean field': Lowry,
          Hollywood Park, p. 12; Betty Gee, 'Betty's "Racey" Narratives',

Australian Women's Weekly, 1 July 1939, p. 22.

p. 302   'real sportsmen at Hollywood Park': AAP report, *Daily Bulletin*, op. cit., p. 3.

p. 303   'if he is ever going to show anything': Paul Lowry, 'Shannon II on spot in Hollypark race today', *Los Angeles Times*, 25 May 1948, p. A9.

p. 303   'race Shannon on the east coast': *Sydney Morning Herald*, 1 March 1948, p. 7.

p. 303   '500 horses in the various barns': '500 horses at Hollywood', *Daily Racing Form*, 6 May 1948, p. 32.

p. 303   'Charlie Howard had the largest string': 'Largest Hollywood String', *Daily Racing Form*, 7 May 1948, p. 5.

p. 304   Hollywood Park's electronic timer: 'Hollywood Park Installs New Electronic Timer', *Daily Racing Form*, 5 May 1948, p. 32.

p. 305   '2 lbs overweight': *Daily Racing Form*, Chart Book.

p. 305   'Shannon is just an Australian champion': 'Shannon Just Another Horse, Mafosta Triumphs', *Los Angeles Times*, 26 May 1948, p. A11.

p. 305   'I'll never pick Shannon to win': *Morning Bulletin*, 27 May 1948, p. 6.

p. 305   'disgusted with Shannon': *Advocate*, 28 May 1948, p. 3.

p. 305   'sick about it all': *Singleton Argus*, 28 May 1948, p. 8.

p. 305   'lack of perseverance': Ibid.

p. 305   McCarthy's cable to Smith: *Sydney Morning Herald*, 29 May 1948, p. 9.

p. 305   'I have owned a lot of horses': *Morning Bulletin*, 27 May 1948, p. 6.

p. 306   'filling all 22,000 parking spaces': *Los Angeles Times*, 1 June 1948, p. A9.

p. 306   'had ever poured into Hollywood Park': 'Record Attendance', *The Blood-Horse*, 12 June 1948, p. 548.

p. 306   'talk to Shannon': AAP report, *Kalgoorlie Miner*, 3 June 1948, p. 6.

p. 307   'Not a single tipster': *Sydney Morning Herald*, 1 June 1948, p. 7.

p. 307   'keeping my fingers crossed': Ibid.

p. 308   'I didn't ride him': AAP report, *Cairns Post*, 2 June 1948, p. 2.

p. 308   'He fits him to a tee': Oscar Otis, 'Between Races', *Daily Racing Form*, 22 June 1948.

p. 308   'not the man to ride this Australian whiz': Hy Schneider's comments in *Examiner*. AAP report, Los Angeles, *Sydney Morning Herald*, 2 June 1948, p. 7.

p. 309   'Longden . . . is not the right jockey for Shannon': George

McCann, 'The Shannon Error', *A.M.* magazine, August 1948, p. 40.

p. 309   'nothing wrong with his speed': AAP report, *Sydney Morning Herald*, 2 June 1948, p. 7.

p. 309   'dead last': Paul Lowry, 'Shannon II Wins Argonaut Before Record 71,789', *Los Angeles Times*, 1 June 1948, p. A9.

p. 309   'Shannon commands new respect': *Morning Telegraph* report, *Argus*, 3 June 1948, p. 12.

p. 309   'stamps Shannon as the horse to beat': *Herald Express*, as reported, Ibid.

p. 309   'Adams seemed to ride the horse perfectly': *Canberra Times*, 2 June 1948, p. 1.

p. 310   'didn't seem quite himself': Lowry, op. cit.

p. 310   '8 June he emerged for a workout': *Morning Bulletin*, 10 June 1948, p. 4.

p. 311   'S. S. *America*': Palmer, *American Race Horses 1948*, p. 44.

p. 311   'George Moore arrived in California': *Daily Racing Form*, 9 June 1948, p. 34.

p. 311   'meet Australia's leading jockey': *Sydney Morning Herald*, 19 June 1948, p. 10.

p. 311   'Molter had to deny them': *Canberra Times*, 10 June 1948, p. 1.

p. 311   'no intentions of piloting Shannon': Paul Zimmerman, 'Sport Scripts', *Los Angeles Times*, 18 June 1948, p. A9.

p. 312   'there's logic to it': Ibid.

p. 312   'seemed to be racing under difficulties': *Sydney Morning Herald*, 19 June 1948, p. 10.

p. 312   'didn't think Shannon looked as well': *Worker*, 2 August 1948, p. 18.

42: For gold and glory

p. 313   'million-dollar line-up': Paul Lowry, 'Field of Nine Goes After Hollypark Gold Cup Today', *Los Angeles Times*, 17 July 1948, p. 10.

p. 313   'he is such an in and outer': Ibid.

p. 314   'society from Pasadena to Santa Barbara': Marie Fenton, 'Society Enjoys Race Amid Floral Backdrop', *Los Angeles Times*, 18 July 1948, p. 18.

p. 314   'Woman of the Year in 1951': Obituary for Rosemary Bullis, *Los Angeles Times*, 22 January 2012.

p. 314   'shared her father's table': Fenton, 'Society Enjoys Race', op. cit.

p. 315   'Molter had thrown Prevaricator in': Lowry, 'Field of Nine', op. cit.

p. 316 'Longden was driving and whistling': Lowry, 'Shannon Captures Hollywood Gold Cup', *Los Angeles Times*, 18 July 1948, p. 121.

p. 316 '$4.30 on the pari-mutuel': Ibid.

p. 316 'hopped up': Ibid.

p. 317 'Shannon II was electrifying': Ibid.

p. 317 'I can't believe it!': Ibid.

p. 317 'The whole American Olympic team': *Sydney Morning Herald*, 19 July 1948, p. 5.

p. 317 'McCarthy's greatest regrets': *Los Angeles Times*, 5 June 1960, p. E17.

p. 317 'hot and cold form': *Argus*, 20 July 1948, p. 12.

p. 317 'half a second faster': *Sydney Morning Herald*, 19 July 1948, p. 5.

p. 317 'first horse to seriously challenge Phar Lap': Sentinel, 'Shannon Threat to Phar Lap', *Daily News*, 21 July 1948, p. 9.

p. 317 'the chief merit of Shannon's success': *Morning Bulletin* editorial, 4 June 1948, p. 3.

43: The lightning strip

p. 318 'God, he was built beautifully': Eddie Arcaro on Citation, Georgeff, *Citation*, p. 62.

p. 318 'He's as strong as a bull': Ibid., p. 60.

p. 320 'The Midstream horse was a miler': Hobson, *Racing's All-Time Greats*.

p. 320 'He ran a good race': *Sydney Morning Herald*, 26 July 1948, p. 5.

p. 321 'relaxed at Del Mar': *Miner*, 2 September 1948, p. 2.

p. 321 'waiting on advice from Neil McCarthy': *West Australian*, 24 July 1948, p. 18.

p. 322 'He's been idle since Hollywood Park': *Miner*, 21 September 1948, p. 6.

p. 322 'odds to $1': *Daily Racing Form*, Chart Book.

p. 323 Information on Jack Westrope supplied by Allan Carter of New York Racing Association Hall of Fame, Saratoga Springs, visit 10 August 2012.

p. 324 'I ain't giving nobody room': Howard Rowe, 'The Rope Enters The Hall Of Fame', *American Turf Monthly*, September 2002, p. 46.

p. 324 'shout the bar': Pamela Westrope Donner's recollection of her father, Hall of Fame ceremony 2002.

p. 324 'all-night binge at La Jolla': Morton Cathro, 'The Final Turn', *The Blood-Horse*, 31 July 1999, p. 4362.

p. 324 'Westrope was fearless': Craig Harzmann, 'Giant Little Man', *The Blood-Horse*, 3 August 2002, p. 4208.

p. 324 'acey deucy': Ibid., p. 4209.

p. 328   Indian Broom's record: 'Fastest Records in Racing', *American Racing Manual*, 1949, p. 675; *Greatest Kentucky Derby Upsets*, Blood-Horse Publications, 2007, Lexington, Kentucky, p. 65.

p. 328   'This Down Under champion blows hot and cold': *West Australian*, 18 October 1948, p. 16.

p. 329   'Molter Trio Favoured': 'Molter Trio Favoured At Golden Gate', *Los Angeles Times*, 23 October 1948, p. B4.

p. 329   'some real running': *Advocate*, 21 October 1948, p. 16.

p. 330   'in the terraces Neil McCarthy was on his feet': 'World Record Equaled: Shannon II Wins Golden Gate 'Cap'. *Los Angeles Times*, 24 October 1948, p. 31.

p. 330   'sending him right over Phar Lap': 'Shannon Passes Phar Lap's Stakes', *Barrier Miner*, 25 October 1948, p. 8.

p. 331   'I need only say': *Canberra Times*, 25 October 1948, p. 4.

p. 331   'the powerful Australian cannonball': *Advertiser*, 25 October 1948, p. 3.

p. 331   'He certainly ran like a racehorse': *Canberra Times*, 25 October 1948, p. 4.

44: 'The white hope of the west coast'

p. 333   'Shannon finished third': *Mercury*, 13 November 1948, p. 20.

p. 333   'I have no excuses for it': *Argus*, 17 November 1948, p. 20.

p. 334   'Citation arrived': *The Modesto Bee*, 15 November 1948, p. 15.

p. 334   'He laid down a few times': 'Weary Citation Steps Off Train at Tanforan', *Los Angeles Times*, 17 November 1948, p. C4.

p. 334   'Those two races at Tanforan': Comment by Eddie Arcaro, Georgeff, *Citation*, p. 133.

p. 335   Shannon's race-day track gallop: *Sydney Morning Herald*, 20 November 1948, p. 10.

p. 335   'It was good work on a track like this': *Courier-Mail*, 20 November 1948, p. 5.

p. 335   'Citation will know he's been in a horse race': Oscar Otis, *Daily Racing Form*, reported in *Townsville Daily Bulletin*, 15 November 1948, p. 3.

p. 335   'Westrope's appraisal of Shannon is keenly interesting': Ibid.

p. 336   '55 cents to $1': *Daily Racing Form*, Chart Book.

p. 337   'hollered the roof off the grandstand': 'Shannon II Roars Home at Tanforan', *Los Angeles Times*, 26 November 1948, p. C4.

p. 338   'They expected 40,000 people': *Townsville Daily Bulletin*, 15 December 1948, p. 3.

p. 338   'The big horse from Down Under': 'Shannon II Roars Home at Tanforan', op. cit.

p. 338   'in California for a dispersal sale': Robert Hebert, 'Slight Earthquake Rocks the Coast', *The Blood-Horse*, 11 December 1948, p. 686.

p. 338   Syndicate members: 'Shannon II Buyers Listed', *The Blood-Horse*, 11 December 1948, p. 668.

p. 339   'crinkle-eyed, silver-haired Texan Clifford Mooers': 'Sport – Before the Big One', *TIME*, 9 May 1949, http://www.time.com/time/magazine/article/0,9171,800233,00.html.

p. 339   '22 applications': Paul Lowry, 'Shannon II Retired After $300,000 Sale', *Los Angeles Times*, 2 December 1948, p. C1.

p. 339   'two conditions': Hebert, 'Slight Earthquake', op. cit., p. 686.

p. 339   'dinner for four with champagne': Paul Lowry, 'Hoofbeats', *Los Angeles Times*, 5 December 1948, p. 31.

p. 339   'no allowances will be given for newspaper clippings': *The Blood-Horse*, 4 December 1948, p. 607.

p. 339   'I told Eugene Mori': *Daily News*, 2 December 1948, p. 8.

p. 340   'Shannon was a far inferior animal to Citation': Lowry, 'Shannon II Retired', op. cit.

p. 340   'By taking a run-out': *Daily News*, 3 December 1948, p. 11.

p. 340   'This is strictly business': *Sydney Morning Herald*, 3 December 1948, p. 9.

p. 340   Letter, Northern California Turf Writers Association: Hebert, 'Slight Earthquake', op. cit., p. 686.

p. 341   Response from McCarthy: Ibid.

p. 341   'scale of weights': American Racing Manual, 1949, p. 521.

p. 341   'I have always supported California racing': Ibid.

p. 342   'Shannon's glory cannot be dimmed': Lowry, 'Shannon II Retired', op. cit.

p. 342   'No one is more disappointed than I am': Hebert, 'Slight Earthquake', op. cit.

p. 342   'never been astride a faster horse': *American Racing Manual*, 1949, p. 44.

p. 342   'Shannon was rated equal fourth': *Mercury*, 25 March 1949, p. 10; *Canberra Times*, 25 March 1949, p. 1.

p. 343   'starting 19 times': 'Review of 1948 Races', *American Racing Manual*, 1949, p. 45.

p. 343   'He led his age division': *American Racing Manual*, 1949, p. 141.

p. 343   'Champion Handicap Horse': The title of 'Champion Handicap Horse' was absorbed in later years to become 'American Champion Older Male Horse' as part of the annual Eclipse Awards. In 1948, Shannon shared the title with Citation, while Citation was also crowned 'Horse Of The Year'.

p. 343   'This is a tribute to him': *Morning Telegraph*, as reported in *Mercury*, 27 December 1948, p. 11.

p. 343   'still in big, black headlines in the newspapers': Hebert, 'Slight Earthquake', op. cit.

p. 344   'friendly as an overgrown puppy': 'The Race That Wasn't', *TIME*, 13 December 1948, pp. 78, 81.

p. 344   'unwind the champion': *Examiner*, 10 December 1948, p. 14.

p. 344   'Shannon trucked out of Tanforan': *Los Angeles Times*, 9 December 1948, p. C4.

p. 344   'Citation's slashing victory in the Tanforan Handicap': This race was one too many for Citation. After its running, he pulled up very sore and was found to have an osselet, a bony growth usually in the fore pasterns. The champion remained out for a year with associated complications, not returning to racing until 1950. He was a shadow of his three-year-old self.

p. 344   'poor crowd that stepped out to witness it': *Sydney Morning Herald*, 13 December 1948, p. 9.

p. 344   'verifying his fertility': *Cairns Post*, 15 December 1948, p. 1.

45: Iron Works Pike

p. 345   '1070 acres': *American Racing Manual*, 1949, p. 1021.

p. 345   '127 acres in 1937': Marshall, *Great Breeders and Their Methods*, op. cit., p. 15.

p. 345   'Everybody said I was a damn fool': *Courier-Journal*; Ibid.

p. 345   'breaking commercial breeding records up and down the United States': Bowen, *Legacies of the Turf: A Century of Great Thoroughbred Breeders* (vol. 2), pp. 129–44.

p. 345   'he would spread grain along the fences': Marshall, *Great Breeders and Their Methods*, op. cit., Wisconsin, 2008, p. 19.

p. 345   'a garrulous showman': Bowen, *Legacies of the Turf*, op. cit., p. 129.

p. 346   'fear of tornadoes', 'slept with a machine gun under his belt': Anecdotes provided by Des Dempsey, marketing manager Spendthrift Farm, visit 6 August 2012.

p. 346   '"Cuzin" Leslie': Marshall, *Great Breeders and Their Methods*, op. cit., p. 19.

p. 346   'It makes fine whisky': Wall, *How Kentucky Became Southern*, p. 55.

p. 346   'Next door was Bernborough': *Examiner*, 22 December 1948, p. 15.

p. 346   'Santa Fe boxcar': The train that carried Shannon to Lexington was an express car of the Santa Fe Railroad, from photographic evidence of the Skeet Meadors collection.

p. 346   'Brora and Avillion': *Canberra Times*, 22 December 1948, p. 1.

p. 347   'poked his nose over the compartment wall': Photographic evidence, collection of Skeet Meadors.

p. 347   'sidled in to a part-time groom position': Crawford, *Kentucky Stories*, p. 43.

p. 347   Tom Harbut: Amy Wilson, 'Groom's Son Remembers Life Growing Up Around Man O' War', *Herald-Leader*, 2 October 2010, http://www.kentucky.com/2010/10/02/1460347/grooms-son-remembers-life-growing.html.

p. 347   'let Shannon meet Bernborough': *Sydney Morning Herald*, 31 May 1949, p. 8.

p. 348   'rather light, a little thin-waisted': 'Review of 1948 Races', *American Racing Manual*, 1949, p. 45.

p. 348   'his later groom, Booker Payne': *Sunday Mail*, 14 February 1954, p. 26.

p. 348   'top-shelf fee of $2500': *Daily Racing Form*, 7 May 1949, p. 16.

p. 348   'Shannon II is a beautifully moving individual': 'Review of 1948 Races', op. cit. p. 45.

p. 348   'On 14 May that year': 'Thoroughbred Obituaries', *American Racing Manual*, 1949, p. 475.

p. 348   'when Payne found him': *Turf Monthly*, December 1958, p. 1.

A note on Shannon's death:

No monument has been erected at Spendthrift Farm to honour Shannon, or mark his final resting place. In Australia, aside from Shannon's instatement to the Hall of Fame in 2006, he is remembered with the Shannon Stakes, run at Rosehill over 1500 metres in the spring.

Appendix A: Shannon's Racing Record

Shannon's career record, including all earnings, was compiled from two primary sources: the *Australasian Turf Register* (issues 1943–1947) and the *American Racing Manual* (1949).

Note on records:
The Australian racing season begins on 1 August and ends on 31 July. The American racing season begins on 1 January and ends on 31 December. sw denotes 'set weights', h'cap denotes 'handicap', qty h'cap denotes 'quality handicap', and wfa denotes 'weight-for-age'. Because Shannon raced in the pre-metric era in Australia, weights are displayed throughout in imperial measures.

Note on earnings:
It is almost impossible to aggregate Shannon's Australian and American earnings into one total owing to the rate of exchange in 1948. However, on an approximate exchange of $2.50 to the Australian £1, Shannon's approximate combined lifetime earnings were $260,000, by far the highest of any Australasian thoroughbred ever at that time.

	Starts	1ˢᵗ	2ⁿᵈ	3ʳᵈ	Unpl.	Earnings
1943–44 Age Two	7	3	3	–	1	£5022
1944–45 Age Three	4	1	–	–	3	£833
1945–46 Age Four	5	4	1	–	–	£5569
1946–1947 Age Five	5	4	1	–	–	£4920/10
1947–1948 Age Six	4	2	2	–	–	£2503
Australian Total	25	14	7	0	4	£18,847/10
1948 Age Seven	19	6	1	5	7	$212,810
Lifetime Totals	44	20	8	5	11	–

Shannon

b.h. 1941, by Midstream (Blandford)–Idle Words, by Magpie

Lifetime records: 44: 20, 8, 5

Owners: Peter Riddle, W. J. Smith, Neil S. McCarthy, Syndicate; Breeder: Percy Miller, Kia Ora Stud (NSW); Trainers: Peter Riddle, Frank Dalton, Willie Molter

Date	Race	Pl.	Dis.	Time	Jockey	Weight (st lbs)	Finish	Margins	Winnings
9 Oct 43	Breeders' Plate, R'wick sw	2nd	5f	1:02½	Shean F	8.5 (53 kg)	Victory Lad 8.5 (53 kg), Shannon, Majesty 8.5 (53 kg)	hd, 4len.	£200
23 Oct 43	Canonbury Stks, R'wick	2nd	5f	0:59	Shean F	8.5 (53 kg)	Majesty 8.5 (53 kg), Shannon, Silver Flare 8.5 (53 kg)	½, 5	£200
20 Nov 43	Two-Year-Old Stks, R'wick	1st	5f 14y	1:01	Shean F	8.5 (53 kg)	Shannon, Tea Rose 8.7 (54 kg), Majesty 8.12 (56 kg)	3, 3	£557
27 Nov 43	Kirkham Stks, R'wick	1st	5f 14y	1:01½	Shean F	8.5 (53 kg)	Shannon, Tea Rose 8.0 (51 kg), Hawk Craig 8.5 (53 kg)	2, 2	£787
18 Mar 44	Services' H'cp, R'wick	4th	6f	1:14¼	Shean F	9.5 (59.5 kg)	Brittanic 7.10 (49 kg), Invictus 7.11 (49.5 kg), Prince Verity 8.3 (52 kg)	4, hd	–
1 Apr 44	Fairfield H'cp, R'wick	2nd	6f	1:13¾	Shean F	8.13 (56.5 kg)	Liberality 7.1 (45 kg), Shannon, Brittanic 8.2 (51.5 kg)	nk, 1½	£150
8 Apr 44	Sires' Produce Stks, R'wick sw	1st	7f	1:25	Shean F	8.10 (55.5 kg)	Shannon, Tea Rose 8.8 (54.5 kg), Bravo 8.1 (55.5 kg)	½nk, 3	£3068
26 Aug 44	Flying H'cp, R'wick	11th	6f*	1:14¼	Shean F	7.6 (47 kg)	Tribal 7.13 (50.5 kg), Main Topic 8.4 (52.5 kg), Tahmoor 8.3 (52 kg)	½nk, 2½	–
2 Sep 44	Hobartville Stks, R'wick	1st	7f*	1:25¾	Munro D	8.10 (55.5 kg)	Shannon, Cold Shower 8.0 (51 kg), Removal 8.1 (55.5 kg)	1½, 2½	£833
23 Sep 44	Rosehill Guineas, R'hill	4th	9f	1:52	Munro D	8.5 (53 kg)	Tea Rose 8.0 (51 kg), Melhero 8.5 (53 kg), Beau Monde 8.5 (53 kg)	2½, nk	–

Date	Race	Pl.	Dis.	Time	Jockey	Weight (st lbs)	Finish	Margins	Winnings
14 Oct 44	AJC Derby, R'wick sw	6th	12f	2:33½	Munro D	8.5 (53 kg)	Tea Rose 8.5 (53 kg), Removal 8.1 (55.5 kg), Prince Verity 8.1 (55.5 kg)	2, 1½	–
25 Aug 45	Campbelltown H'cp, R'wick	1st	6f 20y*	1:12½	Munro D	9.1 (57.5 kg)	Shannon, Warlock 7.12 (50 kg), Silent 7.6 (47 kg)	2, shd	£865
8 Sep 45	Tramway H'cp, R'wick	1st	7f 26y	1:24½	Munro D	9.1 (57.5 kg)	Shannon, Flight 9.1 (57.5 kg), Silent 7.1 (45 kg)	nk, 1	£714
15 Sep 45	Hill Stks, R'hill wfa	1st	8f 110y	1:45	Munro D	9.0 (57 kg)	Shannon, Cold Shower 9.0 (57 kg), Accession 9.0 (57 kg)	2, 2½	£790
29 Sep 45	Epsom H'cp, R'wick	1st	8f	1:36¼	Munro D	8.10 (55.5 kg)	Shannon, Melhero 8.12 (56 kg), Silent 7.8 (48 kg)	½nk, ½nk	£2900
6 Oct 45	Craven Plate, R'wick wfa	2nd	10f	2:03	Munro D	9.0 (57 kg)	Flight 8.13 (56.6 kg), Shannon, Russia 9.4 (59 kg)	2, 1	£300
31 Aug 46	Campbelltown H'cp, R'wick	1st	6f 19y	1:11½	Munro D	9.11 (62 kg)	Shannon, Puffham 8.7 (54 kg), Felstar 8.6 (53.5 kg)	½, 1	£904
21 Sep 46	Theo Marks Qty H'cp, R'hill	1st	7f	1:22½ †	Moore G	9.5 (59.5 kg)	Shannon, Dowborough 7.8 (48 kg), Good Idea 8.11 (56 kg)	½, nk	£669/10
5 Oct 46	Epsom H'cp R'wick	2nd	8f	1:36¼	Munro D	9.9 (61 kg)	Blue Legend 8.9 (55 kg), Shannon, Young Veilmond 7.13 (50.5 kg)	½hd, ½hd	£600
7 Oct 46	George Main Stks, R'wick	1st	8f	1:34½ Δ	Munro D	9.3 (58.5 kg)	Shannon, Flight 8.12 (56 kg), Magnificent 9.0 (57 kg)	6, 4	£1112
12 Oct 46	King's Cup, R'wick qty h'cp	1st	12f	2:29¾	Munro D	9.5 (59.5 kg)	Shannon, Flight 8.7 (54 kg), Good Idea 8.11 (56 kg)	2½, 1¼	£1635
Henceforth owned by W. J. Smith							**Henceforth trained by F. Dalton**		
30 Aug 47	Warwick Stks, R'wick wfa	2nd	7f 19y*	1:25¼	Munro D	9.3 (58.5 kg)	Victory Lad 9.3 (58.5 kg), Shannon, Prince Consort 8.7 (54 kg)	1, ½nk	£200
6 Sep 47	Canterbury Stks, C'bury wfa	1st	6f	1:13½	Munro D	9.2 (58 kg)	Shannon, Deep Sea 8.0 (51 kg), Victory Lad 9.2 (58. kg)	¾, nk	£810
6 Oct 47	George Main Stks, R'wick wfa	1st	8f	1:36½	Munro D	9.3 (58.5 kg)	Shannon, Victory Lad 9.3 (58.5 kg), Puffham 9.0 (57 kg)	½nk, 4	£1093

Date	Race	Pl.	Dis.	Time	Jockey	Weight (st lbs)	Finish	Margins	Winnings
8 Oct 47	Craven Plate, R'wick wfa	2nd	10f	2:02½	Munro D	9.4 (59 kg)	Russia 9.4 (59 kg), Shannon, Columnist 9.4 (59 kg)	½nk, ½	£400
Henceforth owned by Neil S. McCarthy							**Henceforth trained by W. Molter**		
24 Jan 48	overnight h'cp, S'Anita	3rd	7f	1:22⅘	Rich'son N	8.5 (53 kg)	Windfields 8.5 (53 kg), Endeavour 8.5 (53 kg), Shannon II	1¾, 1	$600
3 Feb 48	overnight h'cp, S'Anita	3rd	7f	1:23⅖	Rich'son N	8.3 (52 kg)	Plumper 7.12 (50 kg), Mafosta 8.1 (55.5 kg), Shannon II	½, 3½	$600
14 Feb 48	San Antonio H'cp, S'Anita	8th	9f	1:49⅖	Rich'son N	8.5 (53 kg)	Talon 8.1 (55.5 kg), Double Jay 8.6 (53.5 kg), On Trust 9.0 (57 kg)	nk, 2¼	–
28 Feb 48	Santa Anita H'cp, S'Anita	14th	10f	2:03⅖	Rich'son N	9.0 (57 kg)	Talon 8.1 (55.5 kg), On Trust, 8.9 (55 kg), Double Jay 8.6 (53.5 kg)	nk, 1¾	–
20 Apr 48	Marina Purse, B'Mdws	2nd	6f	1:10⅘	Longden J	8.10 (55.5 kg)	Barbastel 8.0 (51 kg), Shannon II, Stirrup Cup 8.7 (54 kg)	nk, 5	$800
1 May 48	Bay Meadows H'cp, BMdws	7th	9f	1:51	Bailey W	8.4 (52.5 kg)	Mafosta 9.0 (57 kg), Faucon 8.5 (53 kg), Hemet Squaw 7.11 (49.5 kg)	nk, 2¼	–
8 May 48	San Francisco County H'cp, BMdws	1st	9½f	1:55⅗ †	Longden J	8.2 (51.5 kg)	Shannon II, Why Alibi 7.5 (46.5 kg), Please Me 7.12 (50 kg)	12, 1½	$7280
25 May 48	Angelino Purse, H'wood Pk	4th	8f	1:36	Longden J	8.0 (51 kg)	Mafosta 8.6 (53.5 kg), Brabancon 8.0 (51 kg), Flashco 8.6 (53.5 kg)	1¾, 3	$600
31 May 48	Argonaut H'cp, H'wood Pk	1st	8½f	1:42⅖	Adams J	8.0 (51 kg)	Shannon II, Mafosta 8.12 (56.5 kg), On Trust 9.0 (57 kg)	1¼, 1¼	$32,400
17 Jun 48	Riverside County H'cp, H'Wood Pk	3rd	8f	1:36⅗	Adams J	8.6 (53.5 kg)	Mafosta 9.0 (57 kg), With Pleasure 8.12 (56.5 kg), Shannon II	nk, 10	$1200

Date	Race	Pl.	Dis.	Time	Jockey	Weight (st lbs)	Finish	Margins	Winnings
5 Jul 48	American H'cp, H'wood Pk	6th	9f	1:50⅖	Adams J	8.8 (54.5 kg)	Stepfather 7.13 (50.5 kg), Autocrat 8.0 (51 kg), On Trust 9.4 (59 kg)	nk, ¾	–
17 Jul 48	Hollywood Gold Cup, H'wood Pk	1st	10f	2:01⅗	Adams J	8.4 (52.5 kg)	Shannon II, On Trust 9.2 (58 kg), Olhaverry 8.1 (51 kg)	2, 1½	$67,600
24 Jul 48	Sunset H'cp, H'wood Pk	3rd	13f	2:41	Adams J	8.12 (56 kg)	Drumbeat 7.2 (45.5 kg), On Trust 9.0 (57 kg), Shannon II	3, ¾	$7500
24 Sep 48	Walnut Creek H'cp, Gld Gate Flds	3rd	6f	1:10	Longden J	8.10 (55.5 kg)	Mafosta 9.0 (57 kg), Tape Buster 7.12 (50 kg), Shannon II	nk, 1½	$500
2 Oct 48	Golden Gate Mile H'cp, Gld Gate Flds	3rd	8f	1:34⅖	Westrope J	8.10 (55.5 kg)	Prevaricator 8.6 (53.5 kg), Hemet Squaw 7.11 (49.5 kg), Shannon II	hd, ¾	$1500
16 Oct 49	Forty-Niners H'cp, Gld Gate Flds	1st	9f	1:47⅗ † A	Westrope J	8.12 (56 kg)	Shannon II, Mafosta 8.13 (56.5 kg), Autocrat 8.2 (51.5 kg)	1¼, ½	$11,730
23 Oct 48	Golden Gate H'cp, Gld Gate Flds	1st	10f	1:59⅘ †† AA	Westrope J	8.12 (56 kg)	Shannon II, See-Tee-See 8.4 (52.5 kg), Stepfather 7.13 (50.5 kg)	2, ½	$61,000
11 Nov 48	Marchbank H'cp, T'foran	3rd	8½f	1:44	Westrope J	9.1 (57.5 kg)	Please Me 7.11 (49.5 kg), Tropical Sea 7.8 (48 kg), Shannon II	nk, h	$2000
25 Nov 48	San Francisco H'cp, T'foran	1st	9f	1:50⅘ †	Westrope J	9.1 (57.5 kg)	Shannon II, Stepfather 7.13 (50.5 kg), On Trust 9.0 (57 kg)	hd, ¾	$16,800

* Distance recorded as 'about 6f' or 'about 7f' † Track record Δ Australasian record †† Equals world record
A Equals American record AA New American record

Appendix B: Shannon's Pedigree

The following chart traces Shannon's female line from his dam, Idle Words, to Spaewife, via Finland, where the alleged flaw occurred in the case of Shannon's admission to the American Stud Book. The numbers on the left represent the generations removed (e.g., Spaewife was 11 generations removed from Shannon, and so on).

FEMALE LINE OF SHANNON		SIRE OF BROODMARE
1 Shannon (AUS) 1941	by	Midstream (GB) 1933
2 Idle Words (AUS) 1932	by	Magpie (GB) 1914
3 Peptamint (NZ) 1921	by	Finland (AUS) 1897

FEMALE LINE OF FINLAND		
4 Fishwife (AUS) 1884	by	King Of The Anglers (AUS) 1878
5 Nameless (AUS) 1870	by	Panic (GB) 1858
6 Louise (AUS) 1865	by	Peeping Tom (GB) 1854
7 Miss Louey (AUS) 1855	by	Cossack (AUS) 1848
8 Hipped Bessy (AUS) 18--	by	St John (GB) 1834
9 Bessy Bedlam (AUS) 1835	by	Rous' Emigrant (GB) 1822
10 Stella (AUS) 1830	by	Peter Fin (GB) 1819
11 SPAEWIFE (GB) 18--	by	Soothsayer (GB) 1808
12 Selim Mare (GB) 1814	by	Selim (GB) 1802
13 Ringtail (GB) 1801	by	Buzzard (GB) 1787

Appendix B: Shannon's Pedigree

Pedigree of Shannon (AUS) 1941

- **Midstream (GB) 1933**
  - **Blandford (IRE) 1919**
    - **Swynford (GB) 1907**
      - John O' Gaunt (GB) 1901
        - Isinglass (GB) 1890
          - Isonomy (GB) 1875
          - Dead Lock (GB) 1878
        - La Fleche (GB) 1889
          - St Simon (GB) 1881
          - Quiver (GB) 1872
      - Canterbury Pilgrim (GB) 1893
        - Tristan (GB) 1878
          - Hermit (GB) 1864
          - Thrift (GB) 1865
        - Pilgrimage (GB) 1875
          - The Palmer (GB) 1864
          - Lady Audley (GB) 1867
    - **Blanche (GB) 1912**
      - White Eagle (GB) 1905
        - Gallinule (GB) 1884
          - Isonomy (GB) 1875
          - Moorhen (GB) 1873
        - Merry Gal (GB) 1897
          - Galopin (GB) 1872
          - Mary Seaton (GB) 1890
      - Black Cherry (GB) 1892
        - Bendigo (IRE) 1880
          - Ben Battle (GB) 1871
          - Hasty Girl (IRE) 1875
        - Black Duchess (GB) 1886
          - Galliard (GB) 1880
          - Black Corrie (GB) 1879
  - **Midsummer (GB) 1924**
    - **Abbots Trace (IRE) 1917**
      - Tracery (USA) 1909
        - Rock Sand (GB) 1900
          - Sainfoin (GB) 1887
          - Roquebrune (GB) 1893
        - Topiary (GB) 1901
          - Orme (GB) 1889
          - Plaisanterie (FR) 1882
      - Abbots Anne (GB) 1899
        - Right Away (GB) 1887
          - Wisdom (GB) 1873
          - Vanish (GB) 1874
        - Sister Lumley (GB) 1892
          - St Honorat (GB) 1882
          - Lady Lumley (GB) 1875
    - **Dew Of June (GB) 1913**
      - Polymelus (GB) 1902
        - Cyllene (GB) 1895
          - Bona Vista (GB) 1889
          - Arcadia (GB) 1887
        - Maid Marian (GB) 1886
          - Hampton (GB) 1872
          - Quiver (GB) 1872
      - Juana (GB) 1904
        - Velasquez (GB) 1894
          - Donovan (GB) 1886
          - Vista (GB) 1879
        - Ellaline (GB) 1893
          - Bend Or (GB) 1877
          - Dorothy Draggletail (GB) 1885
- **Idle Words (AUS) 1932**
  - **Magpie (GB) 1914**
    - **Dark Ronald (GB) 1905**
      - Bay Ronald (GB) 1893
        - Hampton (GB) 1872
          - Lord Clifden (GB) 1860
          - Lady Langen (GB) 1868
        - Black Duchess (GB) 1886
          - Galliard (GB) 1880
          - Black Corrie (GB) 1879
      - Darkie (GB) 1889
        - Thurio (GB) 1875
          - Cremorne (GB) 1869
          - Verona (GB) 1854
        - Insignia (GB) 1882
          - Blair Athol (GB) 1861
          - Decoration (GB) 1873
    - **Popinjay (GB) 1905**
      - St Frusquin (GB) 1893
        - St Simon (GB) 1881
          - Galopin (GB) 1872
          - St Angela (GB) 1865
        - Isabel (GB) 1879
          - Plebeian (GB) 1872
          - Parma (GB) 1864
      - Chelandry (GB) 1894
        - Goldfinch (GB) 1889
          - Ormonde (GB) 1883
          - Thistle (GB) 1875
        - Illuminata (GB) 1877
          - Rosicrucian (GB) 1865
          - Paraffin (GB) 1870
  - **Peptamint (NZ) 1921**
    - **Finland (AUS) 1897**
      - Bill Of Portland (GB) 1890
        - St Simon (GB) 1881
          - Galopin (GB) 1872
          - St Angela (GB) 1865
        - Electric Light (GB) 1876
          - Sterling (GB) 1868
          - Beachy Head (GB) 1865
      - Fishwife (AUS) 1884
        - King Of The Anglers (AUS) 1878
          - Angler (AUS) 1862
          - Rose De Florence (GB) 1855
        - Nameless (AUS) 1870
          - Panic (AUS) 1858
          - Louise (AUS) 1865
    - **Mint (GB) 1911**
      - Mintagon (GB) 1901
        - Martagon (GB) 1887
          - Bend Or (GB) 1877
          - Tiger Lily (GB) 1875
        - Mimi (GB) 1888
          - Barcaldine (GB) 1878
          - Lord Lyon Mare (GB) 1870
      - Brig Of Ayr (GB) 1907
        - Ayrshire (GB) 1885
          - Hampton (GB) 1872
          - Atalanta (GB) 1878
        - Santa Brigida (GB) 1898
          - St Simon (GB) 1881
          - Bridget (GB) 1888

Appendix C: A note on Shannon's stud record

Shannon entered stud duties at Spendthrift Farm in January 1949, producing seven crops before his premature death in May 1955. During that time, he sired only 132 foals for six stakes winners and six place getters. His complete sire statistics are as follows (courtesy of equineline.com):

Foals of Racing Age: 132
Starters (/foals of racing age): 119 (90%)
Winners (/foals of racing age): 100 (76%)
Stakes Winners (/foals of racing age): 6 (5%)
Stakes Placers (/foals of racing age): 6 (5%)
Starts: 7782
Wins (/starts): 860 (11%)
Placings (/starts): 1795 (23%)
Earnings: $3,230,555
Average Earnings/starter: $27,148
Average Earnings/start: $415
Median Earnings: $11,404
Chief Earner: Clem ($535,681)

Shannon's best progeny were as follows:
CLEM (1954) ch.c Shannon–Impulsive, by Supremus
Lifetime record: 47:12, 8, 13 (8 stakes wins)
Career earnings: $535,681
Major race wins: Arlington Classic (1957), Washington Park Handicap (1958), Woodward Stakes (1958), Withers Stakes (1957), United Nations Handicap (1958)
Major places: Suburban Handicap (1958), Arlington Handicap (1958), Metropolitan Handicap (1958), Toboggan Handicap (1958)
Records: 1 mile, Arlington Park in 1:34; 1 $\frac{3}{16}$ miles, Atlantic City in 1.54.6
Clem was Shannon's most high-profile winner. Bred at Spendthrift Farm

by Louis B. Mayer, he raced for owner Adele L. Rand. A prolific winner on both dirt and turf, Clem is best remembered for his three consecutive defeats of Round Table (the Hall Of Fame champion trained by Willie Molter), beginning with the Washington Park Handicap, then the United Nations Handicap, and finally the Woodward Stakes, all in the space of a month. Clem also raced against Bold Ruler, running him to a close second in the Toboggan Handicap at Belmont Park in 1958.

SEA O ERIN (1951) b.c Shannon–Chantress, by Hyperion
Lifetime record: 85: 19, 12, 10 (15 stakes wins)
Career earnings: $407,259
Major race wins: Citation Handicap (1955, 1956), New Orleans Handicap
(1955), Phoenix Handicap (1955, 1956)
Major places: Citation Handicap (1957), La Salle Handicap (1956),
Phoenix Handicap (1957), Churchill Downs Handicap (1957),
Washington Park Handicap (1956)

SHAN PAC (1954) dk.b.c Shannon–Pacifica, by Puro Habano
Lifetime record: 175: 25, 22, 17 (5 stakes wins)
Career earnings: $182,910
Major race wins: Churchill Downs Handicap (1958), Grassland Turf
Handicap (1958)
Major places: Ohio Derby (1957), Louisiana Derby (1957), Youthful Stakes
(1956), Louisiana Handicap (1958), Phoenix Handicap (1960)
Records: 6f, Detroit Racecourse in 1:09.4; 1 $\frac{1}{16}$ miles, Detroit Racecourse
in 1:42.6; 7f, Churchill Downs in 1:22

COUNTY CLARE (1950) br.c Shannon–Stepwisely, by Wise Councellor
Lifetime record: 46: 11, 4, 8 (5 stakes wins)
Career earnings: $137,450
Major race wins: Atlantic City Turf Handicap (1955), Turf Cup Handicap
(1953), Boardwalk Handicap (1954).
Major places: Meadowland Handicap (1954), Atlantic City Turf Handicap
(1954), Pimlico Futurity (1952)

Appendix D: Shannon's Records

Between 1943 and 1948, Shannon set or equalled many track records across Sydney and California. The following is a list of both his official and unofficial track records.

Official Records

21 September 1946 Theo Marks Quality Handicap (7 furlongs)
Rosehill. 1:22½ new track record.

7 October 1946 George Main Stakes (1 mile, WFA) Randwick.
1:34½ new Australasian record.

7 October 1946 George Main Stakes (1 mile, WFA) Randwick.
Broke 7 furlong Australian record in running.

7 October 1946 George Main Stakes (1 mile, WFA) Randwick.
Equalled 6 furlong track record in running.

8 May 1948 San Francisco County Handicap, Bay Meadows.
1:55 ⅗ new track record.

16 October 1948 Forty-Niners Handicap, Golden Gate Fields.
1:47 ⅗ new track record, equalled American record.

23 October 1948 Golden Gate Handicap, Golden Gate Fields.
1:59 ⅘ new American record, equalled world record.

25 November 1948 San Francisco Handicap, Tanforan.
1:50 ⅘ new track record.

Unofficial Records

5 October 1946 Epsom Handicap (1 mile) Randwick.
1:32½, fastest mile ever recorded at Randwick (clocked by Bob Skelton, confirmed by journalist Bill Whittaker years later).

27 August 1947 half-mile work on the 'screenings', Randwick.
47¾, fastest time ever clocked for the distance on that surface.

6 October 1947 6f track gallop Rosebery.
1:14, fastest time for the distance ever seen at that course.

Weight Conversion Chart

Stones-Pounds	Pounds	Kilograms	Stones-Pounds	Pounds	Kilograms
6 st 5 lbs	89 lbs	40.40 kg	8-8	120	54.43
6-6	90	40.80	8-9	121	54.88
6-7	91	41.30	8-10	122	55.34
6-8	92	41.70	8-11	123	55.79
6-9	93	42.20	8-12	124	56.25
6-10	94	42.60	8-13	125	56.70
6-11	95	43.10	9 st	126 lbs	57.15 kg
6-12	96	43.50	9-1	127	57.61
6-13	97	44.00	9-2	128	58.06
7 st	98 lbs	44.45 kg	9-3	129	58.51
7-1	99	44.91	9-4	130	58.97
7-2	100	45.36	9-5	131	59.42
7-3	101	45.81	9-6	132	59.87
7-4	102	46.27	9-7	133	60.33
7-5	103	46.72	9-8	134	60.78
7-6	104	47.17	9-9	135	61.23
7-7	105	47.63	9-10	136	61.23
7-8	106	48.08	9-11	137	62.14
7-9	107	48.53	9-12	138	62.60
7-10	108	48.99	9-13	139	63.05
7-11	109	49.44	10 st	140 lbs	63.5 kg
7-12	110	49.90	10-1	141	64.00
7-13	111	50.35	10-2	142	64.40
8 st	112 lbs	50.80 kg	10-3	143	64.90
8-1	113	51.26	10-4	144	65.30
8-2	114	51.71	10-5	145	65.80
8-3	115	52.16	10-6	146	66.20
8-4	116	52.62	10-7	147	66.70
8-5	117	53.07	10-8	148	67.10
8-6	118	53.52	10-9	149	67.60
8-7	119	53.98	10-10	150	68.00

Racetrack Distances

Furlongs	Metres (approximate)
5	1000
6	1100
7	1200
8 (1 mile)	1600
9	1800
10 (1¼ miles)	2000
11	2200
12 (1½ miles)	2400
13	2600
14 (1¾ miles)	2800
16 (2 miles)	3200
20 (2½ miles)	4000

A quarter of a mile = two furlongs
A half mile = four furlongs
Three quarters of a mile = six furlongs

Additional note: American distances often work off 'sixteenths' of a mile, e.g. 1 ³⁄₁₆ miles. In that instance, the distance is 8 furlongs and three half-furlongs, making the total distance 9½ furlongs.

Select Bibliography

This book relied on countless primary sources for its information. In Sydney, the State Library of New South Wales, including the Mitchell Library, provided newspaper archives, *Sands Directory* microfiche, as well as rare and out-of-print books and periodicals. While the National Library of Australia's Trove resource was extremely helpful, the following microfilm newspapers were critical: *Sydney Morning Herald, Referee, Truth* (Sydney), *Daily Telegraph, Daily Mirror, The Sun, Sunday Sun and Guardian, Smith's Weekly* and *Town And Country Journal*. All other newspapers and magazines are referenced in the chapter notes.

The library of the Australian War Memorial, Canberra, was key to wartime legislation, as was that of Parliament House. The library of the Australian Turf Club provided racing-calendar information, while the National Racing Museum (Melbourne) assisted with Shannon's Hall Of Fame information. In America, Keeneland Library provided access to photograph archives, while the John A. Morris Research Library at the National Museum of Racing, Saratoga Springs, was critical with Hall Of Fame information on Willie Molter, Johnny Adams, Jack Westrope and Neil S. McCarthy's owner record. Pedigree records came from the Australian Stud Book. The New South Wales State Archives held will and probate information, and the Registry of Births, Deaths and Marriages (New South Wales) provided birth, marriage and death certificates. Weather data for Sydney came from the Bureau of Meteorology for station Observatory Hill, and in California from Jan Null, Certified Consulting Meteorologist at Golden Gate Weather Services, from San Francisco International Airport (for Bay Meadows), Los Angeles International Airport (for Hollywood Park), and San Gabriel Fire Department (for Santa Anita).

Secondary Sources

A Quarter-Century of American Racing and Breeding 1916 Through 1940, The Blood-Horse, Lexington, Kentucky, n.d.

A Second Quarter-Century of American Racing and Breeding 1941 Through 1965, The Blood-Horse, Lexington, Kentucky, n.d.

Ahern, Bill, *A Century of Winners: The Saga of 121 Melbourne Cups*, Boolarong Publications, Brisbane, 1982.

Alvarado, Rudolph, *The Untold Story of Joe Hernandez: The Voice of Santa Anita*, Caballo Press of Ann Arbor, Ann Arbor, Michigan, 2008.

American Racing Manual, Daily Racing Form, Chicago, 1948, 1949, 1956 edns.

Anderson, Joseph, *Tattersall's Club Sydney 1858-1983*, Koorana Ltd, Sydney, 1985.

Auerbach, Ann Hagedorn, *Wild Ride: The Rise And Tragic Fall Of Calumet Farm Inc., America's Premier Racing Dynasty*, Henry Holt & Co, New York, 1944.

Australasian Turf Register (1932, 1933, 1934, 1935, 1936) The Australasian, Melbourne.

Barrie, Douglas M., *The Australian Bloodhorse*, Halstead Press, Sydney, 1956.

—— *Turf Cavalcade: A review of 150 years of horse racing in Australia and of the AJC 100 years at Randwick*, Australian Jockey Club, Sydney, 1960.

—— and Pring, Peter, *Australia's Thoroughbred Idols*, The Discovery Press, Sydney, 1973.

Beckwith, B. K., *The Longden Legend*, A. S. Barnes & Co., New Jersey, 1976.

Beltran, David Jimenez, *The Agua Caliente Story: Remembering Mexico's Legendary Racetrack*, Eclipse Press, Lexington, Kentucky, 2004.

Binney, Keith R., *Horsemen of the First Frontier (1788–1900) and The Serpent's Legacy*, Volcanic Productions, Sydney, 2003.

Bland, E. (ed.), *Flat-Racing Since 1900*, Andrew Dakers Ltd., London, 1950.

The Bloodstock Breeders' Review, The British Bloodstock Agency Ltd, London, 1947.

Boulter Richard, *Forty Years On: The Sydney Turf Club*, Macarthur Press, Sydney, 1984.

du Bourg, Ross, *The Australian & New Zealand Thoroughbred*, Viking O'Neil, Melbourne, 1991.

Bowden, Samuel H., *The History of the Australian Comforts Fund*, Scotow & Presswell, Sydney, 1922.

Bowen, Edward L., *Legacies of the Turf: A Century of Great Thoroughbred Breeders*, vol. 2, Eclipse Press, Lexington, Kentucky, 2004.

—— *Masters of the Turf: Ten Trainers Who Dominated Horse Racing's Golden Era*, Eclipse Press, Lexington, Kentucky, 2007.

Britt, Edgar, *Post Haste*, Pan Macmillan, Sydney, 1967, reprinted 2000.

Broadhead, Fred C., *Here Comes Whirlaway!* Sunflower University Press, Kansas, 1995.

Brown, Greg, *One Hundred Years of Trotting, 1877–1977*, Whitcombe & Tombs, Sydney, 1981.

Cairns, Steve, *'London to a Brick On': A Salute to Australian Race Calling*, The Australian Bloodhorse Review, Richmond, NSW, 1994.

Carter, Isobel, *Phar Lap*, Landsdowne Press, Melbourne, 1964.

Cavanough, Maurice, and Davies, Meurig, *Cup Day: The Story of the Melbourne Cup 1861–1960*, The Specialty Press, Melbourne, 1960.

Church, Michael, *The Derby Stakes: The Complete History 1780–2006*, Raceform, Berkshire, UK, 2006.

Collis, Ian, *Old Sydney: A Pictorial History*, New Holland, Sydney, 2008.

Crawford, Byron, *Kentucky Stories*, Turner Publishing Company, Paducah, Kentucky, 1994.

Curby, Pauline, *Randwick*, Randwick City Council, Sydney, 2009.

Day, William, *Reminiscences of the Turf*, Richard Bentley & Sons, London, 1891.

Elliott, Sumner Locke, *Edens Lost*. Penguin, Melbourne, 1986.

Ellis, Tom, *The Science of Turf Investment*, The Federal Capital Press of Australia, Canberra, 1936.

Eyeman, Scott, *Lion of Hollywood: The Life and Legend of Louis B. Mayer*, Simon & Schuster, New York, 2005.

Fairfax-Blakeborough, J., *The Turf Who's Who 1932*, The Mayfair Press,

London, 1932.

Fitzwygram, F. W., *Horses and Stables*, Longmans, Green & Co., London, 1901.

Georgeff, Phil, *Citation: In A Class By Himself*, Taylor Trade Publishing, New York, 2003.

Gould, Nat, *The Magic of Sport: Mainly Autobiographical*, John Long, London, 1909.

Greatest Kentucky Derby Upsets, Blood-Horse Publications, Lexington, Kentucky, 2007.

Griffiths, Samuel, *A Rolling Stone on the Turf*, Angus & Robertson, Sydney, 1933.

Grose, Peter, *A Very Rude Awakening: The Night the Japanese Midget Subs Came To Sydney Harbour*, Allen & Unwin, Sydney, 2007.

Gross, Michael, *Unreal Estate: Money, Ambition and the Lust for Land in Los Angeles*, Broadway Books, New York, 2011.

Hall, Dixon Henry 'The Druid', *Scott and Seabright,* Rogerson & Tuxford, London, 1862.

Hayes, Capt. M. Horace, *Veterinary Notes for Horse Owners*, Simon & Schuster, New York, 1877, 18th reprint 2002

Hewitt, Abram S., *Sirelines*, Eclipse Press, Lexington, Kentucky, 1977, reprinted 2006.

Hickie, David, *Gentlemen of the Australian Turf*, Angus & Robertson, Sydney, 1986.

Hillenbrand, Laura, *Seabiscuit: An American Legend*, Ballantyne Books, New York, 2001.

Hobson, Warwick, *Racing's All-Time Greats*, The Thoroughbred Press, Sydney, 1986.

Horse Racing's Top 100 Moments, The Blood-Horse Inc., Lexington, Kentucky, 2006.

Horse Racing's Greatest Rivalries, The Blood-Horse Inc., Lexington, Kentucky, 2008.

Howe, Graham, and Esau, Erika, *E. O. Hoppe's Australia*, W. Norton & Co., New York, 2007.

Huntington, Peter, Myers, Jane, and Owens, Elizabeth, *Horse Sense*, Landlinks Press, Melbourne, 2004.

Inglis, Clive, *Horsesense*, Halstead Press, Sydney, 1950.

—— *More Horsesense*, Halstead Press, Sydney, 1959.

Justice, Charles, *The Greatest Horse of All: A Controversy Examined*, Author House, Bloomington, Indiana, 2008.

Kass, Terry, *History of Kia Ora Stud Scone*, Summit Projects Australia, Sydney, 2000.

Laffaye, Horace A., *Polo in the United States*, McFarland, Jefferson, North

Carolina, 2011 [accessed via Google eBooks].

Lawrence, Joan, *Pictorial History: Randwick*, Kingsclear Books, Sydney, 2001.

Lemon, Andrew, *The History of Australian Thoroughbred Racing,* vol. I, Hardie Grant Books, Melbourne, 2008.

—— *The History of Australian Thoroughbred Racing,* vol. II, Southbank Communications Group, Port Melbourne, 1990.

—— *The History of Australian Thoroughbred Racing,* vol. III, Hardie Grant Books, Melbourne, 2008.

Lillye, Bert, *Backstage of Racing*, John Fairfax Marketing, Sydney, 1985.

Lowry, Bill, *Hollywood Park: From Seabiscuit To Pincay*, Hollywood Park, 2003.

Mackaness, Caroline, and Butler-Bowdon, Caroline, *Sydney Then and Now*, Cameron House, Wingfield, South Australia, 2007.

McKay, W. J. Stewart, *Staying Power of the Racehorse*, Hutchinson & Co., London, 1933.

McKernan, Michael, *The Strength of A Nation: Six Years of Australians Fighting for the Nation and Defending the Homefront in WWII*, Allen & Unwin, 2006.

Marshall, Mary, *Great Breeders and Their Methods: Leslie Combs II and Spendthrift Farm*, The Russell Meerdink Company Ltd, Wisconsin, 2008.

Montgomery, E. S., *The Thoroughbred*, Arco Publishing Company, New York, 1973.

Morris, P. A., *Flight: A Story of Courage*, self-published, Sydney, 1947.

Mortimer, Roger Onslow, Richard, and Willett, Peter, *A Biographical Encyclopedia of British Flat Racing*, Macdonald and Jane's, London, 1978.

Names Registered for Racehorses: Vols. I to VIII of Printed List, Registrar of Racehorses (Australian Jockey Club), 1918.

Names Registered for Racehorses, Vols. XVII to XXII of Printed List, Registrar of Racehorses (Australian Jockey Club), 1932.

Nicholson, Rod, *The Track: Australian Racing's Hall of Fame*, News Custom Publishing, Melbourne, 2005.

O'Hara, John, *A Mug's Game, A History of Gaming and Betting in Australia*, University of New South Wales Press, Sydney, 1988.

O'Loghlen, Frank 'Eurythmic', *Champions of the Turf*, F. H. Johnston Publishing Company, Sydney, 1945.

O'Reilly, Tom, *Racegoer*, University of Wollongong, Wollongong, 1997.

Painter, Martin, and Waterhouse, Richard, *The Principal Club: A History of the Australian Jockey Club*, Allen & Unwin, Sydney, 1992.

Palmer, Joe H., *American Race Horses 1948*, The Sagamore Press, New

York, 1948.

Paterson, A. B., *Off Down the Track: Racing and Other Yarns*, Angus & Robertson, Sydney, 1986.

Peake, Wayne, *Sydney's Pony Racecourses: An Alternative History*, Walla Walla Press, Sydney, 2006.

Phipps, Herb, *Bill Kyne of Bay Meadows: The Man Who Brought Horse Racing Back to California*, A. S. Barnes & Co., New Jersey, 1978.

Pierce, Peter, *From Go to Whoa: A Compendium of the Australian Turf*, Crossbow Publishing, Melbourne, 1994.

PIX magazine, vol. 16, no. 8, 3 November 1945.

Poliness, Grania, *Carbine*, Waterloo Press, Sydney, 1985.

Pring, Peter, *Analysis of Champion Racehorses*, The Thoroughbred Press, Sydney, 1977.

Ransom, J. H., *Who's Who and Where in Horsedom: The 400 of the Sport of Kings*, The Ransom Publishing Company, Lexington, Kentucky, 1951.

Reason, Michael, *Phar Lap: A True Legend*, Museum of Victoria, Melbourne, 2005.

Remember the Forties, Parragon, Bath, UK, 2011.

Sharpe, Alan, *Pictorial History: City of Sydney*, Kingsclear Books, Sydney, 2000.

Sharpe, Harry, *The Practical Stud Groom*, British Bloodstock Agency Ltd, London, 1913.

Soldiering On: The Australian Army at Home and Overseas, Australian War Memorial, Canberra, 1942.

Spearitt, Peter, *Sydney's Century: A History*, University of New South Wales Press, Sydney, 2000.

Stallion Register Volume I, The Sydney Morning Herald, Sydney, 1939.

Stearn, Duncan *Bernborough: Australia's Greatest Racehorse*, Mitraphab Press, Kincumber, NSW, 2006.

Thayer, Bert Clark, *Horses in the Blue Grass*, Duell, Sloan & Pearce, New York, 1940.

They're Racing: The Complete Story of Australian Racing, Penguin Books, Melbourne, 1999.

Thoroughbred Champions: Top 100 Racehorses of the 20th Century, The Blood-Horse Inc., Lexington, Kentucky, 1999.

Walker, R. B., *Yesterday's News: A History of the Newspaper Press in New South Wales from 1920 to 1945*, Sydney University Press, Sydney, 1980.

Wall, Maryjean, *How Kentucky Became Southern*, University Press of Kentucky, Lexington, Kentucky, 2010.

Welch, Ned, *Who's Who in Thoroughbred Racing*, Who's Who In

Thoroughbred Racing Inc., Washington, DC, 1946.

Wesch, Hank, *Del Mar: Where the Turf Meets the Surf,* The History Press, Charleston, South Carolina, 2011.

Whittaker, Bill, 'Racing Recollections – Kia Ora Stud – breeding establishment extraordinaire', *Bloodhorse Review*, August 2006, p. 74.

Wicks, B. M., *The Australian Racehorse: An Introduction to Breeding*, Libra Books, Canberra, 1973.

Wilkinson, Michael, *The Phar Lap Story*, Budget Books, Sydney, 1980.

Yater, Wallace Mason, *Fundamentals of Internal Medicine*, D. Appleton-Century Company, Inc., New York, 1944.

Acknowledgements

When I began working on this book in its earliest days, I found very little on Shannon. But like an onion, time peeled back and Shannon revealed himself through the input of hundreds of sources, some technological, many human. I would like to mention a few of them here.

Mardi Henderson, granddaughter of Peter Riddle, was generous and forthcoming with her family's beautiful and personal history. Thank you to her, and her husband Brian, for allowing me in. In 2012 it was my privilege to listen to Edgar Britt recount his memories of 1940s racing, so thank you to him, and also Patricia Campbell. Countless people stepped forward with their recollections of this era and, in particular, of Darby Munro, so my sincere gratitude to Tom O'Reilly, Daryll Cook, John Holmes and Robert Cohen. Thanks also to Arnold House, and to David Crowe for his memories of W. J. Smith. W. J.'s granddaughter, Kate Fraser, was a fabulous interview, along with her son George. John Peck was instrumental in my understanding of the Riddle trotting dynasty, and I thank him sincerely, along with Kathy Gebert of Harness Racing Australia and Olivia Stevens of Kia Ora Stud. At William Inglis & Son, my absolute thanks to Arthur Inglis for his interest (and patience) every time I came knocking, and also Cassandra Simmonds, who found something very special for me.

Max Presnell gave me his ear several times, and this book (and my knowledge bank) is the better for it. Thanks also to the bottomless pit of knowledge that is Graham Caves, and also Wayne Peake, who remembered me any time he came across Shannon. Special mention also to my friend Robert Coleman, 'Mr Hollywood'. Thank you to Mark Shean for information on his grandfather, Shannon's first pilot Fred Shean, and also to Kevin Gates of the Australian Racing Museum, and Margaret Helback and Hannah Hibert of the Australian Turf Club. I make special mention of Michael Ford, Keeper of the Australian Stud Book, who endured my emails about Shannon's ancestors, forcing his resources back some 170 years. He and his staff are marvellous.

I owe a great deal of this book to John Dyer, who remains my fantastic source of treasures. In England, it was my fortune yet again to deal with Lyn Price and, in particular, Rob Marriott of Weatherbys. An entire chapter in this book balanced on Rob's superb research, so thank you to him. My gratitude also to the incredible staff of the State Library of New South Wales, and at Fairfax digital, Aimee Marjurinen and Catherine Reade for wading through millions of negatives in search of my racehorse. Also, thank you to Angus Roland of Sky Racing, and Mark Ewing, who listened to me hash out the merits of Shannon running on dirt. Also, my thanks to Danny Power, whose steady brilliance shows the way.

Much of Shannon's story lies in the US, and here are some of the people who helped me to reconstruct it: Desmond Dempsey of Spendthrift Farm, who left me wide-eyed after my visit, and also Ercel Ellis. Kathy Schenck at the Keeneland Library was critical, along with Allan Carter, historian at the National Museum of Racing in Saratoga. These two, and their organisations, lead the world in the preservation of racing lore. My thanks to Bob Curran and Shannon Luce of the American Jockey Club, and Jan Null, consulting meteorologist at Golden Gate Weather Services, who sent me California weather data faster than the speed of Shannon. Thank you also to delightful Steve Haskin, and his colleagues at *The Blood-Horse*: editor Eric Mitchell, Scot Gillies, and digital archivist Kevin Thompson, who was fabulous. Additional thanks to Lyrical Ballad in Saratoga, and mention must be made of Metchel Fong, who searched and shipped more issues of *The Blood-Horse* than my postman could carry.

There are innumerable others who contributed in small ways to this book, and I can't possibly mention all of them, but their assistance was greatly appreciated. However, I would like to thank the Twitter racing community that has shown enthusiasm for this book (and the last one) since the very beginning. They are a wonderful bunch. Also, thank you to my publisher Alison Urquhart, and my agent Margaret Gee, who stands faithfully in my corner.

Last but by no means least, especial gratitude to Dr Meghan Newcombe for her medical advice on Peter Riddle's health, but more for being the friend that I always dreamed of. And Maurice Lombardo . . . I owe him everything. Finally, I thank the star of this book. Shannon came tentatively out of the shadows for me, until I felt like he was right there, three feet from my keyboard. Let this book be your monument, dear horse.

Jessica Owers, November 2013

Index

Also by Jessica Owers

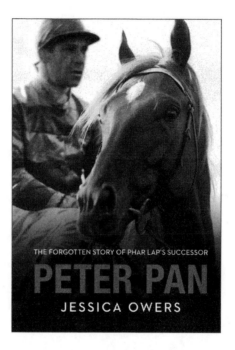

THE FORGOTTEN STORY OF PHAR LAP'S SUCCESSOR

PETER PAN

JESSICA OWERS

In 1932, they said there would never be another Phar Lap. Yet within months there came a racehorse so wildly brilliant that he was instantly compared to the dead champion. He was Peter Pan.

Within months of Phar Lap's death, Peter Pan had won the Melbourne Cup and then two years later won it again – the first horse in 72 years to take home a second. The newspapers of the day called him a 'superhorse' and declared 'another Phar Lap takes the stage'. But over the long years, Australia forgot their new champion.

Casting off the shadow of Phar Lap, this book tells the story of triumph during the Great Depression and the coming of a champion when Australia least expected one. It is time to restore the standing of our other great racing hero.